D1404707

2500 ANECDOTES FOR ALL OCCASIONS

2500 ANECDOTES FOR ALL OCCASIONS

Edited by
EDMUND FULLER

A CLASSIFIED COLLECTION OF THE
BEST ANECDOTES FROM ANCIENT
TIMES TO THE PRESENT DAY

Avenel Books
NEW YORK

Copyright © 1942 © 1970 by Crown Publishers, Inc.
All rights reserved.
This book was originally published as *Thesaurus of Anecdotes*.
This 1990 edition is published by Avenel Books,
distributed by Outlet Book Company, Inc., a Random House Company,
225 Park Avenue South, New York, New York 10003
Printed and bound in the United States of America
Library of Congress Cataloging-in-Publication Data
Thesaurus of anecdotes.
2500 anecdotes for all occasions / edited by Edmund Fuller.
p.   cm.
"Originally published as Thesaurus of anecdotes"—T.p. verso.
Includes index.
ISBN 0-517-05576-7
1. Anecdotes. I. Fuller, Edmund, 1914-   . II. Title.
III. Title: Twenty-five hundred anecdotes for all occasions.
(PN6261.F8   1990)
808.88'2—dc20   9045151
CIP
8   7   6   5   4   3   2   1

INTRODUCTION

Abraham Lincoln speaking:

"They say I tell a great many stories; I reckon I do, but I have found in the course of a long experience that common people, take them as they run, are more easily informed through the medium of a broad illustration than in any other way, and as to what the hypercritical few may think, I don't care."

Anecdotes are stories with points. They are tools—nail-sinkers to drive home arguments firmly. The recognition of their usefulness goes back centuries from Lincoln, America's greatest anecdotist. They are the origin of all teaching.

In their old form they were known as parables. By means of them Jesus Christ taught. The prophets and sages of all ancient religion and wisdom employed the simple, effective parable. "I will liken him unto a wise man, which built his house upon a rock——." "Hearken; Behold, there went out a sower to sow——." "A certain man had two sons——." Thus, stories with points were made to embody profound teachings. So the Greek slave, Aesop, sagely propounded his fables.

Today the true anecdote is still the counterpart of the parable and fable. Time has tended to shorten it somewhat and, as an attribute of our temperament, we have made it often funny. The majority of the anecdotes in this book are humorous. Many are serious and thoughtful. All prove something. The thing to remember is, many jokes are anecdotes but not all anecdotes are jokes.

To see best how to use the wealth of anecdotes in this book for your own needs, for speaking, teaching, preaching, lecturing, arguing or writing, read the rest of this introduction carefully. Study it before you proceed to the selection and adapting of your material.

It will tell you:

1. How to select anecdotes.
2. How to write and tell them.
3. How to vary and adapt them.

HOW TO SELECT YOUR MATERIAL

The Table of Contents will show you the general plan of the book. The anecdotes are classified in ten basic divisions. These are divided and subdivided by logical association. The association of ideas is not only the basis of much humor, it is the key by which stories to drive home your idea may be located. In each main division every story bears a general relation to those immediately before and after it.

A simple and complete system of cross reference is provided. This counteracts the slightly arbitrary trend unavoidable in any method of classification. Many of the subject headings are related to subjects in other parts of the book. These are listed as RELATED SUBJECTS at the end of each group of anecdotes. You will also find, in each case, a list of SEE ALSOS. These refer you to individual stories listed under other headings yet bearing on the subject at hand.

As an example turn to Judges, 2486–2497. Here are 12 anecdotes. If no one of them quite fills the bill try:

1. The preceding subjects, Courts, Trials.
2. The SEE ALSOS at the end.
3. The RELATED SUBJECTS at the end.
4. The following subjects, Witnesses, Juries, etc.

Continue this process until you find the anecdotes you want and as many as you need.

The Index is alphabetical and naturally is much more comprehensive and detailed than the Table of Contents. It is better to look first in the Index when searching for a topic. The numbers are anecdote numbers, not page numbers. If by any chance your topic is not listed try a synonym, a related word, and more general or more specific words.

HOW TO WRITE AND TELL ANECDOTES

In using the written anecdote, if you wish to open with it, begin at once, just as the Lincoln statement is used to open this Introduction. So used, it may serve as the ideal presentation of the subject you are about to discuss and the point which you plan to stress in connection with it.

In making a speech, the telling of a well-chosen anecdote may serve as an attention fixer. Witness the story of the ass and his shadow (No. 776):

> An Athenian crowd demonstrated impatience at a public assembly one day and hissed the orator Demosthenes, refusing to hear him. He said he had but a short story to tell them and began, "A certain youth hired an ass, in the summer time, to go from his home to Megara. At noon, when the sun was very hot, both he who had hired the ass and the owner of the animal were desirous of sitting in the shade of the ass, and fell to thrusting one another away. The owner insisted that he had hired out only the ass and not the shadow. The other insisted that as he had hired the ass, all that belonged to the ass was his." Turning away, Demosthenes made as though to depart, but the mob, which had been piqued by the story, would

not allow him to leave and insisted that he continue. He then turned upon them and demanded, "How is it that you insist upon hearing the story of the shadow of the ass, and will not give an ear to matters of great moment?" He was permitted to deliver the speech for which he had come. And the fine point of the ass and his shadow remains unsettled to this day.

The telling of an anecdote in a speech or conversation requires a certain amount of "build-up," serving first to settle upon the speaker any wandering attention, then to maintain this attention and keep it at a maximum for the climax of the story. By an extension of this principle, the anecdote itself is the "build-up" for the message which is to follow. In addition to this, in speech making, you should use a few generalized opening remarks before beginning the "build-up" for the story. Your remarks to the Chairman, a statement of the pleasure it gives you to be present, or any other such matters will serve. Your first few words are seldom clearly heard. The function of these preliminary remarks is to permit your audience to focus itself upon the sound and pitch of your voice.

The anecdote may be brought into your speech or article at any point. When you have a good story, tell it. It doesn't need an introduction. If you feel that some preface is necessary you can avoid the hackneyed "That reminds me of a story" by simply letting it arise naturally from the association of ideas and subject matter. You need say no more than, "This is like Mark Twain's long-winded missionary," in the case of a story such as that below.

Don't be afraid even to entrust the meat of your message to an anecdote upon occasion. To use a story shrewdly and briefly in this fashion is far wiser than to drift into the pitfall of long-windedness, which may well undo everything for which you have striven.

Mark Twain, after enduring a series of intolerably long drawn out speeches, told a little parable of his own.

"Some years ago in Hartford, we all went to church one hot sweltering night to hear the annual report of Mr. Hawley, a city missionary who went around finding people who needed help and didn't want to ask for it. He told of the life in cellars, where poverty resided; he gave instances of the heroism and devotion of the poor. 'When a man with millions gives,' he said, 'we make a great deal of noise. It's noise in the wrong place, for it's the widow's mite that counts.' Well, Hawley worked me up to a great pitch. I could hardly wait for him to get through. I had $400 in my pocket. I wanted to give that and borrow more to give. You could see greenbacks in every eye. But instead of passing the plate then, he kept on talking and talking, and as he talked it grew hotter and hotter, and we grew sleepier and sleepier. My enthusiasm went down, down, down—$100 at a clip—until finally, when the plate did come around, I stole ten cents out of it. It all goes to show how a little thing like this can lead to crime." (No. 344)

HOW TO ADAPT ANECDOTES TO YOUR OWN
PURPOSE

IF names make news, still more do they make anecdotes. The "anecdotal" quality as against the "joke" quality in a story is primarily its seeming authenticity or its factual nature. Most of the anecdotes in this book are about specific people. Every reader will encounter one or two stories, attributed in the present version to certain persons, which will be familiar to him by other names. This is where skill may be brought into the use of anecdotes.

In the compiling of this book, anecdote No. 1325 came to hand in three versions:

> When the American composer, George Gershwin, died, a man of sentiment combined with musical aspirations wrote an elegy in his honor. He sought out Oscar Levant. Reluctantly Levant granted him a hearing. Eagerly the man rendered the piece with his own hands and then turned expectantly toward Levant, seeking approbation.
> "I think it would have been better," Levant said, "if you had died and Gershwin had written the elegy."

To all listeners to *Information Please* this story will have an authentic ring. Yet it exists currently in a version about Liszt bringing to Rossini an elegy on the death of Meyerbeer, and a version about a lady composer approaching Josef Hofmann with an elegy on the death of MacDowell.

Countless other instances could be cited of one anecdote attributed to a lot of people. In this book all choices have been made favoring names of current interest. As you use the book you must be ingenious for in these stories, with the endless simple variations possible to them, you have the raw material of endless anecdotes on any possible subject. Change names to bring up to date, add names where none are given, change names for the sake of local reference, change place names and scenes for the same purpose. A story about Napoleon and one of his soldiers may serve you as a story about an employee and his boss. A story about a musician may serve for a writer. In each case your need will be served by the *point* of the story. You must be clever in manipulating its framework.

Even the details of subject matter can be changed endlessly to suit occasions, with the effect of creating, for every practical purpose, a brand new story. The story of the shadow of the ass could be placed anywhere and told about anyone. Instead of the ass and its shadow it could be about a dog and its fleas. It could be about a house and its smell; the point could be neatly reversed and made into a pretext for lease-breaking, "I rented the house but I didn't rent the smell." Also the story is precisely the shrewd device of Portia for the confounding of Shylock.

> "This bond doth give thee here no jot of blood;
> Take then thy bond, take thou thy pound of flesh;
> But, in the cutting, if thou dost shed
> One drop of Christian blood, thy lands and goods
> Are, by the laws of Venice, confiscate. . . ."

Thus, any story in this book has latent in it a dozen more.

Anecdotes are no one's property. They are common stock. They are an aspect of folk-lore. They are yours to use as you wish. No matter how shiny the trimmings of modernism it is hard to prove novelty or originality. That story about the man and woman and the automobile was probably told in Athens about a chariot.

> Nicholas Murray Butler and Brander Matthews were discussing stories. Said Matthews, "In the case of the first man to use an anecdote there is originality, in the case of the second there is plagiarism; with the third, it is lack of originality; and with the fourth it is drawing from a common stock."
> "Yes," broke in Butler, "and in the case of the fifth it is research." (No. 1168)

Your judgment should tell you when it is wise to vary an anecdote and when to let it stand. Where the original name and locale are not closely involved with the point, or where the names may be largely forgotten, change often improves the story. Most Lincoln stories, on the other hand, derive a unique value from being Lincoln stories and would be much weakened by omitting or changing this magic name.

Nationalities and dialects, however, are a rich field for variation. No. 332 opportunely makes a brand new Japanese story out of a venerable classic about two merchants of Pinsk.

> It is said that the Japanese inspire no more confidence one in the other than they do in the citizens of the rest of the world. Two merchants of Tokyo once met in the railway station.
> "Where are you going?" asked the first one.
> His friend hesitated, then said, "To Kobe."
> "Oh, you liar!" said the first one angrily. "You tell me you are going to Kobe to make me think you're going to Osaka, but I have made inquiries and I *know* you are going to Kobe!"

Again the *point* is the thing. You can ring these changes for yourself with almost any story in this book. The whole wide world of nationalities, dialects, and localisms is open to you.

A note is necessary on the numbering of the anecdotes. These numbers are not for the purpose of counting but of locating. They are reference numbers. In order to keep the book from becoming frozen by numbers it was necessary to break their numerical sequence, leaving "expansion joints." The practice has been followed, at the end of each subject, of advancing the numbers to begin the next unit of five—thus a 4 to 6, a 16 to 21, a 42 to 46. This has made it editorially practical to readjust and expand this book up to the last minute. It will permit the expansion of further editions without disrupting the entire editorial organization. It is suggested that the constant user may also avail himself of the opportunity to add his own supplementary stories, using the blank numbers to correlate them with the material in this book.

TABLE OF CONTENTS

NOTE: *In order to know how to use this book properly, it is important to read the introduction.*

INTRODUCTION v
How to SELECT YOUR MATERIAL v
How to WRITE AND TELL ANECDOTES vi
How to ADAPT ANECDOTES TO YOUR OWN PURPOSE viii

ANECDOTES 1

(For alphabetical list of subjects, see *Index* page 481)

Numbers in smaller type below are anecdote numbers, not page numbers.

CHARACTER AND MANNERS

PAGE

Behavior 1
Behavior 1
  Eating 6–23
  Sleeping 26–27
  Habits 31
    Drinking 36–55
    Smoking 61–65
    Profanity 66–68
    Gambling 71–74
  Reputation 76–78

Traits 14
Traits
  Absent-Mindedness 81–90
  Accuracy 91–92
  Ambition 96–97
  Boastfulness 101–103
  Boners 106–119
  Borrowing 121–126
  Brevity 131–134
  Carelessness 136
  Cheerfulness 141–143
  Conscience 146–147
  Courage 151–153
  Cowardice 156–160
  Curiosity 161
  Cynicism 166–170
  Devotion 171–173
  Diligence 176–177
  Discretion 181–182

Dullness 186–195
Eccentricity 196–209
Economy 211–213
Endurance 216
Exaggeration 221–226
Extravagance 231–232
Flattery 236–237
Generosity 241–248
Gentlemanliness 251–256
Gratitude and Ingratitude 261–268
Greed 271–276
Helpfulness 281
Honesty 286–294
Honor 296–298
Hypocrisy 301–303
Imagination 306
Kindness 311–316
Lateness 321–324
Laziness 326–327
Liars 331–336
Long-Windedness 341–363
Melancholy 366–368
Memory 371–375
Modesty 376–390
Patience 391
Patriotism 396–407
Pessimism 411
Politeness 416–420
Pompousness 421–427
Practical Joking 431–437

PAGE

Prejudice 441–452
Pride 456–457
Procrastination 461
Quarrelsomeness 466
Quick Thinking 471–492
Rough and Ready 496–507
Rudeness 511–524
Shrewdness 526–541
Snobbishness 546–551
Stinginess 556–566
Stubbornness 571–572
Stupidity 576–583
Tact 586–591
Temper 596–598
Tolerance 601–603
Vanity 606–628
Will Power 631
Worrying 636
Zanies 641–643

Physical Characteristics 113
Physical Characteristics 646–648
Homeliness 651–656
Beauty 661–669

PAGE

Age 671–678
Fatness 681–690
Shortness 691–695
Tallness 696
Handicaps and Afflictions 701–707
Stuttering 711–713
Clothing 716–726
Handwriting 731–733

Social Activities 736
Social Activities 736–737
Parties 741–746
Banquets and Dinners 751–753
Speeches 756–782
Introductions 786–791
Society 796–797
Dueling 801–803
Talking 806–818
Gossip 821–826

Names 145
Names 831–838

Women 147
Women 841–843

LOVE—MARRIAGE—FAMILY

Love 148
Love 846–850
Courtship 851–855
Engagement 856–857
Flirtation 861–863
Friendship 866–867
Old Maids 871–873

Marriage 152
Marriage 876–888
Wedding 891–892
Honeymoon 896–898
Infidelity 901–904
Divorce 906–911
Husband 916–918
Wife 921–933

Mother-in-Law 936–937
Polygamy 941–943

Family 162
Family 946–950
Children 951–952
Babies 956–962
Small Children 966–977
Adoption 981
Father 986–990
Mother 991–993

Home Life 171
Home Life 996–1001
Hospitality 1006–1008
Births, Birthdays 1011–1015

LEARNING AND THE ARTS

Universities and Colleges . . . 175
Universities and Colleges 1016–1022
Professors 1026–1032
Students 1036
College Life 1041
Athletics (See Recreation and
Sports)

Schools 179
Schools 1046–1050

Classrooms 1051–1053
Teachers 1056–1057
Pupils 1061–1066

Erudition 183
Erudition 1071–1076
Learned Men 1081–1095
Critics 1096–1105
Lectures 1106–1111
Scientists 1116–1122

PAGE

Inventors 1126–1131
Experimenters 1136–1138
Explorers 1141–1142
Mathematicians 1146–1154
Common Sense 1156–1157

Literature 200
Literature 1161–1162
Authors 1166–1219
Books 1221–1224
Libraries 1226
Language 1231–1233
Newspapers 1236–1248
Magazines 1251–1252

Art 220
Art 1256
Painting and Drawing 1261–1293
Sculpture 1296–1297
Architecture 1301–1302

PAGE

Music 229
Music 1303–1306
Composers 1311–1326
Conductors 1331–1339
Operas and Concerts 1341–1348
Instrumentalists 1351–1363
Singers 1366–1368
Dancers 1371

Theatre and Film 244
Theatre and Film
Playwrights 1376–1385
Plays 1386–1388
Producers 1391–1397
Directors 1401–1403
Actors 1406–1431
Audiences 1436–1441
Hollywood 1446–1449

RELIGION AND MORALS

Churchmen 259
Churchmen 1451–1456
Ministers 1461–1477
Priests 1481–1483
Rabbis 1486–1488
Bishops 1491–1498
Popes 1501–1504
Evangelists 1511–1516
Missionaries 1521

Churches 271
Churches 1526–1528

Church Services 271
Church Services 1531–1538
Sermons 1541–1559
Collections 1561–1569
Sunday School 1571
Revivals 1576–1578

Bible 281
Bible 1581–1586

Believers 282
Believers 1591–1596
Devout Persons 1601–1602
Prayer 1606–1612
Miracles 1616–1619
Conversions 1621–1625
Bigotry 1626–1629
Superstition 1631–1636

Prohibitions and Restrictions.291
Prohibitions and Restrictions 1641–1642
Sin and Sinners 1646–1647

Atheists and Agnostics 292
Atheists and Agnostics 1651–1659

Pagan Gods 294
Pagan Gods 1661

MEDICINE AND HEALTH

Doctors 295
Doctors 1666–1679
Doctors' Fees 1681
Psychiatrists 1686–1687

Hospitals 299
Hospitals 1691

Dentists 300
Dentists 1696–1697

Sickness 300
Sickness 1701–1707
Poor Health 1711–1712
Hypochondriacs 1716–1720

Diseases 304
Diseases 1721

Medicines 304
Medicines 1726–1731

PAGE

Accidents 305
    Accidents 1736
    Injury 1741

Death 306
    Death 1746–1749

PAGE

Accidental Death 1751
Natural Death 1756–1757
Deathbed Scenes 1761–1775
Funerals 1776–1778
Longevity 312
    Longevity 1781–1782

RECREATION AND SPORTS

Relaxation 313
    Relaxation 1786
Travel 313
    Travel 1791–1796
        Trains 1801–1802
            Porters 1806
        Autos 1811
        Boats 1816
Sports 317
    Sports
        Baseball 1821–1824

Billiards 1826–1827
Bull Fighting 1831
Card Playing 1836–1840
Dancing 1841
Fishing 1846–1854
Football 1856–1858
Golf 1861–1869
Horse Racing 1871–1872
Hunting 1876–1879
Miscellaneous Contests 1881–1883
Prize Fighting 1886–1887
Swimming 1891–1893

GOVERNMENT AND RULERS

Politics 332
    Politics 1896–1901
        Political Parties 1906–1907
        Campaigning 1911–1920
        Elections 1921
        Public Offices 1926
            Presidents 1931–1940
            Congress 1941–1948
            Cabinet Members 1951–1953
            Governors 1956
            Mayors 1961
            Office Seekers 1966–1970
Kings and Emperors 347
    Kings and Emperors 1971–1993
        Parliament 1996–2000
Dictators 353
    Dictators 2001–2011

International Relations 356
    International Relations 2016
        Diplomats 2021–2027
United States 358
    United States 2031–2032
Freedom 359
    Freedom 2036–2042
        Equality 2046
        Woman's Suffrage 2051–2052
Socialism 362
    Socialism 2056–2057
Revolutions 363
    Revolutions 2061–2064

BUSINESS, INDUSTRY AND POSSESSIONS

Buying and Selling 364
    Buying and Selling 2066–2067
        Stores 2071–2072
        Bargaining 2076–2082
        Price 2086
        Salesmen 2091–2097
        Advertising 2101–2108
            Public Relations 2111–2112
        Competition 2116
        Chiseling and Swindling 2121–2132

Insurance 2136–2140
Real Estate 2141–2142
Finance and Wealth 379
    Finance and Wealth
        Stocks and Bonds 2146–2147
        Banks 2151–2158
        Loans 2161–2164
        Credit 2166–2167
        Debt 2171–2174
        Collection 2176–2179

PAGE

Wealth 2181–2187
Taxes 2191–2194
Bankruptcy 2196–2198
Poverty 2201–2211
Begging 2216–2219
Statistics 2221–2222

Employment and Work 392
Employment and Work 2226–2228
Bosses and Executives 2231–2235
Businessmen 2236–2237
Partnerships 2241–2242
Hiring and Firing 2246–2249
Salaries 2251–2254
Working Conditions 2256

PAGE

Manufacturing 2261
Efficiency 2266–2270
Machinery 2271–2272
Servants 2276–2283

Property 403
Property
Horses 2286–2288
Parrots 2291–2293

Hotels and Restaurants 405
Hotels and Restaurants 2296–2302
Waiters 2306–2308

Farmers and Farming 408
Farmers and Farming 2311–2313

WAR AND THE MILITARY

War 410
War 2316–2323
Civil War 2326–2329
Civilians in War 2331–2346
Censors 2351–2355
Rationing 2356–2358
Refugees 2361
Prisoners 2366
Battles 2371–2385
Strategy 2386–2393
Armistice 2396–2397

Army and Navy 428
Army and Navy 2401–2404
Officers 2406–2427
Soldiers and Sailors 2430–2437
Discipline 2441–2442
Regulations 2446
Camp 2451
Marches 2456
Drill 2461–2462
K. P. 2466

LAW AND JUSTICE

Courts 441
Courts 2471–2473
Trials 2476–2485
Judges 2486–2497
Witnesses 2501–2506
Juries 2511–2517
Evidence 2521–2523

Lawyers 451
Lawyers 2526–2537
Lawyers' Fees 2541–2545

Law Enforcement 456
Law Enforcement 2546–2548
Police 2551–2552
Detectives 2556–2557

Jail 2561–2563
Hanging 2566–2568

Criminals 459
Criminals 2571
Murder 2576
Stealing 2581–2590
Stool Pigeons 2591–2592

Laws 464
Laws 2596–2599

Justice 465
Justice 2601

Wills and Testaments 466
Wills and Testaments 2606–2607

INDEX OF NAMES 467

INDEX OF SUBJECTS 481

CHARACTER AND MANNERS

BEHAVIOR

1—George Cheyne, a Scotch physician, when a person was talking about the excellence of human nature, exclaimed:
"Hoot, hoot, man! human nature is a rogue and a scoundrel, or why should it perpetually stand in need of laws and of religion?"

RELATED SUBJECTS
Prohibitions and Restrictions
1641–1642
Sin and Sinners 1646–1647
Chiseling and Swindling
2121–2132
Criminals 2571

EATING

6—At a certain dinner party Daniel Webster found himself preyed upon by that type of hostess who endlessly and mercilessly worries her guests with the insistence that they are not eating enough, that possibly they do not like this or that, will they not have more, is there anything else they would prefer, and so forth.
"You're hardly eating a thing, Mr. Webster," she protested for the umpteenth time.
"Madam," said Webster solemnly, "permit me to assure you that I sometimes eat more than at other times but never less."

7—Bishop Davidson of Winchester was once one of a party of ecclesiastics who went into dinner after a religious conference. One of the others observed in a tone of pompous self-righteousness, "This is the time to put a bridle on our appetites."
"No," returned the Bishop, "this is the time to put a bit in our mouths."

8—One of the chief reasons for Thackeray's visit to America was his great desire to eat some Massachusetts oysters. The publisher James T. Fields knew of the novelist's secret

1

longing, and as soon as he could get Thackeray in his possession he carried him off to a magnificent oyster spread.

Thackeray gazed in delight at the six colossal specimens set before him. Not knowing how to begin the attack he asked his companion in a troubled voice, "How do I do it?" "This way," said Fields promptly, and proceeded to dispatch his first oyster. Then in the midst of a profound silence Thackeray did likewise. After a moment Fields anxiously asked him how he felt. Drawing a deep breath, Thackeray replied: "As if I had swallowed a baby."

9—Swift, in travelling, called at a hospitable house. The lady of the mansion, rejoiced to have so distinguished a guest, with great eagerness and flippancy asked him what he would have for dinner. "Will you have an apple-pie, sir? Will you have a gooseberry-pie, sir? Will you have a cherry-pie, sir? Will you have a currant-pie, sir? Will you have a plum-pie, sir? Will you have a pigeon-pie, sir?"— "Any pie, madam, but a mag-pie!"

10—"Why did I come to Africa?" Cecil Rhodes once remarked to a friend. "Well, they will tell you that I came on account of my health, or from love of adventure—and to some extent that may be true, but the real fact is that I could no longer stand their eternal cold mutton."

11—In his early boarding-house days in Kansas City, Eugene Field was invited to dine at a hospitable house where the best of everything was to be found. Some delicious strawberries were passed. Field gazed at them longingly but shook his head.

"Why, Mr. Field," said his host in surprise, "don't you like strawberries?"

"I dote on them."

"Then why don't you take some?"

"I'm afraid," said the poet sadly, "that if I did, they'd spoil my appetite for prunes."

12—Thomas Hood, tempting Charles Lamb to dine with him, said, "We have a hare."

"And how many friends," anxiously inquired Lamb.

13—John Randolph, the American statesman, said to a waiter, at the same time handing him his cup and saucer: "Take that away—change it."

"What do you want, Mr. Randolph?" asked the waiter, "Do you want coffee or tea?"

"If that stuff is tea," said he, "bring me coffee, if it's coffee, bring me tea. I want a change."

14—Alfred Hitchcock is a man notably fond of food. He is said to have once been a guest at a rather sparsely furnished dinner table, which had yielded him no more than a small portion of one thing or another amounting to a totally unsatisfactory sum. As the coffee was being brought in, his host said, "I do hope that you will soon dine here again."

"By all means," said Hitchcock. "Let's start now."

15—Shelley had "for all the sensualities of the table . . . an ineffable contempt, and, like Newton, used sometimes to inquire if he had dined." He was vegetarian, believing that "abstinence from animal food subtilizes and clears the intellect." Bread was his staff of life. When he felt hungry he would rush into a bake shop, emerge with a loaf under his arm, and stride on—rapidly breaking off pieces and swallowing them greedily. While visiting Shelley, his friend Hogg once ventured to say something about a pudding. "A pudding," said Shelley, "is a prejudice." He did sometimes permit Harriet or Mary to supply a "murdered chicken" for a guest.

16—Will Rogers, invited to dinner by a friend, replied, "No, thanks, I've already et."

"You should say 'have eaten,'" his friend corrected.

"Well," drawled Rogers, "I know a lot of feller's who say 'have eaten' who ain't et!"

17—At the boarding house in Kansas City where he once lived, Eugene Field, the humorist, found the table-fare uninteresting. One day, when hash was served for dinner, he asked his neighbor to, "Kindly pass the Review of Reviews."

18—George Bernard Shaw is noted as a vegetarian. One time, at a dinner party in London, he had before him on his plate the special concoction which was always provided for him, consisting of some greens with a mixture of salad oils.

Sir James Barrie, who was Shaw's neighbor at the table, bent over to him and, in a confidential tone, asked, "Tell me one thing, Shaw, have you eaten that or are you going to?"

19—Mark Twain habitually bemoaned the poor quality of French coffee. It was his insistence that the concoction was brewed by, "rubbing a chicory bean against a coffee bean and dropping the chicory bean in the water."

20—At a Sunday night tea which the author Hamlin Garland attended he was served some fresh mushrooms.

"Are you sure, Madam," he asked his hostess with great concern, "that these are not a poisonous variety of mushrooms?"

The hostess assured him they were harmless and edible. As he still hesitated, looking speculatively into space, his hostess asked him if he was still afraid.

"No," mused Mr. Garland, "I was just thinking of the effect on American letters should you be wrong."

21—The wonderful Madame Ernestine Schumann-Heink, greatest contralto of her time, was seated in a restaurant near the Metropolitan Opera House with an enormous steak before her. Enrico Caruso came in and joined her at the table.

"Stena," he said in mock astonishment, "you're not going to eat that alone?"

"No," said the portly contralto, "no, not alone; with potatoes."

22—Sir Richard Jebb, the famous doctor, was a liberal eater, a high liver. He believed the digestive organs were made to be used, not nursed. The question frequently asked by his patients, "What may I eat, doctor?" was exceedingly annoying to him. On one occasion he gave this answer: "My directions, sir, are simple. You must not eat the poker, shovel, or tongs, for they are hard of digestion; nor the bellows, for they will produce wind in your stomack; but you may eat anything else you please."

23—The old saying that many great inventions are the products of accidents seems to hold true in the culinary field.

There is a tradition surrounding the origin of Melba toast, which was supposedly a creation of the great French master chef, Escoffier. At the Savoy in London, César Ritz was maitre d'hotel and Escoffier was chef. Nellie Melba, celebrated prima donna, was staying there and was strenuously dieting, living largely on toast.

It chanced one day, while the master was preoccupied, that an underling prepared the great lady's toast. It was bungled and was served to her in a thin dried-up state resembling parchment. Ritz beheld with horror his celebrated guest crunching this aborted toast, and hastened over to apologize. Before he could utter a word Madame Melba burst out joyfully, saying, "César, how **clever of** Escoffier. I have never eaten such lovely toast."

SEE ALSO
Eccentricity 198
Imagination 306
Rudeness 511
Tact 589
Fatness 684, 687
Parties 745
Talking 816
Learned Men 1083
Concerts 1345
Sermons 1543
Believers 1594
Psychiatrists 1686
Longevity 1781

RELATED SUBJECTS
Drinking 36–55
Banquets and Dinners 751–753
Hotels and Restaurants 2296–2302
Waiters 2306–2308
K. P. 2466

Advertising 2108
Hotels 2299

SLEEPING

26—Stephen Leacock says, "I often think this 'insomnia' business is about 90% nonsense. When I was a young man living in a boarding house in Toronto, my brother George came to visit me, and since there was no spare room, we had to share my bed. In the morning, after daylight, I said to George, 'Did you get much sleep?'

" 'Not a damn minute,' said he.

" 'Neither did I,' I rejoined. 'I could hear every sound all night.'

"Then we put our heads up from the bedclothes and saw that the bed was covered with plaster. The ceiling had fallen on us in the night. But we hadn't noticed it. We had 'insomnia.' "

27—The old lighthouse-keeper had been at his post continuously for thirty years. During that entire period he had been accustomed to a gun going off, practically under his nose, every six minutes, day and night. This was the method for warning the ships. Naturally, he grew hardened to this periodic explosion, and paid no attention to it. Then, one night, in his 31st year at this post, the gun failed to go off. The old man awoke from a sound slumber. "What was that?" he cried in alarm.

SEE ALSO   RELATED SUBJECTS
Dullness 193   Laziness 326–327
Gratitude 261   Hotels and Restaurants 2296–2302
Introductions 790
Small Children 975
Authors 1194
Sermons 1550, 1557
Doctors 1667
Debt 2157

HABITS

31—In reply to an invitation to lunch with Lady Randolph, George Bernard Shaw wired: "Certainly not; what have I done to provoke such an attack on my well known habits?"
Lady Randolph sent another telegram:
"Know nothing of your habits; hope they are not as bad as your manners."

SEE ALSO   RELATED SUBJECTS
Sleeping 27   Prohibitions and Restrictions
Fatness 690   1641–1642
                           Sin and Sinners 1646–1647

DRINKING

36—One day Dr. Johnson was conversing with Mrs. Williams, a blind friend of his. She was telling him where she had dined the day before. "There were several gentlemen there," said she "and I found that there had been a good deal of hard drinking." She closed this observation with a trite moral reflection: "I wonder what pleasure men can take in making beasts of themselves!"
Dr. Johnson replied, "I wonder madam that you have not the penetration to see that he who makes a beast of himself gets rid of the pain of being a man."

37—A lady once asked Secretary of State Evarts if drinking so many different wines did not make him feel seedy the next day.
"No, madam," he replied, "it's the indifferent wines that produce that result."

38—All teetotallers should be as gracious in their excuses as the Irish poet, George Russell, better known as A. E.
When declining a drink, he would murmur, "No thank you. You see . . . I was born intoxicated."

39—Sir Campbell Bannerman M.P. was once asked his opinion on the liquor traffic. He replied: "The liquor traffic is a large subject, and I can hardly enter on it here. There is an old story of a Highlander who was asked if whiskey was not a bad thing. 'Yes,' said he, 'very bad—especially bad whiskey.'"

40—"I see you're drinking coffee, Judge," someone remarked to Ben Lindsey on a hot summer's day, "Why don't you try something cooling? Did you ever try gin and ginger ale?" "No," said Judge Lindsey, "but I've tried several fellows who have."

41—The story is told about Arthur Sullivan, the composer, that the one faculty which never forsook him was his tonal sense. It is said that he returned one night to his flat in a state of inebriation sufficient to render the row of identical houses in which he lived a difficult problem in identification. Sullivan ambled down the row pausing from time to time and kicking at the metal shoe scrapers by the side of the steps of the houses. Coming to one, he paused, kicked it again, murmured to himself, "That's right. E flat," and entered the door.

42—While Sir Wilfred Lawson was pushing anti-liquor agitation in the House of Lords, some of his waggish enemies passed this story about: During Sir Wilfred's university days he was accused of breaking rules, and the head of his college called him upon the carpet. "Sir," said the dignitary, "I am told you have a barrel of beer in your room, which you should know is contrary to orders."
"Well, sir," the delinquent admitted, "that is true; but the fact is, I am of a weak constitution, and the doctors told me that if I drank this beer I should get stronger."
"And are you stronger?" the head asked sarcastically. "Oh, yes, sir; indeed I am. When the barrel came I could scarcely move it; but it was not long before I could easily roll it around the room."

43—W. C. Fields was suffering from one of his daily hangovers. "May I fix you a Bromo-Seltzer?" suggested the waiter. "Ye gods, no!" moaned Fields, "I couldn't stand the noise."

44—In Texas they like their liquor straight, as witness the case of one old-timer who, upon taking in his hand a small tumbler of whiskey, said, "Blindfold me and hold my nose

—'cause if I see it or smell it, my mouth will water and dilute it!"

45—In one of our Southwestern proverbially dry states a couple of strangers in town asked a man on the street where they could get a drink. "Well," said the man, "in this town they only use whiskey for snake bite. There's only one snake in town, and it's gettin' kind of late. You'd better hurry down and git in line before it gits exhausted."

46—A question of perspective was raised by the case of the drunk, who, while unconscious, had some Limburger cheese rubbed on his mustache. Coming to later, staggering feebly along, he began to say, "Ain't it awful!"
"What is the trouble?" someone asked.
"Ain't it awful!" said the drunk. "The whole world smells."

47—An inebriated gentleman was weaving gently down the street carrying in his hand a box with perforations in the lid and sides. An acquaintance stopped him and said, "My word, what have you got in the box?"
"Shh," said the drunk. "It's a mongoose."
"What on earth for?" asked his friend.
"Well," he said, "you know how it is with me. I'm not very drunk now, but I'll be soon, and when I am I see snakes and I'm scared of 'em, and that's what I got the mongoose for; to protect me."
"But, good heavens," said his friend, "those are imaginary snakes!"
"That's all right," said the drunk reassuringly. "That's all right; this is an imaginary mongoose."

48—The young fellow, slightly green in the ways of the smart set, apologized to his hostess, explaining, "Though I may be slightly under the affluence of incohol, I'm not so think as you drunk I am."

49—At a fashionable bar the main decorations were mounted game and fish. A drunk, fascinated by them, carefully walked from one to the other, mumbling as he went. Suddenly he came upon an enormous stuffed tarpon. Swaying precariously he stared at it for a full minute, then burst forth, "The fella who caught that fish is a liar!"

50—A clergyman told an Indian he should love his enemies. "I do," said the latter, "for I love rum and cider."

51—William Penn was exhorting a drunkard to cast off his habit. The drunkard lamented that this was impossible.

"No," said Penn, "it is as easy as opening thy hand, friend."

"Tell me how this is and I will do as you say," said the drunkard.

"Friend, when thee finds any vessel of intoxicating liquor in thy hand, open the hand that contains it before it reaches thy mouth and thee will never be drunk again."

52—The temperance lecturer, having exhorted the audience with the full force of his eloquence, having demonstrated all the familiar tricks, such as the emersion of an angleworm in a glass of whiskey with its consequent agonies, decided to cap the climax with a homely object lesson: "If I put a pail of whiskey and a pail of water in front of a hard-working donkey toiling in the fields, which would he drink?"

"The water," bellowed a lusty voice in the audience.

"That's true, my friend," said the lecturer. "And why would he drink the water?"

"Because he's a jackass," was the immediate reply.

53—No durance vile could be more pathetic than that suffered by the drunk who was found wandering agonizedly around and around on the sidewalk outside the fence which encloses Gramercy Park, beating upon the bars and screaming, "Let me out!"

54—In the days when Nevada was a territory Bill Nye, the humorist, was appointed Governor. As he journeyed to Carson City to take over his duties in this wild and wide-open silver country, Mark Twain accompanied him.

Word of the new Governor's arrival had reached Carson City, and the boys had gotten together and decided to put the Easterner and his friend in their place by giving them a big banquet and drinking them under the table in short order. The night of the banquet drinks and speeches flowed unceasingly for hours. One by one those present slipped gracefully under their chairs and slumbered noisily beneath the tablecloths.

At a small hour of the night only two men were left in a state of consciousness and seated upright—Bill Nye and Mark Twain.

"Well, Bill," said Twain, stretching and getting up from his chair, "let's go out of here somewhere and get a drink."

55—The representative of an auction house was sent to a home to take an inventory of the goods therein in preparation

for a sale. The inventory had progressed in an orderly
manner through many large items, such as, one walnut
bedroom suite, then listed in detail, one walnut dining-
room suite, likewise listed in detail, and similar items of
household furnishings, until at last came the individual
items of miscellany.

At the top of this list was "One quart Scotch whiskey, full";
the list continued, then appeared the item, "One quart
whiskey, partially full." The list continued; then appeared
the item, "One whiskey bottle, empty."

The final item on the list was, "Two revolving Turkish rugs."

SEE ALSO
Accuracy 92
Boastfulness 103
Liars 333
Quick Thinking 492
Rough and Ready 500
Stinginess 560, 561
Zanies 642
Prejudice 682
Speeches 759
Husband 918
Hollywood 1446
Evangelists 1515
Conversions 1622, 1625
Doctors 1666
Medicines 1731

RELATED SUBJECTS
Eating 6–23
Parties 741–746
Banquets and Dinners 751–753
Prohibitions and Restrictions
   1641–1642
Hotels and Restaurants 2296–2302
Law Enforcement 2546–2548

Billiards 1827
Miscellaneous Contests
   1882
Bosses 2232
Servants 2283
Officers 2416

SMOKING

61—Charles Steinmetz, "the electrical wizard," was an inveterate
smoker. When a notice forbidding smoking was posted in
the General Electric plant where he worked, Steinmetz
ignored it until an executive asked if he was not aware of
the rule. The answer was a cold indifferent stare. The
next day Steinmetz didn't show up, and for two days no
one heard from him, while important work remained untouched. Then began a serious search which ended in the
lobby of a Buffalo hotel where he was found sitting at ease
in a huge chair and puffing a cigar.

Told that the whole company was looking for him, and asked
why he had left so unceremoniously, he calmly replied, "I
came up here to have a smoke." After that the smoking
rule was never applied to him.

62—Thomas Edison was telling Mr. Cary a story one day about the way his friends, when they came into his office, would help themselves to his pure Havana cigars. "They just take 'em by the handful," he said.

"Why don't you lock them up?" asked Mr. Cary.

"Never could remember to do it," returned Edison. "Then, Johnson, my secretary you know, did a clever trick. He had a friend in the cigar business and promised to get him to make me some entirely of cabbage leaves and brown paper. I thought that was a fine scheme. But the cigars didn't come, so I asked him one day about it when I noticed my Havanas disappearing again.

" 'Why, I sent them to you,' he said. 'I left them with your manager.'

"I called the manager in and asked him where those cigars were. 'Why,' he said, 'I put them in your valise when you went to California last month. I didn't know what they were.'

"Do you know, Cary," continued Edison, "I smoked every-one of those damned cigars myself!"

63—This story is told by Max Mueller:

"Tennyson's pipe was almost indispensable to him, and I remember one time when I and several friends were staying at his house, the question of tobacco turned up. Some of his friends taunted Tennyson that he could never give up tobacco. 'Anybody can do that,' he said, 'if he chooses to do it.' When his friends still continued to doubt and to tease him, 'Well' he said, 'I shall give up smoking from tonight.' The very same evening I was told that he threw his tobacco and his pipes out of the window of his bedroom. The next day he was most charming, though somewhat self-righteous. The second day he became very moody and captious, the third day no one knew what to do with him. But after a disturbed night I was told that he got out of bed in the morning, went quietly into the garden, picked up one of his broken pipes, stuffed it with the remains of the tobacco scattered about, and then having had a few puffs, came to breakfast, all right again."

64—A minister was deeply impressed by an address on the evils of smoking given at a synod. He arose from his seat, went over to a fellow minister, and said: "Brother, this morning I received a present of 100 good cigars. I have smoked one of them, but now I'm going home to burn the rest in the fire."

The other minister arose and said it was his intention to accompany his reverend brother.

"I mean to rescue the ninety-nine," he added.

65—When Dr. Creighton was Bishop of London he rode on a train one day with a small, meek curate. Dr. Creighton, an ardent lover of tobacco, soon took out his cigar case, and with a smile, said: "You don't mind my smoking, I suppose?"

The meek curate bowed and answered humbly: "Not if your lordship doesn't mind my being sick".

SEE ALSO	RELATED SUBJECTS
Longevity 1782	Will Power 631
Advertising 2102	Prohibitions and Restrictions 1641–1642

PROFANITY

66—Mark Twain's habit of swearing was revolting to his wife, who tried her best to cure him of it. One day, while shaving, he cut himself. He recited his entire vocabulary and when he was finished, his wife repeated every word he had said. Mark Twain stunned her by saying calmly:

"You have the words, dear, but you don't know the tune."

67—A minister on a fishing trip was delighted to find that his guide was once hired by Bishop Phillips Brooks. They immediately began talking about him, recalling many noble traits and characteristics.

"Yes," said the guide, "He was a fine man 'cept for his swearing."

"What," exclaimed the minister, "Bishop Brooks swear? Impossible!"

"Oh, but he did, sir. Once he hooked a fine big bass. Just as he hoisted him into the boat, the fish slipped and went clean off the hook. So I said to the Bishop, 'That's a damned shame,' and the Bishop come back and said, 'Yes, it is.' But that's the only time I ever heard him use such language."

68—A certain Elector of Cologne, who was at the same time archbishop, had one day made use of profane words and then said to a farmer who could not conceal his astonishment:

"Why do you look so surprised?"

The farmer replied: "Because an archbishop can be so profane."

"I do not swear as an archbishop," replied that person, "but as a prince."

"But Your Highness," answered the farmer, "when the prince goes to hell, what will become of the archbishop?"

The Elector's reply was not reported.

SEE ALSO
Golf 1864
Witnesses 2504
Ministers 2607

RELATED SUBJECTS
Rough and Ready 496–507
Rudeness 511–524
Temper 596–598
Prohibitions and Restrictions
1641–1642

GAMBLING

71—At a large party, Mrs. Henry Clay, chaperoning a young lady, passed through a room where gentlemen were playing cards, Mr. Clay among them. "Is this a common practise?" inquired the young lady.

"Yes," said Mrs. Clay; "they always play when they get together."

'Doesn't it distress you to have Mr. Clay gamble?"

"No, my dear," said the old lady composedly, "he 'most always wins."

72—An ailing bookmaker sent his son to summon the doctor. Instead of the expected man, a stranger arrived. Later, the bookmaker asked for an explanation. "Well," said the boy, "there were a lot of brass plates on the doors, and when I got to the one you told me to go to, it said, 'Consultations, 11 to 12.' The one next to it said, '10 to 1.' And I knew you'd like the one who gave the best odds."

73—The British comedienne, Beatrice Lillie, once won a hundred and fifty thousand francs at Chemin de fer through having the hiccoughs. Her repeated convulsions and noises were interpreted by the croupier as cries of "Banquo."

74—Grandmother was bitterly opposed to gambling games—especially poker—but gave her sanction to the playing of authors. So the grandchildren engaged her interests in the game of her choice. Her enthusiasm increased as the game progressed, and while she knew that the cards used were a deck of authors, she didn't know that the game she was playing was poker, and that grandmother was enthusiastically playing Whittiers wild.

SEE ALSO   RELATED SUBJECTS
Liars 333   Extravagance 231–232
Natural Death 1756   Prohibitions and Restrictions
Deathbed Scenes 1771   1641–1642
Card Playing 1836   Card Playing 1836–1840
Bargaining 2081
Chiseling 2130

REPUTATION

76—One of the powerful figures in Wall Street fell in love with an actress and for many months danced constant attendance upon her and squired her about in the fashionable circles of town. Deciding to marry her, he first prudently put a private detective to the job of looking into her antecedents in order to guard himself against any rash mistake. At last he received his agent's report. "Miss Blank enjoys an excellent reputation. Her past is spotless. Her associates have been irreproachable. The only breath of scandal is that, in recent months, she has been much seen in the company of a business man of doubtful reputation."

77—It is humbling, to all men of note to find themselves at some time outside of the spheres in which their talent and fame are known, and to see themselves as lesser individuals. The great Enrico Caruso once stopped at a farm during a drive through the country. He obtained water and something to eat, and while he was talking in a friendly way with the farmer, the latter chanced to inquire his name. He said his name was Caruso. Instantly the farmer was transfixed. "What an honor," he said, "what an honor to have in my own house that great traveler, Robinson Crusoe."

78—An Irishman was charged with a petty offense. "Have you anybody here who can vouch for your character?" said the judge. "Yes, your Honor, the sheriff there can."
"Why, I do not even know this man," exclaimed the sheriff.
"Observe, Your Honor," said the Irishman triumphantly, "that I've lived twelve years in this county and the sheriff doesn't even know me."

SEE ALSO   RELATED SUBJECTS
Authors 1212   Behavior 1
Politics 1899   Discretion 181–182

Modesty 376–390
Gossip 821–826
Credit 2166–2167

TRAITS

ABSENT-MINDEDNESS

81—The late Dwight Morrow, who was very absent-minded, was once reading earnestly on a train when the conductor asked for his ticket. Frantically Mr. Morrow searched for it.

"Never mind, Mr. Morrow," the conductor said. "When you find it, mail it to the company. I'm certain you have it."

"I know I have it," exploded Mr. Morrow. "But what I want to know is, where in the world am I going?"

82—In his old age, Lessing, the German author became very absent-minded. Coming home one night with his mind on some work he intended to finish, he found the door locked, and discovered that he had not taken his key with him. In answer to his knock, a servant looked out of an upstairs window, and mistaking his master for a stranger, called out, "The professor is not at home."

"Very well," Lessing answered meekly as he turned away. "Tell him that I'll call another time."

83—J. David Stern, former publisher of the New York Post, was sometimes accused of absent-mindedness. Once, as he hastened down the street, he was accosted by a friend who said, "Come, have lunch with me."

"All right," said Stern, "if we go to some place nearby. I am already late."

They entered a restaurant close at hand, and as he ordered, Stern wondered what could be the matter with him for he said, "I am not a bit hungry."

"I beg pardon, sir," the waiter said, "but you just finished lunch five minutes ago."

84—When her daughters were very small girls, Mrs. Dwight Morrow gave a high tea at which one of the guests was to be the senior J. P. Morgan. The girls were to be brought in, introduced and ushered out. Mrs. Morrow's great fear was the possibility that Anne, the most outspoken of them, might comment audibly upon Mr. Morgan's celebrated and conspicuous nose. She therefore

took pains to explain to Anne that personal observations
were impolite, and to caution her especially against making any comment upon Mr. Morgan's nose, no matter
what she might think of it. When the moment came
and the children were brought in, Mrs. Morrow held
her breath as she saw Anne's gaze unfalteringly fix upon
this objective and remain there. Nonetheless, the introduction was made, the little girls curtsied and were
sent on their way. With a sigh of relief Mrs. Morrow
turned back to her duties as hostess and said to her chief
guest, "And now, Mr. Morgan, will you have cream or
lemon in your nose?"

85—"That absent-minded Professor Schmaltz has left his umbrella again. He'd leave his head if it were loose," observed the waiter.
"That's true," said the manager, "I just heard him say he
was going to Switzerland for his lungs."

86—The professor was very absent-minded. "Did you see this?"
his wife asked as he came in. "There's a report in the
paper of your death."
"Dear me," said the professor, "We must remember to send
a wreath."

87—Another story about Dwight Morrow's notorious absent-
mindedness. Getting off the train in New York, he has-
tened into the telegraph office and wired to his secretary:
"Why am I in New York? What am I supposed to do?"
He received a prompt answer; that he was on his way to
Princeton to deliver a lecture.

88—It is said that the late dictator of Greece, General Georges
Metaxas, during an inspection of a Mediterranean air base,
was invited to try out a new flying boat. He undertook to
pilot it himself, and all went well until the commander, his
host, observed that they were about to make a landing on
the airdrome. "Excuse me, General, but it would be better
to come down on the sea; this is a flying boat."
"Of course, Commander, what was I thinking of!" said
Metaxas, suddenly recollecting himself, and making a safe
landing on the water. Rising from the wheel he said,
"Commander, I greatly appreciate the tact with which you
drew my attention to the incredible blunder which I nearly
made." Saying which, he opened the door and stepped into
the sea.

89—"You mean to say," asked the Judge of the defendant, "that you threw your wife out of the second story window through forgetfulness?"

"Yes, sir," replied the defendant. "We used to live on the ground floor and I plumb forgot we moved."

90—Thomas Henry Huxley once arrived late in a town in which he was to deliver an important lecture. Jumping into a cab, he cried to the driver, "Top speed!" In a hurry the cabby whipped his horse into action and the vehicle went bumping along the streets at a wild clip. The lack of dignity and organization in the proceedings then dawned upon Huxley, and above the clatter of the wheels he shouted to the driver, "Here, here, do you know where I want to go?"

"No, your Honor," called the cabby, cracking his whip the while, "but I'm driving as fast as I can."

SEE ALSO
Smoking 62
Books 1223
Churches 1527
Death 1749

RELATED SUBJECTS
Eccentricity 196–209
Memory 371–375
Professors 1026–1032

ACCURACY

91—Cordell Hull is an extremely cautious speaker, striving always for scientific accuracy. One day on a train, a friend pointed to a fine flock of sheep grazing in a field. "Look, those sheep have just been sheared," he said.

Hull studied the flock. "Sheared on this side, anyway," he admitted.

92—The captain of a certain freighter was a martinet who, although technically just, was noted far and wide for the strictness of his interpretation of facts.

On a certain voyage he had a new first mate, an able and conscientious man. Following an occasion of shipboard revelry, the captain entered in the log the note, "The first mate was drunk last night."

Seeing this the mate was greatly distressed and pled with the captain to strike it off the record. He had never been drunk before, he insisted, would not be drunk again; was conscientious in the performance of his duties and had been off duty at the time of the offense anyway. He begged for leniency, pointing out what an unduly detrimental effect on his record such an entry on the log might have.

The captain remained adamant, "You were drunk last night and I can't change the fact. The record will stand."

Much wounded by this the first mate resumed his duties. That night it fell to his lot to make the next entry in the log for the period of his watch. This he did, with what may be called a malicious scrupulousness of accuracy. Accordingly the captain next day found on the log the innocently damning statement, "The captain was sober last night."

RELATED SUBJECTS

Carelessness 136
Diligence 176–177
Liars 331–336
Memory 371–375
Scientists 1116–1122
Mathematicians 1146–1154
Statistics 2221–2222
Evidence 2521–2523

AMBITION

96—Some of Mr. Lincoln's intimate friends once called his attention to a certain member of his Cabinet who was quietly working to secure a nomination for the Presidency, although knowing that Mr. Lincoln was to be a candidate for reëlection. His friends insisted that the Cabinet officer ought to be made to give up his Presidential aspirations or be removed from office. The situation reminded Mr. Lincoln of a story:

"My brother and I," he said, "were once plowing corn, I driving the horse and he holding the plow. The horse was lazy, but on one occasion he rushed across the field so that I, with my long legs, could scarcely keep pace with him. On reaching the end of the furrow, I found an enormous chin-fly fastened upon him, and knocked him off. My brother asked me what I did that for. I told him I didn't want the old horse bitten in that way. 'Why,' said my brother, 'that's all that made him go.'

"Now," said Mr. Lincoln, "if Mr. ——— has a Presidential chin-fly biting him, I'm not going to knock it off, if it will only make his department go."

97—Oliver Herford, the well known humorist, attended a dinner at which he was seated next to a very serious and soulful young lady.

"Tell me, Mr. Herford," she asked, "have you no other ambition beyond making people laugh?"

In the same serious vein, Herford replied, "Yes, I have. And some day I hope to gratify it."

Eagerly the girl asked, "Please tell me. What is it?"

"I want to throw an egg into an electric fan," replied Herford simply.

SEE ALSO	RELATED SUBJECTS
Patriotism 399	Diligence 176–177
Conductor 1332	Laziness 326–327
Efficiency 2269	Campaigning 1911–1920
	Office Seekers 1966–1970
	Salesmen 2091–2097
	Competition 2116

BOASTFULNESS

101—Mark Twain, whenever feats of heroism or ingenuity were being bragged about, would come forth with a little story of his own which usually climaxed the discussion.

"There was a fire in Hannibal one night, and old man Hankinson got caught in the fourth story of the burning house. It looked as if he was a goner. None of the ladders was long enough to reach him. The crowd stared at one another, nobody could think of anything to do.

"Then, all of a sudden, boys, an idea occurred to me. 'Fetch a rope,' I yelled, 'somebody fetch a rope,' and, with great presence of mind, I flung the end of it up to old man Hankinson; 'Tie it around your waist,' I yelled. The old man did so, and I pulled him down."

102—An over-patriotic American gazed at the superb masses of a European cathedral with its marvelous statues and ornaments, and asked the guide how long it had taken to build. "Five hundred years," replied the guide.

The American sniffed, "Five hundred years. Why, we would build a structure like that and have it fall to pieces on our hands all inside of two or three years."

103—A group of men in a bar-room were exchanging wild boasts about their feats of courage and bravery. When the tall tales had almost stretched themselves to the limit, a quiet old Swede who had been silently drinking and listening, spoke up, "I myself never do anything so very brave," said he, "But my brudder, he call Yessie Yames a big s-o-b." The others were appalled.

"What," they cried, "he called Jessie James an s-o-b? Tell us about it."

"My brudder he vas drinking and he get pretty drunk. Yessie Yames in same bar-room. My brudder he go over and say, 'Yessie Yames, you are one great big s-o-b.' "

"What did Jessie James do?" demanded his listeners.

"He shoot my brudder!"

SEE ALSO	RELATED SUBJECTS
Exaggeration 226	Exaggeration 221–226
Baseball 1824	Liars 331–336
Fishing 1846, 1853	Long-Windedness 341–363
Hunting 1877	Modesty 376–390
Miscellaneous Contests	Pompousness 421–427
1883	Pride 456–457
	Vanity 606–628

BONERS

106—While shown the sights of Chicago by the Mayor of that city, M. Cambon, the French Ambassador of another generation, expressed his thanks for the Mayor's kindness. "But," he added, "I am sorry so to cockroach on your time."

"Oh," answered the Mayor, "don't think of that. But you don't mean cockroach M. Cambon; it is encroach, you mean."

"Oh, is it? I see—a difference in gender."

107—As is usual, during public events of any kind, the newspapers hurriedly set up their front pages to describe the inauguration of Theodore Roosevelt.

The evidence of this haste was shown by a New York paper which described the event as follows:

"It was a scene never to be forgotten when Roosevelt, before the Chief Justice of the Supreme Court and a few witnesses, took his simple bath."

108—There is a Congressional legend about the newly elected Congressman who, in his maiden speech on the floor of the House, said, "As Daniel Webster makes clear in his famous dictionary . . ."

He was interrupted from the floor by a cry of, "Noah Webster wrote the dictionary."

"Noah nothing," replied the speaker, "Noah built the ark!"

109—Every newspaper makes its more or less amusing or more or less disastrous typographical errors in headlines or stories. Usually, when these occur, they must be corrected, if caught, in subsequent editions. It is said that recently one of the most important newspapers in Washington reported on its front page a mild indisposition of President Roosevelt with the headline, "President Kept to Rooms by Coed." Most of the run had been printed and had to be destroyed. The President, however, heard of the matter and procured from the paper in question several copies to distribute to his friends.

110—A man stopped at the shop of a Cockney bookseller and asked for Omar Khayyam. "Sorry, sir," said the Cockney, "we 'ave 'is Hilliad and 'is Hodessey but not 'is Khayyam."

111—Benjamin Franklin, being present at the meeting of some literary society in Paris, where many pieces were read, and not well understanding the French when declaimed, but wishing to appear polite, resolved to applaud when he should see a lady of his acquaintance, Mme. de Boufflers, express satisfaction. After the reading was over, his little boy said to him, "But grand-papa, you always applauded, and louder than anybody else, when they were praising you."

112—When Julia Ward Howe died, memorial services were held at San Francisco. The local literary colony attended practically en masse to pay their final tribute. The Mayor was asked to preside. Advancing to the edge of the platform he said.

"Your attendance here, ladies and gents, in such great numbers, shows San Francisco's appreciation of good literature. This meeting is a great testimonial to the immortal author of "Uncle Tom's Cabin"—the late Julia Ward Howard!"

113—"Marse" Henry Watterson used to tell with pleasure of his favorite typographical boner in newspapers. It happened that a New York journal transposed, one day, the headings of its obituary column and the marine and shipping news which had chanced to fall on the same page. As a result a number of respected and deceased citizens were listed under the disconcerting heading, "Passed through Hell Gate today."

114—This was one of Cardinal Gibbons' favorite jokes: Patrick Gilmore, the bandmaster, famous for his rendition of Mozart's "Twelfth Mass," once presented his favorite

number in a small North Carolina town. The reporter
of the one newspaper in town, who was assigned to
"cover" the performance evidently thought that the occasion was one that called upon him to avoid any un-
dignified abbreviations in his write-up of the concert.
He began with this statement: "Gilmore's band rendered
with great effect Mozart's 'Twelfth Massachusetts.'"

115—A young lady, who had recently acquired a large fortune,
invited Paderewski to give a private concert at her
home. Her knowledge of music was by no means as
large as her newly found wealth.

Commenting on one of his selections, she exclaimed, "What
a beautiful piece. Who composed it?"

"Beethoven, Madam," was the reply.

"Ah, yes," she said knowingly, "and is he composing now?"

"No," replied Paderewski gravely, "he is decomposing."

116—A woman whose husband had entered the Navy, gave the
pastor of her church a note just as he was mounting to
the pulpit one Sunday morning. The note said, "John
Anderson, having gone to sea, his wife desires the prayers of the congregation for his safety." The minister in
haste picked up the slip and read aloud, "John Anderson,
having gone to see his wife, desires the prayers of the
congregation for his safety."

117—In the early days of his career the famous writer of short
stories, Bret Harte, was editor of a newspaper in a California mining town. It was his painful duty one time
to write an obituary for the highly respected wife of a
leading citizen. Harte concluded his remarks with the
sentence, "She was distinguished for charity above all
the other ladies in this town."

When the proof of this was handed to him he found that
the compositor had rendered his statement, "She was
distinguished for chastity above all the other ladies of
this town." Carefully, Harte corrected the matter thinking it sufficient to refer the compositor back to the original copy by a large query in the margin. To his horror,
the following day the paper appeared with the statement:
"She was distinguished for chastity (?) above all the
other ladies in this town."

118—A freight agent on the Delaware, Lackawanna and Western received a shipment including a donkey, which was
itemized on the freight bill as, "1 Burro."

He checked over his shipment carefully and then filed his report, concluding with, "short, 1 bureau; over, 1 jackass."

119—A cub reporter was sent to cover the annual class play of the local high school. Being new to his job he described the event in glowing terms, instead of the scant few lines used by a more experienced newspaperman for such an event, and concluded with the words:
"And the auditorium was filled with expectant mothers, eagerly awaiting their offspring."

SEE ALSO
Practical Joking 436
Speeches 772
Introductions 789, 791
Marriage 877
Father 990
Learned Men 1089
Producers 1393
Collections 1567
Billiards 1827

RELATED SUBJECTS
Absent-Mindedness 81–90
Carelessness 136
Stupidity 576–583
Tact 586–591

Dancing 1841
Fishing 1852
Rationing 2358
Officers 2425

BORROWING

121—Mark Twain once went to borrow a certain book from a neighbor.
"Why, yes, Mr. Clemens, you're more than welcome to it," the neighbor told him. "But I must ask you to read it here. You know I make it a rule never to let any book go out of my library."
Some days later the neighbor wished to borrow Twain's lawn mower.
"Why, certainly," the humorist genially assured him. "You're more than welcome to it. But I must ask you to use it here. You know I make it a rule."

122—Charles Lamb meeting an acquaintance, asked him to lend him five shillings; but the friend had only half-a-crown about him, which he handed to Lamb.
Some time after, the acquaintance meeting Lamb, said, "Ah by-the-bye you owe me half-a-crown."
"N-n-not at all," replied Lamb, "y-you owe me h-half-a-crown; f-for d-don't you recollect, I asked y-you for f-five sh-shillings and you only g-g-gave me t-two-and-six-p-pence?"

123—The first time Jerrold saw Tom Dibdin, the song-writer said to him, "Youngster, have you sufficient confidence in me to lend me a guinea?"

"Oh, yes," was the reply, "I've all the confidence—but I haven't the guinea."

124—Mr. Temple Stangan borrowed a sum of money from Joseph Addison the English author and statesman, who soon remarked that his debtor ceased to converse with him on equal terms, and yielded tamely to whatever Addison said. The change displeased Addison and one day when Mr. Stangan had expressed perfect agreement on some topic which had frequently been the subject of keen dispute between them, he exclaimed, heatedly: "Either contradict me, sir, or pay me my money."

125—A visitor in the home of Mark Twain remarked upon the great number of books, many of which were piled about without any adequate provision for them.
"You see," Twain explained, "it is so very difficult to borrow shelves."

126—"I visit my friends occasionally," remarked Hazlitt bitterly, "just to look over my library."

SEE ALSO
Playwrights 1380, 1385

RELATED SUBJECTS
Economy 211–213
Extravagance 231–232
Banks 2151–2158
Loans 2161–2164
Credit 2166–2167
Debt 2171–2174

BREVITY

131—The editor of a small Missouri paper sent a notice to one Bill Jenkins that his subscription had expired. The note came back with the laconic scrawl, "So's Bill."

132—During his administration, President Coolidge was one time taken on a tour of inspection through the fabulously magnificent and variegated horticultural conservatories on the estate of Pierre S. DuPont at Longwood, Pennsylvania.
The marvelous beauties of the spring flowers, the exotically cultivated special fruits, the weird and unreal forms of cacti, the beautiful ferns, the orchids; all these things elicited from the President no word of comment. Stepping into the close and humid atmosphere of the room devoted to tropical trees, the President looked about for a moment and remarked with interest, "Bananas."

133—At one of the White House press conferences various reporters were vainly firing their questions at Calvin Coolidge.

"Have you anything to say about Prohibition?"

"No."

"Have you anything to say about the World Court?"

"No."

"About the farm situation?"

"No."

"About the forthcoming senatorial campaign?"

"No."

The meeting broke up and the reporters began to file out of the room.

"And," called the President, "don't quote me."

134—Bob Burns, the local-boy-who-made-good from Arkansas, is well-known for his stories about his large and amusing family. One day, when chided for his loquaciousness, he explained that not all members of his family were as given to the gift of gab as himself.

"Now take my cousin Wilfred. He was eleven years old before he so much as said one word. One day he was sittin' on a fence, watching his father plow a field. A bull broke through into the pasture and made straight for Wilfred's Pa. All of a sudden, Wilfred's mouth opened and he yelled, 'Hey, Pa! Hey! Look out fer the bull!'

"Soon as his Pa got out of the field he went straight for Wilfred and said, 'Wilfred, you shore done me a right smart favor that time. But how come you're speakin' all of a suddent? You ain't never said nothin' afore.'

" 'Well, Pa,' was Wilfred's reply, 'I jest ain't never had nothin' t' say before.' "

SEE ALSO　　　　　　　RELATED SUBJECTS
Authors 1167　　　　　　Long-Windedness 341–363
　　　　　　　　　　　　Quick Thinking 471–492
　　　　　　　　　　　　Rough and Ready 496–507

CARELESSNESS

136—Heywood Broun was noted for the general carelessness and disarray of his dress and personal appearance. One story has it, that on the occasion when Broun and a number of other war correspondents were presented to General Pershing, the General eyed the journalist with some concern and said, "Have you fallen down, Mr. Broun?"

RELATED SUBJECTS
Gambling 71–74
Extravagance 231–232
Procrastination 461
Laziness 326–327

CHEERFULNESS

141—When they reached Bolt Court Edwards said to Dr. Johnson:
"You are a philosopher, Dr. Johnson. I have tried, too, in my time, to be a philosopher; but, I don't know how, cheerfulness was always breaking in."

142—"Uncle Joe," said Albert Edward Wiggam, the author, meeting an old Negro who was always cheerful in spite of having had more than his share of life's troubles, "how have you managed to remain so cheerful and calm?"
"Well, I'll tell yo," replied Uncle Joe. "I'se jus' learned to cooperate wid de inevitable."

143—When Thomas Hart Benton's house in Washington was burned Benton left Congress and came to the ruin of his house. As he looked at it he said, "It makes dying easier. There is so much less to leave."

SEE ALSO   RELATED SUBJECTS
Cheerfulness 677   Courage 151–153
     Melancholy 366–368
     Pessimism 411

CONSCIENCE

146—There is a tradition to the effect that Noel Coward once sent identical notes to the twenty most prominent men in London, saying, "All is discovered. Escape while you can." All twenty abruptly left town.

147—To a friend who defended the behavior of the upper chamber, saying, "At least you find consciences there," Talleyrand replied: "Ah yes, many, many consciences. Semonville, for example, has at least two."

RELATED SUBJECTS
Honesty 286–294
Honor 296–298
Hyprocrisy 301–303
Devout Persons 1601–1602
Prohibitions and Restrictions
   1641–1642
Sin and Sinners 1646–1647
Chiseling and Swindling 2121–
   2132
Criminals 2571

COURAGE

151—An Athenian, who was lame in one foot, was laughed at by the soldiers on account of his lameness.
"I am here to fight," said he, "not to run."

152—Brasidas, that famous Lacedemonian general, caught a mouse. It bit him, and by that means made its escape.
"Oh!" said he, "What creature so contemptible but may have its liberty if it will fight for it!"

153—As Hugh Latimer and Nicholas Ridley, the English reformers were led to the stake, Latimer said to Ridley:
"Play the man, Master Ridley; we shall this day light such a candle, by God's grace, in England, as I trust shall never be put out."

SEE ALSO
Newspapers 1247
Civilians in War 2336
Battles 2380, 2382
Strategy 2389
Soldiers 2430, 2431

RELATED SUBJECTS
Cheerfulness 141–143
Cowardice 156–160
Endurance 216
Battles 2371–2385

COWARDICE

156—A French colonel had one day punished a young officer, just arrived from Saint-Cyr, for showing fear during his first battle. Marshal Foch to whose notice it came, severely reprimanded the disciplinarian. "Colonel!" said he, "none but a coward dares to boast that he has never known fear!"

157—When Caesar was advised by his friends to be more cautious as to the security of his person, and not to walk among the people without arms or anyone to protect him, he replied: "He who lives in the fear of death, every moment feels its tortures; I will die but once."

158—When a certain politician was spoken of as capable of assassinating anyone, Talleyrand remarked: "Assassinating, no! Poisoning, yes!"

159—The evening before a battle an officer came to ask Marshal Toiras for permission to go and see his father who was at the point of death.
"Go!" said the general who saw through his pretext— "Honor thy father and thy mother, that thy days may be long on earth."

160—Lincoln was often the despair of his generals because of his lenient treatment of cases where soldiers were absent without leave.
"If the good Lord has given a man a cowardly pair of legs," Lincoln reasoned, "it is hard to keep them from running away with him."

SEE ALSO
Officers 2422

RELATED SUBJECTS
Courage 151–153
Battles 2371–2385

CURIOSITY

161—"What made the deepest impression upon you?" inquired a friend one day, of Abraham Lincoln, "when you stood in the presence of the Falls of Niagara, the greatest of natural wonders?"
"The thing that struck me most forcibly when I saw the Falls," Lincoln responded with characteristic deliberation, "was where in the world did all that water come from?"

RELATED SUBJECTS
Imagination 306
Inventors 1126–1131
Experimenters 1136–1138

CYNICISM

166—Dr. Johnson was told that a certain cynic of his acquaintance maintained that there was no distinction between virtue and vice. "If he does really think there is no distinction between virtue and vice," answered Dr. Johnson, "why, sir, when he leaves our houses let us count our spoons."

167—Someone once asked the former Prince of Wales, "What is your idea of civilization?"
"It's a good idea," replied the Prince, "somebody ought to start it."

168—When it was remarked that Fouché, an associate of Talleyrand under Napoleon, had a profound contempt for human nature, Talleyrand replied, "To be sure; he has made a careful study of himself."

169—In one of his travels Mungo Park, the African explorer, traversed a wide extent of uncultivated regions, but at last he chanced upon a gibbet, "The sight of which," said he, "gave me infinite pleasure, as it proved that I was in a civilized society."

170—When the motto of the Hanover Club of Göttingen, to which as a student he had belonged, was quoted to him as applicable to his own life, Bismarck reflected: "Yes, 'No Steps Backwards,' but a good many zig-zags."

SEE ALSO
Gratitude 265
Speeches 782
Husband 916
Authors 1216
Sermons 1547
Politics 1896
Chiseling 2131

RELATED SUBJECTS
Hypocrisy 301–303
Atheists and Agnostics 1651–1659

DEVOTION

171—R. L. Stevenson won the devotion of the Samoans. When the European powers imprisoned Mataafa, one of their chiefs, Stevenson visited him and other political prisoners, bringing them tobacco and other gifts. When they were released they voluntarily built a wide road up to Stevenson's house; and they made him a chief of one of their tribes. Once when Sosimo, his body-servant, had been unusually thoughtful, Stevenson complimented him, "Great is the wisdom." "No," Sosimo replied, "great is the love."

When Stevenson died a group of picked natives bore the coffin to the place of internment on the mountain top. A stranger had appeared at the funeral, to which only close personal friends were invited, a Scotchman who explained that some years before Stevenson had met him on the road as a stranger on a day when he was contemplating suicide, but that Stevenson had dissuaded him. The Samoan chiefs tabooed the use of firearms on the hill of his grave, that the birds might sing there undisturbed.

172—It is said that a great French actress—reproved for wearing bright colors the day after her lover's funeral—replied: "Ah, you should have seen me yesterday; then you would have known what true sorrow is!"

173—Mrs. Isadore Strauss was one of the few women who went down on the Titanic in 1912, and she went down because she could not bear to leave her husband. Both he and she were calm throughout the excitement of loading the lifeboats. Both aided frightened women and children to find places aboard them. Finally, Mr. Strauss, who had been urging his wife again and again to seek safety in a lifeboat, forced her to enter one. She was no more seated, however, than she sprang up and got to the deck before her husband could stop her. There, she caught his arm, snuggling it against her side, exclaiming, "We have been long together through a great many years. We are old now. Where you go, I will go."

SEE ALSO   RELATED SUBJECTS
Kindness 313   Generosity 241–248
                     Kindness 311–316
                     Patriotism 396–407
                     Love 846–850
                     Friendship 866–867
                     Devout Persons 1601–1602

DILIGENCE

176—Abe Lincoln's father was never at a loss for an answer. An old neighbor of Thomas Lincoln was passing the Lincoln farm one day when he saw Abe's father grubbing up some hazelnut bushes and said to him:
"Why, Grandpop, I thought you wanted to sell your farm?"
"And so I do," he replied, "but I ain't goin' to let my farm know it."
"Abe's jes' like his father," the old ones would say.

177—Clarence Darrow was a hard working and energetic man. His clothes were often disheveled. Once he was ragged about this by a group of reporters. He silenced them by saying, "I go to a better tailor than any of you and pay more money for my clothes. The only difference between us is that you probably don't sleep in yours."

SEE ALSO	RELATED SUBJECTS
Instrumentalists 1351, 1356	Ambition 96–97
Hiring 2249	Patience 391
	Procrastination 461
	Stubbornness 571–572
	Will Power 631

DISCRETION

181—"Pray," said a facetious lady, "Mr. Pitt, as you know everything that is moving in the political world tell me some news."

"I am sorry madam," said the discreet premier, "I have not read the newspaper of the day."

182—Secretary of the Navy Knox, was asked by an old friend some casual question about the movement of certain ships in Atlantic waters. The question was thoughtless and Knox leaned over with an air of confidence and said, "Look here, can you keep a secret?"

"Of course, of course," replied the friend eagerly.

"Well," said Knox, "So can I!"

SEE ALSO	RELATED SUBJECTS
Father 989	Carelessness 136
	Modesty 376–390
	Tact 586–591

DULLNESS

186—Lincoln was told of a profound historian, "It may be doubted whether any man of our generation has plunged more deeply into the sacred fount of learning."

"Yes, or come up drier," said Lincoln.

187—One day one of the greatest bores of the Players Club said to Oliver Herford, "Oliver, I have been grossly insulted. Just as I passed that group over there I overheard someone say he would give me $50. to resign from the club."

"Hold out for a hundred," counseled Mr. Herford, "you'll get it."

188—A gentleman who introduced his brother to Dr. Johnson was desirous of recommending him to his notice; which

he did by saying, "When we have sat together some time, you'll find my brother growing very interesting."
"Sir," said Dr. Johnson, "I can wait."

189—To a very thin man who had been boring him, Douglas Jerrold said:
"Sir, you are like a pin, but without either its head or its point."

190—Douglas Jerrold, 19th Century wit, was approached one day by a chatty bore. "Well, well, Jerrold," he said. "What's going on?"
"I am," said Jerrold, and did.

191—An impertinent chatterbox, entertaining Aristotle, the philosopher, with a tedious discourse, and observing that he did not much regard him, made an apology, that he was afraid he had interrupted him.
"No, really," replied the philosopher, "you have not interrupted me at all, for I have not minded one word you said."

192—Talleyrand was asked if a certain authoress whom he had long since known, but who had belonged rather to the last age, was not, "a little tiresome." "Not at all," said he, "she was perfectly tiresome."

193—Sir Walter Scott's faithful servant Tom said to him one day, "Them are fine novels of yours; they are invaluable to me. When I come home very tired, and take up one of them, I'm asleep directly."

194—Speaking of a dull, tiresome fellow whom he chanced to meet, Dr. Johnson said: "That fellow seems to possess but one idea, and that is a wrong one."

195—The modest Joseph Addison was accused by a lady of being dull and heavy in conversation. "Madam," he replied with great dignity, "I have only ninepence in my pocket, but I can draw for a thousand pounds."

SEE ALSO
Practical Joking 432
Snobbishness 547
Parties 686, 742
Authors 1179
Bull Fighting 1831

RELATED SUBJECTS
Long-Windedness 341–363
Stupidity 576–583

ECCENTRICITY

196—There was a tale current in Park Row—how Richard Harding Davis, finding a stranger at his favorite table at Delmonico's, was supposed to have remarked: "I beg your pardon. My name is Richard Harding Davis and you are in my chair."

"Do not mind," replied the usurper. "My name is Jove. Many swear by me. If you are one, sit down."

197—A story of Isadora Duncan's: At the Hotel Trianon D'Annunzio had a gold-fish which he loved. It was in a wonderful crystal bowl and D'Annunzio used to feed it and talk to it. The gold-fish would agitate its fins and open and shut its mouth as though to answer him.

One day when I was staying at the Trianon, I said to the maitre d'hotel:

"Where is the gold-fish of D'Annunzio?"

"Ah, madame, sorrowful story! D'Annunzio went to Italy and told us to take care of it. 'This gold-fish,' he said, 'is so near to my heart. It is a symbol of all my happiness!' And he kept telegraphing: 'How is my beloved Adolphus?' One day Adolphus swam a little more slowly round the bowl and ceased to ask for D'Annunzio. I took it and threw it out of the window. But there came a telegram from D'Annunzio: 'Feel Adolphus is not well.' I wired back: 'Adolphus dead. Died last night.' D'Annunzio replied: 'Bury him in the garden. Arrange his grave.' So I took a sardine and wrapped it in silver paper and buried it in the garden and I put a cross: 'Here lies Adolphus!' D'Annunzio returned: 'Where is the grave of my Adolphus?'

"I showed him the grave in the garden and he brought many flowers to it and stood for a long time weeping tears upon it."

198—Edward W. Bok told how, "I was asked to come to a breakfast at Oscar Wilde's house, and noticed as I sat down that next to me, at my left, had been placed a man instead of the usual rotation. I turned to my left to find my neighbor had pushed his chair back from the table about three feet, and buried his chin in his shirt-bosom and was reaching forth for his eatables, and practically eating them from his lap, his cup resting on his knee. There was something familiar about the features of my neighbor who was eating in the most grotesque fashion I ever saw, and yet I could not place him. I looked for his place-card, but I could see none. So I shoved back my chair and tried to engage him in conversation. But I was not rewarded by even a glance. When I asked a question I received either no answer at all or a grunt. After a few heroic efforts, I gave up the struggle.

"At the close of the breakfast, I asked Wilde: 'Who in the world was that chap at my left?'

" 'I know,' returned Wilde. 'I saw your valiant struggle. He gets that way once in a while, and this morning happened to be one of those whiles. That was Whistler!' "

199—"My rubber," said Nat Goodwin, describing a Turkish bath that he once had in Mexico, "was a very strong man. He laid me on a slab and kneaded me and punched me and banged me in a most emphatic way. When it was over and I had gotten up, he came up behind me before my sheet was adjusted, and gave me three resounding slaps on the bare back with the palm of his enormous hand.

"What in blazes are you doing?" I gasped, staggering.

"No offense, sir," said the man. "It was only to let the office know that I was ready for the next bath. You see, sir, the bell's out of order in this room."

200—Alexander Pope said, "Dean Swift has an odd blunt way that is mistaken by strangers for ill-nature: it is so odd that there is no describing it but by facts. I'll tell you one that first comes into my head. One evening (John) Gay and I went to see him: you know how intimately we were all acquainted. On our coming in, 'Heyday, gentlemen,' (says the doctor), 'what's the meaning of this visit? How come you two to leave all the great lads that you are so fond of, to come hither to see a poor dean?' 'Because we would rather see you than any of them.'

" 'Ay, anyone that did not know you so well as I do might believe you. But since you have come, I must get some supper for you, I suppose?'

" 'No, doctor, we have supped already.'

" 'Supped already? Why it is not eight o'clock yet. That's very strange, but if you had not supped, I must have got something for you. Let me see, what should I have had? A couple of lobsters? Ay, that would have done very well, two shillings; tarts, a shilling. But you will drink a glass of wine with me, though you supped so much before your usual time, only to spare my pocket.'

" 'No, we had rather talk with you than drink with you.'

" 'But if you had supped with me, as in all reason you ought to have done, you must then have drank with me. A bottle of wine, two shillings. Two and two is four, and one is five; just two and six-pence apiece. There Pope, there's half a crown for you; and there's another for you (Gay) Sir; for I won't save anything by you I am determined.'

"This was all said and done with his usual seriousness on such occasions: and in spite of everything we could say to the contrary, he actually obliged us to take the money."

201—Into the bakery shop, the most famous and costly of its kind in New York, came a customer with an order for a cake to be baked in the shape of the letter "s". He insisted on various details of its decoration and specified that it must be ready by a certain date. The day before the deadline the customer dropped around and found that his cake was finished and being decorated. "Oh, this is all wrong," he said, flying into a rage. "You've baked it in the shape of a capital "S". I wanted it especially to be a small "s". The whole thing will have to be done over, and you'll have to have it by tomorrow anyway."

He created such a fuss that the apologetic manager said that they would make every effort to satisfy him; would make it over; felt that it had been a natural mistake; but were willing to accommodate him, and so and so forth.

The following day the customer returned and found his lower case cake decorated in its final details as he desired. "That's fine," he said, much mollified. "That's just right." He drew out his wallet and paid for the cake.

"Now, sir," said the proprietor, "where shall it be sent or do you wish to take it with you?"

"Oh, that's all right," said the customer, with a wave of his hand, "I'll eat it here."

202—The Italians thought Landor the ideally mad Englishman. On one occasion he threw his cook out of the kitchen window and immediately stuck his own head out after him exclaiming, "Good God, I forgot the violets!"

203—In 1766 David Hume, the philosopher and historian, carried off Rousseau to England and tried to get a pension for him from George III. Rousseau was beginning to suffer from the persecution obsession that afflicted his later years, but at first he was purring and grateful. Then his old suspicions, his old hatred of being under obligation, came back upon him and he began to explode nervously. At such times Hume could only pat him on the back, exclaiming:

"What, my dear sir? . . . Eh, my dear sir! . . . What now, my dear Sir?"

204—In one of his lodgings Francis Thompson, the poet, habitually walked around the table all night and went to bed at dawn. Finally he wore out the carpet in a perfect circle round his table. He habitually stayed in bed most of the day and never kept appointments. Wherever he was he always sought the fire and stood against it forever getting his trousers and his coat afire. Once, in his lodging, he set the curtains afire and tipped over the lamp in trying to extinguish it. His hands were badly burned and he walked the streets all night, for, as he later remarked, "The room was quite burned out."

205—Alfred Steiglitz has always been a highly arbitrary and erratic dealer in paintings. Once, at a show of the work of Georgia O'Keeffe, a wealthy woman expressed, with a slightly patronising attitude, a desire to purchase a certain picture. Repelled subtly by the woman's manner, Steiglitz snapped, "Why do you want that painting? Give me some reason why you want it."

The prospective purchaser could think of no satisfactory reason and was refused the picture.

206—A traffic cop will signal Pop Gershwin to stop. Pop has been exceeding the speed limit, perhaps in the unconscious belief that the father of the jazz king has rights that even the police force must respect. "Don't you know who I am?" he asks the officer. "I'm the father of George Gershwin." At the same time, being a New Yorker, he pronounces the first name to rhyme with "judge." (The Jewish-American pronunciations of "George" and "judge" are surprisingly similar.) The officer scratches his head. He doesn't know every judge in Gotham. Perhaps this Judge Gershwin is a big gun up in the Bronx. Better to be safe than sorry. A salute and he lets Pa Gershwin pass. Who now can tell Pa that Gershwin isn't king?

207—In 1874, Sarah Bernhardt was advised to give up acting if she wished to live, but she returned to the theatre as soon as she was able to leave her bed. When she was asked by an admirer what gift he could send her, she replied, "They say I am to die, so you may send me a coffin."

A week later, she was notified by a famous coffin maker that an order had been received for a coffin, to be constructed according to her wishes. Sarah was most particular about its design, finally agreeing that it should be made of rosewood, with handles of solid silver—later changed to gold.

For the remainder of her life this coffin never left her side, even during her travels. She had a trestle made on which it stood at the end of her bed, so she could see it without effort, on awakening.

"To remind me that my body will soon be dust and that my glory alone will live forever," she explained.

208—Gray, the English poet, had an abnormal terror of fire and when he was living at Peterhouse got Wharton to supply him with a sixty-five-foot rope ladder with strong hooks which he fastened to a bar across his window—which bar remains there to this day.

One chill February night some undergraduates, aware of his pyrophobia, shouted, "Fire!" on his staircase. The timid Gray hastily threw out his rope ladder and descended through the darkness and cold in his nightclothes, only to drop into a carefully placed tub of water. He fell to shivering. A night-watchman discovered him and helped him back, up the stairs, to his rooms.

209—A woman visitor to the London Zoo asked a keeper whether the hippopotamus was a male or a female.

"Madam," replied the keeper sternly, "that is a question that should be of interest only to another hippopotamus."

SEE ALSO
Eating 15
Smoking 61
Practical Joking 431
Parties 744
Infidelity 903
Presidents 1934

RELATED SUBJECTS
Absent-Mindedness 81–90
Zanies 641–643

ECONOMY

211—Shortly before sailing back to England, foreign correspondent Quentin Reynolds was received by President Roosevelt in his office at the White House. While he was there the President put through a transatlantic call

to another eminent statesman, Winston Churchill. Mr.
Reynolds was slightly startled when, after a conversation,
the President said: "I'll have to hang up now. My three
minutes are up!"

212—A visitor to the White House during the Coolidge administration said to the President that he would greatly appreciate the gift of a cigar, not for himself but for a friend
who had the eccentricity of collecting cigar bands from
famous smokers all over the world. President Coolidge
thought the matter over for a few seconds, then reached
for a box of cigars. Taking one out, he carefully removed
the band, replaced the cigar in the box, and handed the
band to his visitor.

213—At Lobb's, the famous English bootmaker, one day, I saw
on the floor a heap of 20 or 30 boots, all needing cobbling
badly. "Oh, sir," Lobb explained, "these belong to the
best customer I ever had. He used to come in here and
order 15 or 20 pairs of boots. But when his father died he
left him some £3,000,000. Well sir, since then he has not
ordered a single pair of new boots, but sends the old ones
to be repaired."
"Who is he, Lobb?" I asked.
"An American, sir . . . his name is Pierpont Morgan."

SEE ALSO	RELATED SUBJECTS
Stinginess 559	Carelessness 136
Poverty 2205	Extravagance 231–232
Soldiers 2432	Stinginess 556–566

ENDURANCE
216—In the days of the homestead law a prospective settler
sought out a lawyer friend and asked him to explain the
law and its operations.
"I don't know the exact text of the law," said his friend,
"but I can give you the drift of it. The Government is
willing to bet you 160 acres of land against $14 that you
can't live on it five years without starving to death."

SEE ALSO	RELATED SUBJECTS
Miscellaneous Contests 1881	Courage 151–153
	Diligence 176–177
	Patience 391
	Stubbornness 571–572

EXAGGERATION

221—Mark Twain once asked a baggage handler in the railroad station in Washington, "Is that satchel strong enough to go in the baggage car?"

The baggage man lifted the grip high above his head and smashed it to the ground with all his might. "That," said he, "is what it will get in Philadelphia." He picked it up and bashed it against the side of the car four or five times. "That is what it will get in Chicago," he continued. He next threw it high in the air and when it had landed, jumped on it vigorously. It split open and scattered its contents over the platform. "And that is what it will get in Sioux City," he said, according to Twain. "So if you are going any farther than Sioux City, you'd better take it in the Pullman with you."

222—The Chase National Bank, operating all over the world, receives from its clients some very strange letters.

A short time ago, a furrier in Australia wrote in the following:

"Dear Sirs:

"Am sending draft for a thousand pounds, with which please credit my account. Last year I crossed a kangaroo with a raccoon, and now I'm raising fur coats with pockets."

223—Colonel Cody (Buffalo Bill) used to tell the story of an English visitor to the West. While riding through a Rocky Mountain canyon one day, a tremendous gust of wind swooped down and actually carried the Englishman off the wagon-seat. After he had picked himself up and combed the sand and gravel out of his whiskers, he said, "I say! I think you overdo ventilation in this country!"

224—Bill Nye, the humorist, was not given to mild statements. He had the following to say about liars:

"We have nothing more to say of the editor of the Sweetwater Gazette. Aside from the fact that he is a squint-eyed, consumptive liar, with a breath like a buzzard and a record like a convict, we don't know anything against him. He means well enough, and if he can evade the penitentiary and the vigilance committee for a few more years, there is a chance for him to end his life in a natural way. If he don't tell the truth a little more plentifully, however, the Green River people will rise as one man and churn him up till there won't be anything left of him but a pair of suspenders and a wart."

225—Bear stories are the stock in trade of the Alaskan sourdoughs.

One of them told of his encounter with a giant Kadiak monster. "He was all of two tons and he riz up and come at me. I didn't manage to wound him but just enough to make him mad. But then my rifle jammed. I headed for the nearest tree, but it only had one limb and that was thirty feet off the ground. I got there not more than a foot ahead of the bear and he took a swat at me as I gathered for the leap. He tore my britches but didn't quite get me. But he scairt me so badly I missed the limb."

"What happened?"

"I caught it on my way down."

226—Col. John Cremony was a famous Western figure and known as a yarn spinner. He told one story of a desperate flight from pursuing Indians. "I had a fine horse and managed to keep far enough ahead so their arrows couldn't reach me. I picked 'em off until my last cartridge was gone. Then I headed up a canyon and I'll be doggoned if it didn't end in a sheer wall. I was trapped like a rat with a dozen Apaches closing in on me. And me without as much as a penknife to defend myself."

"What happened, Colonel?" someone in his audience would invariably ask.

"Why, they killed me! Damn them, sir, they killed me!"

SEE ALSO	RELATED SUBJECTS
Baseball 1824	Boastfulness 101–103
Fishing 1846, 1851	Imagination 306
	Liars 331–336

EXTRAVAGANCE

231—After 150 years the truth is out about Benjamin Franklin. "The name 'Poor Richard' might easily have derived from his bank account rather than from his almanac," said William Fulton Kurtz after reading early records of the Bank of North America, where Franklin and many of his illustrious compatriots kept their money. "He was overdrawn at least three days out of every week."

232—When E. H. Harriman, the railroad magnate and millionaire, was dying, reporters were on the spot for the story.

The reporter of one of the metropolitan dailies was notorious for his enormous expense accounts. After the millionaire's death, the reporter's expense account, carefully itemized but out of all just proportions, was handed to the city editor. He looked it over and handed it back, saying, "If this is the will, it's worth a story."

SEE ALSO
Wife 927

RELATED SUBJECTS
Boastfulness 101–103
Imagination 306
Liars 331–336

FLATTERY

236—The politic philosopher Aristippus, by paying court to the tyrant Denys, had acquired a comfortable living and looked down upon his less prosperous fellow sages with no small degree of contempt. Seeing Diogenes washing some vegetables, he said to him disdainfully: "If you would only learn to flatter King Denys you would not have to be washing lentils."

"And you," retorted Diogenes in the same tone, "if you had only learned to live on lentils, would not have to flatter King Denys."

237—A friend once remarked to the famous cartoonist, Ding, "You must get a great deal of praise from all sides."
"No more than I need," he replied.

SEE ALSO
Borrowing 124
Salesmen 2097

RELATED SUBJECTS
Hypocrisy 301–303
Liars 331–336
Vanity 606–628

GENEROSITY

241—Aristotle, on being censured for giving alms to a bad man, answered: "I did not give it to the man, I gave it to humanity."

242—Lafcadio Hearn tells the story of a hero of the Chinese ricefields during an earthquake. From his hill-top farm he saw the ocean swiftly withdrawn, like some prodigious animal crouching for the leap, and knew the leap would be the tidal wave. He saw also that his neighbors working in low fields must be gathered to his hill or swept away. Without a second thought he set fire to his riceribs and furiously rang the temple-bell.

His neighbors thought his farm on fire and rushed to help him. Then, from that safe hill they saw the swirl of waters over fields just forsaken—and knew their salvation and its cost. Afterwards the people of these rice-fields used to go to the temple to worship their neighbor's spirit while he was still alive.

243—On his deathbed Governor Hogg of Texas requested that no monument be placed at his grave; but that instead, there be planted, "at my head a pecan tree, and at my feet an old fashioned walnut and when these trees shall bear, let the pecans and walnuts be given out among the Plains people of Texas, so that they may plant them and make Texas a land of trees."

His wishes were carried out. The first nuts were saved in 1926 and planted in nursery rows. And the same thing has been done each year since. When the saplings are large enough to transplant they are distributed to schools and county boards.

244—When Frederick the Great was seized with his mortal illness, he asked whether "it was necessary to forgive all his enemies." On receiving the proper answer, he said to the queen, "Dorothy, write to your brother that I forgive him all the evil he has done me; but wait till I am dead first."

245—Abe Lincoln was a simple man with honest generous impulses. When he was a candidate for the legislature, it was the practice at that date in Illinois for two rival candidates to travel over the district together. The custom led to much good-natured raillery between them.

On one occasion he had driven out from Springfield in company with a political opponent to engage in joint debate. The carriage, it seems, belonged to his opponent. In addressing the gathering of farmers that met them, Lincoln was lavish in praise of the generosity of his friend.

"I am too poor to own a carriage," he said, "but my friend has generously invited me to ride with him. I want you to vote for me if you will but if not then vote for my opponent, for he is a fine man."

246—"I am rich enough," said Pope to Swift, "and can afford to give away a hundred pounds a year. I would not crawl upon the earth without doing good. I will enjoy the pleasure of what I give by giving it alive and seeing another enjoy it. When I die I should be ashamed to leave enough for a monument if a wanting friend was above ground."

247—An English lover of Brahms' music willed him £1,000. When Joachim sent the news Brahms replied:

"One can experience nothing more beautiful, nothing that does one more good, than what you have just told me. That a perfect stranger, who has, as far as I know, never even written me, should remember me thus, touches me most deeply and intimately. Once before I have had the inestimable joy of experiencing the like. All exterior honors are nothing in comparison.

"As I do not need to 'invest' the money, I am enjoying it in the most agreeable manner, by taking pleasure in its distribution . . ."

248—The despised and rejected often found in this great-hearted man (Brahms) a ready ally. Widmann tells how, one night under the arcades of Bologna, Brahms enthusiastically admired a deaf-and-dumb sidewalk artist who had drawn in the flags a portrait of Cavour. "A plate stood nearby into which one could throw the soldo which one might feel like offering to such art of the highways. But there was a new surprise when the coin, ringing on the hard stone, showed that the plate was not a real one but a well and truly drawn imitation. Brahms could not find words enough to praise this fine idea of the poor artist. And his offering showed how deeply he was moved by learning that in this gifted race, even the street beggar knew how to cover his nakedness with a corner of the hem of Art's sumptuous robe."

SEE ALSO
Tallness 696
Servants 2279
Armistice 2397
Stealing 2588
Wills 2606

RELATED SUBJECTS
Borrowing 121–126
Devotion 171–173
Gratitude and Ingratitude 261–268
Helpfulness 281
Kindness 311–316
Stinginess 556–566
Tolerance 601–603

GENTLEMANLINESS

251—Sir Walter Raleigh would have devised different techniques had he lived today. An authentic descendant of his turned up in Philadelphia as told in the story of the three girls

who were marooned on the curb, after a violent cloud-
burst had left a deep puddle in the poorly drained street
stretching nearly all the way between themselves and the
car which they wished to board. Two of them had jumped
for it only to go in over their ankles. The third was still
standing in despair when a sedan rolled up and stopped
directly in front of her. With a flourish its driver opened
the rear door on her side, then opened the other. Catching
the idea, the young lady proceeded to walk through the
car and on to the trolley. Tipping his hat, the driver
closed his doors and proceeded to drive away.

252—One night a Negro was walking along Forty-second Street
in New York, from the terminal to the hotel, carrying a
heavy suitcase and a heavier valise. Suddenly a hand took
hold of the valise and a pleasant voice said: "Pretty
heavy, brother! Suppose you let me take one. I am going
your way."
The negro resisted, but finally allowed the young white man
to assist him in carrying his burden, and for several
blocks they walked along, chatting like old cronies.
"And that," said Booker T. Washington years afterward,
"was the first time I ever saw Theodore Roosevelt."

253—Charles Lamb once said:
"Don't introduce me to that man! I want to go on hating
him, and I can't hate a man whom I know."

254—It was late at night and the young lady was taking a taxi
home. Checking in her handbag, she was mildly horrified
to discover that she would not have enough money for the
full fare. When the meter had reached the sum which she
had, she called to the driver and told him to let her out,
explaining the situation.
"Listen, lady," said he, "money isn't everything. There's
still what you call chivalry. You just sit still."

255—In 1803 the American Congress granted to General Lafayette, 11,520 acres of land, in what was then called the
Territory of Orleans; but by some inadvertency, a portion
of the same land was afterwards granted to the Corporation of New Orleans. Lafayette was advised to bring
forward his claim; and eminent lawyers assured him it
was perfectly legal. To which the gallant Frenchman
replied:
"I cannot consent even to inquire into the validity of my
title. It was gratuitously bestowed by Congress, and it is

for them to say what was given. I cannot for a moment think of entering into litigation with any public body in the United States."

On this tract that Lafayette relinquished was built the City of New Orleans.

256—Edmund Waller had a tremendous, international reputation for wit, in spite of his "obstinate sobriety." Being shown the Duchess of Newcastle's verses on the death of a stag, he declared that he would give all his compositions to have written them; and being charged with the exorbitance of his adulation answered that "nothing was too much to be given, that a lady might be saved from the disgrace of such a vile performance."

SEE ALSO
Quarrelsomeness 466
Beauty 661
Ministers 1471
Doctors 1668
Credit 2166

RELATED SUBJECTS
Politeness 416–420
Tact 586–591

GRATITUDE AND INGRATITUDE

261—An old deacon, having occasion to spend a night at a hotel, was assigned a room containing three single beds, two of which already had occupants. Soon after the light was extinguished one of these began to snore so loudly as to prevent the deacon from getting to sleep. The tumult increased as the night wore away, until it became absolutely fearful. Some two or three hours after midnight the snorer turned himself in bed, gave a hideous groan, and became silent. The deacon had supposed the third gentleman asleep, but at this juncture he heard him exclaim, "He's dead! Thank God. He's dead!"

262—Dr. Walter Adams, astronomer at Mount Wilson Observatory told a story of gratitude:

"A hunter in the jungle came across an elephant limping. The hunter followed it. Finally it toppled over. The hunter examined its feet. In one there was a large thorn. This he removed.

"Years passed and the hunter was in a cheap seat at a circus. A turn was given by a troupe of performing elephants. One of these elephants reached in its trunk, encircled his waist, and lifted him from his cheap seat and set him down in a seat in a private box."

263—"While fishing one day," said the old-timer, "I ran short of bait and was temporarily at loss as to what to do. Upon looking down near my feet, I noticed a small snake which held a frog in its mouth. I removed the frog and cut it up for bait, feeling very fortunate that my eyes had lighted on the snake at that moment.

"I did, however, feel a bit guilty at relieving the poor reptile of his meal, and in order to give him a slight recompense for my supply of bait, I poured a few drops of whiskey into its mouth. Fortunately for my conscience, the snake seemed to leave in a contented mood, and I turned and went on fishing.

"Some time had passed when I felt something hitting against the leg of my boot. Looking down, I saw the identical snake, laden with three more frogs!"

264—"Are you fond of lobster salad?" asked the hostess of the doctor.

"No," he replied, "I'm not fond of it but I'm grateful to it."

265—"You have much to be grateful for," said the clergyman to the old farmer, "Providence cares for us all. Even the birds of the air are fed each day."

"Yeah," growled the farmer, "off my corn."

266—When told that somebody had spoken something against him, had indeed systematically abused him, Jerrold quietly observed:

"Ah! I suppose I have done him a good turn."

267—In some parts of Mexico hot springs and cold springs are found side by side. The women often boil their clothes in the hot springs and rinse them in the cold springs. A tourist, who had been watching this procedure, remarked to his Mexican friend, "I guess they think old Mother Nature is pretty generous."

"No, señor," the other replied. "There is much grumbling because she supplies no soap."

268—Notwithstanding his long career of snatching killers out of the clutches of the law, Samuel Liebowitz is not an admirer of the class. He considers them unlovable natures and born ingrates. Demonstrating this, he notes that no single one of the 78 men whom he has saved from the chair ever sent him a Christmas card.

SEE ALSO
Generosity 242

RELATED SUBJECTS
Generosity 241–248
Helpfulness 281
Kindness 311–316
Stinginess 556–566

GREED

271—One evening Rachel, the famous French actress, dined at the house of Comte Duchâtel. The table was loaded with the most magnificent flowers; but Rachel's keen eyes presently spied out the great silver centerpiece. Immedi- she began to admire it. The Count, fascinated by her manners, said that he would be glad to present it to her. Being greedy, she accepted it at once, but was rather fearful lest he should change his mind. She had come to dinner in a cab, and mentioned the fact. The Count offered to send her home in his carriage.

"Yes, that will do admirably," said she. "There will be no danger of my being robbed of your present, which I had better take with me."

"With pleasure, Mademoiselle," replied the Count. "But you will send me back my carriage, won't you?"

272—Roland Diller who was one of Lincoln's neighbors in Springfield, tells the following story:

"I was called to the door one day by the cries of children in the street, and there was Mr. Lincoln, striding by with two of his boys, both of whom were wailing aloud. 'Why, Mr. Lincoln, what's the matter with the boys?' I asked. Just what's the matter with the whole world,' Lincoln replied. 'I've got three walnuts, and each wants two.' "

273—Rachel, the celebrated 19th Century French actress, was notorious for her avarice. The younger Dumas once received a ring from her. Immediately he bowed low and returned it to her finger, saying:

"Permit me, Mademoiselle, to present it to you in my turn so as to save you the embarrassment of asking for it."

274—The Mexican War was not a popular one with the American people. Abraham Lincoln, then a member of Congress, opposed it, declaring that those who said that the war was not one of agression made him think of the Illinois farmer who said: "I ain't greedy 'bout land. I only want what jines mine."

275—Rachel, the famous French actress, had a curious way of asking everyone she met for presents and knicknacks, whether they were valuable or not. She knew how to make them valuable.

Once in a studio she noticed a guitar hanging on the wall. She begged for it very earnestly. As it was an old and almost worthless instrument, it was given her. A little later it was reported that the dilapidated guitar had been purchased by a well-known gentleman for a thousand francs. The explanation soon followed. Rachel had declared that it was the very guitar with which she used to earn her living as a child in the streets of Paris.

276—On one occasion P. D. Armour, the meat packer, made a present of a suit of clothes to each of his employes in a certain department. Each man was told that he might order his own suit, and send the bill to Mr. Armour, no restriction being made as to price. In order to avail himself fully of this liberality, one young man ordered evening clothes costing $80. When the bill was sent in, Mr. Armour sent for the clerk to vouch for its accuracy, and finding it right, assured the man it would be paid. As the clerk was leaving, however, Mr. Armour said to him:

"I wish to say to you that I have packed a great many hogs in my time, but I never dressed one before."

SEE ALSO
Wealth 2181
Laws 2596

RELATED SUBJECTS
Ambition 96–97
Competition 2116
Chiseling and Swindling 2121–2132

HELPFULNESS

281—There is a story that tells of a rabbit being chased by a dog, and the people following and telling the rabbit to run hard and escape.

"Thank you for your kind encouragement," said the rabbit, "but for goodness' sake shoot the dog."

RELATED SUBJECTS
Generosity 241–248
Kindness 311–316

HONESTY

286—A beggar asking Dr. Smottett for alms, he gave him, through mistake, a guinea. The poor fellow on perceiving it, hobbled after him to return it; upon which Smollett returned it to him with another guinea as a reward for his honesty, exclaiming at the same time, "What a lodging Honesty has taken up with!"

287—Mirabeau was seldom sincere; Robespierre, nearly always. Once, when Robespierre was speaking, Mirabeau, who had listened attentively, bent his leonine head over to his neighbor and remarked:

"That man will go far; he believes all he says."

288—Pace, jester to Queen Elizabeth, was so bitter in his retorts to her, that she forbade him her royal presence. After he had been absent for some time, a few of his friends interceded for him, assuring the Queen that he would be more guarded in his remarks in the future.

The very first time Pace was as bad as ever. "Come on, Pace," said the Queen in a gracious humor, "now, we shall hear of our faults."

"No, Madam," said Pace, "I never talk of what is discoursed by all the world."

289—A young man, starting out on a business career, was being given some advice by his father, himself a very successful and wealthy man.

"And, remember, son," said the older man, "always keep in mind that honesty always has been and always will be the best policy."

"Oh, yes indeed," agreed the son.

"Oh, and incidentally," were the parting words of his father, "you might read up a bit on corporation law. It's really surprising how many things can be done in a business way, and still be honest."

290—A little boy asked his father, "Papa, what does it mean, business ethics?"

"Well," explained the merchant, "it's like this. Comes into the store a man and makes a purchase. He gives me a bright, new five-dollar bill, which is just the right amount, and he starts out. I'm turning to the cash register when I discover that it's not one, it's two five-dollar bills stuck together. Now comes it in the business ethics—should I tell mine partner?"

291—One day Senator George W. Norris sat taking stock of the situation and puffing a cigar. A visitor came in looking rather smug. He had called because Norris was on the committee on public buildings and grounds. Washington was still in the mushroom stage with land developments in progress. The man wanted to see him about "a little matter" and as soon as he promised to show "appreciation" Norris jumped up and grabbed him, vigorously pushing him out of the room.

292—President Wilson was scrupulous to the degree of fanaticism on the point of avoiding any personal or family favoritism in appointments or the awarding of war contracts.

A caller at the White House quite casually mentioned that the firm headed by a distant relative of the President had received a building contract. Although this might readily have been accepted as a legitimate and purely coincidental transaction, the President said in great agitation, "It must be stopped at once."

The nation could well have used, in his successor's administration, so high a degree of integrity, yet the action created a family breach that was never healed.

293—While visiting his prison at Potsdam, Frederick William I listened to a number of pleas for pardon from prisoners who had grievances against the law's injustice. All said they had suffered imprisonment on account of prejudiced judges, perjured witnesses, unscrupulous lawyers. From cell to cell the tale of wronged innocence continued, until the King stopped at the door of one cell inhabited by a surly inmate who said nothing. Surprised at his silence Frederick said jocosely, "Well I suppose you are innocent too."

"No, your Majesty," was the startling response; "I am guilty and richly deserve all that I get."

"Here, turnkey," thundered Frederick; "come and get rid of this rascal quick, before he corrupts this fine lot of innocent people that you are responsible for."

294—All clients knew that, with Old Abe as their lawyer, they would win their case—if it was fair; if not, that it was a waste of time to take it to him. After listening some time one day to a would-be client's statement, with his eyes on the ceiling, he swung around in his chair and exclaimed:

"Well, you have a pretty good case in technical law, but a pretty bad one in equity and justice. You'll have to get some other fellow to win this case for you. I couldn't do

it. All the time while standing talking to that jury I'd
be thinking, 'Lincoln, you're a liar,' and I believe I should
forget myself and say it out loud."

SEE ALSO

Cynicism 166
Books 1224
Atheists 1652
Advertising 2103
Credit 2166
Partnerships 2242
Judges 2486
Lawyers 2527

RELATED SUBJECTS

Conscience 146–147
Honor 296–298
Hypocrisy 301–303
Liars 331–336
Chiseling and Swindling 2121–
2132
Stealing 2581–2590

HONOR

296—"Why is it," asked a Frenchman of a Swiss, "that you Swiss
always fight for money, while we French only fight for
honor?"

"I suppose," said the Swiss, "that each fight for what they
most lack."

297—A German officer, talking to a senior member of the British
Embassy in Berlin in 1933, made the odd remark that the
British are gentlemen, but the French are not. Asked
what he meant, he explained: "One day in 1920, some of
the Military Control Commission under a French and a
British officer, came to the barracks of which I had
charge. They said they had reason to believe that I had
a store of rifles concealed behind a brick wall, contrary
to the terms of the Peace Treaty. I denied this. 'I give
you my word of honor as a German officer,' I said, 'that
I have no rifles concealed in the barracks.'

"Well, your British officer was a gentleman. He accepted
my word of honor and went away. But the French officer
was not a gentleman. He would not accept my word of
honor. He pulled down the brick wall. And he took away
my rifles."

298—An officious informer came to tell Cardinal Richelieu of
certain free expressions that some persons had used in
speaking of him. "Why how now!" said the Cardinal,
"do you dare to come and call me all these names to my
face, under the pretense of their having been said by
honest gentlemen?"

Ringing his bell, he said to the page in waiting, "Kick that
fellow down stairs."

SEE ALSO
Presidents 1931
Soldiers 2433

RELATED SUBJECTS
Conscience 146–147
Honesty 286–294
Pride 456–457
Stool Pigeons 2591–2592

HYPOCRISY

301—The Bishop of Hereford was once being patronized by a great lord who talked very insolently.

"I never go to church," boasted the lord. "Perhaps you have noticed that, Bishop?"

"Yes, I have noticed it," answered the Bishop gravely.

"Well, the reason I don't go is that there are so many hypocrites there."

"Oh, don't let that keep you away," said the Bishop smiling blandly. "There is always room for one more, you know."

302—An eminent banker from the West End, Boston, once visited Father Taylor's church during a warm revival, and somewhat varied the usual character of the prayer meeting, by an address setting forth the beneficence of the merchant princes, the goodness of the Port Society, and above all the duty of seamen to show their gratitude to the merchants. He was somewhat taken aback when Father Taylor arose, at the close of this rather presumptuous exhortation, and simply inquired: "Is there any other old sinner from up-town that would like to say a word?"

303—Julius Streicher, Hitler's No. 1 Jew persecutor, complained recently to foreign correspondents about the way the foreign press portrays him as a depraved brute. "Of course," he explained, "I do fight the Jews in every way I can, but in private life I'm far from heartless. For example, I have two pet canaries, and whenever I am late coming home I stumble around in the dark rather than turn the light on and wake them up.

SEE ALSO
Rabbis 1486
Equality 2046

RELATED SUBJECTS
Flattery 236–237
Honesty 286–294
Liars 331–336
Believers 1591–1596

IMAGINATION

306—Professor Buckland, the distinguished biologist of the early 19th Century, gave a dinner one day, after dissecting a Mississippi alligator.

"How do you like the soup?" asked the doctor, after having finished his own plate, addressing a famous gourmand of the day.

"Very good, indeed," answered the other; "turtle, is it not? I only ask because I do not find any green fat."

The doctor shook his head.

"I think it has somewhat of a musky taste," said another, "not unpleasant but peculiar."

"All alligators have," replied Dr. Buckland; "the fellow I dissected this morning, and whom you have just been eating—"

There was a general rout of guests. Everyone turned pale. Half a dozen started up from the table and hurriedly left the room.

"See, what imagination is!" exclaimed Dr. Buckland. "If I had told them it was turtle or terrapin, or bird's nest soup, they would have pronounced it excellent."

"Tell me, doctor, was it really an alligator?"

"Alligator!" laughed the doctor. "Stuff and nonsense—it was nothing but a good calf's head."

SEE ALSO
Drinking 47
Painting 1265

RELATED SUBJECTS
Exaggeration 221–226
Liars 331–336
Zanies 641–643

KINDNESS

311—A kindly passer-by assisted a small boy in pushing a heavily loaded cart up a long, steep hill. Reaching the top, and at last getting his wind back, he said indignantly, "Only a scoundrel would expect a youngster to do a job like that! Your employer should have known it was too heavy for you."

"He did," replied the boy, "but he said, 'Go on, you're sure to find some old fool who'll help you up the hill.' "

312—The sentiment of "Woodman, spare that tree," is carried out on an extensive scale by the screen actor, Edward Everett Horton. He has a large ranch which he has converted into an "Old Trees Home." Whenever he discovers a beautiful oak, maple, or elm condemned to be cut down to make way for highways or buildings, he purchases it and has it removed to his sanctuary for unwanted trees.

313—Archibald Rutledge tells this story: "When I was a boy in Carolina, I was cured forever of caging wild things. Not content with hearing mocking-birds sing from the cedars, I determined to cage a young one, and thus have a young musician all my own. On the second day in the cage, he saw his mother fly to him with food in her bill. This attention pleased me for surely the mother knew how to feed her child better than I did. The following morning my pathetic little captive was dead. When I recounted this experience to Arthur Wayne, the renowned ornithologist, he said, 'A mother mocking-bird, finding her young in a cage, will sometimes take it poison berries. She thinks it better for one she loves to die rather than to live in captivity.'"

314—When Grant, knowing Lincoln's attitude of leniency and desiring to be prepared for all eventualities, inquired whether he was to "try to capture Jeff Davis or let him escape from the country if he would," Lincoln explained his stand: "About that I told him the story of an Irishman who had taken the pledge of Father Matthew. He became terribly thirsty, applied to a bartender for a lemonade, and while it was being prepared whispered to him, 'And couldn't ye put a little brandy in it all unbeknown to meself?' I told Grant if he could let Jeff Davis escape all unbeknown to himself, to let him go. I didn't want him."

315—President Lincoln once dropped a few kind words about the Confederates. A woman flashed forth a question of how he could speak kindly of his enemies when he should rather destroy them.

"What, Madam, do I not destroy them when I make them my friends?"

316—Never was a famous composer kinder than Brahms to his young colleagues—where he found genuine talent. With might and main he urged Simrock to publish the works of Knorr, Roentgen, Fuchs, and Novak. He rescued Dvorak from the direst poverty, made Simrock bring out the Slavonic Dances, and helped them to their wide success. Twice he begged Dvorak, with all his heart, to consider the Brahmsian fortune as his own. And when he learned that the Bohemian was a most incompetent proofreader, he himself actually assumed the drudgery of correcting all his friend's proofs.

SEE ALSO	RELATED SUBJECTS
Hypocrisy 303	Generosity 241–248
Homeliness 652	Gratitude and Ingratitude 261–268
Friendship 867	Helpfulness 281
Babies 957	
Horse Racing 1872	
Discipline 2441	

LATENESS

321—At the East India House the head of the office once reproved Charles Lamb for the excessive irregularity of his attendance.

"Really, Mr. Lamb, you come very late!"

"Y-yes," replied Lamb with his habitual stammer, "b-but consi-sider how ear-early I go!"

322—On one occasion, when Lincoln was going to attend a political convention, one of his rivals, a liveryman, provided him with a slow horse, hoping that he would not reach his destination in time. Lincoln got there, however, and when he returned with the horse he said:

"You keep this horse for funerals, don't you?"

"Oh no!" replied the liveryman.

"Well, I'm glad of that, for if you did you'd never get a corpse to the grave in time for the resurrection."

323—A gentleman, having an appointment with another who was habitually unpunctual, to his great surprise found him waiting. He thus addressed him: "Why, I see you are here first at last. You were always behind before, but I am glad to see you have become early of late."

324—On his way to Gettysburg, where he delivered his immortal address, Lincoln was urged by General Fry to hurry in order not to hold up the train. To this Lincoln replied.

"I feel about this as the convict in one of our Illinois towns felt when he was going to the gallows. As he passed along the road in custody of the sheriff the people, eager to see the execution, kept crowding and pushing past him. At last he called out: 'Boys, you needn't be in such a hurry to get ahead. There won't be any fun till I get there.'"

SEE ALSO	RELATED SUBJECTS
Trains 1801	Procrastination 461

LAZINESS

326—Lincoln admitted that he was not particularly energetic when it came to real hard work.

"My father," said he one day, "taught me how to work, but not to love it. I never did like to work and I don't deny it. I'd rather read, tell stories, crack jokes, talk, laugh—anything but work."

327—Judge Davis was going through the docket and came across a long bill in chancery, drawn by an excellent but somewhat indolent lawyer. He exclaimed: "Why Brother Snap, how did you rake up energy enough to get up such a long bill?"

"Dunno, Judge," replied the party addressed. The Judge held up the bill. "Astonishing, ain't it? Brother Snap did it. Wonderful—eh Lincoln?"

This amounted to an order on Lincoln for a joke at this point. He was ready. "It's like the lazy preacher," drawled he, "that used to write long sermons, and the explanation was, he got to writing and was too lazy to stop."

SEE ALSO
Sickness 1705
Longevity 1782

RELATED SUBJECTS
Sleeping 26–27
Carelessness 136
Diligence 176–177
Lateness 321–324
Procrastination 461

LIARS

331—Lord Chatham said of an approaching debate: "If I cannot speak standing I will speak sitting, and if I cannot speak sitting I will speak lying."

"Which he will do in whatever position he speaks," remarked Lord North.

332—It is said that the Japanese inspire no more confidence one in the other than they do in the citizens of the rest of the world. Two merchants of Tokyo once met in the railway station.

"Where are you going?" asked the first one.

His friend hesitated, then said, "To Kobe."

"Oh, you liar!" said the first one angrily. "You tell me you are going to Kobe to make me think you're going to Osaka, but I have made inquiries and I know you are going to Kobe!"

333—Speaker Reed, Ambassador Choate and Senator Westcott were chatting together one evening. Mr. Choate said with great solemnity: "Well, gentlemen, I have not drunk whiskey, played cards for money, or attended a horse race in twenty-eight years."

"My gracious!" exclaimed Senator Westcott admiringly. "I wish I could say that."

"Why don't you?" blandly inquired Mr. Reed. "Choate did."

334—A generation ago, when Prime Minister Winston Churchill was still a member of the Liberal Party, he rose in Commons to defend his party against the charge that they had deliberately misrepresented the Conservative Party. The Liberals had accused the Conservatives of practising slavery in South Africa because they kept Negro laborers behind barbed-wire compounds under severe restrictions. Churchill remarked: "I admit the term 'slavery' might be a terminological inexactitude."

At this Joseph Chamberlain, father of the late Prime Minister Neville Chamberlain, interrupted:

"I prefer the ugly little English three letter word—l-i-e."

335—A minister wound up the services one morning by saying, "Next Sunday I'm going to preach on the subject of liars. And in this connection, as a preparation for my discourse, I should like you all to read the 17th Chapter of Mark." On the following Sunday, the preacher rose to begin, and said, "Now then, all of you who have done as I requested and read the 17th Chapter of Mark, please raise your hands." Nearly every hand in the congregation went up. Then said the preacher, "You are the very people I want to talk to. There is no 17th Chapter of Mark!"

336—A certain young California politician, notorious for lying, had once been unwittingly led into speaking the truth. Noah Brooks was explaining the situation to President Lincoln, who immediately reminded himself of a story, saying that he recalled a similar circumstance about a Negro barber in Illinois, who was a great liar. A crowd in front of a barber shop stood one evening gazing with admiration at the planet Jupiter. "Sho," said the barber, "I've seen that star before. I seen him 'way down in Georgy."

Said Lincoln: "Like your California friend, he told the truth, but thought he was lying."

SEE ALSO
Drinking 49
Honesty 294
Fishing 1848
Golf 1866
Campaigning 1915
Chiseling 2127
Statistics 2222
Censors 2351
Juries 2517

RELATED SUBJECTS
Boastfulness 101–103
Exaggeration 221–226
Honesty 286–294
Hypocrisy 301–303

LONG-WINDEDNESS

341—One of the executives of RKO, Leon J. Bamberger, once spoke at a convention, "I'm having such a good time that I'd just as soon go on speaking all afternoon, but I remember another Monday on which I was addressing a convention. I had hardly begun when I heard someone in the first row lean over and ask his friend, 'Say, what follows Bamberger?' And the answer was, 'Wednesday.'"

342—Sir Josiah Stamp, in a speech at the Chicago Club, expressed a hope that he wasn't talking too long. "I wouldn't like to be in the position of the parson," he explained, "who in the midst of an interminable sermon, suddenly stopped to chide: 'You know I don't mind a bit having you look at your watches to see what time it is, but it really annoys me when you put them up to your ears to see if they are still running.'"

343—At a banquet, a speaker was ranting on about a subject which held very little interest for most of the audience. Unable to stand it any longer, one of them slipped quietly out. Just outside the door he bumped into another sufferer who had gone out just before him.
"Has he finished yet?" he was asked.
"Yes," said the man who had just escaped, "long ago, but he won't stop."

344—The following remarks of Mark Twain may well be taken to heart by the various after-dinner speakers who inflict their long drawn out speeches upon suffering diners.
"Some years ago in Hartford, we all went to church one hot sweltering night to hear the annual report of Mr. Hawley, a city missionary who went around finding people who needed help and didn't want to ask for it. He

told of the life in cellars, where poverty resided; he gave instances of the heroism and devotion of the poor. 'When a man with millions gives,' he said, 'we make a great deal of noise. It's noise in the wrong place, for it's the widow's mite that counts.' Well, Hawley worked me up to a great pitch. I could hardly wait for him to get through. I had $400 in my pocket. I wanted to give that and borrow more to give. You could see greenbacks in every eye. But instead of passing the plate then, he kept on talking and talking, and as he talked it grew hotter and hotter, and we grew sleepier and sleepier. My enthusiasm went down, down, down, down—$100 at a clip—until finally, when the plate did come around, I stole ten cents out of it. It all goes to show how a little thing like this can lead to crime."

345—Burke and Mr. David Hartley of the Ministry arose simultaneously on the floor of the House of Commons. As the speaker granted recognition to Mr. Hartley, Burke settled down for a long wait, as Hartley's speeches were notorious for their length. In the dreary course of three hours' argument, nearly everyone in the House managed to make his escape. At one pause in his speech, Mr. Hartley demanded that the Riot Act be read to illustrate one of the points he was making. "The Riot Act, my dear sir!" Burke exclaimed. "Look at these empty benches. Do you not see that the mob is completely dispersed?"

346—The late "Kingfish" Huey Long had been speaking on a bill in the U. S. Senate for more than two hours, when he called for a glass of water.

"Mr. Speaker, I rise to a point of order," said Senator Johnson of California.

"State your point of order."

"Mr. Speaker," continued Sen. Johnson with a straight face. "I would like to draw the attention of the Senator from Louisiana that it is out of order to run a windmill with water."

347—On one occasion Judge Olin of New York was speaking and in his excitement he walked up and down the aisle passing Thaddeus Stevens' seat. At length Stevens said: "Olin, do you expect to get mileage for that speech?"

348—Much as he hated to give long-winded speeches King Frederick William IV hated even more to have to listen to them. Once after a long and tiresome trip he arrived at a small town in Prussia where the natives had thronged the streets since daybreak waiting for his arrival. As the royal carriage pulled into town the bands began to play, the people shouted and the fat burgomaster, perspiring in a new red coat, came forward, and with a dramatic gesture opened his speech of welcome thus: "Most high and powerful lord! When Hannibal stood before the gates of Carthage—" "He was probably just as hungry as I am." Frederick broke in, putting his hand on the speaker's shoulder, "Come, my friend, let's go and have dinner together."

349—Lord North, once Prime Minister of England, was accustomed to sleep during the parliamentary harangues of his adversaries, leaving Sir Grey Cooper to note down anything remarkable. During a debate on ship-building, some tedious speaker entered on a historical detail, in which, commencing with Noah's ark, he traced the progress of the art regularly downwards. When he came to building the Spanish Armada, Sir Grey inadvertently awoke the slumbering Prime Minister, who inquired at what era the honorable gentleman had arrived. Being answered, "We are now in the reign of Queen Elizabeth." "Dear me, Sir Grey," said he, "why not let me sleep a century or two more?"

350—An Ambassador having come to Sparta from Perinthus, spoke at great length.
"What answer shall I return to the Perinthians?" he asked.
"Say," said the king, "that you talked a great deal, and that I did not utter a word."

351—General Alexander Smyth of Virginia, a man of ability, was an excessively tedious speaker, worrying the House, and prolonging his speeches by numerous quotations. On one occasion when he had been more than ordinarily tiresome he turned to Henry Clay who was sitting near him. "You, sir, speak for the present generation; but I speak for posterity," he said.
"Yes," said Mr. Clay, "and you seem resolved to speak until the arrival of your audience."

352—On one occasion a person who was present at a sitting of the Court of Sessions in England, returned late in the afternoon and found the same case still on and the same advocate talking. He remarked to Lord Cockburn, "Surely he is wasting a great deal of time."

"Time," the jurist replied, "long ago has he exhausted time. Now he is encroaching upon eternity."

353—The late Gilman Marston of New Hampshire was arguing a complicated case, and had looked up authorities back to Julius Caesar. At the end of an hour and a half, in the most intricate part of his plea, he was pained to see what looked like inattention. The judge was unable to appreciate the nice points of his argument.

"Your honor," he said. "I beg your pardon, but do you follow me?"

"I have so far," answered the judge shifting wearily about in his chair, "but I'll say frankly that if I thought I could find my way back, I'd quit right here."

354—And then there was the case of that other counsel, this was an Irishman, who also developed an inexhaustible argument upon an exhaustible case. After he had gone on for four hours the President of the Court said to him, "Mr. Murphy, is it any good for you to continue? Everything you say goes in at one ear and comes out of the other."

"Why not," said the counsel, "there is little enough to stop it."

355—When President Franklin D. Roosevelt was a young lawyer just getting started in New York he was retained to handle a difficult civil case. The opposing lawyer was a very effective jury pleader and completely outshone his youthful rival in the argument to the jury. However, he made one fatal mistake: he orated for several hours. As he thundered on Roosevelt noticed that the jury wasn't paying much attention. So, playing a hunch when his turn came, he rose and said: "Gentlemen you have heard the evidence. You also have listened to my distinguished colleague, a brilliant orator. If you believe him, and disbelieve the evidence you will have to decide in his favor. That's all I have to say."

The jury was out only five minutes and brought in a verdict for Roosevelt's client.

356—Speaking of a lawyer Lincoln said, "He can compress the most words into the smallest ideas better than any man I ever met."

357—When Sheridan was making one of his great displays in Westminster Hall, he observed Gibbon among the auditors, and complimented him by some allusion to his "luminous pen." An acquaintance afterward reproached Sheridan with the sincerity of his compliment, and wondered how he could have used the word "luminous."

"O, it was a mistake," said Sheridan, "I meant voluminous."

358—When Diderot came to visit Voltaire he spoke so much and at such great length that Voltaire couldn't get a word in. When Diderot left, Voltaire chirped, "That man is a great wit, but nature has denied him one great gift—that of dialogue."

359—Elizabeth Barrett, meeting Wordsworth for the first time, wrote ironically, "He was very kind to me and let me hear his conversation."

360—They tell the story of Wilton Lackaye who was scheduled to speak late on the program at a banquet at which all the speakers had been brutally long-winded.

The chairman introduced Lackaye, saying, "Wilton Lackaye, the famous actor, will now give you his address."

Lackaye faced the haggard audience and said, "Mr. Chairman, Ladies and Gentlemen, my address is the Lambs' Club, New York."

He sat down and received a tremendous ovation.

361—A very pretty woman, who was tediously loquacious, complained one day to Madame de Sévigné that she was sadly tormented by her lovers.

"Oh, madam," said Madame de Sévigné to her, with a smile, "it is very easy to get rid of them, you have only to speak."

362—A talkative lady patient came to Dr. Abernathy, the eccentric English physician of another day, and talked tirelessly and tiresomely about her complaint.

"Put out your tongue, madam," barked Dr. Abernathy. The lady complied. "Now keep it there till I've done talking."

363—Sheridan, the playwright, on seeing a Member of the House of Commons, who had already bored everyone with a lengthy speech, stop to drink a glass of water, rose to a point of order,

"What is it?" asked the Speaker.

"Why I think, sir," said Sheridan, "that it is out of order for a wind-mill to go by water."

SEE ALSO
Dullness 191
Speeches 760, 787
Talking 814
Mathematicians 1151
Sermons 1544
Juries 2515

RELATED SUBJECTS
Boastfulness 101–103
Pompousness 421–427
Vanity 606–628
Speeches 756–782
Lectures 1106–1111
Sermons 1541–1559

MELANCHOLY

366—A patient suffering from profound melancholy one day presented himself to Abernathy; after careful examination the celebrated practitioner said, "You need amusement; go and hear the comedian Grimaldi; he will make you laugh, and that will be better for you than any drugs." "My God," exclaimed the invalid, "I am Grimaldi!"

367—Dr. Goldsmith, having been requested by a woman to visit her husband who was melancholy, called upon the patient and told him he would send some pills which he had no doubt would prove efficacious. He immediately went home, put ten guineas into a chip, and sent them to the sick man. The remedy had the desired effect.

368—Philip of Spain was in such a deplorable state of despondency from ill-health, that he refused to be shaved. On the arrival of the famous singer Farinelli, the Queen ordered a concert in a room adjoining the King's chamber. Farinelli sang one of his best airs, which so overcame the King that he desired he might be brought into his presence, when he promised to grant him any reasonable request he might make. The performer, in the most respectful manner, then begged of the king to allow himself to be shaved to which request Philip graciously consented.

SEE ALSO
Relaxation 1786

RELATED SUBJECTS
Cheerfulness 141–143
Pessimism 411
Worrying 636

MEMORY

371—In the days before modern court reporting and our generally efficient and systematized courtroom procedure, an elderly Southern lawyer was the proud owner of a negro slave named Sam, who was endowed with a phenomenal memory. Sam was able to sit in court and, at any point

in the process of a trial, he could reel off every word of
testimony that had transpired before. Sam's reputation
was so great that his evidence "on the record" was accepted in any court in the State. One day the old lawyer
was in his study when the Devil appeared.

"What do you want?" demanded the lawyer.

"I've come for Sam," was the answer. "His time is up and
he's got to go."

"Now, look here," said the lawyer, "I can't spare Sam."

"Can't help it," said the Devil.

"Come now," said the lawyer, "you're a sporting man. I'll
make a little bet with you. If Sam's memory is failing
he's no good to me and you can take him. You go out and
test him, and if you can fool him, he's yours. But if you
can't, he's mine."

"It's a bet," the Devil said, and disappeared.

Sam was then engaged in plowing up his little patch of
ground with a mule. The Devil suddenly appeared before
him and said, "Do you like eggs?"

"Yassah," said Sam. And the Devil vanished.

In less than a year the Civil War broke out. Sam served
first with his master on the Confederate side, was captured and forced to fight on the Northern side, and was
then captured again by the Confederates. He survived
the War with only a minor wound, and after the Emancipation was willingly liberated by his old master, who presented him with the patch of land which he had been accustomed to work for so many years. One day as Sam
was cultivating the little plot that was now his own, the
Devil appeared before him. "How?" said the Devil.

"Fried!" said Sam. Whereupon the Devil vanished and left
him in peace.

372—Memory training by association became a fad in a certain
school. "For instance," the English teacher was explaining, "if you want to remember the name of a poet, Bobbie
Burns, you might conjure up in your eye a picture of a
London policeman in flames. You see, 'Bobbie Burns.' "

"I see," said one of his pupils, "but how is one to be sure
that it doesn't represent 'Robert Browning?' "

373—In order to play in "Rosemary," John Drew shaved off his
mustache, thereby greatly changing his appearance.
Shortly afterward he met Max Beerbohm in the lobby of
a London theatre, but could not just then recall who the
latter was. Mr. Beerbohm's memory was better.

"Oh, Mr. Drew," he said, "I'm afraid you don't recognize me without your mustache."

374—Archbishop Ryan was once accosted on the streets of Baltimore by a man who knew the Archbishop's face, but could not quite place it.

"Now, where in hell have I seen you?" he asked perplexedly.

"From where in hell do you come, sir?"

375—The woman's club was listening, entranced, to the lecture being given by a world-famous traveller. He concluded his remarks with, "And there are some spectacles that one never forgets . . ."

At this point a timid old lady in the audience spoke up shyly, "Pardon me, sir, would you tell me where I could get a pair? I am always forgetting mine."

SEE ALSO	RELATED SUBJECTS
Composers 1323	Absent-Mindedness 81–90
Conductors 1331, 1339	Accuracy 91–92

MODESTY

376—F. W. Wile tells how, "Once when a group of Washington newspapermen wanted Secretary of State Hughes to attend a dinner at which a number of first rank foreign statesmen were to be present, I was a committee of one to ask him where he wished to be seated at table. That was long before Dollie Gann and Alice Longworth all but caused social civil war in Washington over dinner-table precedence. 'You need never worry about that in my case,' Hughes said. 'The only place I ever want to be first is at a fire!' "

377—A characteristic story is told of the great Principal Cairns, one of the most simple-minded and humble of men. Attending a great public meeting on one occasion in Edinburgh, which was densely crowded, his appearance on the platform was received with loud cheers. Never imagining that this was for himself, he turned and saw following him a man of diminutive stature, and totally unknown. Taking him to be the object of popular applause, he stepped aside to let him pass, and as he did so began enthusiastically to join in the clapping. The act, so characteristic of the man, was received with uproarious delight, and fairly brought down the house.

378—In the Netherlands, a few years ago, a publisher decided that his country should follow the lead of other nations and have a Dutch "Who's Who." Immediately he encountered the national feeling that publicity is a state of exposure that the Hollander shuns rather than seeks. The men and women approached for the contemplated book found something positively indecent in the inquisitive request of a publisher that one should write his own life-story. Finally sufficient cooperation was secured to publish such a book but it was obviously incomplete as a record. Then, the Dutch public would not buy it, and the experiment was dropped.

379—When conversation in a company in which Dr. Johnson was present had fallen upon rather a delicate topic, one of the ladies, with an expression of great displeasure, rose and left the room. "That woman," said the doctor, "is the most immodest of all the company."

380—Madame de Genlis carried her purity of manners to such an extent, that she reprimanded the bookseller who had the arrangement of her library, for having placed books written by male and female authors on the same shelf.

381—A man came upon Lincoln blacking his boots in the basement of the White House. He expressed astonishment that the President of the United States should be at such a menial task.
"What! Mr. President," he exclaimed, "are you blacking your own boots?"
"Whose else should I be blacking?" came Lincoln's laconic reply.

382—Cato, the Roman, on observing that statues were being set up in honor of many, remarked: "I would rather people would ask, why is there not a statue to Cato, than why there is."

383—Abraham Lincoln was free from the usual official vanity. He rather shrank from than courted the official title of Mr. President, and generally referred to his office as "this place," "since I have been in this place," or, "since I came here." Referring at one time to the apartment reserved in the Capitol for the Chief Magistrate, he called it "the room, you know, that they call the President's room."
Once he pleaded with some old Illinois friends who addressed his as Mr. President, "Now call me Lincoln, and I'll promise not to tell of the breach of etiquette."

384—Salmon P. Chase, when Secretary of the Treasury, had a
disagreement with other members of the Cabinet, and
resigned.

The President was urged not to accept it as "Secretary
Chase is today a national necessity," his advisers said.

"How mistaken you are!" Lincoln quietly observed. "Yet,
it is not strange; I used to have similar notions. No! If
we should all be turned out tomorrow and could come
back here in a week, we should find our places filled by
a lot of fellows doing just as well as we did, and in many
instances better.

"Now, this reminds me of what the Irishman said. His verdict was that 'in this country one man is as good as
another; and, for the matter of that, very often a great
deal better.' No, this government does not depend upon
the life of any man."

385—At the Lyon assizes, in France, before the trial of a certain
case, the presiding judge remarked on seeing the court
crowded with ladies: "The persons composing the audience are probably not aware of the nature of the case
about to be tried. I therefore feel it incumbent on me to
request all respectable women to withdraw."

Not one of the ladies stirred from her place.

"Usher," the judge continued, "now that all the respectable
women have left, turn the others out."

386—Two ladies, encountering Dr. Johnson soon after the publication of his "Dictionary," complimented him for having
omitted gross, indelicate, and objectionable words.

"What, my dears!" said Dr. Johnson, "have you been
searching for them?"

387—Plato tells a fable of how spirits of the other world came
back to find bodies and places to work. One took the
body of a poet and did his work. Finally, Ulysses came
and said, "All the fine bodies have been taken and all
the grand work done. There is nothing for me."

"Yes," said a voice, "the best has been left for you—the
body of a common man, doing a common work for a
common reward."

388—Thomas Mann was once introduced to a successful American writer who grovelled abjectly before the eminent
novelist, explaining humbly that he was simply a hack
who should hardly call himself a writer in the presence

of so great an artist. Mann was courteous, but later said
to his host, "That man has no right to make himself so
small. He is not that big."

389—In Bonn, the home of Beethoven has been converted into a
memorial museum. In one of the rooms, roped off from
curious hands, is the piano upon which Beethoven composed many of his great works. A Vassar girl, visiting
the shrine with a party of American students, looked upon
the instrument with awe and asked the guard, with the
additional persuader of a generous tip, if she might play
upon it for a moment. The permission was granted and
she sat at the piano and strummed out a few bars of the
"Moonlight Sonata." Departing she remarked to the
guard, "I suppose all the great pianists who have come
here at one time or another have played on it." The guard
said, "No, Miss, Paderewski was here two years ago but
said he was not worthy to touch it."

390—Vasari relates that when Leonardo da Vinci lay on his
death-bed the King came to visit and cheer him. He
raised himself as far up as he could in the royal presence
and lamented "that he had offended God and man in that
he had not labored in art as he ought to have done."

SEE ALSO   RELATED SUBJECTS
Scientists 1120   Discretion 181–182
Inventors 1130   Tact 586–591
Painting 1271, 1277
Presidents 1933

PATIENCE
391—In the reign of Queen Elizabeth, Dr. Thomas Cooper edited
a learned dictionary with the addition of thirty-three
thousand words, and many other improvements. He had
already been eight years in collecting materials for his
edition, when his wife, who was a worthless and malig-
nant woman, going one day into his library, burnt every
note he had prepared under the pretense of fearing that
he would kill himself with study.
The doctor shortly after came in, and seeing the destruction, inquired who was the author of it. His wife boldly
avowed that it was the work of her mischievous hands.
The patient man heaved a deep sigh and said, "Oh Dinah,
Dinah, thou hast given me a world of trouble!"

Then he quietly sat down to another eight years of hard labor, to replace the notes which she had destroyed.

RELATED SUBJECTS
Cheerfulness 141–143
Diligence 176–177
Endurance 216
Tact 586–591
Tolerance 601–603

PATRIOTISM

396—Some time after the conclusion of the revolution, a young American was present in a British playhouse, where an interlude was performed in ridicule of his countrymen. A number of American officers being introduced in tattered uniforms, and barefoot, the question was put to them severally: "What was your trade before you entered the army?" One answered a tailor, another a cobbler, etc. The wit of the piece was to banter them for not keeping themselves in clothes and shoes, but before that could be expressed, the American exclaimed from the gallery: "Great Britain beaten by tailors and cobblers! Hurrah!" Even the Prime Minister, who was present, could not help smiling, amidst a general peal of laughter.

397—I once heard an Irishman say, "Every man loves his native land, whether he was born there or not."

398—In the early part of the Civil War an elderly lady who attended a meeting of the First Vermont Regiment, arose, full of enthusiasm, and said she thanked God that she was able to do something for her country; her two sons, all she possessed in the world, were in the regiment; and the only thing she had to regret was that she could not have known twenty years before that the war was coming —she would have furnished more.

399—When Lieutenant-Governor Patterson was Speaker of the legislature of one of our States, some dozen boys presented themselves for the place of messenger, as is usual at the opening of the House. He inquired their names and into their condition, in order that he might make the proper selection. He came, in the course of his examination, to a small boy about ten years old, a bright-looking lad. "Well, sir," said he, "what is your name?" "John Hancock," was the answer. "What!" said the Speaker, "you are not the one that signed the Declaration of Independence, are you?" "No, sir," replied the lad, stretching himself to his utmost proportions, "but I would be if I had been there." "You can be one of the messengers," said the Speaker.

400—When the Emperor Vespasian commanded a Roman senator to give his voice against the interests of his country and threatened him with immediate death if he spoke on the other side, the Roman, conscious that the attempt to serve a people was in his power, though the event was ever so uncertain, answered with a smile: "Did I ever tell you that I was immortal? My virtue is in my own disposal, my life in yours; you do what you will, I shall do what I ought; and if I fall in the service of my country, I shall have more triumph in my death than you in all your laurels."

401—It was a little boy in an American Sunday-school, who, in reply to his teacher's question, "Who was the first man?" answered, "George Washington," and upon being informed that it was Adam, exclaimed: "Ah, well! If you are speaking of foreigners, perhaps he was."

402—Gladstone remarked that the best example of wit he could recall in the House of Commons was Lord John Russell's reply to Sir Francis Burdett who had changed his political affiliations from Radical to Tory.
Addressing the House one day Burdett declared that there was nothing more odious than the cant of patriotism. To which Lord Russell replied that the cant of patriotism was no doubt very odious, but there was something even more odious and that was the recant of patriotism.

403—Californians are famous for their loyalty to their native state. One of its native sons was once visiting his wife's relatives in the East. While there he had occasion to attend the funeral of a man who was little liked in the community. At the services the minister, who was new to the parish, called upon someone to say a few words about the deceased. A long and significant silence ensued. Finally, the true son of California stood up and said, "Well, since there's no one present who has anything to say about our departed brother, I'd like a few minutes to tell you something about California."

404—Bismarck told a story of an Alpine host who, after pointing out the glories of his native land, asked a Berlin youth if they had any such mountains in Berlin. "No," he replied, "we have not got such mountains, but, if we had, they would be much finer than these."

405—Jerrold was in France, and with a Frenchman who was enthusiastic on the subject of the Anglo-French alliance. He said that he was proud to see the English and French such good friends at last, when Jerrold promptly answered, "Tut! The best thing I know between France and England—is the sea."

406—The leading nobles of Poland addressed a petition to Marie Walewska to accept Napoleon as her lover. They quoted Scripture to reinforce their argument:

"Did Esther, do you think, give herself to Ahasueros out of the fullness of her love for him? So great was the terror with which he inspired her that she fainted at the sight of him. We may therefore conclude that affection had but little to do with her resolve. She sacrificed her own inclinations to the salvation of her country and that salvation it was her glory to achieve. May we be enabled to say the same to you, to your glory and our own happiness!"

407—General Pershing was on a tour of inspection on the Western Front. Stopping at one of the camps that housed the wounded, he happened to notice a very bedraggled looking soldier sitting outside one of the tents. The General was just about to remark sympathetically about his condition, having noticed that he had one arm in a sling and a huge bandage about his head, when he heard the man muttering to himself.

"I love my country," Pershing heard the man say, "I'd fight for my country. I'd starve and go thirsty for my country. I'd die for my country. But if ever this damn war is over, I'll never love another country again!"

SEE ALSO
Boastfulness 102
Quick Thinking 476
Births 1012
Campaigning 1914
Civilians in War 2339
Battles 2382
Soldiers 2430, 2437

RELATED SUBJECTS
United States 2031–2032
Freedom 2036–2042
Equality 2046
Civilians in War 2331–2346
Soldiers and Sailors 2430–2437

PESSIMISM

411—On the subject of calamity howlers, the story is told of the gala crowd that had assembled for the test run of Robert Fulton's outlandish steamboat contraption "The Clermont." For some hours, in the presence of a mass of spectators, the strange craft belched smoke and sparks from its tall, thin stack as his engineers attempted to get up the necessary head of steam. When the time to cast off had come and the engines were being limbered up, the boat quivered and vibrated violently and made a loud racket. A group of doubting Thomases in the crowd had been shouting loudly and scornfully, "She'll never start! She'll never start!" But notwithstanding this, the boat pulled itself together and actually started to move up the river. After a moment of astonished silence, the voices of the scoffers resumed their shouts; this time crying with all the scorn they could muster, "She'll never stop! She'll never stop!"

RELATED SUBJECTS
Cheerfulness 141–143
Melancholy 366–368
Worrying 636

POLITENESS

416—When in this country on a mission during World War I Marshal Foch was buttonholed by a noisy Westerner who launched into a tirade against French politeness.

"There is nothing in it but wind," he sneered.

"There is nothing but wind in a tire," politely countered the Marshal, "but it makes riding in a car very smooth and pleasant."

417—A governor of Virginia, being saluted by a Negro, immediately returned the compliment.

"Can you demean yourself so far," said a slaveholder, "as to raise your hat to a Negro?"

"Undoubtedly," said the governor. "I should be sorry for him to exceed me in politeness."

418—It happens to everybody some time or other. The man and the woman were hastening down the street in opposite directions. They met head on, both veered abruptly to one side, and then to the other confronting each other in a vain effort to untangle themselves and pass. When the difficulty was at last solved, the man tipped his hat and said, "Good-bye, it's nice to have known you."

419—Expressing himself somewhat bitterly on the subject of storytellers who persistently interrupt themselves to ask if one has heard the story, Mark Twain told of an encounter with Henry Irving. The actor asked him if he had heard a certain story and Twain politely said, "No." Irving proceeded and later made the same query. Proceeding almost to the climax of his story, Irving again asked if he had heard it. Twain said, "I can lie once, I can lie twice for courtesy's sake, but I draw the line there. I can't lie the third time at any price. I not only heard the story, I invented it."

420—Henry Clay and John Randolph had had a violent quarrel in the Senate. For a long time they did not speak when they encountered one another outside.

It chanced one day that they found themselves confronted by one another at a very narrow point created by repairs underway on the sidewalk. They stood silently for a moment, faced by the question of which was to step aside and let the other pass. At last Randolph said haughtily, "I never turn out for scoundrels."

"I always do," said Clay, stepping politely out into the mud, giving Randolph the right of way.

SEE ALSO   RELATED SUBJECTS
Critics 1102   Flattery 236–237
                             Gentlemanliness 251–256
                             Kindness 311–316
                             Tact 586–591

POMPOUSNESS

421—To a young speaker Thomas Corwin, the Congressman, gave this advice:

"Never make people laugh. If you would succeed in life, you must be solemn, solemn as an ass. All the great monuments are built over solemn asses."

422—A peddler with a hand-cart full of shrimps was ordered out of the way by a member of Parliament, who was trying to park his limousine.

"Look out yourself," said the coster.

"Do you realize," demanded the other, "that I have an M.P. at the end of my name?"

"So 'as every blarsted shrimp in this 'ere cart!"

423—A pompous young man called on Joseph Choate the prominent lawyer and statesman. The lawyer was busy and asked the young man to take a chair. But the youth was impatient and again interrupted the lawyer with the remark, "I am Bishop Blank's son." "Please take two chairs," said Mr. Choate.

424—When Victor Hugo was an aspirant for the honors of the Academy, and called on M. Royer Collard to ask his vote, the sturdy veteran professed an entire ignorance of his name.

"I am the author of 'Notre Dame de Paris'; 'Les derniers Jours d'un Condamne'; 'Marion Delorme,' etc."

"I have never heard of any of them."

"Will you do me the honor of accepting a copy of my works?"

"I never read new books."

425—To Boston is attributed the credit of having retorted to the superciliousness of Oscar Wilde in kind. "You're Philistines," Wilde accused his Boston audience, "who have invaded the sacred sanctum of Art."

A voice in the audience called out, "And you're driving us forth with the jawbone of an ass."

426—Widmann relates that "when the school-masterish music director of a very small Swiss town graciously assured Brahms that he was familiar with every one of his compositions, the Master motioned him with his hand to be still and listen attentively, as the festival orchestra was just then playing something of his own. It was, however, a military march by Gungl. I can still see the good man before me, how with open mouth and reverent contorted eyes he listened to the rather commonplace fanfares, which he now really held to be a Brahms composition while Brahms, in outrageous glee over his successful trick, whispered to the rest of us: 'Just look at the Basilio!' (the hypocritical dupe in Rossini's 'Barber of Seville')."

427—A Congressman said to Horace Greeley one day: "I am a self-made man."

"That sir," said Greeley, "relieves the Almighty of a great responsibility."

SEE ALSO
Eating 7
Universities 1019
Music 1306
Public Offices 1926

RELATED SUBJECTS
Boastfulness 101–103
Dullness 186–195
Long-Windedness 341–363
Snobbishness 546–551
Vanity 606–628

PRACTICAL JOKING

431—Mark Twain once encountered a friend at the races who said, "I'm broke. I wish you'd buy me a ticket back to town."

Twain said, "Well, I'm pretty broke myself but, I'll tell you what to do. You hide under my seat and I'll cover you with my legs." It was agreed and Twain then went to the ticket office and bought two tickets. When the train was under way and the supposed stowaway was snug under the seat, the conductor came by and Twain gave him the two tickets.

"Where is the other passenger?" asked the conductor.

Twain tapped on his forehead and said in a loud voice, "That is my friend's ticket. He is a little eccentric and likes to ride under the seat."

432—It is said that Dr. Clyde Miller of Columbia University has his way of disposing of dull books occasionally sent to him by publishers. He sends them on to friends with a note, ostensibly from the author, saying, "I hope you will be pleased by the references made to you in this volume, and hope that you will not have any objection to this use of your name." Dr. Miller takes pleasure in the vision of his friends searching vainly through the books for the allusions to them.

433—George Bernard Shaw was poring over a second-hand book-stall of volumes much marked down, when he came across a volume containing his own plays. The book was inscribed, moreover, to a friend, beneath whose name on the fly-leaf, G.B.S. saw, written in his own hand, "With the compliments of George Bernard Shaw." Buying the book, Mr. Shaw wrote under the inscription: "With renewed compliments. G. B. S.," and sent it back to the early recipient.

434—In the days of Kipling's most popular vogue, his literary works yielded him great sums.

An American wit once wrote to him, "I hear that you are

retailing literature for $1.00 a word. I enclose $1.00, for which please send me a sample."

Keeping the dollar, Kipling wrote, "Thanks."

Shortly afterward, he received another letter from his correspondent, saying, "Sold the 'Thanks' anecdote for $2.00. Enclosed please find 45¢ in stamps, being half the profits on the transaction, less postage."

435—A miserly old nobleman wanted Hogarth to paint on his staircase a picture of the destruction of Pharaoh's hosts in the Red Sea. He did so much haggling over the price that Hogarth finally agreed to do the work for about half what it was worth. After two days' work, to the surprise of the nobleman, Hogarth said the picture was ready. When the curtain was removed there was nothing to be seen but the canvas painted red all over. "Zounds!" cried the miser. "What have you here? I ordered a scene of the Red Sea!"

"The Red Sea you have," replied the artist.

"But where are the Israelites?"

"They are all gone over."

"And where are the Egyptians?"

"They are all drowned."

436—Turner, the famous British painter, was much irritated by the fashionable ladies who talked pretentiously about "the masters." One day, when such a woman was gushing ignorantly about Cimabue, Turner interrupted, "Do you seriously think, your ladyship, that any of his works can compare with those of the great Florentine, Mortadella da Bologna?"

Nothing daunted the lady replied, "But how much better is Cimabue's color!"

"Not if you are a connoisseur of Italian sausages, Madame," politely purred the painter to the general hilarity.

437—Brahms once took the most elaborate pains to hoax Gustav Nottebohm, the famous Beethoven scholar. The poverty-stricken scholar often strolled with him in the Prater, and habitually bought his cold supper there from a certain cheese and sausage peddler. Kalbeck amusingly reports how "one evening he received his victuals wrapped in old music paper covered with crabbed notes, apparently in Beethoven's handwriting. Fighting down his excitement, he marched to the next lamppost, unfolded the paper, examined it carefully through his spectacles, smoothed it, and without a word shoved it into his pocket. The cheese he kept in his hand and ate as he walked, assuring the others that he was unusually hungry that day. And never did he drop a syllable about his find—to the huge disappointment of the company who had been let by Brahms into the secret. For the mysterious sheet contained a variation of the latest popular song-hit. That rascal Brahms had fabricated it in masterly imitation of Beethoven's hen scratches, and enjoined the peddler to wrap it around the professor's cheese."

SEE ALSO	RELATED SUBJECTS
Speeches 777	Rough and Ready 496–507
Authors 1204	Zanies 641–643
Sermons 1542	Parties 741–746

PREJUDICE

441—This is the remark William H. Seward made in reply to Douglas, who had been indulging, on the floor of the Senate, in a tirade against "nigger-worshippers." After the debate they walked home together from the capitol, and Mr. Seward, having in view Mr. Douglas's expectation of a nomination from the Democratic party for the Presidency, said: "Douglas, no man will ever be president of the United States who spells Negro with two g's."

442—He was a red-faced, middle-aged Irishman, who had taken just enough to make him officious. He kept a wary eye on the conductor, and a sympathetic one on the unsteady entering passenger; to each "step lively," he would rejoin, "shtiddy, shtiddy, give them toime, give them toime." Opposite the Irishman sat a young man of the most pronounced Hebrew type. He watched Pat with a humorous twinkle in his black eyes.

A good-natured Negro got in, and took the seat next to the Irishman. Pat threw one haughty look at the black man; then, rising with great dignity, he said in terms of unutterable scorn: "a nager!" and sat down next to the young Hebrew. Quick as a flash his new neighbor, with an exact imitation of Pat's tone and manner, said "an Irishman!" and took the vacant seat next to the Negro. A titter went round the car, and one Irishman looked foolish.

443—"You're a Jew, ain't you?" said the bigoted and prejudiced Yankee to the little man he found seated next to him on the train.

"Yes, I'm a Jew," he replied.

"Well, I'm not," said the Yankee arrogantly, "and I'm glad to say that in the little village in Maine where I come from, there ain't a single Jew."

His neighbor replied quietly, "Dot's why it's a village."

444—Meeting Margaret Fuller one day full-gloved in the street, Mrs. Horace Greeley, who had an antipathy to kid coverings, touched Miss Fuller's hand with a shudder and snapped out: "Skin of a beast!"

"Why, what do you wear?" asked Margaret.

"Silk," responded Mrs. Greeley.

Miss Fuller gave a comic shudder and came back with: "Entrails of a worm!"

445—"One day," related Booker T. Washington, the Negro educator, "a poor, ignorant white man came to the polls to vote.

" 'I wish you'd oblige me by voting this ticket,' said a bright mulatto, who was standing near the polls.

" 'What kind of a ticket is it?' asked the poor white man.

" 'Why,' said the mulatto, 'you can see for yourself.'

" 'But I can't read!'

" 'What, can't you read the ballot you have there in your hand and which you are about to vote?' exclaimed the colored man.

" 'No,' said he, 'I can't read at all.'

" 'Well,' said the colored man, 'this ballot means that you are in favor of giving equal franchise to both white and colored citizens.'

" 'It means to let the niggers vote, does it?'

" 'Yes, sir.'

" 'Then I don't want it. Niggers don't know enough to vote.' "

446—Pauline Bonaparte engaged a huge Negro to bathe her every morning. When some one protested, she answered innocently:

"What? Do you call that thing a man?"

She then ordered the Negro to go out and marry at once in order that she might not be compromised.

447—Theodore Roosevelt once said, "While I was Police Commissioner of New York City, an anti-Semitic preacher from Berlin, Rector Ahlwardt, came to New York to preach a crusade against the Jews. Many Jews were

much excited, and asked me to prevent him from speaking
and not to give him police protection. This, I told them,
was impossible; and if possible would have been un-
desirable because it would make him a martyr. The
proper thing to do was to make him ridiculous. Accordingly, I sent a detail of police under a Jewish sergeant,
and the Jew-baiter made his harangue under the active
protection of some 40 police, every one of them a Jew."

448—One day Jack Johnson (the Negro heavyweight champion)
went alone into Bradcock's (in Mexico City), a very
fashionable restaurant run by an American Southerner.
Jack had been told that there was no color line in Mexico,
but in Bradcock's restaurant, after a long wait on his part,
a waitress informed him she had orders never to serve a
Negro.
He went over to El Globo. Two generals at once insisted
on returning with him to Bradcock's. The three of them
seated themselves at a table and asked to see Bradcock
personally.
Bradcock appeared, rubbing his hands ingratiatingly as
though about to present someone with a loving-cup.
"What can we do for you?" he asked solicitously, noticing
the insignia on the uniforms.
"We want four coffees."
"Certainly, certainly." One was never impolite to a Mexican general. "You have another friend coming?"
"No," snorted one of the generals. "We are asking you to
do us the honor of taking coffee with us." He laid his gun
on the table.
Mr. Bradcock, proud Southerner that he was, tamely sat
down.
Afterwards the generals called a policeman, and Bradcock
was fined a hundred pesos for discrimination.

449—In the days of the great Abolition furore, Wendell Phillips
was accosted on a lecture tour by a minister who hailed
from the state of Kentucky, a place with very different
views concerning the ideas of the Abolitionists. The
clergyman, who was more militant on behalf of his prejudices than on behalf of his creed, said, "You're Wendell
Phillips, I believe."
"Yes, I am."
"You want to free the niggers, don't you?"
"Yes, I do."

"Well, why do you preach your doctrines up North? Why don't you try coming down to Kentucky?"

Phillips began to counter-question the man. "You're a preacher, are you not?"

"Yes, I am, sir."

"Are you trying to save souls from Hell?"

"Why yes, sir. That is my business."

"Why don't you go there then?" suggested Mr. Phillips.

450—A man who was once talking with Sir Moses Montefiore at a reception, found the conversation so entertaining that he completely forgot the race of his companion and made some uncomplimentary remark about the Jewish features of a lady who was passing by. The mistake was no sooner made than it was perceived. The unhappy man began to apologize profusely. "I ask a thousand pardons. It was so stupid of me to forget. You look angry enough to eat me. I beg you not to devour me."

"Sir," replied Sir Moses, "it is impossible. My religion forbids."

451—Innocently unaware of the prejudices held against him, an old colored man, staunchly religious, applied for membership in an exclusive church. The pastor attempted to put him off with all sorts of evasive remarks. The old Negro, instinctively becoming aware that he was not wanted, said finally that he would sleep on it and perhaps the Lord would tell him just what to do.

Several days later he returned.

"Well," asked the minister, "did the Lord send you a message?"

"Yessuh, he did," was the answer. "He told me it wan't no use. He said, 'Ah been tryin' to get in that same church myself for ten yeahs an' Ah still can't make it.' "

452—Frederick Douglass, noted Negro author and champion of the rights of his people, was once invited to have tea with President Lincoln at the White House.

Whenever Douglass spoke of this occasion he always said, "Lincoln is the first white man I ever spent an hour with who did not remind me that I am a Negro."

SEE ALSO   RELATED SUBJECTS
Hypocrisy 303   Snobbishness 546–551
Politeness 417   Tolerance 601–603
Prisoners 2366   Equality 2046

PRIDE

456—Diogenes visited Plato one day and perceiving that the floors were beautifully covered with carpets of the richest wool and finest dye, stamped his foot in scorn exclaiming: "Thus do I tread on the pride of Plato!"

"With greater pride," mildly added Plato.

457—Ned Shuter, the 18th Century comedian, was often very poor, and being more negligent than poor, was careless about his dress. A friend overtaking him one day in the street said to him, "Why, Ned, are you not ashamed to walk the streets with twenty holes in your stockings? Why don't you get them mended?"

"No, my friend," said Ned, "I'm above it: and if you have the pride of a gentleman you will act like me, and walk with twenty holes, rather than have one darn."

"How," replied the other, "how do you make that out?"

"Why," replied Ned, "a hole is the accident of the day, but a darn is premeditated poverty."

SEE ALSO
Soldiers 2430, 2436

RELATED SUBJECTS
Boastfulness 101–103
Flattery 236–237
Honor 296–298
Pompousness 421–427
Snobbishness 546–551
Vanity 606–628

PROCRASTINATION

461—Napoleon instructed his secretary, Bourrienne, to leave all his letters unopened for three weeks, and then observed with satisfaction how large a part of the correspondence thus disposed of itself and no longer required an answer.

SEE ALSO
Parliament 2000

RELATED SUBJECTS
Lateness 321–324
Laziness 326–327
Efficiency 2266–2270

QUARRELSOMENESS

466—Keats was a famous little fighter, less in truculent self-assertiveness than by way of high chivalry and defense of the right. According to his schoolfellow, E. Holmes, "He would fight anyone—morning, noon and night, his brother among the rest. It was meat and drink for him."

SEE ALSO
Banquets 752

RELATED SUBJECTS
Profanity 66–68
Boastfulness 101–103
Rudeness 511–524
Stubbornness 571–572
Temper 596–598
Dueling 801–803

QUICK THINKING

471—When Champ Clark was Speaker of the House, Congressman Johnson of Indiana interrupted the speech of an Ohio representative, calling him a jackass. The expression was ruled to be unparliamentary and Johnson apologized.

"I withdraw the unfortunate word, Mr. Speaker, but I insist that the gentleman from Ohio is out of order."

"How am I out of order?" angrily shouted the other.

"Probably a veterinary could tell you," answered Johnson. And this was allowed to enter the record.

472—As Mark Hanna was walking through his office one day he overheard one of his employees remark that he wished that he had Hanna's money and Hanna was in the poorhouse.

Immediately upon reaching his office Hanna sent for the young man.

He told him he had overheard his statement, and then added, "Supposing you had your wish. And you had my money and I was in the poor-house, then what would you do?"

Quickly the boy replied, "Well, I guess the first thing I'd do would be to get you out of that poor-house."

The boy got a raise in salary.

473—Anxious to avoid the clutches of a delegate from a charitable institution, the businessman instructed his secretary to say that he was ill.

Deciding to make the illness a serious and telling factor, the secretary informed the caller, "I'm sorry, but Mr. Johnson cannot see you today. He has a sprained back."

The delegate seemed slightly surprised for a moment and then, looking at the secretary with a mocking gleam in his eye, said, "I didn't come here to wrestle with Mr. Johnson. I just want to talk with him."

474—When Charles (Hell-and-Maria) Dawes was ambassador to Great Britain the story was told of his buying a news-

paper from a London newsboy who charged him the usual
price of a penny.

"I'd have to pay double the price for this paper in America,"
Dawes remarked.

"Well, guv'nor," said the newsboy, "you can pay me double
if it'll make you feel at 'ome."

475—The story was once current in financial circles of New York
of the Negro messenger boy who attempted to deliver a
message personally to J. P. Morgan and was rebuked by
a receptionist who said to him, "You can't go in there,
that is J. P. Morgan of Morgan & Company." "That's all
right," replied the messenger. "I'm the coon of Kuhn,
Loeb & Company."

476—When Voltaire arrived in England in 1727 he found that
feeling ran high against the French, that on the streets of
London he was in grave peril. One day during a walk a
crowd of angry citizens shouted, "Kill him! Hang the
Frenchman!"

Voltaire stopped, faced the crowd and cried:

"Englishmen! You want to kill me because I am a Frenchman! Am I not punished enough in not being an Englishman?"

The crowd cheered wildly, and provided him safe conduct
back to his dwelling.

477—As William Dean Howells and Mark Twain were coming
out of church one morning, it commenced to rain heavily.

"Do you think it will stop?" asked Howells.

"It always has," answered Twain.

478—When Paderewski was visiting Boston some years ago he
was approached by a bootblack who called, "Shine?"

The great pianist looked down at the youth whose face was
streaked with grime and said, "No, my lad, but if you will
wash your face I will give you a quarter."

"All right!" exclaimed the boy looking sharply at him. He
ran to a nearby fountain where he made his ablutions.

When he returned, Paderewski held out the quarter. The
boy took it and then returned it gravely, saying, "Here,
Mister, you take it yourself and get your hair cut."

479—When Daniel Webster was a boy in the district school, he
was not noted for tidiness. Finally the teacher, in despair,
told him that if he appeared again with such dirty hands
she would thrash him. He did appear in the same condi-

tion. "Daniel," she said, "hold out your hand." Daniel
spat on his palm, rubbed it on the seat of his trousers and
held it out. The teacher surveyed it in disgust. "Daniel,"
she said, "if you can find me another hand in this school
that is dirtier than that, I will let you off."
Daniel promptly held out the other hand.

480—De Wolf Hopper was calling down a speaking tube to the
janitor of his apartment in New York. Mr. Hopper, unable to get the information he desired finally blurted out:
"Say, is there a blithering idiot at the end of this tube?"
The reply came quickly: "Not at this end, sir."

481—Sheridan found himself trapped at a house party. A maiden
lady of vinegary mien would not be deterred one day from
her proposal to take a stroll with him. Hard-pressed but
desperate, Sheridan begged off on the pretext of the
threatening weather.
Shortly afterward, sneaking out by a back entrance to walk
alone, Sheridan was accosted by his nemesis.
"So, Mr. Sheridan," said she, "it has cleared up."
"It has cleared up just a little, Madam," said Sheridan
hastily, "enough for one, but hardly enough for two."

482—An astrologer foretold the death of a lady whom Louis XI
passionately loved. She did, in fact, die; and the King
imagined that the prediction of the astrologer was the
cause of it. He sent for the man, intending to have him
thrown through the window, as a punishment. "Tell me,
thou pretendest to be so clever and learned a man, what
thy fate will be?"
The soothsayer, who suspected the intrigues of the Prince,
and knew his foibles, replied: "Sire, I foresee that I shall
die three days before your Majesty."
The King believed him, and was careful of the astrologer's
life.

483—When Killigrew, the celebrated Master of Revels to
Charles II of England, visited Louis XIV in Paris, the
French monarch showed him his pictures. He finally
pointed out to him a picture of the Crucifixion between
two portraits.
"That on the right," said his Majesty, "is the Pope, and that
on the left is myself."
"I humbly thank you your Majesty," replied the English
Court Jester, "for the information; for though I have

often heard that the Lord was crucified between two thieves, I never knew who they were till now."

484—Two Massachusetts State Senators got into an angry debate and one told the other he could "go to hell." The man thus consigned called on Governor Coolidge and asked him to do something about it.

Mr. Coolidge replied:

"I've looked up the law, Senator, and you don't have to go there."

485—"What is the difference between a misfortune and a calamity?" someone asked of Disraeli.

He got the reply, "Well, if Gladstone fell into the Thames, that would be a misfortune; and if anybody pulled him out, that would be a calamity."

486—Bursting into the lawyer's office, the butcher demanded, "If a dog steals a piece of meat from my shop, is the owner liable?"

"Of course," said the lawyer.

"Well, your dog took a piece of steak worth half a dollar about 5 minutes ago."

"All right," said the lawyer, without blinking. "Give me the other half dollar and that will cover my fee."

487—A teacher of psychology, F. L. Thomason of San Francisco, was accosted by a hold-up man late one night. Thinking quickly, Thomason asked the thief for a dime, and started a rambling hard-luck story. Astonished, the bandit admitted his original intention and gave his intended victim a ten-cent piece. The professor went home with his dime and the $200 that was in his wallet.

488—Alexander Pope, sneering at the ignorance of a young man, asked him if he knew what an interrogation was?

"Yes sir," said he, " 'tis a little crooked thing that asks questions."

489—Dr. Robertson observed that Dr. Johnson's jokes were the rebukes of the righteous, described in Scripture as being like excellent oil.

"Yes," exclaimed Edmund Burke, "oil of vitriol!"

490—The Duke of Cumberland being once in company with Samuel Foote, was so delighted with the wit of the actor, that he said, "Mr. Foote, I swallow all the good things you say."

"Do you," replied Foote, "then your royal highness has an excellent digestion, for you never bring any of them up again."

491—When practicing law in Illinois, Lincoln was sent a sub-scription paper in behalf of the worn-out trouser-seat of his opponent. He returned the paper with the remarks, "I refuse to subscribe to the end in view."

492—Douglas, at a gathering at which Lincoln was also present, was repeatedly making remarks about Lincoln's lowly station in life and saying that his first meeting with him had been across the counter of a general store. He finally ended his remarks by saying, "And Mr. L. was a very good bartender too."

There was a roar of laughter at this, but it quieted down considerably when Mr. Lincoln said quietly:

"What Mr. Douglas has said, gentlemen, is true enough; I did keep a grocery, and I did sell cotton, candles and cigars, and sometimes whiskey; but I remember in those days that Mr. Douglas was one of my best customers. Many a time have I stood on one side of the counter and sold whiskey to Mr. Douglas on the other side, but the difference between us now is this: I have left my side of the counter, but Mr. Douglas still sticks to his as tenaciously as ever."

SEE ALSO
Boastfulness 101
Generosity 242
Liars 331
Politeness 420
Prejudice 444
Rudeness 516
Homeliness 653
Beauty 666
Introductions 788
Infidelity 902
Lectures 1111
Ministers 1467, 1473
Salesmen 2092

RELATED SUBJECTS
Rough and Ready 496–507
Shrewdness 526–541
Tact 586–591
Speeches 756–782

Banks 2151, 2157
Rationing 2356
Judges 2490
Lawyers 2526, 2533
Detectives 2556
Hanging 2568
Stealing 2581

ROUGH AND READY

496—When Carter Glass first began to make himself heard in 1913, in caucuses of his party in the Senate, he talked rather ponderously and frigidly. On one such occasion, the subject seemed to warm him up and soon he was not only emphatic but pugnacious. At this point one of his partisans in the caucus shouted:

"Give 'em hell, Carter!"

Mr. Glass's reply has become historic.

"Hell? Why use dynamite when insect powder will do?"

497—It is said that Thomas Hart Benton one day intended to answer a speech of Calhoun's, but hearing that Calhoun was prostrated by illness and could not be present, he announced, "Benton will not speak, today, for when God Almighty lays his hands on a man Benton takes his off."

498—A legend has it that Will Rogers once walked up to the gate of Buckingham Palace and said to the guard, "I am Will Rogers and I have come to see the King." The guards drew themselves up haughtily and Rogers continued, "You tell him that when the Prince of Wales was out my way, he told me to look up his old man sometime, so here I am." Rogers was admitted, had a long chat with the King and stayed to lunch.

499—Charles M. Schwab maintained with some of his old employees in his mills a certain comradeship. Coming into the open hearth room one morning Schwab saw a brawny old laborer, naked from the waist up, glistening with sweat, shining in the lurid glow of the furnaces.

"Pete," said Schwab, "you look like an old Rembrandt."

"Hell," said his employee, "you don't look so hot yourself, Charlie."

500—A badman rushed into a saloon brandishing his guns and shooting to the right and left. He stood in the middle of the floor and shouted, "All you dirty skunks get out of here!" The bar was virtually emptied in one wild burst of confusion, but as the smoke cleared it revealed one imperturbable man calmly finishing his drink at the bar. The badman lumbered over to him. "Well?" he demanded.

"Well," said the other, "there was sure a lot of 'em, wasn't there?"

501—Charles Fox, the English statesman, once asked a tradesman for his vote. The tradesman answered, "I admire your abilities, but damn your principles," to which Fox replied, "My friend, I applaud your sincerity, but damn your manners."

502—Chief-Justice Marshall of the U. S. Supreme Court related that Governor Giles of Virginia once addressed a note to Patrick Henry:

"Sir,—I understand that you have called me a 'bobtail politician.' I wish to know if it be true, and if true, your meaning.—Wm. B. Giles."

Patrick Henry replied:

"Sir,—I do not recollect having called you a 'bobtail politician' at any time, but think it probable I have. Not recollecting the time of the occasion, I can't say what I did mean; but if you will tell me what you think I meant, I will say whether you are correct or not.—Very respectfully, Patrick Henry."

503—At that stage in his political career at which Winston Churchill switched over from the Conservative to the Liberal side of the House, many of his erstwhile adherents were sorely offended. A snippish young lady once said to him playfully, "There are two things I don't like about you, Mr. Churchill."

"Yes?" he inquired.

"Your new politics and your mustache."

"My dear Madam," said Churchill coldly, "you are not likely to come into much contact with either."

504—At a Kentucky political meeting a certain participant in the debate was shot by several of the others at the meeting. The event occurred on the open floor and created a considerable stir in the community.

A Northerner, who was in town, asked an acquaintance, who had been present, why the shooting had occurred.

"He made a motion that was out of order," explained the Kentuckian.

Horrified at this excess of parliamentarianism, "You mean to tell me they shot a man in cold blood on the floor of the meeting just for making a motion that was out of order!"

"Well," drawled his informant, "the motion was toward his hip pocket."

505—An ambitious youth once sent his first manuscript to Dumas, asking the distinguished novelist to become his collaborator. The latter was astounded at the impertinence. Angrily seizing his pen he wrote, "How dare you, sir, yoke together a noble horse and a contemptible ass?"

He received the following reply : "How dare you, sir, call me a horse?"

His anger vanished and he wrote, "Send on your ms., my friend; I gladly accept your proposition."

506—Clyde Fitch tells the following story of Whistler. The artist was in Paris at the time of the coronation of King Edward, and at a reception one evening a duchess said to him: "I believe you know King Edward, Mr. Whistler."

"No, madame," replied Whistler.

"Why, that's odd," she murmured, "I met the King at a dinner-party last year, and he said that he knew you."

"Oh," said the painter, "that was just his brag."

507—Robert Benchley had been shining as the outstanding ladies' man at a certain party in Hollywood, when two matinee idols arrived. The girls began to desert the humorist, one of them exclaiming over the new-comers, "Now, that's my idea of real he-men!"

"He-men!" growled Benchley, "I'll bet the hair of their combined chests wouldn't make a wig for a grape!"

SEE ALSO
Drinking 44
Pompousness 422
Universities 1019
Authors 1173
Actors 1428
Travel 1791
Card Playing 1836
Campaigning 1911
Trials 2481
Witnesses 2504
Law Enforcement 2546

RELATED SUBJECTS
Quick Thinking 471–492
Shrewdness 526–541
Equality 2046

RUDENESS

511—The would-be wit found himself quietly put down several pegs when, at the dinner table, he held up his fork with a piece of meat upon it and asked his hostess, "Is this pig?"

"To which end of the fork do you refer?" asked one of his fellow guests.

512—At a recent gathering of Hamilton College alumni, Alexander Woollcott was interrupted in the telling of a story by a former classmate, who said, "Hello, Alex! You remember me, don't you?"

Mr. Woollcott shook his head:

"I can't remember your name, but don't tell me. . . ." He then went on with his story.

513—At a stuffy English garden party, Beatrice Lillie (Lady Peel), wearing the Peel pearls, was approached by a lady of lineage who said maliciously, "What lovely pearls, Beatrice. Are they genuine?"

Miss Lillie nodded.

"Of course, you can always tell by biting them," said the cat. "Here, let me see."

"Gladly," said Lady Peel, proferring her jewels, "but remember, Duchess, you can't tell real pearls with false teeth."

514—One of Dorothy Parker's more telling retorts was in answer to the snobbish young man who had been discoursing at some length at a party and had finally observed, "I simply can't bear fools."

"How odd," was Miss Parker's reply. "Apparently your mother could."

515—For deadly comments on deadly occasions Beatrice Lillie deserves some kind of accolade. "Don't think it hasn't been charming," she said to her hostess when leaving a party, "because it hasn't."

516—Robert Hall being unsuccessful in securing the hand of a Miss Steel, while smarting under his disappointment, took tea with a company of ladies, one of whom, the lady of the house, said, in bad taste, "You are dull, Mr. Hall, and we have no polished steel to brighten you."

"O, Madam," replied Mr. Hall, "that is of no consequence; you have plenty of polished brass."

517—A celebrity hound approached Groucho Marx at a party. "You remember me, Mr. Marx. We met at the Glynthwaites' some months ago."

"I never forget a face," Groucho replied, "but I'll make an exception in your case."

518—Against the charge of malice, Samuel Rogers defended himself thus:

"They tell me I say ill-natured things. I have a very weak voice; if I did not say ill-natured things no one would hear what I said."

519—When one of the town's most important movie producers had his secretary call the late John Barrymore to invite him to a party, Barrymore politely murmured into the telephone, "I have a previous engagement which I shall make as soon as possible."

520—Hermann Goering accompanied the Fuehrer on one of his visits to Rome. On the crowded railway platform filled with dignitaries and troops, the massive Marshal roughly jostled past an Italian gentleman of aristocratic bearing, who turned and haughtily demanded an apology. Fiercely the Marshal turned upon him and snapped, "I am Hermann Goering." The Italian bowed and replied, "As an excuse that is not enough, but as an explanation it is ample."

521—When a diplomat remarked that he could not understand why he was called ill-natured, for in all his life he had never done but one ill-natured action, Talleyrand asked: "And when will it end?"

522—Oscar Wilde indulged his penchant for baiting Yankees when he met Richard Harding Davis.
"So you are from Philadelphia where Washington is buried?"
"Nonsense, he's buried in Mount Vernon," Davis answered abruptly.
Wilde, miffed, switched the talk to a new French painter. "Do let's hear what Mr. Davis thinks of him," he purred. "Americans always talk so amusingly of art."
Davis answered: "I never talk about things when I don't know the facts."
Wilde's rapier wit flashed back: "That must limit your conversation frightfully."

523—Samuel Johnson was once vexed by the presence of a man at a small dinner party who laughed inordinately and with a great and ostentatious show of appreciation at everything the good Dr. said. Finally, irritated in the extreme, Johnson turned upon the fellow and said, "Pray, sir, what is the matter? I hope I've not said anything that you can comprehend."

524—Oliver Herford was having lunch at his club one day, when a man whom he particularly disliked came up to him. Herford attempted to disregard him but the man, smiling broadly, slapped him on the back and said jovially, "Hello, Ollie, old boy, how are you?"
Herford looked at the man coldly and answered, "I don't

know your name and I don't know your face, but your
manners are very familiar."

SEE ALSO	RELATED SUBJECTS
Memory 374	Gentlemanliness 251–256
Prejudice 450	Prejudice 441–452
Names 836	Quarrelsomeness 466
Actors 1429	Snobbishness 546–551
	Tact 586–591
	Temper 596–598

SHREWDNESS

526—A sidewalk pitch-man was disgusted by his failure to elicit
any profitable response from the large crowd assembled
around him. "You pikers," he said in disgust, "are too
tight to offer me 50¢ for a dollar." "I will," someone
spoke up. "All right," said the pitch-man, "hand over the
50¢." "I ain't taking any chances. Take it out of the
buck and hand me the change."

527—Cornelia Otis Skinner declares that as a child she was so
ugly that her mother used to weep. "But I did have a
genius for something even then," she says. "I was good
at trade and I made money from Dad. He thought I was
a good correspondent. I was; for, for every letter I wrote
him, I received an answer. I cut the 'Cornelia' from the
address on the envelope containing his reply, and sold
the 'Otis Skinner' as my father's autograph. Sometimes
it brought a dime, sometimes a quarter."

528—Otto Kahn, the well-known financier, was one day driving
through the lower East Side of New York when he saw a
large sign reading: "Samuel Kahn, cousin of Otto Kahn."
He immediately called up his lawyer, instructing him to
have the sign changed, sparing no expense. A few days
later, Kahn drove by the place again. The offending sign
had been changed. It read: "Samuel Kahn, formerly
cousin of Otto Kahn."

529—When the films were in their infancy, David Freedman
claimed to have arranged a splendid contract for
Francis X. Bushman by a well conceived stratagem.
Bushman had been playing in Chicago at $250 a week.
Freedman brought him to New York and met him at
Grand Central to take him across to Broadway to the
office of Metro. Freedman carried a sack of 2,000 pennies.

He strewed these along behind him in a thin trickle as they walked. First children and then curious adults began to follow. By the time they had crossed 42nd Street to Broadway and entered the office of Metro, a vast throng was surging in their wake. Looking out the window, the executives of Metro were easily induced to sign Bushman at a thousand dollars a week.

530—A boy, generally known about the village as being not too bright, was annoying the busy blacksmith. Hoping to scare him away, the blacksmith finally held a red-hot piece of iron under the boy's nose.

"If you'll give me half a dollar I'll lick it," said the simple-looking youngster.

The smith held out the coin. Without a word, the boy took the coin, licked it, dropped it in his pocket, and whistling softly, walked away.

531—Rabelais once found himself stranded in a village in southern France without a sou to get him back to Paris. He took this means to obtain quick and easy passage to the French capital. He engaged a room in the only tavern in the town and asked for a secretary to assist him in some writing. The mistress of the inn sent him her son, a sharp lad about twelve years old. Rabelais said to his "secretary":—"My boy, we are about to undertake a very serious business here. I want you to sit down here and print these labels for me,—'Poison for the King, Poison for the Queen, Poison for the Duke of Orleans,' etc. While you are doing this I shall be preparing the poison." While the terrified youngster was busy at his task of printing, Rabelais scraped up the ashes from the grate, mixed them with the contents of his snuff-box and wrapped up the concoction in several neat packages, on which he pasted his labels. He then dismissed his "secretary" with a solemn warning, and the boy at once rushed downstairs and breathlessly told his mother of the whole business. The woman summoned the gendarmes who came to the inn and caught the dangerous guest with his damning evidence. As the suspect could not give an account of himself he was bundled off to Paris. Here he was brought to court and recognized by the king who heard his "case" and of course set him free.

532—Valentine Williams says: "I was walking with Sir Herbert Tree one day when my hat blew off. I was about to hurl myself into the thick of traffic in pursuit when Tree restrained me: 'My brother Max says,' he told me gravely, 'Never run after your hat. Someone is sure to bring it to you.'"

"True enough a moment later, a passerby dashed up breathlessly and restored my hat to me."

533—One sunny May day in Central Park a blind man was seen tapping for attention with his cane and carrying on his chest a sign: "Help the Blind." No one paid much attention to him. A little farther on another blind beggar was doing better. Practically every passer-by put a coin in his cup, some even turning back to make their contribution. His sign said:

"It is May—and I am Blind!"

534—Triboulet was jester to Francis I. A great lord, offended at his sallies, threatened to flog him to death. Triboulet went to complain to his master.

"If he does it," said the King, "I'll hang him a quarter of an hour after."

"Thank ye, cousin," piped the jester, "but if it's all the same to you, couldn't you do it a quarter of an hour before?"

535—Once when a deputation visited Lincoln and urged emancipation before he was ready, he argued that he could not enforce it even if he proclaimed it.

"How many legs will a sheep have if you call the tail a leg?" asked Lincoln.

"Five," they answered.

"You are mistaken," said Lincoln, "for calling a tail a leg don't make it so."

536—A wastrel grandson of Queen Victoria once begged Her Highness by letter for an advance on his allowance. The severe Queen answered with a lengthy rebuke of his way of life, and a great deal of additional advice, exhorting him to thrift and diligence. Although no money had been sent, the good Queen shortly received a letter of thanks from the young man, explaining that he had followed her precepts literally by selling her letter for £25.

537—A certain motorist drove his car to work one day and parked it in front of his office. Coming out some hours later he perceived that it was covered with a number of tickets for an assortment of offenses and violations of parking and traffic rules.

He conceived an ingenious way of extricating himself from the difficulty. Calling the police from his home address, he reported his car as lost. With interest, as time went by, he passed in and out of his office watching the slow accumulation of additional penalties piling upon the forlorn automobile.

It took the police five days to find it.

538—Uncomfortably crowded once in a London bus, Edmund Gosse said to his companion, W. M. Rossetti, "I understand you are an anarchist."

"I am an atheist," replied Rossetti in a loud voice. "My daughter is an anarchist." A sufficient number of people left the bus indignantly to make Gosse and Rossetti comfortable.

539—P. T. Barnum solved the problem of overcrowding in his popular New York museum where customers were prone to linger overlong, by rigging up a corridor toward the doorway to the street and displaying above it prominently the sign, TO THE EGRESS.

540—Marshall Field, 3rd, according to a story that was going the rounds at the turn of the century, bade fair to become a very cautious business man. Approaching an old lady in a Lakewood hotel, he said:

"Can you crack nuts?"

"No, dear," the old lady replied. "I lost all my teeth ages ago."

"Then," requested Master Field, extending two hands full of pecans, "please hold these while I go and get some more."

541—Seeking to raise enough money for a volunteer fire department in Springfield, a committee approached Abraham Lincoln for a subscription. He expressed sympathy for the movement but said, "I'll tell you what, boys. I'll talk it over with Mrs. Lincoln tonight. Here's what I'll say:

"My dear, there's a subscription paper being handed around to raise money for a new hose-cart for the fire department. The committee called on me today and I told them I'd talk it over with you. Don't you think we had better subscribe $50.00?' Then she will look up quickly and say, 'Oh, Abraham, Abraham! Will you never learn? You can't afford it. Twenty-five dollars is quite enough.'"

Mr. Lincoln chuckled as he added, "Bless her dear soul,

she'll never find out how I got the better of her. Come around tomorrow, boys, and get your $25.00."

SEE ALSO	RELATED SUBJECTS
Fatness 681	Ambition 96–97
Speeches 776	Flattery 236–237
College Life 1041	Quick Thinking 471–492
Authors 1217	Tact 586–591
Bargaining 2077, 2078	Bargaining 2076–2082
Chiseling 2123	Competition 2116
Bosses 2232	Chiseling and Swindling 2121–
Salaries 2251	2132

SNOBBISHNESS

546—The Athenian general Iphicrates was the son of a shoemaker. One of his opponents in a suit at law, a descendant of the patriot Harmodius, referred insultingly to Iphicrates' humble birth. With the spirit of a true democrat, the general answered calmly: "Yes, the nobility of my family begins with me; just as that of yours ends with you."

547—A patronising young lord was once seated opposite Whistler at dinner one evening. During a lull in the conversation he adjusted his monocle and leaned toward the artist.
"Aw, y'know, Mr. Whistler," he drawled, "I pahssed your house this mawning."
"Thank you," said Whistler, "thank you very much."

548—Boston dowagers never say die. They are the most supremely right people in America. A visitor was introduced to one such person at a Boston gathering. "Where are you from?" the grand lady asked, just a trifle condescendingly.
"Idaho," replied the stranger.
The Bostonian smiled with a gentle courtesy and said, "I know, dear, that you won't take it amiss if I tell you that here we pronounce it 'Ohio.'"

549—Mount Vernon, the estate of General George Washington, is visited by many people. One day a somewhat snobbish and patronizing young Englishman remarked to Shep Wright, an old gardener employed on the estate, "I say, old man, this hedge. Ah . . . I see that deah old George got this hedge from England."
The old gardener was more than a match for him. Looking

at the young man quizzically for about a minute, he said,
"Yes, reckon he did. And that ain't all. He got this whole
bloomin' country from England."

550—Displaying considerable snobbishness an Englishman remarked to an American friend, "How unpleasant it must
be for you Americans to be governed by people whom
one would never think of asking to dinner."
With scarcely a moment's thought, the American replied
coldly, "No more unpleasant than being governed by
people who wouldn't ask you to dinner."

551—There came to the National Gallery in London, one day,
a gentleman rather shabbily dressed, carrying a picture
under his arm, who asked to see Sir William Boxall, the
governor. He was peremptorily refused an audience, and
only after repeated rebuffs was he granted a moment's
interview. The stranger intimated that he had a picture
in his possession which he wished to give to the National
Gallery, and began to unbuckle the straps to show the
painting within. Sir William, however, brusquely ordered
him either to leave it or take it away altogether, saying
that he was too busy to look at it.
"But you had better have one glance—I ask for no more,"
said the stranger.
Again Sir William refused, and was just on the point of
turning away when the covering fell off the picture and
there was revealed one of Terborch's masterpieces which
the governor himself, some time previously, had failed to
gain, though he had offered for it £6,000.
"My name is Wallace," said the stranger quietly, "Sir William Wallace, and I came to offer this picture to the
National Gallery."
"I almost fainted," related Boxall later.

SEE ALSO	RELATED SUBJECTS
Rudeness 513, 514	Flattery 236–237
Tolerance 603	Pompousness 421–427
Equality 2046	Prejudice 441–452
	Pride 456–457
	Vanity 606–628

STINGINESS

556—A poor German, a relative of John Jacob Astor, once applied to him for charity. Mr. Astor gave him a five dollar
bill.

"Why," said the disconcerted relative, "your son just gave me ten dollars!"

"Well he may!" said the stingy old magnate; "the dog has a rich father."

557—Fénelon had for some time been besieging Richelieu for a contribution to a charity-fund, but all his diplomacy had failed to make the wily French minister "come across." Meeting Richelieu in the Louvre one day, Fénelon remarked, "I have just seen a portrait of you in the other room."

"And did you ask it for a subscription?" replied Richelieu with a polite smirk.

"No,—I knew it was no use," said Fénelon, passing on. "It was a perfect likeness."

558—Russell Sage, the financier, had a wide reputation as a man difficult to separate from his money. A couple of promoters approached him one day and tried to sell him on a scheme they had. Sage talked with them for a while but said he could give them no definite answer as yet. Telling them that he would communicate with them in a few days he showed them out of the office.

One of the promoters seemed quite optimistic and voiced the opinion to his partner that he thought Sage was pretty well sold on their proposition.

"I don't know," replied the other sceptically. "He seemed too suspicious to me. Didn't you notice that, after shaking hands with me, he started to count his fingers?"

559—The young journalist was sent to get a personal interview with the wealthy old Scotch merchant. His paper desired a human interest story on how he had accumulated his riches.

"Weel, it's a long story," said the old man. "And while I'm telling it we may as well save the candle." Wherewith he blew it out.

"Never mind about the story," said the reporter, "I understand."

560—A legend of doubtful authenticity has it that J. P. Morgan was once present with a group of men at a bar in the financial district. Beckoning to the waiter, he ordered a beer; at the same time, saying, "When Morgan drinks, everybody drinks." Everybody had a beer and when Morgan had finished, he slapped a dime upon the table, saying, "When Morgan pays, everybody pays."

561—Jock said to his wife one night, "Weel, Maggie, I think I will go and pay my respects to the new neighbor."

Upon his return some time later, Maggie said, "Weel, Jock, what kind of a mon is the new neighbor?"

"He's a guid mon," replied Jock, "a guid mon and verra lib'ral with his liquor. But verra bad quality. In fact, Maggie, it was that bad, I nearly left some."

562—The story is told of the hard-bitten old Quaker who had died. At the funeral service, those who had gathered were standing silently by, waiting, as was the custom, for anyone who might wish to do so, to make some tribute to the departed. At last one old man spoke up and said, "Well, I can say one good thing about William. He wasn't always as mean as he was sometimes."

563—Two friends were walking down the street. "If you could have any wish," asked one of them, "what would it be?"

"A mountain of gold," said his friend.

"And," said his questioner, "if you had your mountain of gold, surely we're such old friends, you would give me half?"

"I would not," said the other firmly, "nothing would I give."

His friend was deeply hurt. "What," he demanded, "all these years our friendship and this is what I get?"

"Look," said the other practically, "wish yourself a mountain and leave me alone."

564—When Godwin in 1822 was on the point of being sold out to his creditors and a fund was started for him, to which Lamb, Crabbe, Robinson, Byron and Scott contributed, Wordsworth refused to subscribe. The inference is that, while generous enough to inferiors who would be duly grateful, Wordsworth was indifferent to an equal, however needy, especially an arrogant equal like Godwin from whom no gratitude was to be expected.

565—One of the stories circulated about Harry Lauder, as likely as not circulated by himself, has it that he was playing golf one bitter cold day. As he came off the course, he slipped something into the hand of the caddy, saying, "That's for a glass of hot whiskey, lad." The boy opened his hand and found a lump of sugar.

566—James Duke, founder of the tobacco fortune, was one of those eccentrically miserly characters whose accumulation of wealth is a vast storing up and no giving out.

When he had already begun to earn an income of more than $50,000 a year he took pride in living in the cheapest hall bedroom in New York and eating his meals at a Bowery restaurant. At that time he would permit no one associated with the Duke tobacco business, other than himself, to earn more than $1,000 a year.

SEE ALSO	RELATED SUBJECTS
Practical Joking 435	Economy 211–213
Fatness 683	Generosity 241–248
Wife 929	Gratitude and Ingratitude 261–268
Painting 1276, 1282	Greed 271–276
Collections 1565, 1569	Loans 2161–2164

STUBBORNNESS

571—General Grant was known for his tenaciousness. Having once taken a place he never surrendered it. Lincoln once commented on this to General Butler, saying, "When General Grant once gets possessed of a place he seems to hang on to it as if he had inherited it."

572—A man who was extremely successful in dealing with mule teams was once asked by General Booth of the Salvation Army, how he managed the stubborn creatures. "Well General," explained the man, "when they stop and won't go on I just pick up a handful of soil and put it in their mouths. Of course they spit it out, but as a rule they start on."

"Why do you think it has that effect?" asked the General.

"Well, I don't know, but I expect it changes the current of their thoughts," the mule driver replied.

RELATED SUBJECTS
Prejudice 441–452
Pride 456–457
Quarrelsomeness 466
Rudeness 511–524
Will Power 631

STUPIDITY

576—To the city of Washington come all kinds of tourists; from visiting nobility to the representatives of our smallest communities.

A lady from a small upstate New York town was a member of a touring party. Arriving at Washington Monument, the guide took them all to the very top of the structure. Overwhelmed by the many and varied sights, the woman cried in ecstatic and somewhat incoherent tones, "Why —why, there's the White House . . . and—there's the Capitol. Look over there—it's the Lincoln Memorial!" Then, looking about with a slightly bewildered and rather disappointed air, "But—but, where's the Washington Monument?"

577—They tell of the guide showing the visiting Englishman over the battlefield of Bunker Hill. "This is Bunker Hill monument. This is where Warren fell."
The English tourist looked up at the lofty shaft and observed, "Nasty fall. Killed him, of course."

578—Someone once introduced Ed Wynn to the hostess at a gathering.
"That is Ed Wynn, who's not such a fool as he looks."
"That's right," chortled the comedian. "That's right. That's the great difference between me and my friend."

579—The story is told about a wealthy man who was desirous of building a luxurious hunting lodge in the North Woods of Wisconsin. After having his plans drawn up by a famous architect, he dispatched them to a local carpenter with instructions to go ahead and build it according to the blue prints.
Scarcely a day had passed when a post card arrived at the rich man's house, saying, "The plans is all wrong. I can't do nothing till you get them straightened out."
Being in a hurry to get the house finished, the man sent a letter post haste assuring the local workman that the plans were all right and to proceed as ordered.
By return mail came the following:
"I don't aim to saw a plank until I get them plans straightened out. Why if I was to build that house the way it's laid out here you'd have two bathrooms!"

580—There are many versions of the old hill-billy looking-glass story. The oldest war horse of them all is the version in which the mountaineer, finding a mirror, peers at it and remarks, "So—that's the no-count varmint the old lady's taken up with."
Whereupon his wife, finding the mirror where he had left it, snorted in indignation, "So—that's the old hag he's running after."

A somewhat newer version is that of the mountain lad, some 24 years of age, unshaven, untrimmed and unwashed. Peering among the purchases which his father had brought back in the wagon from the settlement he came across a large wall mirror. He burst into laughter. His mother, coming out, demanded to know what he was laughing at.

"Pa's bought a wolf," chuckled the young man.

581—St. Louis, notwithstanding improvements carried out in recent years, has been in its time one of the more famous smoky cities of America.

One of its established city offices was that of Smoke Inspector. This post of such legitimate importance degenerated through the years into a political plum. At last, after one election, it fell into the hands of an appointee of utter incompetence, who shortly after taking office, was shocked to learn that he must make a monthly report.

He submitted thereupon the following:

"Have inspected the smoke of St. Louis for the month of December, 19— and have found it to be of good quality."

582—A lady visiting Stratford-on-Avon, the birthplace of Shakespeare, showed even more than the usual fervor. She had not recovered when she reached the railway station, for she remarked to a friend as they walked on the platform: "To think that it was from this very platform the immortal bard would depart whenever he journeyed to town!"

583—At a party given in honor of Thomas Mann, a noted Glamor Girl found herself dancing with the eminent writer and was duly thrilled. She smiled up at him and purred: "I just love culture, don't you?"

SEE ALSO   RELATED SUBJECTS
Newspapers 1238   Boners 106–119
Conductors 1337   Dullness 186–195
Churchmen 1455   Eccentricity 196–209
Injury 1741   Erudition 1071–1076
Kings 1982   Common Sense 1156–1157
Chiseling 2125
Banks 2155, 2156
Bosses 2231

TACT

586—Once Talleyrand, the French statesman, sat at dinner between Madame de Staël and Madame Récamier, the celebrated beauty. Madame de Staël, whose beauties were certainly not those of the person, jealous of his attentions to her rival, insisted upon knowing which he would save if they were both drowning. After seeking in vain to evade her, he at last turned toward her and said with his characteristic shrug, "Ah, Madame, you know how to swim."

587—When Wu Ting Fang was Minister to the United States from China, he visited Chicago. A native of the Windy City said to him at a reception:

"Mr. Wu, I see there is a movement in China to abolish the pigtails you wear. Why do you wear the foolish thing anyhow?"

"Well," countered Mr. Wu, "why do you wear your foolish mustache?"

"Oh, that's different," said the Chicago man, "you see I've got an impossible mouth."

"So I should suppose," retorted Mr. Wu, "judging from your remarks."

588—At a large party in New York Mrs. Joseph Schildkraut said good-bye to the British consul, then shook many other hands, and finally found herself shaking his hand again. "But you've already said good-bye to me once," he remonstrated.

"Oh, yes, Mr. Campbell," she replied archly, "but it's always a pleasure to say good-bye to you."

589—During the Coolidge administration, an overnight guest at the White House found himself in a hideously embarrassing predicament. At the family breakfast table he was seated at the President's right hand. To his surprise he saw Coolidge take his coffee cup, pour the greater portion of its contents into the deep saucer, and leisurely add a little bit of cream and a little sugar. The guest was so disconcerted that he lost his head. With a panicky feeling that it was incumbent upon him at the White House to do as the President did, he hastily decanted his own coffee into the saucer and followed suit. He was frozen with horror, when he had accomplished this, to see Coolidge take his own saucer and place it on the floor for the cat.

590—"You do not remember my name?" a lady said one time upon meeting Henry Clay. "No," was the prompt and gallant response, "for when we last met long ago I was sure your beauty and accomplishments would very soon compel you to change it."

591—Edmund Gosse had a good story of Browning at a men's dinner given in his honour, at which the only guest without any claim to distinction was a young gentleman whom no one had ever seen or heard of. When the party moved upstairs, it was perceived with consternation that this whipper-snapper had manoeuvred the poet into a position behind the grand pianoforte, from which there seemed no escape. How was he to be rescued? Browning himself solved the difficulty. "But I'm monopolizing you," he said, laying on the youth's shoulder a friendly hand which left him no choice but to yield the pass.

SEE ALSO
Names 838
Courtship 855
Kings 1988, 1990
Salesmen 2097

RELATED SUBJECTS
Discretion 181–182
Gentlemanliness 251–256
Patience 391
Politeness 416–420
Quick Thinking 471–492
Diplomats 2021–2027

TEMPER

596—Some officer had disobeyed or failed to comprehend an order. "I believe I'll sit down," said Secretary Stanton, "and give that man a piece of my mind."

"Do so," said Lincoln, "write him now while you have it on your mind. Make it sharp. Cut him all up." Stanton did not need a second invitation. It was a bone crusher that he read to the President.

"That's right," said Lincoln. "Why, that's a good one."

"Whom can I send it by?" mused Stanton.

"Send it!" replied Lincoln. "Why, don't send it at all. Tear it up. You have freed your mind on the subject, and that is all that is necessary. Tear it up. You never want to send such letters; I never do."

597—It being reported that Lady Caroline Lamb had, in a moment of passion, knocked down one of her pages with a stool, the poet Moore to whom this was told by Lord Strangford, observed: "Oh! nothing is more natural for a literary lady than to double down a page."

"I would rather," replied his Lordship, "advise Lady Caroline to turn over a new leaf."

598—Henderson, the actor, was seldom known to be in a passion. When at Oxford, he was one day debating with a fellow student, who, unable to keep his temper, threw a glass of wine in the actor's face. Henderson took out his handkerchief, wiped his face, and coolly said, "That, sir, was a digression; now for the argument."

RELATED SUBJECTS
Patience 391
Quarrelsomeness 466
Rudeness 511–524

TOLERANCE

601—When Abe Lincoln used to be drifting around the country, practicing law in Fulton and Menard counties, Illinois, an old fellow met him going to Lewiston, riding a horse, which, while it was a serviceable enough animal, was not of the kind to be truthfully called a fine saddler. It was a weatherbeaten nag, patient and plodding, and it toiled along with Abe—and Abe's books, tucked away in saddlebags, lay heavy on the horse's flank.

"Hello, Uncle Tommy," said Abe.

"Hello, Abe," responded Uncle Tommy. "I'm powerful glad to see ye, Abe, fer I'm goin' to have sumthin' fer ye at Lewiston co't, I reckon."

"How's that, Uncle Tommy?" said Abe.

"Well, Jim Adams, his land runs 'long o' mine, he's pesterin' me a heap, an' I got to get the law on Jim, I reckon."

"Uncle Tommy, you haven't had any fights with Jim, have you?"

"No."

"He's a fair to middling neighbor isn't he?"

"Only tol'able, Abe."

"He's been a neighbor of yours for a long time, hasn't he?"

"Nigh on to fifteen year."

"Part of the time you get along all right, don't you?"

"I reckon we do Abe."

"Well, now, Uncle Tommy you see this horse of mine? He isn't as good a horse as I could straddle, and I sometimes get out of patience with him, but I know his faults. He does fairly well as horses go, and it might take me a long time to get used to some other horse's faults. For all horses have faults. You and Uncle Jimmy must put up

with each other as I and my horse do with one another."
"I reckon, Abe," said Uncle Tommy, as he bit off about four
ounces of Missouri plug, "I reckon you're about right."
And Abe Lincoln, with a smile on his gaunt face, rode on
toward Lewiston.

602—St. Francis De Sales, being consulted by a lady on the pro-
priety of wearing rouge, replied, "Some persons may object to it, and others may see no harm in it, but I shall
take a middle course, by allowing you to rouge on one
cheek."

603—Sir Walter Scott, once happening to hear his daughter Anne
say of something that it was vulgar, gave the young lady
the following temperate rebuke: "My love, you speak like
a very young lady; do you know, after all, the meaning
of this word vulgar? It is only common. Nothing that is
common, except wickedness, can deserve to be spoken of
in a tone of contempt."

SEE ALSO	RELATED SUBJECTS
Drinking 38	Generosity 241–248
	Kindness 311–316
	Patience 391
	Prejudice 441–452
	Freedom 2036–2042
	Equality 2046

VANITY

606—Scrope Davies was on very intimate terms with many of the
great men of the period, and he had such admiration for
the author of "Don Juan" (Byron) that he could gain admission to his rooms at all hours. On one occasion he
found the poet in bed with his hair "en papillote," upon
which Scrope cried in great glee, "Ha, ha, Byron, I have
at last caught you acting the part of the Sleeping Beauty."
Byron, in a rage, exclaimed, "No, Scrope; the part of a
damned fool, you should have said."
Upon which Scrope answered: "Anything you please—but
you have succeeded admirably in deceiving your friends,
for it was my conviction that your hair curled naturally."
"Yes, naturally every night; but do not, my dear Scrope,
let the cat out of the bag, for I am as vain of my curls as
a girl of sixteen."

607—A magnificent ball was given in Paris. Pauline Bonaparte
decided "to blot out every woman there." She entered the

ballroom when all the guests had already assembled. At sight of her the music stopped, silence fell upon the assemblage. Her costume was of the finest muslin bordered with golden palm leaves. Four bands, spotted like a leopard's skin, were wound about her head, while these in turn were supported by little clusters of golden grapes. She had copied the headdress of a Bacchante in the Louvre. All over her person were cameos, and just beneath her breasts she wore a golden band held in place by an engraved gem. She had, indeed, "blotted out" her rivals.

Nevertheless, Mme. de Coutades, who hated her, took a sly revenge. She went up to Pauline, who was lying on a divan to set off her loveliness, and began gazing at the princess through a double eye-glass. Pauline felt flattered for a moment, and then became uneasy. The lady who was looking at her said to a companion, in a tone of compassion:

"What a pity! She really would be lovely if it weren't for that!"

"For what?" asked her escort.

"Why are you blind? It's so remarkable that you surely must see it."

Pauline was ·beginning to lose her self-composure. She flushed and looked wildly about, wondering what was meant. Then she heard Mme. de Coutades say:

"Why, her ears! If I had such ears as those I would cut them off!"

Pauline gasped and fainted away.

608—A young man, who had come to the city from a small rural community, had toiled diligently until at last he had attained some prominence in the banking world. Belatedly he returned for a visit to his old home town, half expecting that the greater part of the community would be marshalled out to meet him at the station, and that some considerable fuss would be made over the local boy who had made good. To his disappointment, there was not a soul around when he alighted at the station platform. He waited doubtfully as several people came and went, none of them giving him so much as a glance. At last he was recognized by an old baggage handler who shuffled forward and looked at him with some interest. "Hello, George," he said at last, "goin' away?"

609—One of Disraeli's admirers, speaking about him to John Bright, said: "You ought to give him credit for what he has accomplished, as he is a self-made man."

"I know he is," retorted Mr. Bright, "and he adores his maker."

610—Miss Frances Keller of the Women's Municipal League of New York illustrated at a dinner party a point she wished to make in reply to a man who had said, "Women are vainer than men."

"Of course," Miss Keller answered, "I admit that women are vain and men are not. There are a thousand proofs that this is so. Why, the necktie of the handsomest man in the room is even now up the back of his collar." There were six men present and each of them put his hand gently behind his neck.

611—Henry James, the novelist, once lived near the estate of a millionaire jam manufacturer, retired. This man, having married an earl's daughter, was ashamed of the trade whereby he had piled up his fortune.

The jam manufacturer one day wrote Mr. James an insolent letter, vowing that it was outrageous the way the James' servants were trespassing on his grounds. Mr. James wrote back:

"Dear Sir: I am sorry to hear that my servants have been poaching on your preserves.

"P.S.—You'll excuse my mentioning your preserves, won't you?"

612—When Jack London was in Korea reporting the Russo-Japanese War, an official came to his hotel one day and told him that the entire population was gathered in the square below to see him. London felt enormously set up to think his fame had spread to the wilds of Korea. But when he mounted the platform that had been erected for him, the official merely asked him to take out his bridge of artificial teeth. The crowd watched closely as he did it. And then for half an hour they kept him standing there, taking out his teeth and putting them back again, to the applause of the multitude.

613—A Chicago matron was recently seated next to a Mrs. Cabot at a Boston tea party. During the crisp exchange of conversation, Mrs. Cabot advanced the information that "in Boston, we place all of our emphasis on breeding." To which the Chicago matron responded: "In Chicago, we think it's a lot of fun, but we do manage to foster a great many outside interests."

614—P. T. Barnum craved free publicity. When he was near death the "Evening Sun," of New York, asked the great showman's publicity agent if Barnum would object to having his obituary published before he died. The agent said, "The old man will be delighted." The next day Barnum read four columns about his own death, and he loved it.

615—Theodore Roosevelt, at the height of his prominence in American public life, was once approached by a man on the street who tipped his hat and said, "Mr. Brown, I believe?"
Roosevelt looked at the man and replied bluntly, "Sir, if you believe that, you will believe anything."

616—Oscar Levant is said to have once asked George Gershwin, "Tell me, George, if you had it to do all over, would you fall in love with yourself again?"

617—When Coolidge was Governor of Massachusetts he was once host to a visiting Englishman of some prominence. The latter ostentatiously took a British coin from his pocket, saying, "My great, great grandfather was made a Lord by the King whose picture you see on this shilling."
Coolidge laconically produced a nickel. "My great, great grandfather," he said, "was made an angel by the Indian whose picture you see on this coin."

618—An English newspaper once printed the following bit of gossip: "James McNeill Whistler and Oscar Wilde were seen yesterday at Brighton, talking as usual about themselves." Whistler sent the paragraph to Wilde with a note saying: "I wish these reporters would be accurate: If you remember, Oscar, we were talking about me."
Wilde sent him a telegram saying: "It is true, Jimmie, we were talking about you, but I was thinking of myself!"

619—"Gershwin," observed Oscar Levant, "was the happiest man on earth. He was in love with himself and didn't have a rival on earth."

620—A little fable was formerly current about Theodore Roosevelt. The great man, after his death, was supposed to have ascended to Heaven. There he bustled about and made himself a nuisance by insisting that he be entrusted with some major responsibility. At last, wearily the higher powers instructed St. Peter to authorize T. R. to organize and train a celestial choir to replace the old one, which it was felt, had gone to seed. T. R. continued to be a nuisance by the fierce persistence with which he pressed his requisitions.

"I must have 10,000 sopranos," he told the bewildered and weary St. Peter, "and 10,000 contraltos, and 10,000 tenors. And hurry—hurry! Everything is waiting on you."

"Yes," said St. Peter, "how about the basses?"

Roosevelt fixed him with a scornful glare. "I'll sing bass!" he bellowed.

621—It was one of his own sons who so aptly characterized Theodore Roosevelt, saying, "Father always had to be the center of attention. When he went to a wedding, he wanted to be the bridegroom; and when he went to a funeral, he wanted to be the corpse."

622—There is a good story told of the way Disraeli got rid of an unfortunate applicant for a baronetcy upon whom, for many reasons, it was impossible to confer the honor. "You know I cannot give you a baronetcy," said Disraeli, "but you can tell your friends I offered you a baronetcy and that you refused it. That's far better."

623—In an interview between President Lincoln and Petroleum V. Nasby, the name came up of a recently deceased politician of Illinois whose merit was blemished by great vanity. His funeral was very largely attended.

"If General ———— had known how big a funeral he would have had," said Mr. Lincoln, "he would have died years ago."

624—Oscar Levant is noted for his self-esteem. Occasionally he would tell this story on himself. "Once I was saying to an old friend how remarkable was our congeniality since we had practically nothing in common."

"Oh, but we have," replied the friend, "I think you're wonderful and you agree with me."

625—Henry IV enacted some sumptuary laws, prohibiting the use of gold and jewels in dress; but they were for some time ineffectual. He passed a supplement to them which completely answered his purpose. In this last he exempted from the prohibitions of the former after one month, all prostitutes and pickpockets. Next day there was not a jewel nor golden ornament to be seen.

626—In London D'Annunzio, the Italian poet, asked a policeman to direct him to his destination and remarked: "I am D'Annunzio!" The bobby did not understand. Whereupon the genius burst forth into oaths and commanded his secretary to present that ignorant lout with copies of all his works.

627—While D'Annunzio was living in France, a letter was addressed to him simply with the words: "To Italy's Greatest Poet." He declined to accept it, saying that he was not Italy's greatest poet—he was the world's greatest poet.

628—A young girl came to the late Father Healey of Dublin and confessed that she feared she had incurred the sin of vanity. "What makes you think that?" asked her father confessor. "Because every morning when I look into the mirror I think how beautiful I am."
"Never fear, my girl," was the reassuring reply. "That isn't a sin, it's only a mistake."

SEE ALSO
Devotion 172
Modesty 388, 389
Tolerance 602
Fatness 687
Shortness 691
Society 796
Husband 916
Family 948
Composers 1312
Concerts 1342
Directors 1403
Audiences 1438
Dictators 2003
Servants 2282

RELATED SUBJECTS
Boastfulness 101–103
Flattery 236–237
Pompousness 421–427
Pride 456–457
Snobbishness 546–551

WILL POWER

631—A young man, contemplating marriage, was almost shocked out of his future state by overhearing the following conversation.
Several young women, discussing their husbands, were talking of their men's vices and how they had succeeded in curing them.

"Incidentally," said one of them to a very pretty young thing standing by, "I hear that John has given up smoking. He used to smoke a great deal. That must have taken a strong will."

In contrast to her frail prettiness, the young woman was heard to say, "It certainly did. But that's the kind of will I've got."

SEE ALSO   RELATED SUBJECTS
Smoking 63   Habits 31
                             Conscience 146–147
                             Diligence 176–177
                             Endurance 216
                             Stubbornness 571–572

WORRYING

636—Secretary of the Treasury Chase happened to remark, "Oh, I am so sorry that I did not write a letter to Mr. So-and-so before I left home!"

President Lincoln promptly responded: "Chase, never regret what you don't write; it is what you do write that you are often called upon to feel sorry for."

RELATED SUBJECTS
Conscience 146–147
Cowardice 156–160
Melancholy 366–368
Handicaps and Afflictions 701–707
Debt 2171–2174
Bankruptcy 2196–2198

ZANIES

641—Riding on the subway during a fairly crowded hour a man was startled to see sitting opposite him in the car a man reading his newspaper and paying no attention whatever to a pair of pigeons which were seated one on each of his shoulders. Many stations further on, when the crowd had thinned out somewhat, he could repress his curiosity no longer. Stepping across the aisle he accosted the man, saying, "I beg your pardon, but would you mind telling me what those pigeons are doing on your shoulders?"

The man looked up from his paper and said, "I don't know. They got on at 14th Street."

642—A man stepped briskly up to a swanky cocktail bar at the Waldorf in New York and snapped at the barkeeper, "Martini!"

He got the drink and the bartender was astounded to see him toss the contents over his left shoulder and then proceed to nibble off the rim of the glass. Having finished this crispy morsel he slapped down the remains and said, "Another."

Another was served and the performance was repeated.

"Say," said the bartender, leaning over the bar, "are you crazy?"

"No," said the man snappily, "It's simply that I like only the rim of the glass."

"But," said the barkeeper, "the stem's the best part!"

643—One day at Ebbets Field Leo Durocher was accosted by a large and well-groomed horse, who said, "I'd like to join the Dodgers if you've got any place for me."

"What can you do?" asked Durocher scornfully.

"Well, I can bat," said the horse.

"Pick out a bat and show me," said the manager.

The horse looked over the pile of bats, selected one and stepped out to the plate with the bat between his teeth. Casey was pitching. The horse hit the first ball that came over and knocked it out of the field.

"Pretty good," said Durocher, "What else can you do?"

"I'm a mighty good first baseman," said the horse.

"Get over there," said Durocher.

The horse again proved its mettle.

"I'm a pretty good shortstop," the horse next volunteered, and again demonstrated its prowess.

"All right," said Durocher, at last convinced. "Can you pitch?"

"Oh," said the horse in disgust, "who ever heard of a horse pitching!"

RELATED SUBJECTS
Boners 106–119
Eccentricity 196–209
Exaggeration 221–226
Liars 331–336
Practical Joking 431–437

PHYSICAL CHARACTERISTICS

646—Mark Twain often received photographs from men whose friends had made them believe that they looked like him. Discovering that his house was beginning to run over with pictures of these aspirants to fame, Mark determined to relieve himself of the burden of answering the heavy correspondence, and so had his printer strike off a few hundred copies of the following form letter: "My dear Sir: I thank you very much for your letter and your photograph. In my opinion you are more like me than any other of my numerous doubles. I may even say that you resemble me more closely than I do myself. In fact, I intend to use your picture to shave by.

Yours thankfully,
S. Clemens"

647—Lincoln once dreamed he was in some great assembly, and the people drew back to let him pass, whereupon he heard some one say, "He is a common-looking fellow." In his dream Lincoln turned to the man and said, "Friend, the Lord prefers common-looking people; that is the reason why he made so many of them."

648—A simple youth coming to Rome from the country, was observed to resemble Augustus so much that it was the subject of general conversations. The emperor ordered him to appear at court, and inquired of him if his mother had ever been in Rome.

"No," answered the innocent youth, "but my father has."

SEE ALSO	RELATED SUBJECTS
Dullness 189	Homeliness 651–656
Memory 373	Beauty 661–669
Rudeness 517	Age 671–678
Children 951	Fatness 681–690
Painting 1283	Shortness 691–695
Diplomats 2025	Tallness 696
	Handicaps and Afflictions 701–707

HOMELINESS

651—Lincoln delighted to tell stories on himself. One of his favorites was the following:

"In the days when I used to be on the circuit (traveling on horseback from one county court to another) I was once accosted by a stranger, who said:

"'Excuse me, sir, but I have an article which belongs to you.'

"'How is that?' I asked, considerably astonished.

"The stranger took a jack-knife from his pocket.

"'This knife,' said he, 'was placed in my hands some years ago, with the injunction that I was to keep it until I found a man homelier-looking than I am myself. I have carried it from that time until this; allow me to say, sir, that you are fairly entitled to the property.' "

652—Lincoln's great love for children easily won their confidence.

A little girl, who had been told that the President was very homely, was taken by her father to see the President at the White House.

Lincoln took her upon his knee and chatted with her a moment in his merry way, when she turned to her father and exclaimed:

"Oh, Pa! he isn't ugly at all; he's just beautiful!"

653—An acquaintance came to Jerrold and said, indignantly, "I hear you said my nose was like the ace of clubs!"

Jerrold looked thoughtful. "No, I did not," he drawled; "but now that I look at it, I see it is—very like."

654—The day following the adjournment of the Baltimore Convention, at which President Lincoln was renominated, various political organizations called to pay their respects. While the Philadelphia delegation was being presented, the chairman of that body, in introducing one of the members said: "Mr. President this is Mr. S. of the second district of our State, a most active and earnest friend of yours and the cause. He has, among other things, been good enough to paint, and present to our league rooms a most beautiful portrait of yourself."

President Lincoln took the gentleman's hand in his, and shaking it cordially said, with a merry voice: "I presume, sir, in painting your beautiful portrait, you took your idea of me from my principles and not from my person."

655—Said the brash traveling salesman to the farmer, "My God, that's certainly a homely woman!"

"That's my wife, young man," said the farmer, "and you might remember that beauty is only skin deep."

"Then," said the salesman, "for Heaven's sake, skin her!"

656—A farmer, making his nightly rounds, saw a shadowy figure holding a lantern and standing somewhat furtively by the side of the house.

Knowing that all his family was in the house, he shouted, "Hey, there. Who are you?"

Holding the lantern head high, the figure laughed and said, "It's only me. Albert."

"Why I thought you were in bed long ago. What are you doing out so late?"

"Well," said Albert, shifting about a bit as though in embarrassment, "I'm courtin' Annie."

The farmer chuckled. "Why the lantern? Why, when I was courtin' my missus, I didn't take a lantern."

The young man hesitated for a minute, then said in all seriousness, "Yes, sir. I know. We can all see that, sir."

SEE ALSO	RELATED SUBJECTS
Vanity 628	Physical Characteristics 646–648
Tallness 696	Beauty 661–669

BEAUTY

661—As the beautiful Duchess of Devonshire was one day stepping out of her carriage, a dustman who was accidentally standing by, and was about to regale himself with his accustomed whiff of tobacco, caught a glance of her countenance, and instantly exclaimed, "Love and bless you, my lady, let me light my pipe in your eye!" It is said the Duchess was so delighted with this compliment, that she frequently afterwards checked the strain of adulation which was constantly offered to her charms, by saying, "Oh! after the dustman's compliment, all others are insipid."

662—Fontenelle, at the age of 97, after saying many amiable and gallant things to a beautiful young lady, passed before her without seeing her, to place himself at table.

"See," said the lady, "how I ought to value your gallantries, you pass without looking at me."

"Madam," replied the old man, "if I had looked at you I could not have passed."

663—Lord Chesterfield and Voltaire were attending a reception in Paris. Noticing that the Englishman was being assailed by some of the ladies, the French wit said to him, "My Lord, it is said that you possess keen discrimination; tell me now, who are the more handsome, the French women or the women of your own country?"

"As to that," replied Chesterfield, "I must admit I cannot say, as I am no connoisseur in the art of painting."

664—Curran, speaking of Madame de Staël who was by no means handsome, but a splendid conversationalist, said she "had the power of talking herself into a beauty."

665—Someone once noted to Samuel Goldwyn the beauty of his wife's hands.

"Yes," Goldwyn said, "she has such beautiful hands, I'm thinking of having a bust made of them."

666—Chesterfield and Voltaire were once attending a ball in London. A celebrated beauty was there, much berouged and painted. This lady concentrated a great deal of her attention very flatteringly upon the renowned Frenchman. Chesterfield accosted Voltaire and cautioned jokingly, "Sir, take care that you are not captivated."

"My Lord," said Voltaire, "I scorn to be taken by an English craft with French colors."

667—Lady Randolph Churchill was canvassing among the voters of Woodstock on behalf of her husband, the then chancellor of the Exchequer. Interviewing a workingman she asked for his support.

"No, certainly not," he replied. "I should never think of voting for a lazy fellow who never leaves his bed until dinner-time."

The lady assured him that he was wrongly informed, adding, "As I happen to be his wife, my evidence ought to be conclusive."

"Lor, ma'am," he at once replied, "if you were my wife I should never want to get up."

668—One of the finest compliments ever offered was the compliment by Sir Joshua Reynolds to Mrs. Siddons, the Queen of Tragedy, whose portrait he painted. When it was finished Mrs. Siddons noticed a peculiar brocaded effect upon the corner of the robe, and found on closer examination that it was the painter's name inscribed upon it. Turning to the artist she was met with a stately bow.

"I could not resist the opportunity," Sir Joshua explained, "of sending down my name to posterity on the hem of your garment."

669—It was at one of those Selfridge election parties that Max Beerbohm was heard to make one of his delightful remarks. He and his wife had been asked to come to the party, which was attended by nearly all London. There were beautiful girls from the stage, striking ladies from the film studios and others both beautiful and striking from addresses Mayfair.

He looked gravely round at the faces near him. All were painted, not with the art that conceals art, but with the determination to gain attention. This elderly exquisite looked again and shuddered, then he turned to his wife. "My dear," he said, "you are looking so charming tonight that I simply must talk to you."

SEE ALSO   RELATED SUBJECTS
Long-Windedness 361   Physical Characteristics 646–658
Tact 590   Homeliness 651–656
Vanity 607
Handicaps 703

AGE

671—Fabia Dollabella saying she was thirty years of age, Cicero answered: "It must be true, for I have heard it these twenty years."

672—When Oliver Wendell Holmes was still on the Supreme Court bench, he and Justice Brandeis took walks every afternoon. On one of these occasions Holmes, then 92, paused to gaze in frank admiration at a beautiful young girl who passed them. He even turned to look at her as she continued down the street. Then, turning to Brandeis, he sighed: "Oh! What wouldn't I give to be 70 again!"

673—A farmer called out to Colonel Thomas Hart Benton and inquired to know his age. The Colonel replied, "According to the Calendar my age is seventy-four, but when anything is to be done I am thirty-five years old, sir."

674—"Youth," said Bernard Shaw, "is a wonderful thing. What a crime to waste it on children."

675—The opposition of Pitt to the ministry, in a short time became so annoying, that Sir Robert Walpole meanly deprived him of his commission. Horace Walpole also taunted him bitterly on account of his youth, although he was then thirty-two, and sneeringly observed, that the discovery of truth was little promoted by pompous diction and theatrical emotion. Pitt replied:
"I will not attempt to determine whether youth can be imputed to any man as a reproach, but I will affirm that the wretch, who after having seen the consequences of repeated errors continues still to blunder, and whose age has only added obstinacy to stupidity, is surely the object of either abhorrence or contempt, and deserves not that his gray head should secure him from insult. Much more

is he to be abhorred, who, as he has advanced in age, has seceded from virtue, and become more wicked with less temptation; who prostitutes himself for money which he cannot enjoy, and spends the remains of his life in the ruin of his country."

676—"I do not approve of shadows in painting," said Queen Elizabeth to Daniel Meyers. "You must strike off my likeness without shadows."

The Queen was near sixty when she said this and the "shadows," as she charitably called them were wrinkles big enough to have had a straw in them.

677—In his extreme old age John Quincy Adams was slowly and feebly walking down a street in Boston. An old friend accosted him and shaking his trembling hand asked, "And how is John Quincy Adams today?"

"Thank you," said the ex-President, "John Quincy Adams is well, quite well, I thank you. But the house in which he lives at present is becoming quite dilapidated. It is tottering upon its foundations. Time and the seasons have nearly destroyed it, Its roof is pretty well worn out. Its walls are much shattered, and it trembles with every wind. The old tenement is becoming almost uninhabitable, and I think John Quincy Adams will have to move out of it soon. But he himself is quite well, quite well."

678—Stirred by the patriotic fervor that swept over the country, an Irishman of 41 tried to enlist in the army. Although the recruiting sergeant saw that this man would make a good soldier, he could not accept any man over 38.

"Listen, fella," said the sergeant, "are you sure of your age? Suppose you go home and think it over, and then come back tomorrow."

Next day the Irishman returned.

"Well, how old are you now?" asked the sergeant.

"I was wrong yesterday," said the hopeful recruit. "Sure, I'm 38; it's me old mother who's 41."

SEE ALSO   RELATED SUBJECTS
Divorce 907   Physical Characteristics 646–648
Authors 1201   Longevity 1781–1782
Hypochondriacs 1720
Insurance 2136

FATNESS

681—One night William Howard Taft, then a young law reporter, finished studying a case in Somerville, Ohio, and discovered that he could not get back to his office that night unless he could stop a through express. He wired division headquarters:

"Will you stop through express at Somerville to take on large party?"

Promptly came back the reply: "Yes."

When the train arrived, the conductor said to Mr. Taft: "Where's the large party we were to take on?"

Mr. Taft regarded his own comfortable bulk ruefully and laughed. "I'm it," he said, stepping aboard the train.

682—The celebrated Gibbon, notwithstanding his shortness and rotundity, was very gallant. One day, being tête-a-tête with Madame de Cronzas, Gibbon wished to seize the favorable moment, and suddenly dropping on his knees, he declared his love in the most passionate terms. Madame de Cronzas replied in a tone likely to prevent a repetition of such a scene. Gibbon was thunderstruck, but still remained on his knees, tho' frequently desired to get up and resume his seat.

"Sir," said Madame de Cronzas, "will you have the goodness to rise?"

"Alas! Madame!" replied the unhappy lover, "I cannot!" His size preventing him from rising without assistance. Upon this Madame de Cronzas rang the bell, saying to the servant, "Lift up Mr. Gibbon."

683—"Would you mind walking the other w'y and not passing the 'orse?" said a London cabman with exaggerated politeness to a fat lady who had just paid a minimum fare.

"Why?" she inquired. "Because if 'e sees wot 'e's been carryin' for a shilling 'e'll 'ave a fit."

684—The English artist C. R. W. Nevinson tells, "Sisley Huddleston and I were great friends. He was a man of enormous stature. We have dined and wined together in all parts of Paris, roared with laughter, and teased 'the girls.' On one occasion Sisley, Clive Bell, and I had eaten chicken and rice and had drunk wine with it. Being a large man, Sisley had a large appetite. We took one of those tiny Parisian taxis to the Boulevard St. Germain and when we arrived outside we discovered that the rice had swelled so much inside Sisley that it was impossible for him to get out of the door. We pushed and we pulled, but he seemed to be growing larger before our eyes; and at length the driver opened the roof, and Sisley came out through that and over the back. By that time he and I and the driver were so hysterical with merriment that they refused us admission to the Brasserie Lipp's in the belief that we were drunk; and Clive Bell, who had stood by, shocked and exquisite, was furious because he had a rendezvous there with Derain."

685—Marie Dressler used to tell the story of her first trip to Paris, when her French was one step removed from nothing. She was seeking the house of a friend, and the cab driver, whom she hired to convey her there, was attempting to tell her that the address was directly behind the hotel where she was staying.

"C'est derrière l'hotel," the driver kept saying. Miss Dressler did not know the word and kept repeating, "Que signifie derrière?"

They exchanged these remarks futilely for some moments until at last, in despair, the cab driver shrugged his shoulders and said, "If Madame does not know the meaning of derrière, nobody does!"

686—"Oh, I just love nature!" gushed the dowager with more than the usual number of shoulder-straps and chins.

"That's loyalty," mused Groucho Marx, "after what nature did to her!"

687—According to his friend Trelawney, "Byron's terror of getting fat was so great that he reduced his diet to the point of absolute starvation. When he added to his weight, even standing was painful, so he resolved to keep down to eleven stone, or shoot himself. He said everything he swallowed was instantly converted into tallow and deposited on his ribs. He was the only human being I ever met with who had sufficient self-restraint and resolution to resist his proneness to fatten. As he was always hungry, his merit was the greater. Occasionally he relaxed his vigilance, when he swelled apace. I remember one of his old friends saying, 'Byron how well you are looking!' If he had stopped there it had been well, but when he added, 'You are getting fat,' Byron's brow reddened, and his eye flashed—'Do you call getting fat looking well, as if I were a hog?' and turning to me he muttered, 'The beast, I can hardly keep my hands off

him.' I don't think he had much appetite for his dinner
that day, or for many days, and he never forgave the man.
He would exist on biscuits and soda-water for days
together, then, to allay the eternal hunger gnawing at his
vitals, he would make up a horrid mess of cold potatoes,
rice, fish, or greens, deluged in vinegar, and gobble it up
like a famished dog. Either of these unsavoury dishes,
with a biscuit and glass or two of Rhine wine, he cared
not how sour, he called feasting sumptuously. Upon my
observing he might as well have fresh fish and vegetables
instead of stale, he laughed and answered: 'I have an
advantage over you, I have no palate; one thing is as good
as another to me.' "

688—President Taft was fond of telling of an occasion upon
which he was enjoying the ocean at a beach in New
England. "Let us go in," said one of a group of acquaintances on the sand.

"How can we?" asked a youngster who was among them,
"The President is using the ocean."

689—Years ago, when one of her sons was a cadet at Culver,
Madame Schumann-Heink went to visit him. She was
told where his dormitory was and, wishing to surprise
him, she decided to go to his room unannounced. Arriving at the dormitory she found it to be still under construction. As she went through a doorway a sliver of
wood caught on her dress and tore a small hole in it. A
cadet, who happened to be passing by at the time, called
out impudently, "Madame, you should have gone through
that door sideways."

Without taking offense, the heavily built singer laughed
heartily. "Mein Gott, child, I have no sideways."

690—Taft always relished humor at his own expense. He liked
to tell of a small boy who had had the habit of biting his
nails. His nursemaid, seeking to frighten him out of it,
told him that if he did not stop he would swell up like a
balloon. Considerably impressed, the boy desisted from
his habit.

A few days thereafter Taft appeared at his home for a
luncheon. Marching straight up to the President, the boy
accused, "You bite your nails."

SEE ALSO	RELATED SUBJECTS
Producers 1397	Physical Characteristics 646–648
Sermons 1548	Shortness 691–695
	Tallness 696

SHORTNESS

691—Napoleon was one day searching for a book in his library, and at last discovered it on a shelf somewhat above his reach. Marshal Moncey, one of the tallest men in the army, stepped forward, saying:

"Permit me, Sire—I am higher than your Majesty."

"You are longer, Marshal," said the Emperor with a frown.

692—Alexander H. Stevens, Senator from Georgia and, subsequently, Vice-President of the Confederate States, was short of stature and weighed less than 80 lbs. A big Congressman from the West, in a heated debate, once said, "Why, I could swallow you and never know I'd et a thing."

"In that case, you'd have more brains in your belly than you ever had in your head," snapped Stevens.

693—Dr. Busby of Westminster, who was very short, was one day accosted in a public coffee-room by an Irish baronet of colossal stature with: "May I pass to my seat, O Giant?"

When the doctor politely making way, replied: "Pass, O Pigmy!" the baronet apologized. "Oh, Sir, my expression alluded to the size of your intellect."

"And my expression, Sir," retorted the doctor coldly, "to the size of yours."

694—Archbishop Laud was a man of very short stature. Charles the First and the Archbishop sat down to dinner one day when it was agreed that Archie, the King's jester, should say the Grace for them, which he did in this fashion: "Great praise be given to God, but little Laud to the Devil!" For this sally, Archbishop Laud was weak enough to insist upon Archie's dismissal.

695—A group of men were discussing Stephen Douglas and his physical peculiarities. Abraham Lincoln happened to join the men at this point and, turning from the specific subject under discussion, one of them asked the President how long he thought a man's legs should be.

"Well," drawled Lincoln, "I should think a man's legs ought to be long enough to reach from his body to the ground."

RELATED SUBJECTS
Physical Characteristics 646–648
Fatness 681–690
Tallness 696

TALLNESS

696—When Lincoln heard that a general who was supporting
McClellan's Presidential candidacy had been relieved of
his command the President countermanded the order,
saying, "Supporting General McClellan for the Presidency is no violation of army regulations, and as a question of taste in choosing between him and me—well, I'm
the longest, but he's better looking."

SEE ALSO   RELATED SUBJECTS
Shortness 693   Physical Characteristics 646–648
                            Fatness 681–690
                            Shortness 691–695

HANDICAPS AND AFFLICTIONS

701—The Reverend Whitefield having remarked in a sermon that
everything made by God was perfect, "What think you of
me?" said a deformed man in a pew beneath who arose
from his seat, and pointed at his own back.
"Think of you," reiterated the preacher. "Why sir, you are
the most perfect hunchback my eyes ever beheld."

702—Madame Bernhardt had a subtle sense of humor. Shortly
after recovering from the amputation of her leg, she received a cable from the manager of the Pan-American
Exposition at San Francisco. He had the temerity to ask
permission to exhibit her leg at the Exposition, offering
her $100,000. She cabled back only two words: "Which
leg?" That ended the matter.

703—During one of Hobhouse's visits to Byron—Hobhouse was
a college friend—at his villa near Genoa, and whilst they
were walking in the garden, his lordship suddenly turned
upon his guest, and, apropos of nothing, but always having his deformity in his mind, exclaimed: "Now I know
Hobhouse you are looking at my foot!"
Upon which Hobhouse kindly replied, "My dear Byron,
nobody thinks of or looks at anything but your head."

704—Junius Brutus Booth, the tragedian, had a broken nose.
"You're such a wonderful actor, Mr. Booth," said a lady
upon being introduced to him, "but to be perfectly frank
with you, I can't get over your nose."
"There's no wonder, Madam," Booth replied, "the bridge is
gone."

705—When Milton's enemies mocked his blindness, the poet with
great heat replied:

"I prefer my blindness to yours, yours is sunk into your deepest senses, blinding your minds, so that you can see nothing that is sound and solid. Mine takes from me only the color and surface of things, but does not take away from the mind's contemplation what is in those things of true and constant. Moreover how many things are there which I would not see. How many which I can be debarred the sight without repining! How few left which I much desire to see! Vile men! Who mock us! The blind have a protection from the injuries of men, and we are rendered almost sacred."

706—Thomas Edison was deaf but only a few of his friends were aware that in his case deafness was more psychological than physical. Once a specialist in diseases of the ear called upon Mr. Edison and unfolded a plan of treatment which he was sure would restore his hearing. To the proposition that he submit to treatment, however, Mr. Edison opposed an emphatic negative.
"What I am afraid of," said he, "is that you would be successful. Just think what a lot of stuff I'd have to listen to that I don't want to hear! To be a little deaf and be the only one who knows just how deaf you are has its advantages. I prefer to let well enough alone."

707—A British veteran of the Boer War was discharged from the army in a hopeless condition; he had lost a leg and an arm, and one eye was gone. In his distress he was obliged to solicit alms on the London streets. One day an Irishman who spied him showered coins upon the unfortunate man with both hands.
"Why do you do that?" demanded a bystander. "Don't you see that the man is a British soldier—a foe to Ireland?"
"I do," retorted the Irishman. "But he can have all I've got. He is the first Englishman I have ever seen that was trimmed up to suit me."

SEE ALSO
Wife 931
Church Services 1536
Sermons 1547, 1554
Insurance 2140
Trials 2480

RELATED SUBJECTS
Physical Characteristics 646–648
Stuttering 711–713
Sickness 1701–1707
Poor Health 1711–1712

STUTTERING

711—Henry Guy Carleton, wit, journalist, and playwright, had an impediment in his speech about which he used to joke. Meeting Nat Goodwin, the comedian, one day he asked: "G-G-Goodwin, c-c-an you g-g-give m-m-me f-f-fifteen m-m-minutes?"

"Certainly," replied the comedian, "what is it?"

"I w-want to have a f-f-five minutes' c-c-conversation with you."

712—Stammering, says Coleridge, is sometimes the cause of a pun. Someone was mentioning in Lamb's presence the cold-heartedness of the Duke of Cumberland, in restraining the Duchess in rushing up to the embrace of her son, whom she had not seen for a considerable time, and insisting on her receiving him in state. "How horribly cold it was," said the narrator. "Yes," said Lamb in his stuttering way, "but you know he is the Duke of Cu-cum-ber-land."

713—A big hulk of a man, somewhat sinister in appearance, accosted a small dapper gentleman on the street, and asked, "C-c-c-can you t-t-tell me how to g-g-get to C-c-city Hall?"

The small man paled and, turning on his heels, fled down the street. Angered and exasperated, the big man pursued him. They raced for several blocks until the little man's wind gave out and he was overtaken and captured. The big man seized him by the arm and cried angrily, "W-w-what do you m-m-mean—running away w-w-when I ask you a c-c-civil question?"

The little man looked up and gasped, "D-d-do you t-t-think I w-w-wanted my block knocked off?"

SEE ALSO	RELATED SUBJECTS
Borrowing 122	Physical Characteristics 646–648
Lateness 321	Speeches 756–782
Babies 956	Talking 806–818
Authors 1186, 1203	
Church Services 1533	

CLOTHING

716—H. G. Wells has such a big head that he has trouble getting hats to fit. Once when he found one that balanced nicely on his head he just walked off with it, and blandly penned a note to its owner, E. S. Peck of Cambridge, Mass.

"I stole your hat," wrote the author, "I like your hat; I shall keep your hat. Whenever I look inside it I shall think of you and of your excellent sherry and of the town of Cambridge. I take off your hat to you."

717—Whistler was standing bareheaded in a London hat-shop while a clerk was looking for his size hat. A short red-faced man with a large waistline burst into the door and, mistaking Whistler for a clerk, exploded: "See here, you, this hat doesn't fit."

The artist casually eyed the man from head to foot, then drawled out: "Well, neither does your coat. What's more, if you'll pardon my saying so, I'll be hanged if I care much for the color of your trousers."

718—Sheridan made his appearance, one day, in a pair of new boots. These attracting the notice of some of his friends, "Now guess," said he, "how I came by these boots." Many probable guesses then took place. "No," said Sheridan, "no, you've not hit it, nor ever will. I bought them and paid for them."

719—A young lady on her way to business was standing in a crowded New York bus going down Fifth Avenue one morning. She was worrying over the age-old problem of whether or not her slip was showing. Unable to twist around sufficiently to see, she put the question directly to a small boy standing next to her. "No ma'am," he informed her politely. A few blocks farther she alighted and started to move briskly along crowded Fifth Avenue. Then, to her horror, she was hailed by the voice of the little boy, calling to her as the bus went by, yelling at the top of his lungs, "Your slip is showing now, lady, it's showing now!"

720—There are numerous stories of the embarrassing predicaments that have ensnared public speakers at one time or another. Probably no worse fate ever befell any of them than that of the lecturer who, with some trepidation, had finally consented to address a banquet at a nudist colony. Upon his arrival at the extensive premises, he was greeted by large numbers of men and women in their pristine natural state. He was shown into the headquarters building and it was suggested that he might like to prepare for dinner.

Upstairs in the room to which they allotted him, he felt that there was nothing he could do except face the fact that he was expected to divest himself of his garments. In extreme mental anguish he determined to be equal to the situation. At last, hearing the bell for dinner, he marched downstairs as bare as Adam, to discover, to his horror, that the colonists had all assumed formal dress in deference to the speaker.

721—When the great Duke of Argyle was one night at the theatre in a side-box a person entered the same box in boots and spurs. The Duke arose from his seat and with great ceremony, expressed his thanks to the stranger who, somewhat confused, desired to know for what reason he received those thanks. The Duke gravely replied, "For not bringing your horse into the box."

722—After the death of Nelson, English ladies were fond of wearing the Trafalgar garter, on which was inscribed the memorable signal: "England expects every man to do his duty."

723—Old Mrs. Smith of South Orange, N. J., who kept a small shop in Washington during the Civil War, said:
"Abraham Lincoln came in one day asking for socks. I said, 'What color?'
"'Colour? Why, I don't know, I'm sure.'
"Finally he stooped down and took hold of the end of his pants. 'Why I guess this colour is good enough for me.'
"He pulled it up. I looked for the sock—and saw—his bare skin."

724—In his early days in New York Floyd Odlum and his wife were invited to a dinner. The only pair of shoes he happened to own at the time were bright yellow. In order to render them appropriate to the occasion he and his wife painted them black on the day of the party. During dinner, their hostess, sniffing perplexedly, said to her son, "Charlie, I smell paint. Did you upset the paint in the cellar?"
A fruitless discussion ensued in which everyone spoke of the smell of paint except the Odlums who protested that they smelled nothing.

725—Mark Twain, cherishing his comfort above his appearance, was very often wont to visit his friends and neighbors without wearing either a collar or tie. His wife objected strenuously to this habit and, meeting him one day returning from a neighborly visit without any sign of a collar or tie, scolded him soundly.

Mark returned home, searched out a collar and tie, wrapped them up and sent them to the neighbor's house with the following note:

"A little while ago I visited you without my collar and tie for about half an hour. The missing articles are enclosed. Will you kindly gaze at them for 30 minutes and then return them to me?"

726—Before the birth of the son of Marie Antoinette and Louis XVI, the fashion of pregnancy spread through the court. The Queen's ladies-in-waiting wore skirts stuffed with cushions to make themselves appear enceinte; "skirts of the season" were created, with titles such as "fourth month skirt," etc., their voluminousness adjusted to the progress of the Queen.

SEE ALSO	RELATED SUBJECTS
Carelessness 136	Physical Characteristics 646–648
Devotion 172	
Diligence 177	
Greed 276	
Gossip 826	

HANDWRITING

731—Horace Greeley is another instance of a famous man noted for the illegibility of his handwriting. He once wrote the following letter:

"Mr. M. B. Castle,
Sandwich, Ill.

Dear Sir: I am overworked and growing old. I shall be 60 on next February the 3rd. On the whole, it seems I must decline to lecture henceforth except in this immediate vicinity. If I go at all, I cannot promise to visit Illinois on that errand, certainly not now.
                    Yours truly,
                    Horace Greeley"

A few days later he received this answer:

"Horace Greeley,
New York Tribune.

Dear Sir: Your acceptance to lecture before our association next winter came to hand this morning. Your penmanship not being the plainest, it took some time to trans-

late it; but we succeeded and would say your time,
February 3rd, and the terms, $60, are entirely satisfac-
tory. As you suggest, we may be able to get you other
engagements.

Respectfully,
M. B. Castle"

732—John Calhoun's handwriting, though it looked neat, was
almost undecipherable. Once a friend sent him back one
of his letters because it was too difficult to read. Calhoun
replied: "I know what I think on this subject but cannot
decipher what I wrote."

733—The actor, Macready, was notorious for the illegibility of
his handwriting. He frequently was called upon to scrawl
a chit for the free admission of friends and acquaintances
to performances. Although unrecognizable, they were
familiar to the doorman and served their purpose. One
day, however, a friend of the actor jestingly took one of
Macready's scrawled passes to a pharmacist and gravely
handed it over as a prescription to be filled. The latter
unhesitatingly compounded a potion from various phials
and powder boxes, and handing it across the counter to
the waiting customer, observed, "A cough mixture, and
a very good one. Fifty cents, please."

SEE ALSO   RELATED SUBJECTS
Marriage 888   Physical Characteristics 646–648

SOCIAL ACTIVITIES

736—Bernard Shaw one day received an invitation from a celebrity hunter: "Lady X will be at home Thursday between
four and six."
The author returned the card; underneath he had written:
"Mr. Bernard Shaw likewise."

737—Said Marie Antoinette, "My tastes are not the same as those
of the king, who cares only for hunting and blacksmith
work. You will admit that I should not show to advantage in a forge. I could not appear there as Vulcan, and
the part of Venus might displease him even more than
my tastes."

RELATED SUBJECTS
Parties 741–746
Banquets and Dinners 751–753
Society 796–797

PARTIES

741—Dorothy Parker once attended a party at which the greater number of people seemed to be the rakings of Bohemia. Her companion said to her, "Where on earth do these people come from and where do they stay the rest of the time?"

"I think," Miss Parker said thoughtfully, "that after it's over they crawl back into the woodwork."

742—"I've had a wonderful evening," said Groucho Marx to his hostess as he was leaving a dull Hollywood party, "but this wasn't it!"

743—Once, it is said, Margot Asquith gave a party in London: a big party. She received the guests with graciousness, set them spinning into the rhythm of pleasure and then retired to an upper room to play bridge.

Next day, a well-meaning, but tactless woman fluttered up to her in a restaurant and said: "Oh, Lady Asquith, I was at your party last night."

"Thank God I wasn't," answered Margot, and moved on.

744—Thomas A. Edison was once reluctantly persuaded by his wife to attend one of the brilliant social functions of the season in New York. At last the inventor managed to escape the lionizers who had crowded about him, and sat alone unnoticed in a corner. Edison kept looking at his watch with a resigned expression on his face. A friend edged near to him unnoticed and heard the inventor mutter to himself with a sigh, "If there were only a dog here!"

745—Oliver Wendell Holmes, having been at an afternoon tea, authoritatively defined such functions for all time as, "Giggle—gabble—gobble—git."

746—Dorothy Parker, completely bored by a country week-end, wired a friend: "Please send me a loaf of bread—and enclose a saw and file."

SEE ALSO
Rough and Ready 507
Rudeness 513, 514,
   515, 517, 519
Tact 588, 591
Talking 806
Marriage 884

RELATED SUBJECTS
Social Activities 736–737
Society 796–797
Hospitality 1006–1008
Birth, Birthdays 1011–1015

BANQUETS AND DINNERS

751—At the dinner-parties which the poet Sam Rogers gave he
started the custom of having no candles on the table, all
the lights being attached to the walls and ceiling. This
novelty created quite a buzz of comment in London
society. While Sydney Smith was dining with Rogers
one evening, the host asked him to say what he thought
of the illumination of the table. "For my part, I don't
fancy it at all, Rogers," returned the candid guest. "It's
too uncomfortably like the Day of Judgment. Here we
are, a flood of light on all above, and below nothing but
darkness and gnashing of teeth."

752—At dinner one day Douglas Jerrold was forced to listen to
a noisy argument between an admirer of the Prince of
Orange and a henchman of William III. Having exhausted the political issues of the debate, they entered
upon the personal phases of the question. One of the
arguers finally brought his fist down on the table and
exclaimed: "Bah! to you, sir; I spit upon your Prince of
Orange!"

The other, determined not to be outdone, rose to his feet
and screamed, "And I, sir, spit upon your King William!"

Hereupon Jerrold, unable to endure the racket longer, rang
the bell and shouted to the waiter, "Here, boy—spittoons
for two!"

753—It is said of Charles Fox that from infancy to manhood it
was the practice of his father, Lord Holland, to show him
the most unlimited indulgence. The following story is
told in proof of it. Master Charles, when six or seven
years of age, one day strolled into the kitchen; and while
dinner was cooking, and a pig roasting at the fire, he
amused himself with making water upon the unresisting
porker. It was a standing order of the house to contradict
him on nothing, so there was nothing to be done—but to
let the pig be so basted. The cook, however, thought it
fair to give the guests warning of the sauce to it, which
he did by sending up the following lines upon a label in
its mouth.

> If strong and savory I do taste,
> 'Tis with the liquor that did me baste,
> While at the fire I foam'd and hiss'd,
> A Fox's cub upon me ————.

SEE ALSO
Eating 6, 14, 18
Drinking 54
Imagination 306
Modesty 376
Rudeness 511
Clothing 720, 724
Parties 746
Speeches 756
Talking 816
Diplomats 2022
Stealing 2583

RELATED SUBJECTS
Eating 6–23
Social Activities 736–737
Parties 741–746
Speeches 756–782

SPEECHES

756—At a banquet at Princeton University, the great Chinese
diplomat, Dr. Wellington Koo, was the guest of honor
and main speaker. As one of a number of representatives
of the student body on this occasion, a burly member of
the Princeton football team found himself seated next to
Dr. Koo. Very embarrassed by the formality of the occasion and utterly at a loss for conversation, the young man
turned to Dr. Koo during the soup course and said,
"Likee soup?"

Dr. Koo urbanely bowed his head and grinned. Later he
arose and delivered a polished, thoughtful and witty
address. Sitting down amidst applause, Dr. Koo turned
to the chagrined student and said smiling, "Likee
speech?"

757—Dean Briggs was once one of the speakers at a formal
banquet at Radcliffe College. In preparation for the
event, among other things, the chairs had been given a
new coat of varnish. The evening was hot and humid and,
as the speakers rose to deliver their remarks, it was with
some difficulty. The Dean was more than equal to the
occasion. "Ladies and gentlemen," he said, with a rueful
backward glance, "I had expected to bring you this
evening a plain and unvarnished tale, but circumstances
make it impossible to fulfill my intentions."

758—When J. M. Barrie addressed an audience of one thousand
girls at Smith College during his American visit, a friend
asked him how he had found the experience.

"Well," replied Mr. Barrie, "to tell you the truth, I'd much
rather talk one thousand times to one girl, than to talk
one time to a thousand girls."

759—Henry Ward Beecher was once in the midst of an address. A drunken spectator interrupted him by crowing like a rooster. Beecher was imperturbable; looking at his watch he said, "What! morning already? I would never have believed it, but the instincts of the lower animals are infallible."

760—Dr. MacNamara on one occasion, while speaking in a marquee at Bridlington, during a torrential rain, said to the audience, "I'm afraid I've kept you too long."
"Go on, sir, it's still raining," a voice in the rear replied.

761—General Sam Carey, the great Ohio orator, was finishing up an exceptionally fiery oration: "You cannot keep me down," he shouted, "Though I may be pressed below the waves I rise again; you will find that I come to the surface, gentlemen."
An old whaler, who happened to be in the audience, said, and not too quietly, "Yes, you come to the surface to blow."

762—Congressman Fred Landis of Indiana had made a reputation for himself as an orator. Speaking at the unveiling of a monument to President Lincoln, he uttered the phrase: "Abraham Lincoln—that mystic mingling of star and clod." This was loudly applauded.
After the speech a friend of Landis approached him and, repeating the phrase, said: "Fred, what in the name of heaven does that mean?"
Landis replied: "I don't know, really, but it gets 'em every time."

763—The story is told in London that God-fearing Prime Minister Stanley Baldwin was going over with the cabinet the speech he was subsequently to make in the House of Commons upon the accession of King Edward VIII. Afterward Mr. Baldwin's secretary gathered up the manuscript and observed a marginal note by the Prime Minister, "Refer again to A.G." Promptly the speech was rushed to the Attorney-General. The hour was late and in some puzzlement the A.G. and his staff scrutinized the wholly innocuous phrases, wondering what Mr. Baldwin could possibly have thought might be indiscreet or dangerous. It turned out next morning that Orator Baldwin had meant to remind himself by his marginal note to "Refer again to Almighty God."

764—Rev. Samuel J. May: Mr. Garrison, you are too excited—
you are on fire!

William Lloyd Garrison: I have need to be on fire, for I
have icebergs around me to melt.

765—At the laying of a cornerstone, while President, Mr.
Coolidge turned a spadeful of earth and then remained
silent. The gathering expected him to speak. The master
of ceremonies suggested that a few words would be
fitting.

Mr. Coolidge looked over the upturned earth.

"That's a fine fishworm," said he.

766—During a parliamentary discussion on curtailing debate
Sir Campbell Bannerman remarked that "it was reasonable that Members should wish to let off a certain amount
of intellectual steam."

"Is that a polite way of describing debate in this House?"
interposed Balfour.

"I thought steam was a motive power," replied Bannerman.

"Not when it's let off," retorted Balfour amidst the laughter
of the House.

767—Some years ago Winston Churchill highly amused his
fellow Members in the House by distributing among them
printed copies of his recent speeches. A Liberal Member
for one of the Devonshire constituencies acknowledged
the gift in the following manner:

"Dear Mr. Churchill, Thanks for copy of your speeches
lately delivered in the House of Commons. To quote the
late Lord Beaconsfield: 'I shall lose no time in reading
them.'"

768—Secretary of State William Maxwell Evarts once was asked
to address the guests at a Thanksgiving dinner. He began, "You have been giving your attention to a turkey
stuffed with sage; you are now about to consider a sage
stuffed with turkey."

769—On one occasion, when George III came out of the House
of Lords after opening the session of Parliament, he
addressed Lord Eldon thus: "Lord Chancellor, did I
deliver the speech well?"

"Very well indeed, sir," was the enthusiastic answer.

"I am glad of that," replied the king; "for there was nothing
in it."

770—Joseph Chamberlain, Prime Minister of England, told this story about himself. He was guest of honor at a banquet. The mayor of the city presided and when coffee was being served he leaned over and touched Mr. Chamberlain saying, "Shall we let them enjoy themselves a little longer or had we better have your speech now?"

771—Eamon de Valera was once arrested at Ennis in the middle of a political speech. A year later he was released. He went forthwith to Ennis, and began to speak again with the words, "As I was saying when I was interrupted—."

772—William Lyon Phelps tells, "Having to speak at a public dinner in Chicago, I found my place at the pillory of torment, the speakers' table; and there, seeing a magnificent man in evening dress, I gave him my name and grasped his hand with what cordiality I could command.
"'I'm the headwaiter, sir,' he replied.
"'Shake hands again, old man,' I cried. 'You don't know how I envy you!'"

773—When Dr. Walter Williams spoke in a Chinese university, an interpreter translated into Chinese symbols on a blackboard. Dr. Williams noted that the interpreter stopped writing during most of the speech and at the conclusion he asked why. "We only write when the speaker says something," was the blithe reply.

774—Andrew Jackson, before he became President, was once making a stump speech in a small village. Just as he was finishing, a friend who sat near him whispered, "Tip 'em a little Latin, General; they won't be contented without it." The man of iron will instantly thought upon the few phrases he knew, and in a voice of thunder wound up with "E pluribus unum, sine qua non, ne plus ultra, multum in parvo." The effect was tremendous, and the shouts of the Hoosiers could be heard for miles.

775—At a banquet in connection with the war effort, the toastmaster opened the speaking with the assurance that all the guests had promised to make brief addresses. It chanced that the first to be called upon was the heavyweight champion, Private Joe Louis, who rose to his feet and said, "The toastmaster must have known my speed," and sat down.

776—An Athenian crowd demonstrated impatience at a public assembly one day and hissed the orator Demosthenes, refusing to hear him. He said he had but a short story to tell them and began, "A certain youth hired an ass, in the summer time, to go from his home to Megara. At noon, when the sun was very hot, both he who had hired the ass and the owner of the animal were desirous of sitting in the shade of the ass, and fell to thrusting one another away. The owner insisted that he had hired out only the ass and not the shadow. The other insisted that as he had hired the ass, all that belonged to the ass was his." Turnaway, Demosthenes made as though to depart, but the mob, which had been piqued by the story, would not allow him to leave and insisted that he continue. He then turned upon them and demanded, "How is it that you insist upon hearing the story of the shadow of the ass, and will not give an ear to matters of great moment?" He was permitted to deliver the speech for which he had come. And the fine point of the ass and his shadow remains unsettled to this day.

777—Chauncey Depew once played a trick upon Mark Twain on an occasion when they were both to speak at a banquet. Twain spoke first for some 20 minutes and was received with great enthusiasm. When Depew's turn came, immediately afterwards, he said, "Mr. Toastmaster, Ladies and Gentlemen, before this dinner, Mark Twain and I made an agreement to trade speeches. He has just delivered mine and I'm grateful for the reception you have accorded it. I regret that I have lost his speech and cannot remember a thing he had to say."
He sat down with much applause.

778—The ability of various public speakers was being discussed in Sydney Smith's club. Someone said that Archbishop Whatley was gifted with unusual oratorical powers. Smith granted that there were some things he could indeed admire in the worthy doctor's discourses, remarking with emphasis of one particular speech, "There he had some splendid flashes of silence."

779—President Lincoln was attending a dinner at which many personages were asked to give speeches. Many and flowery were the phrases that were tossed about the table. At last the President was called upon to add his remarks to all that had gone before.
"I appear before you, fellow-citizens," said Lincoln, "merely to thank you for this compliment. The inference is a very

fair one that you would hear me for a little while at least, were I to commence to make a speech. I do not appear before you for the purpose of doing so, and for several substantial reasons. The most substantial of these is that I have no speech to make. In my position it is somewhat important that I should not say any foolish things. (At this point a voice was heard to say, 'If you can help it.'— but the President went on without appearing to have noticed it.) It very often happens that the only way to help it is to say nothing at all. Believing that is my present condition this evening, I must beg of you to excuse me from addressing you further."

780—The distinguished Senator from Minnesota (Cushman K. Davis), a member of the Peace Commission, said in the Senate: "We stand in the vestibule of a century full of miracles, and, following the metaphor of the English orator who eloquently proclaimed, 'The British lion, whether it is roaming the deserts of India or climbing the forests of Canada, will not draw in its horns or retire into its shell,' so the American eagle will continue to guard whatever territory comes under the shadow of its wings so long as it chooses to hold it."

781—William Lloyd Garrison, the Abolitionist, had much unhappy experience with mobs and missiles. At a dinner given him by the British Anti-Slavery Society he was presented with a watch.
"Well, gentlemen," he said, "if this had been a rotten egg I should have known what to do with it, but as it is a gold watch, I have nothing to say."

782—Jules Janin, at a banquet, was given the toast, "Long live success!"
"Yes," he retorted, "it is the only thing that succeeds!"

SEE ALSO
Long-Windedness
   342, 343
Introductions 787
Common Sense 1156
Newspapers 1242
Kings 1978
Miscellaneous Contests
   1882
Parliament 1997, 1998
Jail 2561

RELATED SUBJECTS
Long-Windedness 341–363
Banquets and Dinners 751–753
Introductions 786–791
Talking 806–818
Lectures 1106–1111
Sermons 1541–1559
Campaigning 1911–1920
Trials 2476–2485

INTRODUCTIONS

786—During one of his campaigns, William Jennings Bryan spoke in a city in one of the northwestern states. The chairman, in presenting the speaker, made an embarrassing fulsome and eulogistic introduction of Bryan, in such bad taste that many wondered how Bryan would succeed in overcoming the unfortunate effect of it. Bryan, however, was not easily dismayed: "The very kind observations of the chairman," said he, "bring to my mind the case of the man at a formal banquet table, who impulsively put into his mouth a large forkful of steaming, hot baked potato, which he instantly spat out upon his plate. Looking about at his disconcerted fellow guests and at his hostess, he remarked blandly, 'Some damn fools would have swallowed that.'"

787—"Long introductions when a man has a speech to make are a bore," said former Senator John C. Spooner, one of the great Senate leaders. "I have had all kinds, but the most satisfactory one in my career was that of a German mayor of a small town in my state, Wisconsin.

"I was to make a political address and the opera house was crowded. When it came time to begin the mayor got up.

"'Mine friends,' said he, 'I hafe asked been to introduce Senator Spooner who is to make a speech, ja. Vell, I haf dit so, und he vill now do so.'"

788—"I had expected to find Mr. Lloyd George a big man in every sense," playfully remarked the chairman when introducing the statesman to a meeting, "But you see for yourselves he is quite small in stature."

Lloyd George was no whit abashed. "In North Wales," he remarked, "we measure a man from his chin up. You evidently measure from his chin down."

789—The lady from Arkansas, Senator Hattie Caraway, was about to address a gathering of her constituents. The chairman introduced her with a prolonged and lavish eulogy, culminating thunderously with the words, "Ladies and Gentlemen, I now present to you the most notorious woman in Arkansas!"

790—When Woodrow Wilson was President of Princeton he was called upon to be the chief speaker at an educators' banquet in New York. Dr. Nicholas Murray Butler of Columbia was toastmaster. When the time came to introduce the principal speaker, Dr. Butler presented him as "A sleepy man from a sleepy little college in a sleepy little town."

Wilson rose and opened his remarks by saying, "The charge of sleepiness could never be brought against Dr. Butler, for is it not said in the Scriptures, 'Lo, he that keepeth Israel shall neither slumber nor sleep.'"

791—At a banquet in Dublin a toastmaster was delivering a eulogy of Sir Henry Irving. "Sir Henry," he said, "is not only an artist of the first rank, the first of his profession to be honored with a knighthood, but is also a man of the utmost integrity and highest honor. It would not be too much to say that his has been a life of unbroken blemish!"

SEE ALSO	RELATED SUBJECTS
Lectures 1107	Speeches 756–782
	Campaigning 1911–1920

SOCIETY

796—At a fashionable salon in London appeared a young gentleman, the son of his majesty's printer who had the patent for publishing Bibles. He was dressed in green and gold. Being a new face, and extremely elegant, he attracted the attention of the whole company. A general murmur prevailed in the room, to learn who he was. Colley Cibber, the outrageous wit, who was present, instantly made reply, loud enough to be heard by everybody: "Oh, don't you know him? It is young Bible, bound in calf and gilt, but not lettered."

797—Lord Balfour was visiting friends in Scotland. One evening, while attending a dinner given in his honor, he noticed that the little daughter of his host was eyeing him covertly. He smiled to her and she, plucking up courage, asked him:

"Are you really and truly an English Lord?"

"Yes," he answered gravely, "really and truly."

"I have often thought I should like to see an English lord," she went on, "and—and—"

"And now you are satisfied?" he asked her.

"N-no," she answered slowly, "I'm not satisfied; I'm a good deal disappointed."

SEE ALSO	RELATED SUBJECTS
Newspapers 1239	Snobbishness 546–551
Concerts 1345	Social Activities 736–737
Wealth 2186	

DUELING

801—On one occasion Lord Alvanley fought a duel with Morgan O'Connell on Wimbledon Common. It appears that several shots were fired without effect, and the seconds then interfered and put a stop to any further hostilities. When his hackney coach drove up to his door Alvanley gave the coachman a sovereign. Jarvey was profuse in his thanks, and said: "It's a great deal for only having taken your lordship to Wimbledon."

"No, my good man," said Alvanly, "I give it to you, not for taking me, but for bringing me back."

802—When Professor Rudolf Virchano, famous German scientist, criticized Bismarck severely in his capacity as Chancellor, Bismarck challenged him to a duel. "Well, well," said the scientist to the Iron Chancellor's seconds, "as I am the challenged party, I suppose I have the choice of weapons. Here they are." And he held up two large sausages which looked exactly alike.

"One of these," he continued, "is infected with the deadly germs of trichinosis, the other is perfectly sound. Let His Excellency do me the honor to choose whichever he wishes, and eat it. I will eat the other."

Within an hour the Iron Chancellor had decided to laugh the duel off.

803—Mirabeau the French statesman received many challenges to duels. He always answered this way: "Sir, your favor is received, and your name is on my list, but I warn you that the list is long and that I grant no preferences."

SEE ALSO   RELATED SUBJECTS
Soldiers 2433   Quarrelsomeness 466
                         Rudeness 511–524

TALKING

806—At a party, someone observed to Dorothy Parker that their hostess was outspoken. "By whom?" asked Miss Parker.

807—Mark Twain met Winston Churchill in 1900, when the latter was just coming into prominence as a young statesman. The occasion was a dinner in London. Churchill and Twain went out for a brief time to have a smoke. Sir William Vernon Harcourt observed, as they departed, that whichever one got the floor first would keep it. He speculated that, inasmuch as Twain was an older and

more experienced hand, Churchill's voice would get the
first good rest that it had had in years.

When the two men returned, Harcourt asked Churchill
whether he had enjoyed himself, and the young man replied, "Yes," most enthusiastically. Turning to Twain,
Sir William put the same question. Twain hesitated and
said, "I have had a good smoke."

808—A talkative barber was trimming the beard of King Archelaus, and asked, "How shall I cut?"
"In silence," replied the king.

809—King Archelaus, perpetrator of that ancient joke about replying, "in silence," to the barber who asked him how he
should cut his hair, would be pleased to know that his
tradition is being carried on in the modern era.
A man, who might well stem from this kingly line, handed
the barber a coin and then climbed into the chair.
"Why, sir, thank you," said the astonished barber, "never
before have I been tipped in advance."
"That is not a tip," snarled the customer. "It's hush money."

810—The need to talk to someone finds its expression in everything from friendly confidences, to the confessional, to
the psychoanalyst. Recently it has been commercialized
by an organization calling itself, The Southern Listening
Bureau of Little Rock, Arkansas.
Their advertisement proclaims: "We offer well trained and
experienced listeners who will hear you as long as you
wish to talk, and without interruptions, for a nominal fee.
As our listeners listen, their faces portray interest, pity,
fellow feeling, understanding; where called for, they exhibit hate, hope, despair, sorrow or joy. Lawyers, politicians, club leaders, reformers can try their speeches on
us. You may talk freely about your business or domestic
problems without fear of having any confidence betrayed.
Just let off steam into the discreet ears of our experts and
feel better."

811—Dr. Johnson was one day in conversation with a very talkative lady, of whom he appeared to take very little notice.
"Why, Doctor, I believe you prefer the company of men
to that of the ladies."
"Madam," replied he, "I am very fond of the company of
ladies; I like their beauty, I like their delicacy, I like their
vivacity, and I like their silence."

812—A lady stepped into a taxicab at Grand Central. The driver swung out into traffic, and at the same time asked, "Do you want the radio, lady, or shall we just talk?"

813—A prominent Washington society woman was sitting next to President Coolidge at a smart party.

"Oh, Mr. President," she said gushingly, "you are so silent. I made a bet today that I could get more than two words out of you."

"You lose," the President replied.

814—Samuel Rogers had a reputation for quiet, venomous wit. Knight was a great talker and a bad listener. When Rogers was told that Knight was going deaf, he remarked: "It is from lack of practice."

815—It was Mark Twain, on a balmy day of Spring, who was hailed by every passing acquaintance with some observation on the state of the weather. Upon arriving at his destination and being greeted with, "Nice day, Mr. Twain," he replied drily, "Yes, I've heard it very highly spoken of."

816—When Coolidge was Vice-President, he was invited to attend many dinners. Always he was the despair of his hostess because of his utter disregard of the art of conversation. One lady felt that she had solved this problem by placing him next to Alice Roosevelt Longworth who was a most brilliant conversationalist.

Mrs. Longworth began to chat in her usual charming fashion, but failed to elicit any response from the silent Mr. Coolidge.

Finally, exasperated out of her generally calm demeanor, she acidly asked, "You go to so many dinners. They must bore you a great deal."

Calmly Coolidge replied without lifting his eyes from the contemplation of the plate before him, "Well, a man has to eat somewhere."

817—A debutante went to visit her grandmother. The old lady was distressed by what she considered the girl's wild and unruly manners and speech. Not wishing to appear stern and demanding she decided nevertheless that she should reprimand her granddaughter.

One evening as they were sitting together the old lady said gently, "Dear, there are just two words I want you to refrain from using. One is 'swell' and the other is 'lousy.' "

"All right," replied the debutante agreeably, "What are they?"

818—Diderot came to Catherine the Great in 1773 and remained for five months. On certain afternoons he conversed with her from three to five. "I listened more than I talked," she said. Discoursing vehemently, he would gradually draw his chair up to her knees. In his excitement he would pound them until they were blue, compelling her to place before her a table on which he could vent his punctuation.

SEE ALSO
Eating 9
Borrowing 124
Brevity 134
Long-Windedness 358, 359
Rudeness 518
Beauty 664
Parties 745
Newspapers 1240

RELATED SUBJECTS
Dullness 186–195
Long-Windedness 341–363
Stuttering 711–713
Speeches 756–782
Gossip 821–826

GOSSIP

821—"How this world is inclined to slander," said a maiden lady to an English nobleman. "Can you believe it, sir, some of my malicious acquaintances reported that I had twins." "Madam, I make it a rule to believe only half of what I hear!" replied his lordship.

822—Mrs. Graham Fair Vanderbilt had been displeased by a number of things which the late Maury Paul had written about her in his Cholly Knickerbocker column.
Upon meeting him one time at a night club, she said, "You're a rude, scurrilous man."
"Yes," confessed Paul, "I am. But I'd rather make a living that way than by selling bonds."

823—Once when Mme. de Staël was praising the British Constitution, Talleyrand explained in an aside: "Above all she admires the habeas corpus."

824—The society gossip purveyor, Maury H. B. Paul, had been writing a number of familiar and impertinent items about Mrs. Cornelius Vanderbilt for many years. Then one day Vincent Astor unexpectedly introduced Paul to the mighty lady. With a gasp he said, "I'm not really the disreputable person you think I am, Mrs. Vanderbilt."

Mrs. Vanderbilt replied, "My dear Mr. Paul, from what you have been writing about me, I was under the impression that you thought I was the disreputable person."

825—The late Maury H. B. Paul, better known as Cholly Knickerbocker, in the course of his career as a society columnist had frequently aroused the ire of those about whom he had written. Every so often some such individual confronted him in a public place and demanded, "Just what did you mean by what you wrote about me?"

Mr. Paul had found a standard answer to this demand. He blandly retorted, "Just what do you think I meant," which invariably silenced further discussion.

826—Due to the exigencies of his position as purveyor of tasty news items on the doings of the upper crust, Maury Paul, widely known as Cholly Knickerbocker, had incurred many enemies. Toward these he felt no rancor.

He once said, "Even when people snub me I feel like saying to them, 'Thank you for just existing. I wouldn't be wearing solid gold garter clasps if it weren't for you.'"

SEE ALSO	RELATED SUBJECTS
Honesty 288	Discretion 181–182
Honor 298	Talking 806–818

NAMES

831—John Barrymore, at the height of his fame, went into the shop of a swanky men's clothier in Hollywood. He left an order and started to leave.

"Your name, please?" the clerk asked.

The Barrymore brows arched high, "Barrymore," he replied coldly.

"Which Barrymore, please?"

"Coolness turned to solid ice. "Ethel," he said.

832—When George Burns assumed his professional name, George Jessel remarked to him, "Well, Georgie, you can change your name to Burns but you will never get the salami out of your stomach."

833—Says Walter Winchell, "Shortly before our son was born, I remarked in the newspaper that if our new baby was a boy he would be named 'Reid' Winchell, and if a girl,

'Sue' Winchell. To which a reader-heckler telegraphed: 'Boy or girl it should be called Lynch Winchell.'"

834—A stranger in town passed the grocery store bearing on its window the name of its proprietor, "A. Swindler." Amused, the stranger entered the store and asked the grocer if he did not think that his full name would make a better impression. "No," said the grocer, "it would be worse. My first name is Adam."

835—At one time both Montague Matthews and Matthew Montague were members of the British House of Commons. Mr. Matthews was a big, powerful giant of a man. Mr. Montague was thin and emaciated. The Speaker frequently confused the two.
"I can't understand it," said Montague Matthews. "There's as much difference between us as there is between a horse chestnut and a chestnut horse."

836—One time, talking with Lord Beaverbrook, Sinclair Lewis kept on saying, "What do you think, Max?" Beaverbrook grew tired of this form of address after the eighth time and suddenly snapped at him, "What do you think, Sinc?"

837—A man named Longworth was once presented to Longfellow, and remarked upon the similarity of their names. "Yes," said Longfellow, "and I believe the advantage is yours, for as Pope has said, 'Worth makes the man, the want of it, the fellow.'"

838—"I've made up my mind what we'll call the baby," the young mother announced. "We'll call her Eulalia."
The father did not care for this choice but he was shrewd. "That's fine," he said. "The first girl I loved was named Eulalia, and it will evoke pleasant memories." The wife was silent for a moment. "We'll call her Mary after my mother," she said.

SEE ALSO   RELATED SUBJECTS
Reputation 77   Family 946–950
Rudeness 512
Tact 590
Marriage 888
Small Children 966
Debt 2171

WOMEN

841—When Madame de Staël published her celebrated novel "Delphine," she was supposed to have painted herself in the person of the heroine, and M. Talleyrand in that of an elderly lady, who is one of the principal characters.

"They tell me," said he, the first time he met her, "that we are both of us in your novel, in the disguise of women."

842—One day at Mr. Kipling's home in Sussex he read to Edward W. Bok his latest poem, and at its conclusion said: "You can never publish that. The 'Journal' ('The Ladies Home Journal') sisters would break all your windows with the stones they would fire at you. You wouldn't have a whole pane left."

The poem was "The Female of the Species."

843—Edwin Booth was very shy about women. He tells of a harrowing experience that once befell him on a tour, when he had lain down to rest in his room and failed to lock his door. "I heard a sound and opened my eyes. The door was being stealthily opened. I felt it was a woman. I couldn't move. She came in—the most determined woman I ever saw. She was tall, and gaunt, and strange. She couldn't help seeing I was trembling. She came to the bed, looked down upon me. Without smiling she bent over me—kissed me on the mouth. She didn't say a word. She walked out of the room. I never was so frightened in my life. I bolted the door when it was too late, but I'm not over it yet. I've tried to reason it out, but I can't. She was not silly. She looked to be the last woman on earth to care for kissing. I should say she was a hard woman."

RELATED SUBJECTS
Love 846–850
Old Maids 871–873
Wife 921–933
Mother 991–993
Woman's Suffrage 2051–2052

LOVE—MARRIAGE—FAMILY

LOVE

846—A woman told her husband that she had read "The Art of Love" on purpose to be agreeable to him.
"I would rather have love without art," he said.

847—The witty Oliver Herford has defined a kiss as, "A course of procedure, cunningly devised, for the mutual stoppage of speech at a moment when words are superfluous."

848—When Madame de Staël was writing her memoirs a female friend asked her how she would manage to portray herself and her amours.
"Oh!" answered Madame de Staël, "I shall give only a bust of myself."

849—A French clergyman catechising the youths of his parish, put the first question from the catechism of Heidelberg to a girl: "What is your only consolation in life and in death?"
The poor wench smiled, but did not answer. The priest insisted. "Well then," said she, "since I must tell, it is the young shoemaker of Agneaux Street."

850—A group of actors, Samuel Foote among them, was discussing the marriage of a too well-known woman-about-town, whose pre-marital life had been, to say the least, adventurous.
"It is a very good match that she has made," one of the group observed. "And they say she made to her husband a full confession of all her past affairs." "What honesty she must have had," another remarked. "What courage!" "Yes," put in Foote, "and what a memory!"

SEE ALSO
Kindness 313
Long-Windedness 361
Infidelity 901
Sickness 1705

RELATED SUBJECTS
Devotion 171–173
Courtship 851–855
Engagement 856–857
Marriage 876–888
Wedding 891–892
Honeymoon 896–898

COURTSHIP

851—It is said that Edwin C. Hill, the journalist and radio commentator, encountered upon his first arrival in New York an experience that outdoes O. Henry. Looking around the city he took a sight-seeing ride on the Elevated. His eye was attracted by the charming young lady seated across the car from him. In the vicinity of Columbus Circle he had ventured to move over and strike up a conversation with her. They found an astonishing congeniality between them, and pursued the conversation intensely.

At last they reached City Hall; left the train, and, going over to the City Hall, got married.

852—One of the most unusual beginnings of a romance in the world is the well-known case of the great Wagnerian tenor, Lauritz Melchior. When the singer was a young music student he was sitting in the garden of his pension in Munich, studying a role. According to his own story, he sang the lines, "Come to me, my love, on the wings of light," when, to his utter astonishment, a young lady literally dropped out of the sky at his feet. The heavenly visitant was Maria Hacker, a Bavarian actress who had been doing a stunt for a movie thriller. She had parachuted from a plane right into his arms. They were married.

853—One day Nicholas Schenck, movie millionaire, about to board Tom Meighan's yacht, saw a slip of a girl standing on the edge of the wharf.

"For some inexplicable reason," Mr. Schenck recalls, "I had an uncontrollable impulse to push her into the water. To my horror—I did. I had no idea if she could swim. I expected an infuriated young woman. Instead, she came to the surface, blinked the water out of her eyes and smiled a brilliant smile.

"By God!" I said to myself, "that's the girl I'm going to marry!" And he did.

854—When Aaron Burr was seventy-eight Mme. Jumel attracted him. One day, as he was about to lead her in to dinner he said:

"I give you my hand, madam; my heart has long been yours."

Much fluttered and no less flattered she uttered a sort of "No" which was not likely to discourage a man like Aaron Burr.

"I shall come to you before very long," he said, "accompanied by a clergyman; and then you will give me your hand because I want it."

855—Dr. Samuel Johnson, when paying court to Mrs. Porter, confessed that his family was not without stain, as he had had an uncle who had been hanged.

Mrs. Porter, with a woman's true tact, set the good Doctor's mind at rest by assuring him that, although this was not the case with her, she had in her family at least fifty who deserved hanging.

SEE ALSO

Reputation 76
Patriotism 406
Rudeness 516
Homeliness 656
Fatness 682
Stores 2072
Juries 2514
Detectives 2557

RELATED SUBJECTS

Love 846–850
Engagement 856–857
Flirtation 861–863

ENGAGEMENT

856—When George IV of England went to meet his future bride, Princess Caroline of Brunswick, he kissed her hand gallantly, and then, suddenly recoiling, he whispered to one of his friends:

"For God's sake, George, give me a glass of brandy!"

857—In breaking his engagement to Agathe von Siebold, Brahms wrote her:

"I could not love thee, dear, so much if I did not love my freedom more."

RELATED SUBJECTS

Love 846–850
Courtship 851–855
Wedding 891–892

FLIRTATION

861—Gilbert Stuart, the early American portrait painter, once met a lady on the street in Boston who saluted him with,

"Ah! Mr. Stuart, I have just seen your miniature, and kissed it, because it was so much like you."

"And did it kiss you in return?"

"Of course not!" she answered, laughing.

"Then," said Stuart, "it was not like me."

862—Near eighty, Aaron Burr, after he was married to Mme. Jumel, engaged in flirting with the country girls near the Jumel mansion.

One day the postmaster at what was then the village of Harlem was surprised to see Mrs. Burr drive up before the post office in an open carriage. He found her in a violent temper and with an enormous horse-pistol on each cushion at her side.

"What do you wish, Madam?" said he.

"What do I wish?" she cried. "Let me get at that villain Aaron Burr!"

863—Talleyrand once said, "Mme. de Genlis, in order to avoid the scandal of coquetry, always yielded easily."

SEE ALSO	RELATED SUBJECTS
Learned Men 1082	Discretion 181–182
	Love 846–850
	Courtship 851–855
	Infidelity 901–904

FRIENDSHIP

866—Anacharsis, coming to Athens, knocked at Solon's door, and told him that he, being a stranger, was come to be his guest, and contract a friendship with him; and Solon replying, "It is better to make friends at home," Anacharsis replied, "Then you that are at home make a friendship with me."

867—Thousands of appeals for pardon came to Lincoln from soldiers involved in military discipline. Each appeal was as a rule supported by letters from influential people. One day a single sheet came before him, an appeal from a soldier without any supporting documents.

"What!" exclaimed the President, "has this man no friends?"

"No, sir, not one," said the adjutant.

"Then," said Lincoln, "I will be his friend."

SEE ALSO	RELATED SUBJECTS
Vanity 624	Devotion 171–173
Authors 1198	Love 846–850

OLD MAIDS

871—At a recent dinner the Reverend Dr. Minot J. Savage told a story of a lady who was asked "Do you ever think of getting married?"

"Think?" she answered, with asperity, "I worry."

872—Maude Adams, the famous actress, was in her dressing room
preparing for a performance. Her old colored maid was
dressing her hair when, without warning, she said:
"When you gwine to git married, Miss Maudie?"
"Oh," replied the star laughingly, "I don't think I'll ever
get married."
"Well," said the old servant, in a soothing tone as though
to comfort her mistress, "they do say old maids is the
happies' kind after they quits strugglin'."

873—It was the maid's day off and the lady of the house was doing her own marketing. On her way home she happened
to meet the girl who was wheeling a baby carriage which
contained a smiling set of twins. Stopping to pet the children she casually asked the maid, "And whose children
are these?"
"Mine, ma'am."
"Yours, Sally, why I always thought you were an old maid."
"Well, ma'am, I is. But I ain't a fussy old maid."

> RELATED SUBJECTS
> Gossip 821–826
> Women 841–843

MARRIAGE

876—When Socrates was asked whether it was better for a man
to marry or remain single, he answered:
"Let him take which course he will, he will repent of it."

877—Archbishop Ryan was one time attending confirmation in
a small parish. The local pastor was giving the prepara-
tory questions to one rather frightened little girl. He
asked her to define the state of matrimony. "It's a state
of terrible torment which those who enter are compelled
to undergo for a time to prepare them for a better world,"
she replied.
"No, no," chided the rector, "that's not matrimony. That's
the definition of Purgatory."
"Leave her alone," said the Archbishop, "perhaps the child
has been shown the light."

878—Miss Drummond, the famous preacher among the Quakers
some time ago, was asked if the spirit had never inspired
her with thoughts of marriage.
"No, friend," said she, "but the flesh often has."

879—Like many tourists, Lewis Cotlow, president of the Adven-
turers' Club, wondered why Mexican peons always ride

on burros while their wives walk along behind. Finally he stopped a peasant and asked him the reason. The Mexican, looking very surprised, replied, "But Señor, my wife doesn't own a burro."

880—Lord Lansdowne was speaking to Samuel Rogers about the marriage of a friend they both knew. "She has made a good match," Lansdowne ventured to remark.
"I am not so sure about that," returned Rogers dubiously.
"No, why not? All her friends approve it."
"Then," said Rogers, "she is able to satisfy everyone. Her friends are pleased and her enemies are delighted."

881—A gentleman who had been very unhappy in marriage married a second time, immediately after his first wife died. Dr. Johnson said of him: "His conduct was the triumph of hope over experience."

882—George Ade was fond of telling the following story, "I was sitting with a little girl of eight one afternoon. She looked up from the copy of Hans Andersen she was reading, and asked innocently, 'Does m-i-r-a-g-e spell marriage, Mr. Ade?' 'Yes, my child,' said I."

883—An old gentleman, who had never attended a football game, allowed himself to be persuaded by a fan to accompany him. "Now then," said his friend, as the game was about to begin, "you're going to see more excitement here for a couple of dollars than you ever saw before." "I doubt it," said the old timer, "that's all I paid for my marriage license."

884—At a Hollywood party the guests were playing a game which required each one to write an epitaph for himself. A much married actress was sitting next to Robert Benchley and complained that she did not know what to write for herself. Benchley said, "I'll write it for you." He did so, and passed on her slip with his to be read out. The epitaph when read was, "At last she sleeps alone."

885—A celebrated wit was asked why he did not marry a young lady to whom he was much attached. "I know not," he replied, "except the great regard we have for each other."

886—A widower in his great bereavement, expressed his feelings by having engraved on the tombstone of his wife the line, "My light has gone out." As he was about to marry again, he asked the advice of Bishop Henry C. Potter as to whether or not he should have the inscription erased, as it seemed at variance with the new conditions. "Oh, no," said the bishop, "I wouldn't have it taken off; just put underneath it, 'I have struck another match.'"

887—Socrates' marital difficulties are well known. Out of them he coined this sage advice: "By all means marry. If you get a good wife, you will become very happy; if you get a bad one you will become a philosopher—and that is good for every man."

888—Into the office came a negress to collect her weekly wages. In signing for them, she drew a circle.

"How it is, Mandy," she was asked, "that you make a circle instead of your usual cross?"

"Why," she said, "I done got married agin and changed my name."

SEE ALSO	RELATED SUBJECTS
Devotion 173	Courtship 851–855
Will Power 631	Engagement 856–857
Love 850	Wedding 891–892
Babies 959	Honeymoon 896–898
Instrumentalists 1355	Divorce 906–911
Actors 1427	Husband 916–918
Sunday School 1571	Wife 921–933
Woman's Suffrage 2052	Mother-in-Law 936–937
	Polygamy 941–943

WEDDING

891—Bridegrooms are known for their nervousness; but here is one who managed to retain his diplomacy in the midst of all the hurry and tension of the ceremony and the departure for the honeymoon trip.

Finally, seated in the car which was to take them to the railroad station, the bride asked if he had remembered the tickets. He reached into his pockets and pulled out— one ticket. Hurriedly gathering his thoughts, remembering his flustered feelings when he had gone to purchase the tickets, he said, "Dear me. Look, only one ticket. You see, darling, I forgot all about myself."

892—Here is Marie Antionette's rather dreary account of her wedding and honeymoon, from her diary:

Sunday, 13—Left Versailles. Supper and slept at Compignée, at the house of M. de Saint-Florentin.

Monday, 14—Interview with Mme. la Dauphine.
Tuesday, 15—Supped at La Muette. Slept at Versailles.
Wednesday, 16—My marriage. Apartment in the gallery.
  Royal banquet in the Salle d' Opera.
Thursday, 17—Opera of "Perseus."
Friday, 18—Stag-hunt. Met at La Belle Image. Took one.
Saturday, 19—Dress-ball in the Salle d' Opera. Fireworks.
Thursday, 31—I had indigestion.

SEE ALSO   RELATED SUBJECTS
Vanity 621   Marriage 876–888
                      Honeymoon 896–898

HONEYMOON

896—When Cary Grant, the film actor, recently married Barbara
  Hutton, the couple did not depart for a wedding trip because it was necessary for Grant to report on the lot for
  the filming of "Once Upon a Honeymoon."

897—After a whirlwind courtship, the loving couple had eloped
  and married. After a few days of the honeymoon, the
  fact came out that the wife was a snake-charmer. Slightly
  appalled, the husband said in reproachful astonishment,
  "How is it that you never told me you were a snake-
  charmer?"
Said his wife, "You never asked me."

898—While on her honeymoon the young bride had gone out
  alone one afternoon to make a few purchases. Coming
  back to the hotel where she had been accustomed to trust-
  fully following her husband's guidance, she got off the
  elevator at the wrong floor. She went down the corridor
  until she reached what she supposed to be the door of
  her room. Finding it locked and having no key with her
  she knocked upon it and called out softly, "Honey, oh
  Honey."
There was no response. After a while she knocked again,
  calling somewhat more loudly, "Honey, oh Honey."
When this had occurred a number of times, a blatant male
  voice roared out from within, saying, "Madam, this is
  not a beehive, it's a bathroom."

RELATED SUBJECTS
Marriage 876–888
Wedding 891–892

INFIDELITY

901—Pauline Bonaparte was in love with Fréron, a commissioner of the Convention. She wrote him:

"I love you always and most passionately. I love you forever, my beautiful idol, my heart, my appealing lover. I love you, love you, love you, the most loved of lovers, and I swear never to love any one else!"

Soon after she fell in love with Junot who became a field marshal.

902—Charles Coghlan, the actor, was known not only for his great wit and resourcefulness, but also for his fondness for the ladies. One day his wife left him to go on a weekend trip. She had scarcely left the house when Coghlan contacted a very charming young lady, inviting her to come to his home for dinner.

Mrs. Coghlan, forgetting something of importance, returned home just in time to see her husband help the girl from a cab. No whit dismayed, Coghlan blandly introduced the two women. "My dear," said he, turning to his wife, "allow me to present Miss Johnson. Miss Johnson, Mrs. Coghlan."

The two ladies glared speechlessly at each other, while Coghlan said:

"I know you two ladies have ever so many things you want to say to each other, so I will ask to be excused."

Whereupon he lifted his hat, stepped into the cab and was driven away.

903—When Shelley was undoubtedly carrying on an affair with Jane Williams, he got his obsession of death by water mixed up with his search for the absolute in terms of women. He took Jane rowing far out to sea. Suddenly he went into a trance, then leapt forward and cried; "Now let us solve the great mystery together." Jane, who was a brilliant woman and one of the most congenial of his "sisters," had to exercise the greatest tact to keep him from upsetting the boat, and he did upset it after they were in shallow water.

904—Percy Bysshe Shelley, in a letter to his wife, telling her he had eloped with Mary Godwin, and asking her to join them:

"Please bring my flute."

SEE ALSO   RELATED SUBJECTS
Flirtation 862   Flirtation 861–863
                           Divorce 906–911

DIVORCE

906—"A large number of divorces indicate that America is still the land of the free," someone observed.

"Yes," said his friend, "but the steady level of the marriage rate shows that it's still the home of the brave."

907—When Mrs. Pierre Riendeau, 79 years old, asked for a legal separation from her 86-year old husband, the judge asked how long they had been married, "Sixty years," she replied.

"Why are you seeking a separation after all this time?" the court asked.

"Enough's enough," she said.

908—After the manner of Hollywood's "civilized" social practices, Lewis Browne, the writer, and his ex-wife appeared together at a party and listened to an announcement of their divorce by a radio commentator. Leopold Stokowski was among the guests, and said to Browne, "It's very indecent of you to be having such a good time. At least when my wife and I were divorced, we quarreled."

909—Ilka Chase likes to tell a story of the aftermath of her divorce from Louis Calhern. His next wife was Julia Hoyt. Miss Chase, going through a trunk, found a box of handsome, engraved cards, bearing simply the name, Mrs. Louis Calhern. Feeling it a shame that they should go to waste, she wrapped them up and sent them to her successor, with the little note: "Dear Julia, I hope these reach you in time."

910—After the death of Jane Seymour, Henry VIII had some difficulty in getting another wife. His first offer was to the Duchess Dowager of Milan, but her answer was, "She had but one head: if she had two, one should have been at his service."

911—Hollywood is a great place. To it came a young man from a small Western town who succeeded in making himself a noted screen lover. His own town became famous as his birthplace. Tourists, passing through, would invariably remark upon its distinguished former citizen. "Tell me," one passer-by asked of the old codger who was station master, "does he ever come back?"

"Sure, sure," said the old timer, "once in a while he comes back for quite a stay. Five times he's been back."

"Is that so? Came back for a stay, did he? And did he ever bring his wife?"

"Yes, sir, each time, and five prettier girls you never see."

RELATED SUBJECTS
Marriage 876–888
Infidelity 901–904

HUSBAND

916—When General Leclerc, unloved husband of Pauline Bonaparte, died in Haiti, she had him placed in a costly coffin and cut off her beautiful hair and buried it with him.

"What a touching tribute to her dead husband!" said someone to her brother Napoleon.

The Emperor smiled cynically:

"Hm! Of course she knows that her hair will come in longer and thicker for being cropped."

917—Henry William Anglesea, a British peer and soldier who died in 1854, was angrily beating his wife. She pointed to a house maid and cried out, "How much happier is that wench than I am!"

Her husband immediately kicked the maid downstairs and then said, "Well there is at least one grievance removed."

918—Late one night a drunken husband, after spending his whole time at his club, set out for home. "Well," said he to himself, "if I find my wife up I'll scold her; what business has she to sit up, wasting fire and light, eh? And if I find her in bed, I'll scold her; what right has she to go to bed before I get home?"

SEE ALSO   RELATED SUBJECTS
Prayer 1607   Marriage 876–888
                            Wife 921–933
                            Mother-in-Law 936–937
                            Father 986–990

WIFE

921—Of a lady, more insipid than offensive, Dr. Johnson once said, "She has some softness indeed; but so has a pillow. For my part, I do not envy a fellow one of those honeysuckle wives; as they are but creepers at best, and commonly destroy the tree they so tenderly cling about."

922—When surprise was expressed at his choice of a wife, Talleyrand replied: "A clever wife often compromises her husband; a stupid one only compromises herself."

923—"Well," said Lincoln on a certain occasion, "I feel about that a good deal as a man whom I will call 'Jones' whom I once knew, did about his wife. He was one of your meek men, and had the reputation of being badly henpecked. At last one day his wife was seen switching him out of the house. A day or two afterwards, a man met him in the street, and said:

" 'Jones, I have always stood up for you, as you know; but I am not going to do it any longer. Any man who will stand quietly and take a switching from his wife deserves to be horsewhipped.'

"Jones looked up with a wink, patting his friend on the back.

" 'Now don't,' said he; 'why it didn't hurt me any: and you've no idea what a power of good it did Sarah Ann!' "

924—Loyalty sometimes proves embarrassing. A case in point is that of the wife whose husband was unusually late, who wired to five of his friends, "Jack not home. Is he spending night with you?" The unfortunate Jack arrived home shortly afterwards, and was followed by five telegrams all saying, "Yes."

925—By mistake a letter directed to a newly married motion picture star was delivered to the house of a poor workingman. Upon being opened, it proved to contain a threat that unless a substantial sum of money was paid, his wife would be kidnapped. The workingman immediately wrote a reply, "Sir, I don't have much money, but I'm mighty interested in your proposition."

926—A man, being suspected of impotency, met a friend one day, who had railed him on it, to whom he said, "My good Sir, for all your wit, my wife was yesterday brought to bed."

"What of that," said his friend, "nobody ever suspected your wife."

927—A person told Samuel Foote he had laid out a thousand pounds upon his dear wife.

"Indeed," said Foote, "she is truly your dear wife."

928—Cato, the elder, having buried his wife, married a young woman: his son came to him and said: "Sir, in what have I offended that you have brought a step-mother into your house?"

"Nay, son," answered the old man, "quite the contrary; you please me so well that I should be glad to have more such."

929—A niggardly farmer lost his wife and scrimped as much as he could on each phase of the funeral expenses down to the bitter end, when he lingered in the graveyard after the mourners had gone, and asked the gravedigger, "How much do I owe you?"

"Ten dollars," said the gravedigger, who was just beginning to fill in the grave.

"That's overmuch for such light sandy soil," said the farmer speculatively.

"Light sandy soil or rich loamy soil, ten dollars," said the gravedigger firmly, "or up she comes."

The farmer hastily paid.

930—A French general's wife, whose tongue-lashing ability was far-famed, demanded that an old servant, who had served with her husband during the wars, be dismissed.

"Jacques," said the general, "go to your room and pack your trunk and leave—depart!" The old Frenchman clasped his hands to his head with dramatic joy. "Me—I can go!" he exclaimed in a very ecstasy of gratitude. Then suddenly his manner changed as with the utmost compassion he added: "But you, my poor general, you must stay."

931—When the poet Milton was blind he married a shrew. The Duke of Buckingham called her a rose. "I am no judge of colors," replied Milton, "and it may be so, for I feel the thorns daily."

932—A celebrated French preacher, in a sermon upon the duty of wives, said: "I see in this congregation a woman who has been guilty of the sin of disobedience to her husband, and in order to point her out to universal condemnation, I will fling my breviary at her head."

He lifted his book, and every female head instantly ducked.

933—"I have no sympathy," bellowed the judge, "for a man who beats his wife."

"That's right, your Honor," said the policeman who stood beside the culprit. "Any man who can beat his wife don't need sympathy."

SEE ALSO
Profanity 66
Absent-Mindedness 89
Boners 116
Patience 391
Shrewdness 541
Will Power 631
Homeliness 655
Love 846
Authors 1180
Evangelists 1516
Doctors 1673

RELATED SUBJECTS
Marriage 876–888
Husband 916–918
Mother-in-Law 936–937
Mother 991–993

Deathbed Scenes 1765
Banks 2155
Trials 2478

MOTHER-IN-LAW

936—One of the witticisms of Lord Russell of Killowen was his answer to a question from a distinguished counsel who asked what the heaviest penalty for bigamy was.

"Two mothers-in-law," said Russell promptly.

937—When Marshal Foch visited the Grand Canyon, Colonel John R. White, who spoke French fluently, hung breathlessly on the Marshal's words as he turned to him after a long scrutiny of the depths below. "Now," thought the Colonel, "I shall hear something worthy of passing along to my children and my grandchildren."

Observed the Marshal, "What a beautiful place to drop one's mother-in-law!"

RELATED SUBJECTS
Marriage 876–888
Husband 916–918
Wife 921–933

POLYGAMY

941—A story is told about Mrs. Amos Pinchot who dreamed one night that she had written a poem more beautiful and more fundamentally profound than any ever written before. She had awaked in one of those semi-trance-like states in the middle of the night; fumbled for a pencil at her bedside table and written it down.

When she finally awoke in the morning, she had at first forgotten the matter. Suddenly all came back to her as she saw the scrawl on the table beside her. She picked it up to see the masterpiece that she had written in her semi-conscious state. It was:

> Hogamus Higamus
> Men are Polygamous
> Higamus Hogamus
> Women Monogamous.

942—A Mormon acquaintance once inveigled Mark Twain into an argument on the issue of polygamy. After he had been beaten about the ears with long and tedious expositions justifying the practice, the climax was capped by the Mormon's demand that he cite any passage of Scripture expressly forbidding polygamy.

"Nothing easier," Mark replied. " 'No man can serve two masters.' "

943—In his old age, after he quit the warpath, Quanah Parker, the famous chief of the Comanches, adopted many of the white man's ways. But in one respect he clung to the custom of his fathers. He continued to be a polygamist.

He was a friend and admirer of Theodore Roosevelt and on one occasion when Roosevelt was touring Oklahoma he drove out to Parker's camp to see him. With pride Parker pointed out that he lived in a house like a white man, that his children went to a white man's school, and he himself dressed like a white man. Whereupon Roosevelt was moved to preach him a sermon on the subject of morality. "See here chief, why don't you set your people a better example? A White man has only one wife, he's allowed only one at a time. Here you are living with five squaws. Why don't you give up four of them and remain faithful to the fifth?"

Parker stood still a moment, considering the proposition. Then he answered: "You are my great white father, and I will do as you wish—on one condition."

"What's the condition?" asked Roosevelt.

"You pick out the one I am to live with and then you go kill the other four."

SEE ALSO   RELATED SUBJECTS
Mother-in-Law 936   Marriage 876–888

FAMILY

946—Speaking of his ancestry Lincoln once humorously remarked, "I don't know who my grandfather was, but I am much more concerned to know what his grandson will be."

947—The elder Dumas was once interviewed by an enterprising
reporter, who, like many other admirers of the novelist,
was curious about his ancestry. "Is it true that you are a
quadroon, M. Dumas?" he asked.

"I am, sir," Dumas replied.

"So your father—?"

"Was a mulatto."

"And your grandfather—?"

"Was a negro."

Dumas' patience was running out but the reporter was a
bold man. He continued: "And may I inquire who your
great-grandfather was?"

"A baboon, sir!" thundered Dumas. "A baboon! My ancestry begins where yours ends!"

948—The story is told that Mark Twain was once a guest of an
Englishman who took him, with some pride, into a mano-
rial hall hung with a huge tapestry depicting the judging
of King Charles the First. The host placed his fingers
with great pride upon the figure of one of the obscure
clerks of the court and said, "An ancestor of mine."

Twain, always offended by such ostentation, casually put
his finger upon one of the judges seated on the tribunal
and remarked, "An ancestor of mine but it is no matter,
I have others."

949—To a man who had proudly said, "My ancestors came over
in the Mayflower," Will Rogers retorted, "My ancestors
were waiting on the beach."

950—Mark Twain, whenever confronted by people who were
haughty about their ancestry, was fond of saying, "My
grandfather was cut down in the prime of his life. My
grandmother always used to say that if he had been
cut down fifteen minutes earlier, he could have been
resuscitated."

SEE ALSO   RELATED SUBJECTS
Physical Characteristics   Marriage 876–888
  648   Children 951–952
Kings 1980   Father 986–990
Insurance 2137   Mother 991–993
Poverty 2208   Home Life 996–1001

CHILDREN

951—There is a legend about the fervent message George
Bernard Shaw received from Isadora Duncan expressing

the opinion that by every eugenical principle they should
have a child.

"Think what a child it would be," she said, "with my body
and your brain."

Shaw sent the following response, discouraging the proposition, "Think how unfortunate it would be if the child
were to have my body and your brain."

952—Two Irishmen were discussing their families. One was
boasting about his seven sons, saying that he had never
had any trouble with any of them:

"Yes, indade," he said, "they are just about the finest boys
in the world. An' would ye believe it, I nivver laid violent
hands on any one of 'em except in self-defense."

SEE ALSO   RELATED SUBJECTS
Age 674   Babies 956–962
Mother 993   Small Children 966–977
Battles 2383   Adoption 981
                            Father 986–990
                            Mother 991–993
                            Births, Birthdays 1011–1015

BABIES

956—Mrs. K., after expressing her love for her children, added
tenderly, "And how do you like babies, Mr. Lamb?"

His answer, immediate, almost precipitate, was, "B-b-boiled,
ma'am."

957—When a baby in a crowded Washington horse car was
screaming, Walt Whitman took it from its mother, into
his own arms; the infant stared at him a long time, then
snuggled against him and fell asleep. Presently the conductor got off the car to get his supper, and Whitman
acted as conductor the rest of the trip, still holding the
sleeping baby.

958—Eleanore Duse, the great actress, once offered to look after
the year-old baby of some friends while the family went
for a walk.

"What will you do if she cries?" they asked.

"Do? I'll sing to her," said the resourceful Duse. "I have
lots of tricks to entertain babies."

When the parents returned, they found the baby sitting
quietly in her carriage, her eyes fixed with a hypnotic
stare upon the sofa. There lay the great actress, her head
drooping, her mouth open, her eyes shut. She was snoring—regularly, sonorously snoring.

Slowly she opened her eyes. "Sh!" she said. "If I stop for a second, she'll cry."

Then she explained: "I sang for her; I danced for her; I made faces at her; I acted the whole of "Paolo and Francesca" to her, and she hated it all. But the snoring— from the first faint sign—she loved it!"

959—Mme. de Staël (to Napoleon): General who is the woman you would love the most?

Napoleon: My own.

Mme. de Staël: But what woman would you admire the most?

Napoleon: The best housekeeper.

Mme. de Staël: But with you, who would be the first among women?

Napoleon: She who has had the most babies.

960—During gold rush days in California, a lady took her infant to the theatre one evening and it started crying just as the orchestra began to play.

"Stop those fiddles and let the baby cry," called a man in the pit. "I haven't heard such a sound in ten years!"

The audience applauded the sentiment wildly, the orchestra was stopped, and the baby continued its performance amid unbounded enthusiasm.

961—The six-year-old wandered into the room where the brand new baby was being nursed. Because of her interest in the process, the mother carefully explained how mother animals furnish milk for their babies, even the human species. The child was satisfied on all but one point. "But Mother," she demanded, "is it pasteurized?"

962—Burdened with the care of a new baby the young mother sent her little brother to the department store to get some things for the new arrival.

He managed to get everything without too much trouble. The last item on his list was diapers. He went to the counter where they were sold, stated his wishes, and in the space of a few minutes the salesgirl returned with a bundle.

"That will be sixty cents for the diapers and two cents for the tax."

"Ah, never mind the tacks," said the youngster, "Sis puts them on the baby with safety pins."

SEE ALSO   RELATED SUBJECTS
Names 838   Children 951–952
Old Maids 873   Births, Birthdays 1011–1015
Actors 1412
Church Services 1537

SMALL CHILDREN

966—When he was in nursery school Woody, the young son of
Heywood Broun, was constantly annoyed by grown-up
visitors to whom he had been pointed out, who kept
coming up to him and asking in saccharine tones, "And
whose little boy are you?"

To one such inquirer, when his patience was exhausted,
Woody peremptorily replied, "You know damned well
whose little boy I am!"

967—Themistocles had a son who was the darling of his mother.
"This little fellow," said Themistocles, "is the sovereign
of all Greece."

"How so?" said a friend.

"Why, he governs his mother, his mother governs me, I
govern the Athenians, and the Athenians govern all
Greece."

968—Napoleon the Third was practising a Spartan method of
education for the little five-year-old Louis Napoleon.

One day, in pursuance of this course, at Biarritz the child
was given a swimming lesson by being tossed head first
into the water. He was quite terrified and was severely
reproached for this. He, a corporal, who could face a
loaded cannon without wincing, and yet was afraid of the
water!

"Well," whimpered little Louis, "I am in command of the
cannon but I am not in command of the sea."

969—Generally Byron suffered a moody and irritable childhood,
between his cruel nurse whom he hated and feared, and
his eccentric and tempestuous mother. In his fourth year
he bit a large piece out of a china saucer "in a silent rage."
Coming into the title at ten, he burst into tears when first
called "dominus" at school.

970—The late Sir Josiah Stamp, the economist, was fond of a
story about a Parliamentary candidate who approached a
house in his constituency and saw two small children of
identical size and appearance standing hand in hand be-

fore the cottage door. Jovially he asked them if they were twins.

"No, sir," they answered.

"You're brothers, aren't you?" he inquired.

"Yes," they said.

"Well, how old are you?"

"We're both five."

"Well, my goodness, if you're both five and you're brothers, you must be twins."

"Please, sir," said one of them, "we're triplets. Billie's in doors."

971—The little young lady of the house, by way of punishment for some minor misdemeanor, was compelled to eat her dinner alone at a little table in a corner of the dining room. The rest of the family paid no attention to her presence until they heard her audibly delivering Grace over her own repast, with the words, "I thank Thee Lord for preparing a table before me in the presence of mine enemies."

972—A mother was reproving her little girl one day, in the presence of Degas, for making mistakes in spelling.

"Why do mistakes in spelling matter?" the child protested.

"Why do they matter? Because they do, and it is very naughty in a little girl to make them, isn't it Monsieur Degas?"

"Very naughty," agreed Degas.

Then when the mother had left them, Degas said to the child: "Which would you like best: to know how to spell or have a box of candy?"

"Candy!" cried the little girl without hesitation.

"Well, so would I," replied Degas.

973—"I like to hear a child cry," jocosely said the Abbé Morold.

"Why?"

"Because then there is some hope of his being sent away."

974—In animated conversation, the adults of the family and their guests around the dinner table had completely forgotten for the time being the presence of four-year-old Dorothy, who had been automatically excluded. After a time she tentatively plucked at her mother's sleeve, and asked, "Remember me?"

975—A very small boy spoke at the breakfast table about a dream he had had the night before. "Johnny," asked his mother, "do you know what dreams are?"

"Sure," he said, "moving pictures that you see when you're asleep."

976—A certain small boy had tumbled into bed, leaving his room in a characteristic state of disorder. His mother, coming in to bid him Good-Night, chided gently, saying, "Now, I wonder who it was who didn't hang up his clothes before going to sleep."

"Adam," said the little boy, and promptly pulled the covers over his head.

977—Mark Twain used to tell a pathetic story of his childhood. It seems, according to the story, that Mark was born twins. He and his twin looked so much alike, that no one, not even their mother, could tell them apart. One day, while the nurse was bathing them, one of them slipped in the bathtub and was drowned. No one ever knew which twin it was that was drowned—"And therein," says Mark, "was the tragedy. Everyone thought I was the one that lived, but I wasn't. It was my brother who lived. I was the one that was drowned."

SEE ALSO
Absent-Mindedness 84
Greed 272
Quick Thinking 478, 479
Shrewdness 540
Homeliness 652
Fatness 690
Marriage 882
Babies 961
Mother 991
Birthdays 1014
Schools 1046, 1047, 1050
School Classrooms 1052
Scientists 1121
Language 1233

RELATED SUBJECTS
Children 951–952
Babies 956–962
Births, Birthdays 1011–1015

Actors 1407
Kings 1985
Chiseling 2124
Lawyers 2532

ADOPTION

981—There is the story of the Hollywood star who had a Mexican gardener. He once informed his employer that he had adopted a baby and would like to display him. He turned up forthwith with an unmistakably Jewish child.

"How is it," the surprised actor asked, "that you didn't adopt a Mexican child?"

"Not me," said José firmly, "a Jewish child for me. Jewish children take care of their parents when they are old."

RELATED SUBJECTS
Family 946–950
Children 951–952

FATHER

986—Paul Bourget: Life can never become entirely dull to an American. When he has nothing else to do he can always spend a few years trying to discover who his grandfather was.

Mark Twain: Right, your Excellency. But I reckon a Frenchman's got his little standby for a dull time too; he can turn in and see if he can find out who his father was!

987—A father was walking with his young son. The boy said, "Daddy, what is electricity?"

"Well now, I don't really know," said the father. "I never knew much about electricity. All I know about it is that it makes things run."

A little farther on, the boy said, "Daddy, how does the gasoline make the automobiles go?"

The father replied, "Well, I don't know. I don't know much about motors."

Several more questions followed with much the same result; until at last, the boy said, "Gee, I hope you don't mind my asking so many questions?"

"Not at all, son," said his father, "you go right ahead and ask. How else will you ever learn anything!"

988—Part of Aaron Burr's reputation for profligacy was due, no doubt, to that vanity respecting women of which Davis himself speaks. He never refused to accept the parentage of a child.

"Why do you allow this woman to saddle you with her child when you know you are not the father of it?" said a friend to him a few months before his death.

"Sir," he replied, "when a lady does me the honor to name me the father of her child I trust I shall always be too gallant to show myself ungrateful for the favor."

989—In 1814 Shelley, being then twenty-two, and the father of two children by Harriet . . . visited the family at Field Place for the first time since his expulsion from Oxford. A reconciliation would then have been easy, but instead

Timothy made his son feel unwelcome. Indeed, so panicky was this patriotic M.P. of being detected harboring a liberal and an atheist—albeit his son—that he compelled Bysshe to masquerade under the name of "Captain Jones," and to wear, when on the public highways, the uniform of a young officer then visiting the Shelleys.

990—Getting on a trolley car, a kindergarten teacher sat down next to a man who appeared familiar to her. Smiling pleasantly, she turned as if to speak to him. Noticing his lack of response, she realized her error, and said, "Oh, excuse me. I mistook you for someone else. I thought you were the father of two of my children."
He got out at the next corner.

SEE ALSO   RELATED SUBJECTS
Diligence 176   Husband 916–918
Children 952   Family 946–950
Actors 1424   Children 951–952
Priests 1483   Mother 991–993
Chiseling 2131

MOTHER

991—Two small boys were hesitant about approaching their mother for a permission which was almost certain to be denied. They felt that they must take the long shot, however. "You ask her," said Billy to his younger brother. "No, you." At this point the mother chanced to overhear the balance of the conversation. "Oh, go on, you ask her," urged Billy. "No, you do it," said the younger, "you've known her longer than I have."

992—John D. Rockefeller, Sr. was reared with strict discipline. Upon one occasion, while being punished, he succeeded in convincing his mother that he was not guilty of the offense for which he was being whipped.
"Very well, son," his mother replied with grim humor, "but we have gone so far that we may as well proceed. It will be credited to your account for next time."

993—A number of years ago my little girl said to her mother, in one of those bursts of confidence that children sometimes have, "Mama, I am nearer to you than I am to papa." Her mother asked, "Why, what do you mean, my dear?" "Why," she replied, "I am your own little girl, but I am only related to papa by marriage."

SEE ALSO
Civilians in War 2346

RELATED SUBJECTS
Wife 921–933
Family 946–950
Children 951–952
Father 986–990

HOME LIFE

996—When asked how she made her soft voice heard above the notorious roars of her husband and eight sons, Rider Haggard's delicate little mother replied: "That's very simple. I whisper. In the Haggard family a whisper is so unusual that everyone listens to it with profound surprise."

997—The wife of an Iowa farmer, whose place was isolated in the vastness of the prairie, suddenly went out of her mind and was carted away in a strait-jacket by an ambulance from the nearest State hospital. An attendant remained behind to get the data on the case from the puzzled and distressed husband, who lamented, "Now what do you suppose could o' went wrong with the old woman? Why, man alive, she ain't been out of the kitchen in 20 years!"

998—We are told a story of a girl of the roaring 20's who said to a real estate agent when he wanted to sell her a house: "A home? Why do I need a home? I was born in a hospital, educated in a college, courted in an automobile, and married in a church. I live out of the delicatessen and paper bags. I spend my mornings on the golf course, my afternoons at the bridge-table, and my evenings at the movies. And when I die I am going to be buried at the undertaker's. All I need is a garage."

999—In the course of his pastoral visitations, Rev. Dr. Chalmers called upon a worthy shoemaker who, in recounting his blessings, said that he and his family had lived happily together for thirty years without a single quarrel. This was too much for the doctor, who struck his cane on the floor and exclaimed:
"Terribly monotonous man! Terribly monotonous!"

1000—Two young benedicts, married about a year, were discussing their various marital problems.
"I'm the head of my house," said one, "I think I should be; after all, I earn the money."
"Well," said the other, "my wife and I have a perfect

agreement. I decide all the major matters and she takes care of all minor matters."

"And how is that working out?"

Somewhat ruefully the other replied, "Well, so far, no major matters have come up."

1001—An Athenian (as was customary with that people) had caused the following inscription to be placed over the door of his house:

"Let nothing enter here but what is good."

Diogenes asked: "Then where will the master of the house go in?"

SEE ALSO	RELATED SUBJECTS
Small Children 969	Marriage 876–888
	Family 946–950
	Servants 2276–2283

HOSPITALITY

1006—Alice James, wife of William James, says that often during evenings her husband would exclaim, "Are we never to have an evening alone? Must we always talk to people every night?" And she would answer, "I will see that whoever calls tonight is told that you are strictly engaged." So they would settle down to their quiet evening. Presently the doorbell would ring and Alice would go to the entry, to make sure that her instructions were carried out; but close behind her would be William, exclaiming, "Come in! Come right in!"

1007—Daniel Webster was once bested by one of the farmers of his native state. He had been hunting at some distance from his Inn, and rather than make the long trip back, he approached a farmhouse some considerable time after dark and pounded on the door. An upstairs window was raised and the farmer, with head thrust out, called, "What do you want?"

"I want to spend the night here," said Webster. "All right. Stay there," said the farmer. Down went the window.

1008—Andrew Lang at one time lived in the very far reaches of a London suburb. Inviting a friend to dinner, he instructed him how to get to the house. After long and explicit explanations he wound up by saying: "Just walk right along Cromwell Road. Keep on walking until you drop dead of exhaustion, and my house is just opposite."

SEE ALSO
Friendship 866
Actors 1428

RELATED SUBJECTS
Generosity 241–248
Parties 741–746
Home Life 996–1001

BIRTHS, BIRTHDAYS

1011—One night in New York friends of Mark Twain, remembering that it was the author's birthday, decided to send him a letter of congratulation. But no one knew in what corner of the globe he happened to be, so they addressed it: "Mark Twain, God Knows Where." Several weeks later they received a note from Italy which consisted of two words: "He did."

1012—When Lincoln went to the Legislature in 1854, after an absence of 12 years from that body, he got the indorsement of the Whigs and the Know-Nothings. He rejected their support in the following manner:

"Who are the native Americans? Do they not wear the breech clout and carry the tomahawk? We pushed them from their homes, and now turn upon others not fortunate enough to come over as early as we or our forefathers. Gentlemen, your party is wrong in principle." Then he told this story: "I had an Irishman named Patrick cultivating my garden. One morning I went out to see how he was getting along. 'Mr. Lincoln, what do yez think of these Know-Nothings?' he asked. I explained what they were trying to do, and asked Pat why he had not been born in America. 'Faith,' he replied, 'I wanted to but my mother wouldn't let me.'"

1013—Voltaire (writing to Frederick the Great): Madame du Chatelet is not yet delivered; it gives her more trouble to produce a child than a book.

Frederick the Great (replying to Voltaire): Since Madame du Chatelet writes books, I do not think she will produce her child in a moment of distraction. Tell her to hurry, for I wish to see you.

1014—A young lady of 8 or 9 years was almost overcome with joy when the occasion of her birthday netted her the two gifts which she had most ardently desired, a wristwatch and a bottle of perfume. She chattered about the new possessions all day long, wearying her parents of the subject. Guests were expected for dinner and the Mother gently admonished the child in advance, saying,

"Now, dear, everybody knows about your presents and everybody is very happy for you. But now we mustn't go on talking about them all the time."
The little girl held her peace at the table throughout the greater part of the meal. A lull occurred in the conversation and, unable to restrain herself any more, she burst forth, "If anyone hears anything or smells anything, it's me !"

1015—A gentleman whose wife was delivered of a boy six months after marriage, asked a physician the reason for this. "Make yourself easy," said the latter, "this often happens in the case of the first child, but never afterwards."

SEE ALSO
Clothing 726
Names 833

RELATED SUBJECTS
Family 946–950
Children 951–952
Father 986–990
Mother 991–993

LEARNING AND THE ARTS

UNIVERSITIES AND COLLEGES

1016—When Woodrow Wilson was President of Princeton University he deplored the promiscuous giving of honorary degrees.

"Our universities have learned of late," he said, "to distribute honorary degrees judiciously. But in the past—well, in the past I met an uncouth person at a dinner, and, being told by an acquaintance that he had three degrees, I asked why it was.

"'Well,' said my friend, 'the third was given because he had two, the second because he had one, and the first because he had none.'"

1017—Dr. Charles W. Eliot, the eminent educator of Harvard whose fate it has been to be dubiously immortalized by a five-foot shelf of books, was once asked how Harvard had gained its prestige as the greatest storehouse of knowledge in the nation.

"In all likelihood," said Dr. Eliot slyly, "it is because the freshmen bring us so much of it, and the seniors take away so little."

1018—Attorney-General Seymour of Virginia snorted at the establishment of William and Mary College, which was founded not only to inculcate learning but to save souls. "Souls?" he cried. "Damn your souls. Make tobacco."

1019—Sir William B——, being at a parish meeting, made certain proposals which were objected to by a farmer. Highly enraged, "Sir," said he to the farmer, "do you know, sir, that I have been at two universities, and at two colleges in each university?"

"Well, sir," said the farmer, "what o' that? I had a calf that sucked two kye, an' the observation I made was, the mair he sucked the greater calf he grew."

1020—When James A. Garfield was president of Hiram College a man brought up his son to be entered as a student. He wanted the boy to take a course shorter than the regular one.

175

"My son can never take all those studies," said the father. "He wants to get through more quickly. Can't you arrange it for him?"

"Oh, yes," said Mr. Garfield. "He can take a short course; it all depends on what you want to make of him. When God wants to make an oak he takes a hundred years, but he takes only two months to make a squash."

1021—A guide, new at his business, was showing a group of tourists around Oxford. Conscientiously, he pointed out all the places of interest. Coming in front of one of the buildings he paused and said, "And this is Trinity Hall, where the president of the college, the famous Benjamin Jowett, lives."

Glancing around at the upturned faces, the guide then stooped and picked up a handful of gravel and threw it at a second story window. A red-faced and furious man opened the window almost immediately and peered out.

"And that is President Jowett himself," said the guide in a tone of voice as though he had just completed a task well done.

1022—Hendrik Willem Van Loon was visiting Cambridge. "That," said someone who was showing him around the university, "is Miss Jones," pointing to a formidable looking female striding along before them. "She's the mistress of Ridsley Hall."

"Who," asked Van Loon, "is Ridsley Hall?"

SEE ALSO	RELATED SUBJECTS
Rudeness 512	Professors 1026–1032
Speeches 756, 757, 758, 773	Students 1036
	College Life 1041
Introductions 790	Schools 1046–1050
Learned Men 1087	Erudition 1071–1076
Churchmen 1455	Learned Men 1081–1095
Travel 1793	
Lawyers 2534	
Ministers 2607	

PROFESSORS

1026—William Lyon Phelps, on a pre-Christmas examination paper, found written, "God only knows the answer to this question. Merry Christmas."

He returned the paper with the notation, "God get's an A; you get an F. Happy New Year."

1027—A certain University professor was about to depart on his sabbatical and addressed a few parting words to his students. "This parting is very melancholy to me. I wish there might be a window in my breast that you might see the innermost recesses of my heart."
"Professor," called a young man from the class, "would a pane in the stomach do?"

1028—The celebrated Prof. Maclaurin, the famous mathematician of Edinburgh College and the able expounder of Newton's "Principia," always dislocated his jaw, and was unable to shut his mouth whenever he yawned. His pupils took advantage of this physical affliction. When tired of his lecture, they either began to yawn or open their mouths in imitation of that act, and the professor began to yawn, too, by unconscious imitation. He stood before them with his mouth open and could not proceed till he rang for his servant to come and shut it. In the meantime, the mischievous enemies of Euclid effected their escape.

1029—Told by John Erskine: "At the end of my university studies when I was leaving for my first professorial job, I went to say goodbye to my old teacher, William Peterfield Trent. 'I can give you no theoretical advice in pedagogy,' he said, 'but I'll tell you one thing from experience. It will frequently happen when you are holding forth that some boy in the class will disagree. He will probably shake his head violently. You will be tempted to go after him and convert him then and there. Don't do it. He is probably the only one who is listening.' "

1030—Professor Parson, in a dispute, so exasperated his opponent by the dryness of his sarcasm that the latter at length exclaimed: "Mr. Parson, I beg leave to tell you, sir, that my opinion of you is a perfectly contemptible one."
Parson replied: "I never knew any opinion of yours, sir, which was not contemptible."

1031—Harvard's famous Professor, Charles Townsend Copeland, for many years occupied a couple of cramped, dusty rooms on the top floor of Hollis Hall. He was frequently urged to move to more comfortable and fitting quarters.
"No," he always said, "I shall always live on the top floor. It is the only place in Cambridge where God alone is above me. He's busy—but he's quiet."

1032—Interrupted by the sound of the bell announcing the end of the class, the professor was annoyed to see the students noisily preparing to leave although he was in the very middle of his lecture.

"Just a moment, gentlemen," he said, "I have a few more pearls to cast."

SEE ALSO
Quick Thinking 487

RELATED SUBJECTS
Universities and Colleges 1016–1022
Teachers 1056–1057
Erudition 1071–1076
Learned Men 1081–1095
Lectures 1106–1111

STUDENTS

1036—In the days when Dora Russell and others were journeying about giving out student questionnaires on sex life at most of our leading colleges, the story was told of a Wellesley girl who became tired of the endless round of intimate questionnaires. Summoned one day to a personal interview with the visiting psychiatrist, she meekly answered the many questions fired at her, and upon rising to leave, guilelessly asked, "Oh, doctor, tell me. Does it mean anything that I am so passionately fond of pancakes?" The doctor laughed heartily with professional geniality. "Why, my dear girl, of course not. I'm very fond of them myself."

"Oh, I'm so glad," replied the girl, "over in my room, I've a whole bureau drawer full and I love to take them out and stroke them."

The young lady was never troubled again by questionnaires, but reported that from time to time, the housemother dropped in and quietly went through her bureau drawers.

SEE ALSO
Speeches 756
Experimenters 1137

RELATED SUBJECTS
Universities and Colleges 1016–1022
College Life 1041

COLLEGE LIFE

1041—A tradition of Haverford College centers around the administration of its famous President, Dr. William Wistar Comfort. On the occasion of the erecting upon the campus of a beautiful metal sign proclaiming the name of the college, an enterprising group of seniors stole the sign and concealed it. It was missing for many days, during which Dr. Comfort instituted a search, located the sign, and caused it to be removed to a place of concealment of his own. Thereupon he announced that a joke was a joke but that unless the culprits returned the sign by the following Saturday night, all privileges of the senior class would be indefinitely revoked. The dismay of the culprits was great when they were unable to find their trophy and comply with the ultimatum. Accordingly, an extremely glum and down-in-the-mouth body of seniors assembled in chapel the Sunday morning after the deadline. Dr. Comfort stepped into the pulpit, surveyed the faces before him, and opened the great Bible for the reading of the morning text, which was, "A wicked and adulterous generation seeketh for a sign and there shall be none given unto them."

RELATED SUBJECTS
Universities and Colleges 1016–1022
Professors 1026–1032
Students 1036

ATHLETICS (SEE RECREATION & SPORTS)

SCHOOLS

1046—After a lecture by the late Francis Wayland Parker, great Chicago educator, a woman asked:
"How early can I begin the education of my child?"
"When will your child be born?"
"Born?" she gasped. "Why, he is already five years old!"
"My goodness, woman," he cried, "don't stand here talking to me—hurry home; already you have lost the best five years."

1047—"What are your eyes for?" the little child in kindergarten was asked.
"To see with."
"And your nose?"
"To smell with."
"And what are your ears for?" was the last question.
"To keep clean," the child replied.

1048—A little girl who was attending a progressive school had a cold one morning and her mother suggested that she remain home from school. "But I can't, Mother," the child insisted, "this is the day when we start to make a clay model of a cow and I'm chairman of the udder committee."

1049—A certain mother wished to enter her five-year old daughter in a kindergarten, the age requirement of which was six. To the disapproving teacher the mother explained, "She can easily pass the six-year old test."

"Say some words," the teacher said rather skeptically to the child.

The little girl surveyed the teacher with dignity, and turning to her mother, asked, "Purely irrelevant words?"

1050—As a special treat, a teacher took her class to visit the museum of natural history. The children returned home very excitedly, and rushing into his house, one of the little boys greeted his mother exuberantly, saying, "What do you think we did today, Mother! The teacher took us to a dead circus."

SEE ALSO	RELATED SUBJECTS
Boners 119	Universities and Colleges 1016–
Memory 372	1022
Quick Thinking 479	Classrooms 1051–1053
Small Children 966	Teachers 1056–1057
Wealth 2185	Pupils 1061–1066

CLASSROOMS

1051—The small boy had created a disturbance in kindergarten. All the methods of the teacher had failed. The child was in revolt, and determined to go home. The teacher got the child's mother on the telephone and, after explaining the situation, put the culprit himself on the line. Clearly, as evidenced by his side of the conversation and his increasingly weaker protests, he was losing his case. At last the child said in despair, "All right then. If you want me to be a damned bead-stringer!" and hung up.

1052—The day of a big snowstorm, the country school teacher felt called upon to warn her charges against playing too long in the snow. She said, "Now, children, you must be careful about colds and over-exposure. I had a darling little brother only seven years old. One day he went out in the snow with his new sled and caught cold. Pneumonia set in and three days later he died."

The room was silent and then a youngster in the back row raised his hand and asked, "Where's his sled?"

1053—A young woman named Murphy was the teacher of the kindergarten grade in a Massachusetts school. She had taught her class to repeat together the 23rd Psalm. As the little voices chorused out, she seemed somewhere to detect a false note. She heard the children one by one, until at last she came across one little boy who was concluding the Psalm with the words, "Surely good Miss Murphy shall follow me all the days of my life."

> RELATED SUBJECTS
> Schools 1046–1050
> Teachers 1056–1057
> Pupils 1061–1066

TEACHERS

1056—There is the story about the famous Dr. Busby, headmaster of Westminster who, while showing Charles II of England over the school, apologized to that merry monarch for keeping his hat on in the presence of royalty, "For," said he, "it would not do for my boys to suppose that there existed in the world a greater man than Dr. Busby."

1057—In the classroom the teacher was trying, without success, to quell what looked like a small riot. The principal, passing through the hall, stopped and asked what all the noise was about.

The pretty young teacher was almost in tears. "I was explaining the difference between concrete and abstract, stating that abstract is something you can't see, and concrete is something you can see. Then I asked James to give me an illustration.

"'My pants are concrete. Yours are abstract,' he answered."

The principal, attempting to repress a smile, helped the teacher restore order to her class, and then, going into the hall, finally gave vent to the laughter he could no longer restrain.

SEE ALSO　　　　RELATED SUBJECTS
Father 990　　　　Schools 1046–1050
Judges 2494　　　　Classrooms 1051–1053
　　　　　　　　　Pupils 1061–1066

PUPILS

1061—In English class a small boy was told to write an essay about King Alfred, but was warned not to elaborate overly much on the familiar story of the cakes. The boy delivered his essay which, after summing up the chief historical facts, concluded with "There is another incident in King Alfred's life. One day he visited a house where a certain woman lived—and the less said about that, the better."

1062—For sheer lucidity of description, it is difficult to match the young lady who wrote on her examination paper the following in reply to the question, "What is a bolt and what is a nut?"

"A bolt is a thing like a stick of hard metal, such as iron, with a square bunch on one end and a lot of scratches going round and round the other end. A nut is similar to the bolt only just the opposite, being a hole in a little square of iron sawed off short with rings also around the inside of the hole."

1063—A certain young man came home with a grievously unsatisfactory report card in January. "Oh, dear," said his mother, "what is the trouble?"

"There isn't any trouble," said the youngster, "you know how it is yourself; things are always marked down after the Holidays."

1064—When the pupils were assigned the task of writing an essay on "the most beautiful thing I ever saw," the least esthetic young man in the class handed in his paper first with astonishing speed. It was short and to the point— "The most beautiful thing I ever saw was too beautiful for words."

1065—When Theodore Roosevelt was in school, he was one day called upon to deliver an assigned recitation, beginning, "When Greece, her knees in suppliance bent—."

When he essayed to deliver the recitation, he found himself unable to get past the first few words. He said, "When Greece, her knees—" and again, "When Greece, her knees—"; and, after a few more false starts, gave up hopelessly.

His teacher said severely, "Roosevelt, grease her knees again and then perhaps she'll go."

1066—Given the assignment of writing a composition about what they would do if they had a million dollars, all of the children in the class except Willy were busily writing away.

The teacher, becoming aware of his idleness, said severely, "Willy, don't you know that you are supposed to tell what you would do if you had a million dollars?"

"Well," said the boy, lazily leaning back on his chair, "this is exactly what I would do if I had a million dollars."

RELATED SUBJECTS
Schools 1046–1050
Classrooms 1051–1053
Teachers 1056–1057

ERUDITION

1071—President Woodrow Wilson would sit down beside his green-shaded lamp and take up one paper after another —and so work until the small hours. Approval was designated by "Okeh, W. W." on the margin of a paper. Someone asked why he did not use the "O.K." "Because it is wrong," Mr. Wilson said. He suggested that the inquirer look up "Okeh" in a dictionary. That he did, and discovered that it is a Choctaw word meaning "It is so."

1072—Once, during the progress of Mr. Hastings' trial, Charles Fox, struck by the solemnity of Lord Thurlow's appearance, said to the speaker, "I wonder if any man is as wise as Thurlow looks."

1073—Mark Twain once observed sagely, "One should be careful to get out of an experience only the wisdom that is in it—and stop there; lest we be like the cat that sits down on the hot stove lid. She will never sit down on a hot stove lid again—and that's well; but also she will never sit down on a cold one any more."

1074—Someone once rudely taunted John Maynard, Lord Commissioner of the Great Seal of England, with having grown so old as to forget his law.

"True, Sir," he replied, "I have forgotten more law than you ever learned."

1075—When Bernardo Tasso remonstrated with his son, the immortal Torquato, on his injudicious preference of philosophy to jurisprudence, and angrily demanded: "What has philosophy done for you?" Torquato replied: "It has taught me to hear with meekness the reproofs of a father."

1076—One time when the little Louis Napoleon was racking his brains over a pile of Latin dictionaries and grammars, Napoleon the Third entered the room. He looked at him with sympathy and said, "It is a grind, translating Latin. I never could."

The tutor spoke up in astonishment, "But, your Majesty's translation of Caesar's 'Commentaries'?"

"It wasn't mine," said the Emperor, and went off.

SEE ALSO	RELATED SUBJECTS
Speeches 774	Professors 1026–1032
Children 951	Learned Men 1081–1095
	Common Sense 1156–1157

LEARNED MEN

1081—Ralph Waldo Emerson had read philosophy, science, poetry and histories, but none of them had said anything about an effective and harmonious way of pushing a female calf into a barn. His son Edward grasped an ear, the father pushed diligently from behind, and together they tried to propel the animal. The heifer resisted with calm obstinacy. The pale face of the sage reddened and perspiring beads gathered on his high white forehead. And then an Irish servant girl came by. With an amused glance she thrust a finger into the animal's mouth, and the calf, seduced by this maternal imitation, at once followed her into the barn. Edward grinned, but Emerson was already absorbed in thought. After cleansing his hands of their hairy, bovine smell, he recorded this telling declaration in his journal: "I like people who can do things."

1082—It is related of Noah Webster that his wife, coming suddenly into the pantry one day, caught him in the act of embracing the chambermaid. "Mr. Webster," she said, "I'm surprised."

The great lexicographer gazed upon her in mild reproof. "No, my pet," he replied, "you are amazed. It is we who are surprised."

1083—A nobleman observing a person eminent for his philosophical talents, intent on choosing delicacies at table, said to him:

"What! do you philosophers love dainties?"

"Why not—do you think my Lord, that the good things of this world were only made for blockheads?"

1084—The Duke of Newcastle, when Prime Minister, once told the author of "Tristram Shandy," that men of wit were not fit to be employed, being incapable of business.

"They are not incapable of business, my Lord, but above it," replied Sterne. "A sprightly generous horse is able to carry a pack-saddle as well as an ass, but he is too good to be put to the drudgery."

1085—"Bury me on my face," said Diogenes, and when he was asked why, he replied, "Because in a little while everything will be turned upside down."

1086—Talleyrand, on being told that the Abbé Sieyes was a very profound man, replied:

"Profound! Yes—he is a perfect cavity."

1087—In one of the ancient academies the students had a three years' course. In the first year they were called the wise men; in the second they were called the philosophers— those who wished to be wise men; in the third year they were called disciples, learners.

1088—When the mighty Alexander the Great asked the ragged philosopher Diogenes what favor he could grant him, the Cynic, who was reclining on the ground, remarked quietly:

"Now please move a little out of my sun."

1089—A committee of the French Academy employed in the preparation of the Academy Dictionary, defined the word "crab" as follows: "Crab: a small red fish which walks backwards." Commenting on this definition the celebrated naturalist Cuvier said: "Your definition, gentlemen, would be perfect, only for three exceptions. The crab is not a fish, it is not red and it does not walk backwards."

1090—When Dante was at the court of Signor della Scala, then sovereign of Verona, that prince said to him one day.

"I wonder, Signor Dante, that a man so learned as you should be hated by all my court, and that this fool should be so beloved."

Highly piqued Dante replied, "Your Excellency would wonder less if you considered that we like those best who most resemble ourselves."

1091—Noah Webster once undertook to write out a letter for an illiterate servant. Before concluding, he asked, "Is there anything else you wish to add?"

His serving man replied, "Well, you might just ask him to excuse the poor scholarship and want of sense the letter shows."

1092—At a convention of teachers in Chicago several of the learned men became heatedly involved in a discussion on a number of abstruse points of information. They split over an issue which could only be solved by reference to authority. Hastening downstairs one of the savants approached the desk clerk and said, "Is there an Encyclopedia Britannica in the house?"

"No, sir," said the clerk blandly, "what is it you wish to know?"

1093—Cottle, the Bath bookseller, recorded:

"I removed the harness . . . , but . . . could not get off the collar. In despair I called for assistance. Mr. W. (Wordsworth) first brought his ingenuity into exercise, but, after several unsuccessful efforts, he relinquished the achievement as altogether impracticable. Mr. Coleridge now tried his hand, but . . . after twisting the poor horse's neck, almost to strangulation, and the great danger of his eyes, he gave up the useless task, pronouncing that 'the horse's head must have grown (gout or dropsy!) since the collar was put on! for it was a downright impossibility for such a huge os frontis to pass through so narrow a collar!' At about this juncture the servant girl appeared, turned the collar upside-down, and removed it."

1094—One of Emerson's rural neighbors at Concord borrowed from him a copy of Plato. "Did you enjoy the book?" asked Emerson, when it was returned.

"I did that," replied his neighbor. "This Plato has a lot of my ideas."

1095—Queen Christina of Sweden complimented the celebrated Vossius by saying that he was so well learned as not only to know whence all the words came but whither they were going.

SEE ALSO
Cheerfulness 141
Dullness 186
Pompousness 424
Shortness 693
Churchmen 1452
Efficiency 2266

RELATED SUBJECTS
Professors 1026–1032
Erudition 1071–1076
Scientists 1116–1122
Mathematicians 1146–1154
Common Sense 1156–1157

CRITICS

1096—According to Richard Aldington: "In the early days of Dada (predecessor of Surrealism) I received for review a book which contained the following 'poem':

        A B C D E F
        G H I J K L
        M N O P Q R
        S T U V W X
          Y Z.

"On which I commented:

        1 2 3 4 5
        6 7 8 9 10.

"I still think that was the most snappy review I ever wrote; but unfortunately 'The Times' refused to print it."

1097—A man said he was afraid he was going to be of no use in the world because he had only one talent. "Oh, that need not discourage you," said his pastor. "What is your talent?"

"The talent of criticism."

"Well, I advise you," said his pastor, "to do with it what the man of one talent in the parable did with his. Criticism may be useful when mixed with other talents, but those whose only activity is to criticize the workers might as well be buried, talent and all."

1098—Jerrold admired Carlyle, but objected that he did not give definite suggestions for the improvement of the age which he rebuked.

"Here," said he, "is a man who beats a big drum under my windows, and when I come running downstairs, has nowhere for me to go."

1099—Richard Aldington tells that, "An American friend of mine was then editing the 'Outlook,' and asked me to write an article telling his readers about young writers and picking out those I thought would make a name. I made a choice which I modestly think wasn't bad for 1919: James Joyce, T. S. Eliot, D. H. Lawrence, Aldous Huxley, and Marcel Proust. I received a letter from the editor in these terms:

" 'For God's sake, Richard, can't you think of somebody who has been heard of or is ever likely to be heard of?'

"I protested, and my article was submitted to the judgment of that eminent expatriate, Mr. Logan Pearsall Smith, who decided that my writers never would be heard of; and the article was rejected. If I had chosen such mediocrities as Jack Squire, Hugh Walpole, Frank Swinnertown, I should have received a cheque and a crown of wild parsley."

1100—A shallow poet took Piron into his confidence and entrusted to him a long manuscript, assuring the critic that the verses contained therein were the best he had ever written. With an air of condescension he asked Piron to put a cross before each line which he thought might possibly be improved. When he asked for his manuscript a few days later Piron handed it to him without a word. Leafing hastily through it, the author exclaimed delightedly: "Why, I don't see a single cross on my paper."

"No," returned Piron dryly, "I didn't want to make a graveyard of it."

1101—When Michelangelo had completed his great sculptural work, the David, the Gonfalonière Soderini of Florence who had ordered it came to inspect his purchase. Among his other criticisms he objected to the nose, pronouncing it to be out of all due proportion to the rest of the figure, and added, that he wished some reduction should take place in its size. Angelo knew well with whom he had to deal; he mounted the scaffold for the figure upwards of twelve feet high, and giving a few sonorous but harmless blows with his hammer on the stone, let fall a handful of marble dust which he had scraped up from the floor below; and then descending from his station turned to the Gonfalonière with a look expectant of his approbation. "Ay," exclaimed the sagacious critic; "now you have given it life indeed."

Michelangelo was content, and receiving his four hundred scrudi for his tasks, wisely said no more. It would have been no gratification to a man like him, to have shown the incapacity of a presumptuous critic like Soderini.

1102—Professor Brander Matthews was a great stickler for proprieties. At an opening night he had gone to review a play. The next day he was asked for his opinion by one of his students at Columbia University.

"Well, gentlemen," said Prof. Matthews, "the play was in four acts, and I was there as the guest of the author.

After the first act the audience sat silent and I applauded. After the second act I sat quiet while the audience hissed."

The Professor took a long-drawn and reminiscent pull at his cigarette, then held it at arm's length and flicked off the ashes.

"And the third act?"

"Well, gentlemen," and there was a gleam of satisfaction in the Professor's eye, "after the third act I went out and bought standing room and came back and hissed too."

1103—When Bernard Shaw wrote dramatic criticisms for the "London Saturday Review" he commented about a certain play in his column as follows:

"I am in a somewhat foolish position concerning a play at the Opera Comique, whither I was bidden this day week. For some reason I was not supplied with a program; so that I never learned the name of the play. At the end of the second act the play had advanced about as far as an ordinary dramatist would have brought it five minutes after the first rising of the curtain; or say, as far as Ibsen would have brought it ten years before that event. Taking advantage of the second interval (intermission) to stroll out into the strand for a little exercise, I unfortunately forgot all about my business, and actually reached home before it occurred to me that I had not seen the end of the play. Under these circumstances, it would ill become me to dogmatize on the merits of the work or its performance. I can only offer the management my apologies."

1104—While he was dramatic critic on the old "Denver Post," Eugene Field was given an assignment to report on a performance of "King Lear." His review was brief but pointed:

"Last night at the Tabor Opera House, So-and-So played King Lear. He played it as though under the premonition that someone was about to play the Ace."

1105—A friend of Dr. Johnson's, in conversation with him, was lamenting the disagreeable situation in which those persons stood who were eminent for their criticisms. As they were perpetually expected to be saying clever things, it was a heavy tax on them.

"It is, indeed," said Dr. Johnson, "a very heavy tax on them; a tax which no man can pay who does not steal."

SEE ALSO   RELATED SUBJECTS
Sculpture 1296, 1297   Learned Men 1081–1095
Playwrights, 1377, 1379   Art 1256
Actors 1421   Music 1303–1306
                           Plays 1386–1388

LECTURES

1106—Professor Agassiz, the naturalist, had declined to deliver a lecture before some lyceum or public society, on account of the inroads which previous lectures given by him had made upon his studies and thought. The gentleman who had been deputed to invite him continued to press the invitation, assuring him that the society was ready to pay him liberally for his services.

"That is no inducement to me," replied Agassiz, "I cannot afford to waste my time in making money."

1107—Artemus Ward was once about to lecture on "American Wit and Humor," but the chairman spoke at such length on the subject that when Artemus rose, he said: "The chairman has said all that needs to be said on 'American Wit and Humor,' so instead of taking that subject, I shall lecture on 'Indian Meal.'" And he did.

1108—The German philosopher and theologian, Friedrich Schleiermacher, once attempted to explain to a questioner the type of people who composed his audiences. "My audience is composed mainly of students, young women, and soldiers. Students come because I'm a member of the Board of Examiners. The young women come because of the students. And the soldiers come because of the young women."

1109—After a great deal of urging, Mark Twain's friends in San Francisco persuaded him to give a lecture on the interesting things he had seen in the Hawaiian Islands during his visit in the fall of 1866. In order to encourage the new lecturer they promised to place hearty laughers at strategic points among the audience. "Tell them not to investigate my jokes, but to respond at once," Clemens said. When he came out on the platform his knees were shaking so violently that his backers thought he wouldn't last long enough for the hearty laughers to get into action. But Clemens needed no support, for he won the day by his inimitable opening, "Julius Caesar is dead, Shakespeare is dead, Napoleon is dead, Abraham

Lincoln is dead, and I am far from well myself." When the lecture was over, the audience had been laughing so much they were too weak to leave their seats.

1110—Mark Twain in his lecturing days, reached a small Eastern town one afternoon and went before dinner to a barber's to be shaved.

"You are a stranger in town, sir?" the barber asked.

"Yes, I am a stranger here," was the reply.

"We're having a good lecture here tonight, sir," said the barber, "a 'Mark Twain' lecture. Are you going to it?"

"Yes, I think I will," said Mr. Clemens.

"Have you got your ticket yet?" the barber asked.

"No, not yet," said the other.

"Then, sir, you'll have to stand."

"Dear me!" Mr. Clemens exclaimed. "It seems as if I always do have to stand when I hear that man Twain lecture."

1111—On the occasion of a lecture which Charles Lamb was once delivering, a loud hiss emanated from somewhere in the audience. There was an embarrassed silence. Lamb, not turning a hair, said, "There are only three things that hiss—a goose, a snake and a fool. Come forth and be identified."

SEE ALSO	RELATED SUBJECTS
Memory 375	Speeches 756–782
Clothing 720	Introductions 786–791
Handwriting 731	Professors 1026–1032
Authors 1211	Learned Men 1081–1095
Audiences 1438	

SCIENTISTS

1116—When Gustavus III of Sweden was in Paris, a deputation of French scientists called on him. It congratulated him on the happy fortune, that had given him so great a man as Scheele, the discoverer of magnesium, as his subject and fellow countryman.

The king, who took small interest in the progress of science, felt somewhat ashamed that he should be so ignorant as never even to have heard of the renowned chemist.

He dispatched a courier at once to Sweden with the laconic order: "Scheele is to be immediately raised to the dignity of a count." "His Majesty must be obeyed," said the Prime Minister, "but who in hell is Scheele?"

A secretary was told to make inquiries. He came back with very full information. "Scheele is a good sort of fellow," said he, "a lieutenant in the artillery, a capital shot, and a first-rate hand at billiards."

The next day the lieutenant became a count, and the illustrious scientist was completely forgotten by King and court.

1117—A botanist found a beautiful plant by the wayside. He sat down to analyze it. He pulled it apart and examined every part under a microscope.

When he had finished he could tell the color of the flower, its classification, and the number of stamens and pistils and petals and bracts, but the life and the beauty and the fragrance were gone.

1118—They tell the story of a celebrated biologist who tried for months to train a monkey to play ball. As a last resort, he shut up the little creature by itself in a room with a bat and ball. After some considerable time had elapsed he finally stooped and peered through the keyhole. He was disconcerted to find himself staring into an intent brown eye.

1119—A Cambridge lecturer on the history of chemistry thus describe the celebrated Mr. Boyle: "He was a great man, a very strong man; he was the father of modern chemistry, and brother of the Earl of Cork."

1120—Lord Kelvin, the great physicist, once paid an unexpected visit to an extensive electrical plant. He had not disclosed his identity and was shown through the plant by a young foreman who painstakingly explained all the rudiments of electrical science, as here manifested, to the great man.

When the tour was completed, Kelvin asked him quietly, "What then is electricity?" His guide was stumped. "No matter," Lord Kelvin said kindly, "that is the only thing about electricity which you and I do not know."

1121—The great naturalist, Charles Darwin, was once approached by two small boys of the family whose guest he was. They had caught a butterfly, a centipede, a beetle, and a grasshopper. Taking the centipede's body, the butterfly's wings, the beetle's head and the grasshopper's legs, they had glued them together to make an alarming and original insect.

"We caught this bug in the field," they said innocently. "What kind of a bug is it, Mr. Darwin?"

Darwin examined it with great solemnity. "Did you notice whether it hummed when you caught it, boys?" he asked gravely.

"Yes, sir," they answered, trying to conceal their mirth.

"Just as I thought," said Darwin. "It is a humbug."

1122—The wife of the great physicist, Robert A. Millikan, happened to pass through the hall of her home in time to hear her maid answer the telephone. "Yes," Mrs. Millikan overheard, "this is where Dr. Millikan lives, but he's not the kind of doctor that does anybody any good."

SEE ALSO	RELATED SUBJECTS
Dueling 802	Learned Men 1081–1095
Inventors 1127	Inventors 1126–1131
Common Sense 1157	Experimenters 1136–1138
Bigotry 1628	Explorers 1141–1142
Army and Navy 2401	Mathematicians 1146–1154
Stool Pigeon 2592	Doctors 1666–1679

INVENTORS

1126—One of the most interesting incidents of a business nature is that which concerns the first steamboat fare paid to Robert Fulton. The narrator of this, who was also one of the actors on the scene, says:

I chanced to be at Albany on business when Fulton arrived there, in his unheard-of craft, which everybody felt so much interest in seeing. Being ready to leave and hearing that this craft was going to return to New York, I repaired on board and inquired for Mr. Fulton; I was referred to the cabin, and there found a plain, gentlemanly man, wholly alone, and engaged in writing.

"Mr. Fulton I presume."

"Yes, sir."

"Do you return to New York with this boat?"

"We shall try to get back, sir."

"Can I have a passage down?"

"You can take your chance with us, sir." I inquired the amount to be paid, and, after a moment's hesitation, a sum, I think six dollars was named, the amount in coin, I laid it in his open hand, and, with eye fixed upon it, he remained so long motionless, that I supposed there might be a miscount, and said to him, "Is that right, sir?"

This question roused him as from a kind of reverie, and as he looked up to me the big tear was brimming in his eye, and his voice faltered as he said:

"Excuse me sir; but memory was busy as I contemplated this, the first pecuniary reward I have ever received for all my exertions in adapting steam to navigation. I should gladly commemorate the occasion over a bottle of wine with you, but really I am too poor, even for that just now."

1127—Thomas A. Edison never forgot his role as a business man. The profit motive was an essential part of his temperament. Once he said practically to a friend, referring to a newspaper article which discussed him as a scientist, "That's wrong. I am not a scientist. I am an inventor. Faraday was a scientist. He didn't work for money, he said he hadn't time. But I do. I measure everything I do by the size of a silver dollar. If it don't come up to that standard, then I know it's no good."

1128—The late Thomas A. Edison had a very beautiful summer residence in which he took great pride. One day he was showing his guests about, pointing out all the various labor-saving devices on the premises. Turning back toward the house it was necessary to pass through a turnstyle which led onto the main path. The guests soon found out that it took considerable force to get through this device.

"Mr. Edison," asked one of his guests, "how is it that with all these wonderful modern things around, you still maintain such a heavy turnstile?"

Said Mr. Edison, his eyes lighting up with laughter, "Well, you see, everyone who pushes the turnstile around, pumps eight gallons of water into the tank on my roof."

1129—"I got fired twice," said Edison. "The first time was when I was a telegraph operator. It was my fault, all right, but I got so interested in the dinged machine and its workings that I began to see how I could improve it. But I forgot all about the messages that were coming over the wire, and I left a lot of messages unsent and undelivered. Of course, they discharged me, and I didn't blame them," he added.

"Then," he laughed again, "I got a job in an office, and

there were a fearful lot of rats; terribly old office, you
know. I got up a thing that killed them like flies—the
same with cockroaches. The floor used to be covered
with dead roaches, and they fired me for that!"

1130—A step which seems obvious after it has been taken is frequently obscure before the way has been pointed out,
no matter how close to it we may have been led by the
slow and painful processes of learning and experimentation. Just such a step was taken by Thomas A. Edison
in one of the processes of subdividing an electric current.
Subsequently a patent suit arose over the matter in
which the famous English physicist, Tyndall, was called
upon to testify.

He mentioned that he had followed the same course taken
by Edison and had hesitated before the final step which
now seemed so childishly clear. One of the attorneys
demanded of him, "When the next step was so obvious,
why did you not take it?"

"Because," said Tyndall, "I was not Thomas A. Edison."

1131—Thomas A. Edison told, himself, about the invention of the
phonograph:

"I was working on the telephone, developing the carbon
button transmitter. My hearing wasn't too good and I
couldn't get the sounds as clearly as I wanted to, so I
fixed a short needle on the diaphram of the receiver.
When I let my finger rest lightly on this needle the
pricks would show me its amplitude and that's what I
wanted to find out.

"One day when I was testing this way it occurred to me
that if I could indent a yielding substance with these
vibrations I could reverse the process and reproduce the
sounds. I sat down and made a sketch of a machine that
I thought would do the trick.

"Then I called in John Kruesi, my chief mechanic. I explained the mechanism and asked him what he would
charge me for making it. He said he would make it for
thirty dollars, and I told him to go ahead. Then he asked
me what it was for, and I told him it was going to talk.
He thought I was joking and went away laughing.

"When he finished the machine and brought it back to me
I put the tinfoil on, started her up, and recited 'Mary
had a little lamb.' When I reversed and the words began
to come back, Kruesi nearly fell over.

"That was the only one of my inventions that was perfect from the start. When we began to manufacture it we didn't have to alter a single detail."

SEE ALSO   RELATED SUBJECTS
Pessimism 411   Scientists 1116–1122
Experimenters 1136   Experimenters 1136–1138
Devout Persons 1601
Bargaining 2079
Wealth 2183

EXPERIMENTERS

1136—"Results!" exclaimed Edison to an assistant marveling at the bewildering total of his failures—50,000 experiments for example, before he succeeded with a new storage battery. "Results? Why, man, I have gotten a lot of results. I know fifty-thousand things that won't work."

1137—Shelley's lifelong interest in science, especially chemistry, was aroused by a quack lecturer who visited his first school, Sion House. At Eton he was forbidden to study chemistry, and so performed experiments in his room. One day his tutor, Mr. Bethel, heard strange noises from his room, entered and found Shelley enveloped in blue flames.
"What on earth are you doing, Shelley?" asked the teacher.
"Please, sir, I am raising the devil."
The startled tutor put his hand on some apparatus which, being a leyden jar, gave him a bad shock.

1138—Edison's school of scientific experimentation was essentially empirical. Once he was seeking a solvent for hard rubber. Many scientists, seeking it through theory or formula, were yet helpless. Edison went to his impressive and remarkably complete storeroom of chemicals. He immersed a small fragment of hard rubber in a vial of each one of these many chemicals. It was an enormous number. But Edison found his solvent.

SEE ALSO   RELATED SUBJECTS
Exaggeration 222   Scientists 1116–1122
                             Inventors 1126–1131

EXPLORERS

1141—When Captain Cook discovered Australia, his sailors brought a strange animal aboard ship whose name they did not know. Sent ashore to inquire of the natives, they came back and said, "It is a kangaroo." Many years passed before it was known that when the natives were asked to name the animal and said, "Kangaroo," they meant, "What did you say?"

1142—Robert Falson Scott, the explorer, applied to Lloyd George for assistance in the financing of his last and fatal Polar expedition. The then Chancellor referred him to a certain wealthy man, also of some prominence in the political scene. "How did you succeed," asked Lloyd George, when the explorer again called on him.

"He gave me a thousand pounds," was the reply, "but he has undertaken to raise 20 thousand pounds if I can persuade you to come with me, and a million if I manage to leave you there."

SEE ALSO   RELATED SUBJECTS
Cynicism 169   Scientists 1116–1122
Pagan Gods 1661   Travel 1791–1796

MATHEMATICIANS

1146—When the Greek philosophers found that the square root of 2 is not a rational number, they celebrated the discovery by sacrificing 100 oxen.

1147—Pascal's genius for geometry began to appear before he was even twelve years old, in the room where he passed his hours of play; he procured a piece of charcoal, and drew diagrams on the floor, trying to make a circle, perfectly round, a triangle with equal sides and angles, a perfect parallelogram and like things. He discovered all this unaided, and then turned his attention to the properties of these figures and their mutual relations and proportions. But as his father had with such great care concealed from him all mathematical works, the poor boy did not even know the names of the figures he drew. Compelled to make his own definitions, he called a circle "a round," and a line "a bar," etc., and with these very primitive definitions proceeded to construct his axioms, till at last he wrought out complete demonstrations!

Step by step he advanced in his studies, one discovery opening the door to another; and so far did he push his researches, that without ever seeing a mathematical work, he got to the thirty-second proposition of the book of Euclid.

1148—The sculptor Jacob Epstein tells this story: "When I was doing Professor Albert Einstein's bust he had many a jibe at the Nazi professors, one hundred of whom had condemned his theory of relativity in a book. 'Were I wrong,' he said, 'one professor would have been enough!'"

1149—Edison approached the mathematical aspects of his science with that same practical instinct and native ability that characterized every other phase of his work. He often succeeding in beating the mathematicians on his staff to the draw in the search for correct formulae, seeming to arrive at his conclusions through infallible instinct and native genius.

"These mathematicians make me tired," he often said, "You ask them to work out a sum and they take a piece of paper, cover it with rows of a's and b's and x's and y's; decorate them with a lot of little numbers, scatter a mess of fly specks around them and then give you an answer that's all wrong."

1150—This story is told of, and possibly by, Alfred Einstein, who was asked by his hostess at a social gathering to explain his theory of relativity. Said the great mathematician, "Madam, I was once walking in the country on a hot day with a blind friend, and said that I would like a drink of milk.

"'Milk?' said my friend, 'Drink I know; but what is milk?'

"'A white liquid,' I replied.

"'Liquid I know; but what is white?'

"'The color of a swan's feathers.'

"'Feathers I know; what is a swan?'

"'A bird with a crooked neck.'

"'Neck I know; but what is this crooked?'

"Thereupon I lost patience. I seized his arm and straightened it. 'That's straight,' I said; and then I bent it at the elbow. 'That's crooked.'

"'Ah!' said the blind man, 'Now I know what you mean by milk!'"

1151—At a gathering of mathematicians, someone undertook to discourse upon the meaning of Einstein's theories. After he had run on tediously for nearly an hour, someone interrupted to say, "I think you are greater than Einstein himself. Twelve men understand Einstein—but nobody understands you."

1152—Sir William Rothenstein was in Berlin doing a portrait of Einstein. The mathematician was always accompanied to the studio by a solemn, academic looking individual who sat in a corner throughout the sittings. Einstein, not wishing to waste any time, was putting forth certain tentative theories, to which the silent companion replied only by an occasional nod or shake of the head. When the work was concluded, Rothenstein, who was curious, asked Einstein who his companion was.

"That's my mathematician," said Einstein, "who examines problems which I put before him and checks their validity. You see, I am not myself a good mathematician."

1153—Asked one day for a mathematical formula for success in life, Albert Einstein gave the following:

"If a is success in life, the formula is, a equals x plus y plus z, x being work and y being play."

"And what is z?" he was asked.

"Z," he said, "is keeping your mouth shut."

1154—Once the Gershwin family happened to be discussing the Einstein theory. "Imagine," began George, "working for twenty years on an idea and then being able to write it down in three pages!"

"It was probably very small print," was Pop Gershwin's comment.

SEE ALSO
Professors 1028
Wealth 2184

RELATED SUBJECTS
Learned Men 1081–1095
Scientists 1116–1122
Statistics 2221–2222

COMMON SENSE

1156—Lincoln once said to Chauncey Depew, "They say I tell a great many stories; I reckon I do, but I have found in the course of a long experience that common people, take them as they run, are more easily informed through the medium of a broad illustration than in any other way, and as to what the hypercritical few may think, I don't care."

1157—This is one of the favorite stories of Dr. Karl Compton, the noted physicist of M. I. T. His sister lives in India. She was having a simple electrical installation done by a native electrician. He troubled her so much for instructions that she at last said irritably, "You know what I want; just use your common sense and do it."

The electrician salaamed politely and said, "Madam, common sense is a rare gift of God. I have only a technical education."

SEE ALSO
Machinery 2272

RELATED SUBJECTS
Stupidity 576–583
Erudition 1071–1076
Learned Men 1081–1095

LITERATURE

1161—Two passengers were overheard in a literary discussion on the Brooklyn express.

"Whatcher favorite readin'?"

"Popeye, Superman, and Flash Gordon."

"Howcha like O. Henry?"

"Naw, the nuts get in my teeth."

1162—The magazine which published "The Old Curiosity Shop" came to America by sailing vessel. As interest in Dickens' story mounted from week to week, the crowds became larger on the New York wharf waiting to buy copies as soon as the boat docked. By the time the story reached its last chapter these crowds had grown to such numbers and to such a pitch of suspense that they swarmed, five or six thousand strong, upon the wharf and could not wait until the ship docked. When they spied the captain on the deck they called out across the narrowing water the question that burned in everyone's heart: "Did little Nell die?"

SEE ALSO
Eating 20
Critics 1096
Authors 1216

RELATED SUBJECTS
Authors 1166–1219
Books 1221–1224
Libraries 1226
Language 1231–1233
Newspapers 1236–1248
Magazines 1251–1252
Art 1256
Music 1303–1306
Plays 1386–1388

AUTHORS

1166—Meeting one's literary idol face to face is sometimes a sad experience, according to George Dolby, who was Dickens' lecture manager.

"During the progress of a reading," he tells, my attention was drawn to a gentleman who was in a most excited state. Imagining him to be ill and wanting assistance, I said, 'What's the matter with you?'

" 'Say, who's that man on the platform reading?'

" 'Mr. Charles Dickens,' I replied.

" 'But that ain't the real Charles Dickens, the man as wrote all them books I've been reading all these years?'

" 'The same.'

" 'Well, all I've got to say about it then is that he knows no more about Sam Weller'n a cow does of pleating a shirt, at all events that ain't my idea of Sam Weller, anyhow.' And he clapped his hat on his head and left in a state of high dudgeon."

1167—The Emily Dickinson house in Amherst has been converted into a shrine, preserving the memory and relics of the distinguished American poetess. During his administration, President Coolidge, chancing to pass through Amherst, stopped off at the Dickinson shrine to do it honor.

In deference to the President he was shown throughout the house and permitted to see and handle many relics carefully shut away from the general public. At last, in the small upper room in which Emily Dickinson had done much of her writing, the greatest special privilege was conferred upon him. Stooping down, his guide opened a locked chest and removed from it a packet of the holograph manuscripts of some of her most famous poems. These were put into Coolidge's hand. He examined them with interest and handed them back making, at the same time, his only comment on the entire tour, "Wrote with a pen, eh? I dictate."

1168—Nicholas Murray Butler and Professor Brander Matthews of Columbia University were having a conversation, and Prof. Matthews was giving his ideas as to plagiarism, from an article of his own on that subject.

"In the case of the first man to use an anecdote," he said, "there is originality; in the case of the second there is plagiarism; with the third, it is lack of originality; and with the fourth it is drawing from a common stock."

"Yes," broke in President Butler, "and in the case of the fifth, it is research."

1169—Henry James could never rest content with the phrases that came to his tongue. He simply couldn't leave the English language alone; he would extract a word from his verbal storehouse, drop it, substitute another, then a third, and so on until he had constructed a veritable pyramid of synonyms. This terrible word-malady broke out once at Prince's Restaurant as he gave the waiter his order:

"Bring me . . . fetch me . . . carry me . . . supply me . . . in other words (I hope you are following me) serve—when it is cooked . . . scorched . . . grilled I should say—a large . . . considerable . . . meaty (as opposed to fatty) . . . chop."

1170—While Voltaire was living in retirement in Geneva, he was visited by the Italian Casanova. Voltaire had been reading some recent works by Haller, the Bernese savant, and praised him to his guest. "That is commendation which is indeed ill requited," said Casanova. "I have heard that Haller, far from returning your compliment says that your writing is more than half nonsense." "Ah well, then," returned the famous wit with a wry smile, "it may be that we were both mistaken in our judgment."

1171—One day Dr. Johnson received a message from Oliver Goldsmith that his landlady had called in an officer to arrest him for non-payment of his bill. Johnson immediately sent him a guinea and himself proceeded to the scene of battle at his own best speed. When he arrived Goldsmith had already broken the guinea to procure a bottle of Madeira, and being well stimulated by the contents, was berating his landlady soundly when Johnson entered. The heavy angel interrupted his eloquence to inquire if he had any means of raising money, whereat Goldsmith produced the manuscript of a novel. This Johnson pocketed, hurried away to Newberry the bookseller, and returned shortly with £60. This was the "Vicar of Wakefield."

1172—On the last three days of July the genius of English narrative stood in the pillory—in Cheapside first and then in the Temple. He had a triumph there. The notable "Hymn to the Pillory," which he had composed in prison, was chanted by the crowd. The flower-girls of the district wreathed the pillory with chaplets of their own weaving. Money, said to have been subscribed by the High Church faction "for his torment," circulated mysteriously among the audience, who spent it in liquor with which they drank his health. Still we are not to forget that the creator of "Crusoe" stood three times in the pillory, victim of clerical hatred.

1173—Lord Craven during the reign of King James I was anxious to meet Ben Jonson, the poet. When the latter learned of it he proceeded to call on his lordship. He was in a very shabby condition and the porter insulted him and asked him to go about his business. The poet, enraged, returned the compliments. Lord Craven, hearing the disturbance came out to inquire about it.

"I understand your lordship wishes to see me," said the poet.

"You, friend!" exclaimed Lord Craven. "Who are you?"

"Ben Jonson."

"No, no—you can't be Ben Jonson who wrote "The Silent Woman"; you look as if you could not say Boo to a goose."

"Boo, then!" cried Ben.

His lordship laughed and profusely apologized: "You are Ben Jonson after all."

1174—Sir Walter Scott told this story: "One morning last Spring I opened a huge lump of a despatch . . . the contents proved to be a MS play, by a young lady of New York who kindly requested me to read and correct it, equip it with prologue and epilogue, procure for it a favorable reception from the manager of Drury Lane, and make Murray or Constable bleed handsomely for the copyright; and inspecting the cover I found that I had been charged five pounds odd for the postage. This was bad enough,—but there was no help, so I groaned and submitted. A fortnight or so after, another packet, of not less formidable bulk arrived, and I was absent enough to break its seal too without examination.

Conceive my horror when out jumped the same identical tragedy of 'The Cherokee Lovers,' with a second epistle from the authoress, stating that, as the winds had been boisterous, she feared the vessel entrusted with her former communication might have foundered, and therefore judged it prudent to forward a duplicate."

1175—At an unguarded moment Piron was buttonholed by a poetaster who, standing his victim in a corner, announced that he was going to read to him the five entire acts of a tragedy he had just dashed off. After hearing the first scene, Piron perceived that the play was nothing but a potpourri of verses pillaged from other poets. So as he stood wearily listening he took off his hat and made a low bow to each quotation he recognized. The author at length lifted his eyes, observed Piron's repeated salutation, and asked him why he bowed so often. "Why," said Piron as he edged away, "that is the way I am accustomed to recognize old friends when I find them."

1176—Albert Smith once wrote an article in "Blackwood's," signed "A.S."

"Tut," said Douglas Jerrold, on reading the initials, "what a pity Smith will tell only two-thirds of the truth."

1177—Self-criticism is an admirable human trait. It is demonstrated in this story about Samuel Goldwyn. A ghost writer, who had been doing a series of articles purporting to be by Goldwyn, became sick and one of the pieces was done by a substitute ghost. Goldwyn, upon reading this article, expressed some dismay, saying, "This is not up to my usual standard."

1178—Bernard Shaw's name first became familiar to the general public as the result of scurrilous attacks, disguised as interviews, made upon him by a section of the London evening press. The interviewer would force his way into Shaw's modest apartment, apparently for no other purpose than to bully and insult him.

Many people maintained that Shaw must be an imaginary personage. Why did he stand it? Why didn't he kick the interviewer downstairs? Failing that why didn't he call the police? It seemed difficult to believe in the existence of a being so Christian as this poor persecuted Shaw appeared to be. Everyone talked about him.

As a matter of fact, the interviews were written by Shaw himself.

1179—When Jean Baptiste Rousseau wrote his ode "To Posterity," Voltaire, doubtful of its quality, remarked, "This poem will not reach its destination."

1180—Nathaniel Hawthorne, having lost his government position, went home, dejected and almost desperate. His wife, after a time, learning the reason for his gloom, instead of giving way to reproaches, set pen and ink on the table, and, lighting a fire in the grate, put her arms about his shoulders and said, "Now you will be able to write your book."

He took heart of grace and the world was enriched with "The Scarlet Letter."

1181—When Spenser had finished the "Faërie Queen," he carried it to the Earl of Southampton, the great patron of the poets of those days. The manuscript being sent up to the Earl, he read a few pages, and then ordered the servant to give the writer twenty pounds. Reading further, he cried in rapture, "Carry that man another twenty pounds!"

Proceeding still, he said, "Give him twenty pounds more." But at length he lost all patience, and said, "Go, turn the fellow out of the house, for if I read on I shall be ruined."

1182—Dr. Johnson was asked by Miss Brooke, a would-be authoress, to read a play she had just written, called "The Siege of Sinope." In an offhand manner she informed the Doctor that she wanted his criticism because she had too many irons in the fire to give her play the correction that she felt it might need. Without expressing any curiosity about the manuscript, the Doctor replied: "In that case, Madam, I would say: Put your tragedy where your irons are."

1183—Dryden and Otway lived opposite each other in Queen Street. Otway coming one night from the tavern, chalked upon Dryden's door, "Here lives John Dryden; he is a wit."

Dryden knew his handwriting, and, next day, chalked on Otway's door: "Here lives Tom Otway; he is oppo-site."

1184—The record of Shakespeare's wit is hardly hilarious. There was the pun àpropos of his god-paternity to one of Ben Jonson's children. Ben found him in an attitude of thought and asked him the reason. Will replied that he was pondering what to give his godchild and had just decided:

"I' faith, Ben, I'll e'en give him a dozen of good latten spoons, and thou shalt translate them."

1185—On one occasion a group was assembled, including Oscar Wilde and Frank Harris. Harris, it seems, was addicted to plagiarism in his conversation and on this occasion told as his own an anecdote which every one recognized as a paraphrase of a story of Anatole France. A silence followed the story, which Wilde at last broke. "Frank," he said gravely, "Anatole France would have spoiled that story."

1186—When Wordsworth said to Lamb, "I believe I could write like Shakespeare, if I had a mind to try it." "Yes, n-nothing is w-wanting but the m-mind," came Lamb's answer as swiftly as the stutter would allow.

1187—An Englishman being left alone with Richardson, observed to him "he was happy to pay his respects to the author of "Sir Charles Grandison," for at Paris and at the Hague and in fact, at every place I have visited it is much admired." Richardson appeared not to notice the compliment, but when all the company were assembled addressed the gentleman with, "Sir, I think you were saying something about 'Sir Charles Grandison.'"

"No sir," he replied, "I do not remember ever to have heard it mentioned."

1188—Queen Elizabeth, being much enraged against Dr. Heyward, author of the "Life of Henry the Fourth," had ordered her law officers to proceed against him, and, amongst others, inquired of Lord Bacon "if there was not treason in the book."

Bacon readily answered, "No, madam, I cannot answer for there being treason in it, but I am certain it contains much felony."

"How?" eagerly exclaimed her Majesty, "how, and wherein?"

"In many passages," replied Bacon, "which he has stolen from Tacitus."

1189—Lillah McCarthy asked George Bernard Shaw why he had come to live in England instead of seeking his inspiration among the Dublin poets—George Moore, A. E., Yeats and the others. He answered: "Lord bless you, I'm old enough to be A. E.'s father; and George Moore had not discovered Ireland then. He was in Paris studying painting. He hadn't even discovered himself. The Ireland that you know did not exist. I could not stay there, dreaming my life away on the Irish hills. England had conquered Ireland; so there was nothing for it but to come over and conquer England. Which, you will notice, I have done pretty thoroughly."

1190—William Dean Howells once read a poem which had been brought to him by an aspiring young writer. "This is a magnificent poem," said Howells. "Did you write it unaided?"

"Yes, sir," said the young man. "Every word of it."

Mr. Howells rose and said, "I'm very glad to meet you, Lord Byron. I was under the impression that you had died at Missolonghi a good many years ago."

1191—Boswell, dining one day with Dr. Johnson, asked him if he did not think that a good cook was more essential to the community than a good poet.

"I don't suppose," said Dr. Johnson, "that there's a dog in the town but what thinks so."

1192—An American had been crying aloud for an opportunity to meet H. G. Wells, the author, for whose works he had an ardent admiration. At one of these luncheons, it was arranged that he should sit next to Mr. Wells, and all through the luncheon he had a wonderful time talking to the source of his admiration. After the luncheon a friend said to him: "Well, you had your opportunity at last to meet your patron saint, didn't you?"

"Who is that?" he blandly asked.

"H. G. Wells," was the answer.

"H. G. Wells?" he echoed in surprise. "I haven't met Wells. I wish I could."

"Well," was the reply, "you certainly talked enough to him during the luncheon."

"What?" he gasped in sheer amazement. "You don't mean to say that was H. G. Wells, the author? . . . Good Heavens, man, I told that man the whole plot in detail of "Mr. Britling Sees It Through," and when I asked him if he had ever read the book, he said he had not."

1193—Sir Lewis Morris was complaining to Oscar Wilde about the neglect of his poems by the press. "It is a complete conspiracy of silence. What ought I to do, Oscar?"

"Join it," replied Wilde.

1194—The main pattern of Shelley's life was an alternation of sleeping and reading. He was, in fact, always fatigued from night reading, and had a habit of falling asleep by day, anywhere, suddenly, like a child. At Oxford he read about sixteen out of every twenty-four hours, his eyes always in a book when eating or when walking, whether in country lanes or on the streets. . . . It was his habit at this time to read standing, where possible. Trelawney reported that he left Shelley at ten one morning, standing at the mantel in his study, reading and returning at six, found him in the same position still reading, looking pale and exhausted.

1195—Some of the admirers of the 18th Century German poet Klopstock made a journey from Gottingen to Hamburg to ask him to explain a difficult passage in his works. Klopstock received them graciously, read the passage, and said: "I cannot recollect what I meant when I wrote it, but I remember it was the finest thing I ever wrote, and you cannot do better than devote your lives to the discovery of its meaning."

1196—John Erskine one time went to lecture at the University of Pennsylvania. The President of the University had never met Dr. Erskine, and did not immediately succeed in finding him when he went to meet him on the station platform. When the two men had at last identified one another, the President of the University said, "I asked one gentleman if he were Dr. Erskine, and he said emphatically, 'I should say not!' I asked another one and he said, 'I wish I were.' That proves that at least one of them had read your books."
"Yes," said Erskine. "But which one!"

1197—When D'Angeau, a Parisian writer, heard that all rank and merit were threatened with destruction on the breaking out of the Revolution, he exclaimed: "Well, come what will, I have two hundred verbs well conjugated in my escritoir!"

1198—When George Bernard Shaw, as a young man, emerged from his native Ireland and moved to England he began writing a column for a London weekly publication. At that time Oscar Wilde was enjoying his vogue as a wit and an epigram-maker. One evening an acquaintance, calling upon Wilde, happened upon a copy of the paper to which Shaw was a contributor and reading therein one of Shaw's characteristic articles which was signed with the author's initials, said to his host:
"I say, Wilde, who is this chap G. B. S. who's doing a department for this sheet?"
"He's a young Irishman named Shaw," said Wilde. "Rather forceful, isn't he?"

"Forceful," echoed the other, "well, rather! My word, how he does cut and slash! He doesn't seem to spare anyone he knows. I should say he is in a fair way to make himself a lot of enemies."

"Well," said Wilde, "as yet he hasn't become prominent enough to have any enemies. But none of his friends like him."

1199—Soon after Goldsmith's death, some people dining with Dr. Johnson were commenting freely on some parts of Goldsmith's works which in their opinion, showed neither talent nor originality. To this Dr. Johnson listened for some time, when at length his patience being exhausted he arose with great dignity, looked them full in the face, and exclaimed, "If nobody were allowed to abuse poor Goldsmith but those who could write as well, he would have few censors."

1200—Goldsmith and Johnson one time had an argument on the merits of Warburton, the writer. Goldsmith asserted that Warburton was a weak writer. Dr. Johnson refuted this, saying, "Warburton may be absurd, but he will never be weak; he flounders well."

1201—Sophocles wrote tragedies to the very end of his long life. On account of this zeal for writing he seemed to be neglecting his business affairs so his sons summoned him to court that a jury might pronounce him incompetent to manage his estate on the ground of senility. Then the old man is said to have recited to his judges a play which he had just finished and had in his hands, the "Oedipus at Colonnus," and to have asked whether the poem seemed the work of a man in his dotage. After his recitation he was freed by the vote of the jurors.

1202—Somebody told Jerrold that a friend of his, a prolific writer, was about to dedicate a book to him.

"Ah!" replied Jerrold gravely, "that's an awful weapon he has in his hands!"

1203—Barry Cornwall tells how he once said something in Lamb's presence which he thought possessed some smartness.

Lamb commended him with a stammer.

"Very well, my dear boy, very well; Ben" (taking a pinch of snuff) "Ben Jonson has said worse than that—and b-b-better."

1204—At the Garrick Club in London the witty librettist, W. S. Gilbert, was once making light of Shakespeare, to the horror of most of those surrounding him. "All right then," said Gilbert in answer to their protests. "Let us take this passage for example:
    'I would as lief be thrust through a quickset hedge,
    As cry, "Plosh," to a callow throstle.' "
"Why, that's perfectly clear," insisted one of his hearers, rising to the defense of the Bard. "It just means that this bird-lover would rather get himself all scratched up in the thorny bush than disturb the bird's song. What play is the passage from?"
"No play," said Gilbert, "I made it up—and jolly good Shakespeare too."

1205—Frank Harris, Whistler and Oscar Wilde were playing billiards one day. Whistler uttered a bon mot. Whereupon Wilde enviously said, "I wish I had said that."
"Don't worry, Oscar," retorted Harris, "you will."

1206—Dryden, when about to compose, had himself "blooded and purged."

1207—William Blake, English mystic, poet, and artist said, "I write when commanded by the spirits, and the moment I have written I see the words fly about the room in all directions. It is then published and the spirits can read. My manuscripts are of no further use. I have been tempted to burn my manuscripts, but my wife won't let me."

1208—Stevenson's prose tales often came to him as dreams. "In the small hours one morning," writes his wife, "I was awakened by cries of horror from Louis. Thinking he had a nightmare I awakened him. He said angrily: 'Why did you awaken me? I was dreaming a fine bogey tale.' "
This was "Dr. Jekyll and Mr. Hyde."

1209—The power of the pen is excellently illustrated by an incident in the war between the ancient Greeks and Romans. A group of Athenians were seized and held captive at Syracuse. To help pass the time they enacted many scenes from the plays of Euripides. Their captors were so favorably impressed by the beauty of the verses that instead of treating their prisoners cruelly as was their custom, they persuaded them to continue their play-acting and held them as honored guests.

Upon their return to Athens, the former captives went to the home of Euripides and informed him of the effect of his plays upon the supposedly heartless men of Syracuse. So great was their gratitude toward the great dramatist that they treated him as though he had actually rescued them in combat on the field of battle.

1210—Boileau, in presenting a poet to M. d'Hemery, addressed him, "Sir, I present to you a person who will give you immortality; but you must give him something to live upon in the meantime."

1211—DuBose Heyward was once lecturing in Detroit. After his talk, a group of local women insisted upon questioning him as to his opinion of their local laureate, Edgar A. Guest. After vainly seeking to side-step the issue, Heyward was at last driven to acknowledge that he did not consider Mr. Guest's work poetry. Great indignation resulted.

"Mr. Heyward," snapped one fearsome lady, "what kind of car do you drive?"

The poet and novelist was compelled to admit that he drove none.

"Eddie Guest," said the lady cuttingly, "drives a Packard."

1212—"Doctor," said Frederick Reynolds, the dramatist, to Dr. Baillie, the celebrated physician, "don't you think that I write too much for my nervous system?"

"No, I don't," said Dr. Baillie, "but I think you write too much for your reputation."

1213—In his later years a lady called upon Mark Twain to express her enthusiasm for his work. She wanted to kiss his hand. He accepted it with perfect dignity and seriousness. "How God must love you!" said the lady. "I hope so," said Mark Twain gently. After she had gone, he observed as gently and without a smile, "I guess she hasn't heard of our strained relations."

1214—An author was reading some bad verses in his poem to a friend in a very cold apartment. The critic cried out in a shaking fit:

"My dear friend, either put fire into your verses or your verses into the fire or I shall not be able to stand here any longer."

1215—After coming out of jail Frank Harris decided that he
would rather commit suicide then go in again; and as
he always had a contempt for Court orders and ignored
everything, he felt liable to arrest at any moment. So
that he might not again suffer indignity, he carried with
him a small packet of cyanide of potassium, which he
proposed to swallow before the hand of the Law could
touch him.

On his last trip to New York he was packing up at quaran-
tine when a steward came along and told him he was
wanted by the captain. Harris' heart fell. Here it was.
He concealed the packet of poison in his right hand and
followed the steward, and when he saw the captain talking to a tall, smooth, well-fed man he knew it could
only be the worst.

"You wanted me?" gulped Frank.

The captain inclined his head toward the third man, who
was eyeing Frank keenly.

"Mr. Frank Harris?" asked the American.

Frank wished he wasn't, but admitted the stigma.

"Pleased to meet you, Mr. Harris," said the large man, extending his hand. "I'm the mayor, and I've come right
off the tug-boat to tell you . . . that we are honored to
offer you the freedom of our great city."

Hastily Frank changed the poison packet into his left hand
and greeted the mayor.

1216—Shortly after the sensational reception accorded the publication of his marvelous translation of "The Arabian
Nights," Sir Richard Burton made the following statement:

"For thirty years I served Her Majesty at home and
abroad without acknowledgment or reward. I publish a
pornographic book, and at once earn 10,000 pounds and
fame. I begin at last to understand the public and what
it wants."

1217—At one time, before they had achieved the fame that later
came to them, Dorothy Parker and Robert Benchley
shared a tiny office in the Metropolitan Opera House
building. When Benchley was out in the search for
Eldorado, Miss Parker frequently found herself oppres-
sively lonely in the gloomy cubby-hole. No one ever
came to see them.

She solved this problem adroitly, and procured for herself

no end of company by inducing the sign painter to put on the office door, instead of their names, the word "Gentlemen."

1218—On the subject of proof reading some authors are a menace to their publishers, while others suffer from legitimate grievances. In one such instance an author, Ward Dorrance, wrote to his publishers on the subject of the proofs of his book: "In all the proof that has reached me windrow has been spelled window. If, in the bound book, windrow still appears as window, then neither rain nor hail nor gloom of night nor fleets of riot squads will prevent me from assassinating the man who is responsible. If the coward hides beyond my finding, I shall step into Scribner's and merely shoot up the place, Southern style."

1219—The import of Thomas Hardy's birth was so little appreciated that he was thrown aside for dead. Presently he must have been so in fact, had not the nurse glancing up from attending the mother, cried out suddenly, "Dead! Stop a minute. He's alive enough, sure!"

SEE ALSO
Dullness 193
Eccentricity 202, 208
Gentlemanliness 256
Long-Windedness 357
Modesty 386, 388
Patience 391
Practical Joking 433, 434
Quarrelsomeness 466
Rough and Ready 505
Vanity 626
Women 841
Infidelity 904
Births, Birthdays 1011, 1013
Critics 1099

RELATED SUBJECTS
Literature 1161–1162
Books 1221–1224
Playwrights 1376–1385

Newspapers 1244
Magazines 1251
Painting 1288
Miracles 1616
Deathbed Scenes 1764, 1775
Swimming 1892
Taxes 2193
Poverty 2202, 2206, 2211
Stealing 2590

BOOKS

1221—It was an Englishman, met in a train somewhere in Europe, who startled Mark Twain by saying abruptly, "Mr. Clemens, I would give ten pounds not to have read your 'Huckleberry Finn'!" And when Mark looked up, awaiting an explanation of this extraordinary remark, the Englishman smiled and added: "So that I could have again the great pleasure of reading it for the first time."

1222—Sir John Malcolm once asked Warren Hastings, who was a contemporary and a companion of Dr. Johnson and Boswell, what was his real estimation of Boswell's "Life of Johnson"?

"Sir," replied Hastings, "it's the dirtiest book in my library." Then proceeding, he added: "I knew Boswell intimately; and I well remember when his book first made its appearance, Boswell was so full of it that he could neither think nor talk of anything else: so much so, that meeting Lord Thurlow hurrying through Parliament Street to get to the House of Lords, where an important debate was expected, for which he was already too late, Boswell had the temerity to stop and accost him with: "Have you read my book?"

"Yes, damn you!" replied Lord Thurlow, "every word of it; I could not help myself."

1223—Coleridge was always a tremendous reader. While he was a student at Christ's Hospital, he used to spend his free time wandering aimlessly about London, shivering in front of the windows of book-shops and print-shops. Once, while so standing, he got, in his own words "absent-mindedly involved" with "the coat-tail pocket" of a stranger, who "at first took him for a thief, then was so charmed by his conversation that he made him free of a library in Cheapside." Thenceforth "he would run all risks in skulking out to get the two volumes to which he was entitled daily."

1224—When Dr. Johnson was told that Rousseau's "Confessions" would contain every motive that had induced him to act in every situation—"Then," replied he, "if he was an honest man, his book will not be worth a farthing."

SEE ALSO   RELATED SUBJECTS
Borrowing 125   Literature 1161–1162
Practical Joking 432   Authors 1166–1219
Censors 2354   Libraries 1226

LIBRARIES

1226—The famous American orator, Robert Ingersoll, was the owner of a remarkable and celebrated library of atheistical books. An interviewer once asked Ingersoll what the library had cost him. Thinking it over a moment, Ingersoll replied, "It certainly cost me the Governorship of Illinois, and possibly even the Presidency of the United States."

SEE ALSO
Borrowing 126
Modesty 380
Books 1223
Bigotry 1629

RELATED SUBJECTS
Literature 1161–1162
Books 1221–1224

LANGUAGE

1231—On New Year's Eve, a Negro in Harlem added a new word to the language. He stood on a street corner and shouted: "Hallalouyear!"

Before morning revelers all over the city were shouting "Hallalouyear!"

1232—"Why don't you buy a dictionary?" asked the man whose friend repeatedly consulted him as to the spelling of certain words.

"What would I do with a dictionary?" was the reply. "If I can't spell the words, I couldn't find 'em, and if I can spell 'em, I don't need a dictionary."

1233—"What's status quo, Daddy?"

"Son," said his father gravely, "that's just the name of the mess we're in."

SEE ALSO
Bishops 1495

RELATED SUBJECTS
Speeches 756–782
Talking 806–818
Literature 1161–1162

NEWSPAPERS

1236—Booth Tarkinton, while stopping at a little Indiana town, lost one of his dogs.

"Have you a newspaper in town?" he asked of the landlord.

"Right across the way, there, back of the shoemaker's," the landlord told him. "The 'Daily News'"——best little paper of its size in town.

The editor, the printer, and the printer's devil were all busy doing justice to Mr. Tarkington with an "in-our-midst" paragraph when the novelist arrived.

"I've just lost a dog," Tarkington explained after he had introduced himself, "and, I'd like to have you insert this ad for me: 'Fifty dollars reward for the return of a pointer dog answering to the name of Rex. Disappeared from the yard of the Mansion House Monday night.'"

"Why, we were just going to press, Sir," the editor said, "but we'll be only too glad to hold the edition for your ad."

Mr. Tarkington returned to the hotel. After a few minutes he decided, however, that it might be well to add, "No questions asked" to his advertisement, and returned to the "Daily News" office.

The place was deserted, save for the skinny little freckle-faced devil, who sat perched on a high stool, gazing wistfully out of the window.

"Where is everybody?" Tarkington asked.

"Gawn to hunt th' dawg," replied the boy, without removing his gaze from the distant fields.

1237—They called Eleanor Roosevelt "God's gift to newspaper women" because she made it easier for women to get news of the White House, and because she made jobs for them by making much news which only women could get. No previous First Lady held press conferences or gave news directly. Nevertheless, there was painful truth as well as humorous fiction in the Women's National Press Club skit in which a frazzled inmate of the "Eleanor Roosevelt Home for Exhausted Newspaper Women" clasped her hands, and petitioned Heaven: "Dear God, let me pray the prayer they say that Franklin (Roosevelt) prays. Just for one day, God, please make her tired! Dear God, just for one day!"

1238—A Metropolitan paper once chartered a locomotive to rush a green reporter to a near-by town to scoop all rivals with first news of a fire that was burning the place down. A couple of hours later the managing editor got a telegram from the bright young man reading: "Have arrived at the fire. What shall I do?"

The editor replied: "Find the place where the fire is hottest and jump in!"

1239—One of the first big assignments that fell to Maury H. B. Paul as a young society editor was the covering of the seasonal opening of the Metropolitan Opera House. He had not been long in New York and was not familiar enough with the personalities to identify the occupants of the lavish boxes.

He resorted to the device of slipping around the corridor during the act and copying the names from the brass plates on the doors. The following day he was summoned to the office of his employer, Frank Munsey.

"I have just had a telephone call from Mrs. Stuyvesant Fish," said Munsey. "She has read your account of the Metropolitan première. She thought you might be interested to know that you have succeeded in opening half the graves in Woodlawn Cemetery."

Thus Mr. Paul learned, the hard way, that the name of the original box-owner is usually left on the door no matter who subsequently may occupy it.

1240—When Heywood Broun, as a cub reporter, once went to interview Senator Smoot for the "N. Y. World," the legislator from the Mormon State pompously said, "No, I have nothing to say."

"I know," coldly replied young Broun, "now let's get down to the interview."

1241—In an upstate New York town, certain busybodies began to carp about the carelessness of the grammar and general diction of the editor of the local weekly newspaper. Having heard echoes of this, that dignitary rose at the next town meeting and said, "I hear I been criticised somewhat by some of you folks for usin' poor grammar. I have three good reasons for it. To begin with, I don't know any better. If I did, none of you would know the difference; and more than that, if I spoke and wrote any better than I do, I'd be managing editor of a big New York paper at a decent salary and you farmers would lose the best darned editor in Herkimer county."

1242—Wendell Phillips once addressed an abolitionist meeting in Boston where the audience was hostile to him. They yelled and sang and completely drowned his voice. The reporters were seated in a row just under the platform. Phillips made no attempt to address the howling audience, but bent over and seemed to be speaking in a low tone to the reporters. By and by the curiosity of the audience was excited; they ceased to clamor and tried to hear what he was saying to the reporters. Phillips looked at them coldly and said:

"Go on, gentlemen, go on. I do not need your ears.

Through these pencils I speak to thirty millions of people."

1243—A man who considered himself a humorist sent a selection of his original jokes to the editor of a newspaper, and confidently awaited a check. He was much elated when, a few days later, he received a letter bearing the imprint of the newspaper. Upon opening it, however, instead of a check, he found a brief note: "Dear Sir: Your jokes received. Some we have seen before, some we have not seen yet."

1244—When Robert Bridges came back from America, he told how when he evaded the interviewers who met him on the boat, they got back at him by printing in their papers in their largest caption: "The King's Canary Refuses to Sing."

1245—While in Denver on the "Tribune," Eugene Field hung on the wall: "God bless our proofreader. He can't call for him too soon."

1246—The editor of a tiny small-town newspaper had cherished for many years a set of old-fashioned wooden scarehead type of some 60 point size. On more than one occasion his assistants had tried to induce him to use it, but he always firmly vetoed the idea.

One summer the old man went away for a short fishing trip. In his absence a cyclone struck the town; tore the steeple off the church, unroofed several houses, sucked a couple of wells dry, and scattered a few barns around. No bigger calamity had hit the town in years. So, figuring "Now's our chance," his assistants got down the 60 point type from the shelf and set up a sensational front page headline with it.

Two days later the editor came storming into the office in a high dudgeon. "Balls of fire!" he shouted. "What d'ye mean by taking down that type for a cyclone? All these years I've been savin' that type for the Second Coming of Christ!"

1247—It was at the Yale-Princeton game on Thanksgiving day, 1890, that Richard Harding Davis risked his job. His managing editor, Arthur Brisbane, had a sidelines ticket but he was accompanied by a friend who was behind the fence without one. Let Reporter Davis turn over his pass to the friend and retire to the stands. Davis refused pointblank and with undiplomatic emphasis. He was reporting this game, it was best done from the sidelines, there was his post, and there he was staying, he informed his chief. Otherwise, he remarked, McClay would take his head off. Rather than the fury of his city editor, he would chance the wrath, once removed, of his managing editor. Brisbane and guest relegated themselves to the stands.

When Brisbane told the story at the office that night, a subordinate asked him if Davis was to be fired.

"No," said the editor, "raise his salary!"

1248—Out of newspaper offices come some very extravagant yarns. There is the one told about Chapin, famous New York editor, who made it a strict rule that his employees were not to hang around the office on "days off."

A certain reporter on his staff fell in with a friend on his day off, Thursday, and they went on a "bat" that lasted for six days. On the seventh day, a trifle weak but cold sober, the reporter, realizing that he was in for trouble, decided that the best thing to do would be to go to the office and get it over with.

When the boss came in the reporter was waiting in his office. Without waiting for an explanation, Chapin shouted, "What the hell are you doing here on your day off? Get out of here and don't come back until tomorrow at nine."

SEE ALSO	RELATED SUBJECTS
Boners 107, 109, 113, 114, 117, 119	Literature 1161–1162
	Magazines 1251–1252
Brevity 131, 133	
Exaggeration 224	
Extravagance 232	Sickness 1701
Patriotism 403	Death 1747
Vanity 614, 618	Cabinet Members 1953
Gossip 825, 826	Advertising 2101

MAGAZINES

1251—"Dear Jack London," wrote the editor of a well-known magazine, "If I don't receive your story within twenty-four hours, I'll come up to your room and kick you downstairs. And I always keep my promises."

London sent this reply:

"Dear Dick: If I did all my work with my feet, I'd keep my promises too."

1252—The distinguished editor, the late George Horace Lorimer, was obliged, as are all editors, to reject by far the greater number of stories sent to him.

In the early days of his career when a great burden of editorial reading fell to him he once received a letter from an indignant woman, who said, "Last week you rejected my story. I know that you did not read it for, as a test, I pasted together pages 15, 16 and 17, and the manuscript came back with the pages still pasted. You are a fraud and you turn down stories without even reading them."

Mr. Lorimer replied: "Madam, at breakfast when I open an egg, I don't have to eat the whole egg to discover it is bad."

SEE ALSO
Women 842
Literature 1162

RELATED SUBJECTS
Literature 1161–1162
Authors 1166–1219
Newspapers 1236–1248

ART

1256—Someone called, "Monsieur Degas!" It was Vibert, the well-known painter of "The Cardinals."

"You must come to see our exhibition of watercolors," he said. Then he gave a sidelong glance at the old mackintosh Degas was wearing, and added: "You may find our frames and rugs a little too fancy for you, but art is always a luxury, isn't it?"

"Yours, perhaps," retorted Degas; "but mine is an absolute necessity."

RELATED SUBJECTS
Literature 1161–1162
Painting and Drawing 1261–1293
Sculpture 1296–1297
Architecture 1301–1302
Music 1303–1306
Plays 1386–1388

PAINTING AND DRAWING

1261—Of Correggio the painter it is told that upon seeing one of the works of Raphael, he could only express his feelings by exclaiming with a noble pride in their common art: "And I too am a painter!"

1262—Tolstoy tells the following story about Brulov, the Russian artist.

"One day, in correcting a sketch made by one of his pupils, he added a stroke or two with his own brush, and immediately put the breath of life into what had been a very mediocre piece of work. 'But my sketch is entirely changed,' said the pupil, 'and all you've done is to add a few strokes to it.'

" 'The reason for that,' answered Brulov, 'is that Art entered the thing just where those strokes began.' "

1263—Degas rarely ever indulged in anything more than mildly biting repartee except when art or "the established order" was attacked. Bonnet, for instance, was showing him a picture by one of his pupils, representing a warrior drawing his bow.

"Just see how well he aims!" said Bonnet.

"Aiming at a prize—isn't he?" replied Degas.

1264—Although the French public at first said only that cubism was crazy, a leading art merchant added, "I am now buying Picasso not because I have any taste for him but because he will be worth a lot of money someday."

1265—Honoré de Balzac lived many years in a cold and all but empty attic. There was no flame in his fireplace, no picture on his wall. But on one wall he inscribed with charcoal: "Rosewood paneling with commode;" on another, "Gobelin tapestry with Venetian mirror," and in the place of honor over the fireless grate, "Picture by Raphael."

1266—When someone asked the famous painter Orpen: "How do you mix your colors?" he answered: "With brains, sir."

1267—When Tintoretto was a little boy he entered Titian's studio, but that master could not foresee the artistic in the boy and sent him home after three days, with the message, "He will never be anything but a dauber."

1268—The artist Turner invited Charles Kingsley, the author, to his studio to view his picture of a storm at sea. Kingsley was wrapt in admiration.

"How did you do it, Turner?" he exclaimed.

"I wished to paint a storm at sea," answered Turner, "so I went to the coast of Holland and engaged a fisherman to take me out in his boat in the next storm. The storm was brewing, and I went down to his boat and bade him

bind me to its mast. Then he drove the boat out into
the teeth of the storm. The storm was so furious that I
longed to be down in the bottom of the boat and allow
it to blow over me. But I could not; I was bound to the
mast. Not only did I see that storm and feel it, but it
blew itself into me till I became part of the storm.
And then I came back and painted that picture."

1269—Cézanne observed that Ambroise Vollard was looking
with some curiosity at a row of big druggist's pots set
out on the floor, and bearing abbreviated Latin inscrip-
tions: Jusqui., Aqu., Still., Ferug., Rib., Sulf., Cup., and
volunteered:
"That, Monsieur, is my paint box. I am going to show 'em
that with drugs I can paint beautiful things, while they,
with their fine colors, make nothing but drugs!"

1270—Orozco is a deeply embittered soul; a veritable glare comes
from behind the very thick lenses of his glasses. He is
one-armed; his body has a tortured twist. But in personal relations Orozco is never bitter. He is the kindliest
man I know, solicitous toward other folk, warmly com-
passionate . . . His early work, not sufficiently academic, was derided in Mexico. Disheartened, he decided
to go to the United States where artistic experimentation seemed to have more of a chance. But at the American border a comprehensive set of drawings was seized
in the customs and declared indecent. They were torn
up and ground under the feet of our outraged officials,
who in those days of contempt for Mexico saw no reason
for being considerate of any Mexican, and least of all an
artist with dubious drawings. Only half a dozen of those
early drawings—the House of Tears series—survived,
and they are among the finest things Orozco has ever
produced.

1271—At a period of Donatello's life he went to Pisa to execute
some works there which were found so wonderful that
the Pisans broke out into transports of delight, praising
the artist to the skies. Oddly enough, however, this excessive praise proved distasteful to the sculptor. He declared that he must go back to Florence for the whim-
sical reason, that where he was praised by everybody he
would soon forget all he knew, grow lazy and self-
satisfied, whereas at home in Florence he was noto-
riously abused and found fault with and thus forced

always to produce his best, "the constant blame forcing him," as he put it, "to study and consequently to greater achievements."

1272—Samuel F. B. Morse, who was a painter before he invented the telegraph, once asked a physician friend to look at his painting of a man in death agony. "Well," Morse inquired after the doctor had scrutinized it carefully, "what is your opinion?"

"Malaria," said the doctor.

1273—Alfred Steiglitz, the husband of Georgia O'Keeffe, has also always been the exclusive handler of her paintings. In most cases he has been reluctant to part with them at all. Occasionally he would name, in a sort of irritation, a sum which he regarded as safely beyond the pale. He once demanded $25,000 for a series of five flower paintings. To his astonishment the price was accepted without question. Miss O'Keeffe was so dumbfounded that for three months she was unable to paint.

1274—In 1906, Gertrude Stein, posed eighty times for Picasso's portrait of her, after which he wiped the face off, saying he couldn't "see" her any more, and then finished the likeness in Spain, where he couldn't see her at all. He also gave her this portrait because, as he later said, at that time in his career the difference between a gift and a sale was, after all, negligible. He also said, when friends complained that the portrait didn't look like her, that someday she'd look like the portrait.

1275—A philosopher called upon a young art student who had just set to work in his first studio after a brilliant course in the art schools of Europe. They talked of the problems relating to beauty, ideals and ambitions. Upon his departure the philosopher paused upon the threshold of the studio and said to the young painter:

"Your art will cease to be great art unless you keep in touch with humanity."

1276—A rich merchant of Genoa commissioned Donatello to carve for him a colossal head. When the model was finished the Genoese objected to the price, saying that he had been engaged only a month on it, and that the sum asked was equal to half a florin a day.

Donatello, turning round, exclaimed that it was possible in a moment to destroy the work of a year, and with a sudden push he threw the head to the ground, where it broke into a hundred pieces.

"It was clear," he said, "that the purchaser ought to confine himself to vegetables and leave art alone."

1277—The works of of Millais, the painter, had been collected in a gallery in London, and a friend, Lady Constance Leslie, went early in the day to the exhibition. Going up the stairs, she encountered the painter going out with head bowed down. As she greeted him and he looked up she saw tears in his eyes. "Ah, dear Lady Constance," he said, "you see me unmanned. Well, I'm not ashamed of averring that in looking at my earliest pictures I have been overcome with chagrin that I so far failed in my maturity to fulfill the full forecast of my youth."

1278—When Sir Humphry Davy returned from a visit to Paris he was asked how the picture galleries had impressed him. "The finest collection of frames that I ever saw," he said.

1279—Mark Twain once visited the artist Whistler in his studio and was looking over his pictures. He started to touch one canvas. "Oh," cried Whistler, "don't touch that! Don't you see, it isn't dry yet?"

"I don't mind," said Mark Twain, "I have gloves on."

1280—The fine American painter, Georgia O'Keeffe, was slow in appreciating the monetary value of her work, and has never ceased to be somewhat indifferent to it. Characteristic of her reactions was the day when the first sale of one of her pictures occurred. The canvas brought $400. Miss O'Keeffe, who was standing nearby while the transaction was completed, became pale; not because of the sum of money but at the thought that she would never see her painting again.

1281—Whistler once undertook to get a fellow painter's work into the autumn salon. He succeeded and the picture was hung. But the painter, going to see his masterpiece with Whistler on varnishing day, uttered a terrible oath when he beheld it! "Good gracious," he groaned. "You're exhibiting my picture upside down."

"Hush," said Whistler, "the committee refused it the other way."

1282—Correggio was yet in the prime of life when he completed his great work, "The Assumption of the Virgin," which he painted on the ceiling of the dome of the cathedral at Parma. So ignorantly unappreciated was his masterly performance by the canons, his employers, that they not only refused the unfortunate artist the price they had agreed upon, but paid him five hundred crowns, which was all they would allow, in copper. Correggio was carrying home this money to his family who were living in great poverty in a neighboring village, when overcome by the heat of the weather, and the weight of his coppers, he was tempted to slake his thirst at a spring by the wayside, and the consequence was an inflammatory attack, which soon proved fatal.

1283—The great moral satirist, Hogarth, was once drawing in a room where many of his friends were assembled, and among them a young lady. As she stood by Hogarth, she expressed a wish to learn to draw caricature. "Alas! young lady," said Hogarth, "it is not a faculty to be envied. Take my advice, and never draw caricature—by the long practice of it I have lost the enjoyment of beauty. I never see a face but distorted. I have never the satisfaction to behold the human face divine."

1284—Abe Lincoln was shown a picture done by a very indifferent hand, and asked to give an opinion of it.
"Why," said Lincoln, "the painter is a very good painter and observes the Lord's commandments."
"What do you mean by that, Mr. Lincoln?"
"Why, I think," answered Lincoln, "that he hath not made to himself the likeness of anything that is in the heaven above, or that is in the earth beneath or that is in the waters under the earth."

1285—On one occasion a woman said to Whistler: "I just came up from the country this morning along the Thames, and there was an exquisite haze in the atmosphere which reminded me so much of your little things. It was really a perfect series of Whistlers."
"Yes, madam," responded Whistler gravely, "Nature is creeping up."

1286—Degas stopped to look at each canvas, and presently gave a little exclamation of disgust.
"To think," he remarked, "that not one of these fellows has

ever gone so far as to ask himself what art is all about!"
"Well, what is it all about?" countered the critic.
"I have spent my whole life trying to find out. If I knew
I should have done something about it long ago."

1287—Whistler completed a portrait for a wealthy and highly
placed client, who was dissatisfied with the finished
work. "I really think, Mr. Whistler," he explained, "that
it's a bad work of art."
Whistler shrugged and looked coolly at the man. He said,
"But then you must admit that you're not a good work
of nature."

1288—Whistler once admired a picture Rossetti was painting,
and some time afterward asked him how it was going.
"All right," said Rossetti. "I have ordered a stunning
frame for it."
Later Whistler saw it framed, but not at all advanced in
execution. "You've done nothing to it since I saw it,
have you?"
"No-o," said Rossetti, "but I've written a stunning sonnet
on the subject."
"Then," replied Whistler, "take out the picture and frame
the sonnet."

1289—A painter was advised to turn physician: for now all his
faults were seen; then they would be buried.

1290—Whistler detested Turner. Unwittingly, a lady approached
him one day requesting, "Mr. Whistler, my husband has
discovered in an auction shop what he thinks are two
genuine Turners. Would you be kind enough to come
and tell us whether they're genuine Turners or imitation
Turners."
"Madam," said Whistler, "that's a fine distinction."

1291—Helen Westley, the actress, while playing in a Theatre
Guild show in Chicago, decided to see the sights of the
city. Some days later, a culture-bitten colleague en-
thusiastically raised the subject of her visit to the gal-
leries of the Art Institute. "The room of contemporary
American painters is superb!" she chanted.
"I prefer the Rembrandt Room," commented Frank
Reicher. Then everyone turned questioningly to the
noted character actress.
"And which room in the Museum do you prefer, Helen?"

"I?" remarked the incorrigible Miss Westley, without blinking an eyelash, "why I prefer the Ladies Room."

1292—At a showing of the work of Rockwell Kent, a woman, who had been gazing at one of his celebrated angels, approached him and said, "No angel ever looked like that!"

"Have you ever seen an angel, Madam?" asked Kent.

1293—Ambroise Vollard once told Degas of a painter who had come to him, exclaiming, "At last I have found my true style!"

"Well," said Degas, "I'm glad I haven't found my style yet. I'd be bored to death."

SEE ALSO
Eccentricity 205
Generosity 248
Modesty 390
Practical Joking 435, 436
Rough and Ready 499, 506
Snobbishness 551
Beauty 668
Age 676
Flirtation 861
Churchmen 1451
Popes 1501

RELATED SUBJECTS
Art 1256
Sculpture 1296–1297
Architecture 1301–1302

Doctors 1669
Deathbed Scenes 1765
Advertising 2107
Real Estate 2142
Poverty 2205, 2206
Civilians in War 2340, 2344

SCULPTURE

1296—A cobbler detected a fault in the shoe-latchet of one of Apelles' sculptures and the artist, recognizing his superior information, rectified the fault. The cobbler, blown up by his success, next ventured to criticize the legs, for which he was indignantly kicked out. "Keep to your trade," said the sculptor. "Let not a cobbler overstep his last."

1297—This is a story told by Anatole France. Rodin had just finished an imposing statue of the poet, Victor Hugo, standing upright on the crest of a rock, with Muses and Ocean deities circling about him. One morning the sculptor brought a troupe of journalists to his studio to contemplate the new work. Unfortunately, the evening before, he had left the window open and, as a terrible storm had broken out during the night, a stream of

water had reduced the huge group to a formless pulp.
Victor Hugo had flopped down into a sea of mud.

Rodin opened the door and allowed his guests to go in
first. Suddenly he beheld the disaster. He all but tore
his beard with despair. But the chorus of praise had
already begun:

"Wonderful! Marvelous! Victor Hugo rising from this
bed of slime, what a symbol! Master, it is a stroke of
genius! You have tried to represent the ignominy of
an epoch in which the inspiration of the bard alone survived, noble and pure. How beautiful!"

"Do you think so?" Rodin asked timidly.

"Of course! It is the masterpiece of masterpieces."

SEE ALSO   RELATED SUBJECTS
Critics 1101   Art 1256
Atheists 1653   Painting and Drawing 1261–1293
Deathbed Scenes 1773   Architecture 1301–1302
Battles 2378

ARCHITECTURE

1301—That celebrated landmark of Paris, the Eiffel Tower, has
been the butt of much abuse in its time. Balzac is said
to have fled screaming from the sight of it, saying that
he could not endure its colossal vulgarity.

William Morris, the English poet, appears to have shared
a somewhat similar view. During a long stay in Paris
he very nearly cloistered himself in the restaurants of
the Eiffel Tower, not only taking all his meals but even
doing much of his writing there.

"You're certainly impressed by the Tower," someone once
remarked to him.

"Impressed," said Morris, "I stay here because it's the only
place in Paris where I can avoid seeing the damn thing!"

1302—An Egyptian architect was commissioned by one of the
Pharaohs to build a lighthouse at the mouth of the Nile.
On a piece of rock, duly selected, Cnidus, the architect,
erected the house of light. Engraved upon the cement
which covered the outside of the lighthouse was the
name of Pharaoh.

In a few years the effect of wind and rain had worn the
cement away and Pharaoh's name had vanished. Then
it was discovered that the wily Cnidus had engraved his
own name in the masonry beneath.

RELATED SUBJECTS
Art 1256
Painting and Drawing 1261–1293
Sculpture 1296–1297

MUSIC

1303—"No, Madam," replied Dr. Johnson to the lady who had asked him if he liked music, "but of all noises, I think music is the least disagreeable."

1304—President Ulysses S. Grant had a violent dislike of music. One time during a concert at Peabody Institute in Baltimore he turned to Robert Winthrop sitting next to him and said, "Why, Mr. Winthrop, I know only two tunes. One is, 'Yankee Doodle' and the other isn't."

1305—At the first performance of the celebrated "Miserere" of Lully before the Court of Louis XIV in the chapel of Versailles, the monarch being on his knees during the whole time, necessarily kept his Court in the same position. At its conclusion the King asked the Count de Grammont his opinion of it. "Sire," he replied, "the music is very soft to the ears, but very hard to the knees."

1306—The musical world is full of smart alecs, tricksters and faddists; such as the so-called tune detectives, who delight in singling out musical phrases which may appear identically in the work of a number of different composers.

Such men ignore the fact that music is a form of language in which the words and phrases are common stock, to some degree, much as with the spoken word. Moreover it is by no means uncommon for a composer to pay some colleague the compliment of quotation, again as practiced in the literary world. This is sometimes carried to the length seen in some of the notable variations upon themes.

Brahms waited until the rich maturity of his talents before composing his first symphony. When this great work was in its final rehearsal, before the première playing, there was in the auditorium a certain officious musical upstart fond of seizing opportunities to display his great musical learning. This person hastened to the podium at the end of the rehearsal and, pulling at Brahms' coat-tail, said "Meister, in the fourth movement

there is a theme which is very similar to that used by
Beethoven in the fourth movement of the Ninth Symphony."

Brahms wheeled majestically upon the upstart. "Any ass
knows that!" he roared.

SEE ALSO   RELATED SUBJECTS
Boners 114   Literature 1161–1297
                          Art 1256
                          Composers 1311–1326
                          Conductors 1331–1339
                          Operas and Concerts 1341–1348
                          Instrumentalists 1351–1363
                          Singers 1366–1368
                          Dancers 1371
                          Plays 1386–1388

COMPOSERS

1311—"I feel," said Max Dreyfus to George Gershwin, "that you
have some good stuff in you. It'll come out. It may take
months, it may take a year, it may take five years, but
I'm convinced that the stuff is there. I'll tell you what
I'm willing to do: I'll gamble on you. I'll give you
thirty-five dollars a week, without any set duties. Just
step in every morning, so to speak, and say, 'Hello.'
The rest will follow."

1312—Something of this unwinking poker-faced, toneless com-
icality is in the routine George—the George Gershwin
away from his ruled paper, his old Steinway grand. He
will inform the reporters that he has just received the
$50,000 he demanded of the movie people for the rights
to use his "Rhapsody in Blue" in Whiteman's film, "The
King of Jazz." "That's more than Beethoven or Schubert
ever got for a composition, eh? I guess that wouldn't
make them turn over in their graves!"

1313—The Master's (Brahms') intolerance, however, was of
longer standing than his last illness. A generation before, in the middle seventies, this quality lost him his
warm friend and zealous propagandist, the conductor
Hermann Levi. Brahms was visiting Levi in Munich
when, in the course of a musical conversation, Levi mentioned the names of Gluck and Wagner in the same
connection. Whereupon the Master shouted angrily:
"One doesn't pronounce these two names like that, one

after the other!" He rushed from the room, and left town the following day.

1314—Toward the end of his life Brahms confided to a friend: "Recently I started various things, symphonies and so on, but nothing would work out well. Then I thought: I'm already too old, and resolved energetically to write no more. I considered that I had all my life been sufficiently industrious and had achieved enough; here I had before me a care-free old age and could enjoy it in peace. And that made me so happy, so contented, so delighted—that all at once the writing began to go."

1315—Mascagni, the composer of Cavalleria Rusticana, once heard an organ-grinder playing excerpts from his opera underneath his window. The composer, annoyed by the slow tempo of the playing, rushed into the street.
"Here, here," he cried to the street-musician, "I am Mascagni—I will show you how to play this music correctly." Thereupon, he gave the crank-handle of the barrel-organ a few rapid turns.
The next day Mascagni, hearing the barrel-organist again, put his head out of the window and read the following sign over the hurdy-gurdy: "Pupil of Mascagni."

1316—Mendelssohn's friend Madame Frege sang to him a song with the words:
"Time marches on by night as well as day,
And many march by night who fain would stay."
"Oh, that has a dreary sound!" the composer cried with a shudder—"but it is just what I feel."
He then suddenly rose, as pale as death, and paced the room hurriedly, complaining that his hands were as cold as ice.
He died within a month.

1317—A lad once asked Mozart how to write a symphony.
Mozart said, "You're a very young man. Why not begin with ballads?"
The aspirant urged, "You composed symphonies when you were 10 years old."
"Yes," replied Mozart, "but I didn't ask 'how?'"

1318—Robert Fuchs, a reminiscent composer, was present one day when a highly Brahmsian composition of his was played to Brahms, and nearly fainted with embarrassment when the Master, assuming innocent bewilderment, asked him: "But what piece of mine is that?"

1319—Brahms attended a rehearsal of his clarinet quintet, and was so touched that tears came to his eyes. To cover his emotion he marched across the room, closed the first violin part and growled: "Stop the terrible music!"

1320—When Nietzsche one day observed to Wagner that in "Figaro" Mozart had invented the music of intrigue, Wagner replied: "On the contrary! In 'Figaro' Mozart dissolved the intrigue in music."

1321—While George Gershwin was at work on the "Rhapsody in Blue," his father thrust his head into the room. "Make it good, George," he counselled, "it might be important." So, indeed, it proved as Pa Gershwin was able to demonstrate irrefutably to a doubting Thomas. "Of course it's a great piece! Doesn't it take fifteen minutes to play?"

1322—Brahms hated to be called Meister (Master) or Tonkunstler (musical artist), for, he contended, "You might as well call me 'Cobblemaster' or 'Maker of Clay Stoves,' and have done with it!"

1323—The composer, Gounod, had a fabulous memory. When he was about 19 he had attended a rehearsal of "Roméo et Juliette," which was still in manuscript and was being directed by the composer, Berlioz. The next day he called upon Berlioz, sat at the piano and proceeded to play the entire finale of the opera from memory. The composer stared at him in terror and astonishment. Had his work been pirated? Was it some incredible coincidence?
"Where the devil did you get that music?" he demanded.
"At your rehearsal yesterday," replied Gounod.

1324—Irving Thalberg once sought to persuade the composer, Arnold Schoenberg, to write the score for the film, "The Good Earth." The producer's representative found the composer unenthused over the idea, and tried to work him up about its possibilities.
"Think of it," he said, "you've got a scene with a terrific buildup; a storm, wheat fields swaying in the wind. The earth trembles. In the midst of the earthquake and storm O-Lan gives birth to a baby. What an opportunity for music."

"With so much going on," said Schoenberg, "What do you want with music?"

1325—When the American composer, George Gershwin, died, a man of sentiment combined with musical aspirations wrote an elegy in his honor. He sought out Oscar Levant. Reluctantly Levant granted him a hearing. Eagerly the man rendered the piece with his own hands and then turned expectantly toward Levant, seeking approbation.

"I think it would have been better," Levant said, "if you had died and Gershwin had written the elegy."

1326—At the premiere performance of César Franck's symphony the gentle, benign old composer, who had seldom ventured out of his organ loft, was seated in the audience. The stupid and blasé assemblage were hostile to this fine work which did not until later find its proper appreciation. One pompous and arrogant woman, who chanced to be seated directly behind the composer, remarked loudly in the interim between two of the movements, "Who is the creature who writes this abominable music?"

The gentle Franck turned around in his seat and said courteously, "Madam, it is I."

<table>
<tr><td>SEE ALSO</td><td>RELATED SUBJECTS</td></tr>
<tr><td>Drinking 41</td><td>Music 1303–1306</td></tr>
<tr><td>Boners 115</td><td>Operas and Concerts 1341–1348</td></tr>
<tr><td>Eccentricity 206</td><td></td></tr>
<tr><td>Generosity 247</td><td></td></tr>
<tr><td>Kindness 316</td><td></td></tr>
<tr><td>Pompousness 426</td><td></td></tr>
<tr><td>Practical Joking 437</td><td></td></tr>
<tr><td>Deathbed Scenes 1766</td><td></td></tr>
</table>

CONDUCTORS

1331—One of the great traditions of contemporary music is the astounding and infallible memory of Arturo Toscanini. One time early in his career, when Toscanini was a cellist, he formed an acquaintance with the violinists, Romanini and Enrico Polo, and with Bolzoni, the composer. Bolzoni once composed an Adagio which the group performed on a special occasion. More than a year later the two violinists and Toscanini again met. But Bolzoni was absent. "What a pity," exclaimed some-

one, "that Bolzoni has the score. If he had left us a copy
we might have had that quartet we liked so much."
Toscanini said, "Give me a pencil and paper."
Whereupon he proceeded to write down all four parts of
the Adagio from memory.

1332—The fine conductor, Bruno Walter, is a man of a gentle
and sensitive temperament. The first time that he conducted the New York Philharmonic the noted cellist,
Alfred Wallenstein, occupied the first cellist's chair.
Walter was annoyed and embarrassed by the fact that
Wallenstein ignored him throughout rehearsal and con-
certs alike, gazing everywhere in the auditorium, except
at the conductor, while playing. Where another man
might have flown into a rage, Walter merely asked that
Wallenstein come to speak privately with him.
"Tell me, Mr. Wallenstein," said Walter mildly, "what
is your ambition?"
"I should like some day to be a conductor."
"Well," said Walter gently, "I only hope you never have
Wallenstein in front of you."

1333—The eminent conductor, Malcolm Sargent, was conducting
a Royal Choral Society rehearsal of "The Messiah." He
was displeased with the women's section's rendering of
"For Unto Us a Child is Born." Calling for attention, he
begged, "Just a little more reverence, please, and not so
much astonishment."

1334—When Basil Cameron, the conductor, was starting on his
musical career he looked round for a good name and decided on Von Hindenburg. And a good name it was, up
to the beginning of August 1914, when Von Hindenburg
quietly disappeared like so many "Germans" of the period. In his case, however, the public was astounded to
hear that the brilliant young conductor they had admired
was commanding the German Army.

1335—A certain young violinist came to Leopold Stokowski with
a very forceful and impressive letter of introduction from
an old and respected friend of the notable conductor.
"I'm very sorry that there's no opening for you now in
the orchestra," Stokowski explained, "but if you can stay
in Philadelphia for a while, I'll be glad to place you at
the first opportunity."
The chance came little more than a week later, when the
second violinist was rushed to the hospital for an ap-

pendectomy only a few hours before a concert. Stokowski called the young aspirant and said, "We're playing
a Beethoven cycle. Can you manage the second violin in
the Seventh and Eighth Symphonies?"

Eagerly the young man assured him he could. In the opening passages of the Seventh Symphony that night the
conductor listened sharply for the strains of the second
violin and noted that the new-comer seemed to be doing
well. Glancing at him, he was shocked to see an expression of great agony and anguish on the violinist's face.
"Heavens," he thought, "there must be a curse on the
second violin. Will he be able to last out the program!"

As the symphony progressed from movement to movement, the second violinist appeared to writhe and gri-
mace in increasing torture. Stokowski's concern began
to change to anger and irritation. At the intermission,
seeking to control himself, he went to the musician's
dressing room and demanded, "Are you sick?"

"Why, no," said the young man.

"Is there anything paining you?"

"Not at all."

"Then," shouted Stokowski angrily, "you must not approve of my conducting."

"Oh, sir," said the musician, "it's a privilege to play under
you."

"Then why on earth were you making such outlandish
faces?"

"Oh, that—" said the young man. "Well, you see, sir, I
just don't like music."

1336—The first time the musical instrument called "the Serpent"
was used at a London concert over which the German
composer Handel presided, he was so much surprised at
the coarseness of its tones that he called out sharply:
"Vat de devil is dat?" On being informed it was the
Serpent, he replied: "It never can be de serpent vat
seduced Eve."

1337—The noted conductor, Eugene Goosens, is fond of a story
about a titled Englishman of no real musical education
or ability, who desired to be a conductor. He hired a
symphony orchestra and a costly concert hall and, willy-
nilly, began conducting a rehearsal in preparation for
the launching of a great concert. He had no ability
whatsoever to control the orchestra and the musicians

found themselves struggling to keep time against the erratic and vague gestures of their conductor. The rehearsal got nowhere and, after a couple of hours, everyone was hot, tired and irritable. At this time, in the midst of a slow, stately passage, the kettle drummer, who was rattled, anticipated an attack by some 12 bars and came crashing in. Flying into a fury, the conductor hurled down his baton, glared at the players, and shouted, "Who did that?"

1338—During a rehearsal a second violinist grazed the string next to the one he had intended to play. The sound of this slip was almost inaudible. Few people would have noticed it. But Toscanini stopped the orchestra, pointed his baton at the culprit without hesitation, and cried out sharply, "One string will be quite enough, if you please."

1339—Once, when the Philharmonic was rehearsing César Franck's Symphony under the direction of Toscanini, he interrupted the rehearsal and protested that the clarinetist was playing a wrong note. The clarinetist denied the charge, and repeated the passage from his score before him.

"The note is A," Toscanini said, "Not A Flat."

"No, no," said the clarinetist, and came forward with his score to prove it. Toscanini peered nearsightedly at the page.

"This is an error," he said, and, sending for the full conductor's score, which he never used, he opened it and demonstrated the error of which the clarinetist himself was innocent, an error in the part-copyist's work.

RELATED SUBJECTS
Music 1303–1306
Operas and Concerts 1341–1348

OPERAS AND CONCERTS

1341—Walking with a friend one day, Fritz Kreisler passed a large fish shop where a fine catch of codfish, with mouths open and eyes staring, were arranged in a row. Kreisler suddenly stopped, looked at them, and clutching his friend by the arm, exclaimed:

"Heavens! That reminds me—I should be playing at a concert!"

1342—So dependent on the adulation of his audiences was Franz Liszt that he is said to have paid women 25 francs to faint at his concerts. The swoon was always timed to occur just before the climax of his most popular run. Liszt would leap from his piano-stool, pick up the swooner and leave the rest of the audience impressed by his brilliance and dismayed by their own stolidity. Once, however, the hired fainter forgot to faint. Liszt's fingers flew up the keys—but he could not finish the run. So he fainted himself.

1343—Joseph Choate, the lawyer, had no taste for music. Once he was persuaded by his daughter to accompany her to the opera. He looked at the libretto helplessly and said, "Helen, expound to me this record lest I dilate with the wrong emotion."

1344—After his concert in a Midwestern town, Paderewski was found backstage in a silent, preoccupied mood. One of his aides asked if he were ill.

"No, no," the great musician replied, "but some friends were missing. The gray-haired couple. They were not in their usual seats in the fourth row."

The aide was surprised. "I didn't know you had friends in this town. Did you know them well?"

"I knew them very well," Paderewski explained, "but I never met them. I liked the way they listened. Every time I have played here for 20 years I have always played for them." He shook his head gravely. "I hope there is nothing seriously wrong."

1345—According to C. R. W. Nevinson, "It was a privilege to paint Mark Hambourg, a dear friend. Never have I met a man with such a gift for penetrating to the heart of things and by the use of a few vivid phrases he will lift any conversation out of the ordinary. I remember sitting beside him at an after-dinner concert, when Moiseivitch was playing. The audience, all men and women of 'culture,' were anything but attentive, smoking, drinking, coughing, picking, wriggling, but the waiters and waitresses stood entranced, their eyes on the master. 'Look,' said Mark. 'Look at the effect of education. It kills all concentration. The lower classes are the only people left who can listen, and can respond to the highest emotions.' "

1346—In Boston the famous tenor, Beniamino Gigli was singing "Faust." The stage of the Boston Opera House was not as adequately equipped as that of the Metropolitan. There was a trap door which sank down in order that Mephistopheles might conduct Faust to Hell. As Gigli stepped on this and began to sink, something went wrong and he became stuck midway and could not get any further, though he made every effort to squeeze through. In the midst of the predicament which was now clearly evident to all the audience, the voice of a slightly inebriated Irishman roared from the top gallery, "Thank God. I'm safe at last! Hell is full!"

1347—Brahms' kindness often revealed a finely imaginative quality. During his concert tour in Hungary with Joachim, the audience one evening consisted of a solitary man. The violinist was all for giving him back his money and closing before the start. "No," said Brahms, "our unique partisan does not deserve such disrespect. Let us go on with the program." So they began, and soon were enthusiastically playing whatever their fortunate solo audience suggested.

1348—A story is told by Deems Taylor about the first performance in Carnegie Hall of the extremely modernistic "Ballet Méchanique" by George Antheil. The composition might be classed as an extreme of extremes; and among the unorthodox instruments augmenting the orchestra were 10 grand pianos, 6 xylophones, a player piano, a fire-alarm siren, an airplane propeller and several automobile klaxons.

The audience, which had been attentive and quiet previously, began to fidget after the start of the music. The general excitement and consternation mounted, until finally, after eight minutes of the composition, a man in one of the front rows raised a white handkerchief tied to his cane. Whereupon the entire audience burst into laughter.

SEE ALSO
Newspapers 1239

RELATED SUBJECTS
Music 1303–1306
Composers 1311–1326
Conductors 1331–1339
Instrumentalists 1351–1363
Singers 1366–1368
Dancers 1371

INSTRUMENTALISTS

1351—Once when Paderewski played before Queen Victoria, the sovereign exclaimed with enthusiasm, "Mr. Paderewski, you are a genius!"

"Ah, Your Majesty," he replied, "perhaps, but before I was a genius, I was a drudge."

1352—Sam Ward told this story of Paganini. "The master held a guitar across his lap. 'Your young friend is musical?' enquired he. 'Fanatico!' replied Gear. 'Then, he shall hear me practice for tomorrow night's concert.' Taking the guitar he converted that little-understood instrument into an orchestra of bewildering and harmonic sonority. Now it seemed a battle, with the clash of swords, shouts of combatants, the roll of the drum. Then wails of pain and grief appeared to emerge from the sounding board over which his fingers flew like what the Westerners call 'greased lightning.' The performance lasted perhaps half an hour, and the dampness of his dishevelled locks indicated the intensity of the emotion and the exertions that expressed it.

"When the maestro received, with a sad smile, our frantic applause, I inquired whether he was going to rehearse on the violin his programme for the morrow. He shook his head: 'I never rehearse the violin. My practice is the gymnastics of the guitar, to be sure of my suppleness of finger and delicacy of touch. My violin never fails me.'"

1353—A musical lady was playing once on the harpsichord for Dr. Johnson who appeared very much bored with the proceedings. As she finished she turned apologetically to him:

"Do you know, doctor, that selection is very difficult?"

"Difficult, madam," answered Dr. Johnson. "Would to heaven it had been impossible."

1354—Paderewski was once traveling incognito through Germany. He stopped for the night at a small Inn in the Black Forest. In the main room of the Inn was an old battered piano. Paderewski asked the landlord if he might try it. Upon doing so, he found that the instrument was not only badly out of tune but that a number of the keys were stuck and would strike no sound at all. He remarked upon this to the landlord. The latter, offended at the criticism of his piano, replied, "If you were a good pianist you could skip over those keys so it wouldn't matter."

1355—A young lady called one day on Rubinstein, the great pianist, who had consented to listen to her playing.

"What do you think I should do now?" she asked when she had finished.

"Get married," was Rubinstein's answer.

1356—Dr. Axel Munthe, seated in the lounge of the Victoria Louise, was enthusiastically hailed by a brother physician.

"What a genius you are!" Thus the brother physician ended a long eulogy.

But Dr. Munthe smiled and said: "A genius, eh? Well, at his villa in Biarritz Sarasate was once called a genius by a famous critic. But Sarasate frowned and shook his head.

"'A genius!' he said. 'For thirty-seven years I've practiced fourteen hours a day, and now they call me a genius!'"

1357—Paderewski once explained that he practiced faithfully every day. "If I miss one day's practice," said he, "I notice it. If I miss two days, the critics notice it. If I miss three days, the audience notices it."

1358—Fritz Kreisler, the violinist, found himself in Hamburg one evening with an hour to spare before taking his boat to London where he was to play the following evening. So he wandered into a music shop. The proprietor asked to see his violin which he carried under his arm. In a moment he disappeared, to reappear with two policemen. One laid his hand on Kreisler's shoulder and said, "You are under arrest."

"For what?" asked Kreisler.

"You have Fritz Kreisler's violin."

"Well, I am Fritz Kreisler."

"Come, come," said the policeman, "you cannot pull that one on us. Come to the station."

Kreisler's boat sailed in an hour. He had to do some quick thinking.

"I looked around," he says, "and in the corner I saw a victrola. I asked the proprietor if he had any of Fritz Kreisler's records; he produced "The Old Refrain," put it on for me, and played it through. 'Now,' I said, 'let me have my violin.' Then, with whatever skill I may command I played "The Old Refrain." When I was through I said, 'Are you satisfied now?' "

With profuse apologies they bowed him out to freedom.

1359—It is said that Jascha Heifetz and Mischa Elman were dining together in a restaurant much frequented by artists. The waiter approached the table with an envelope which bore simply the inscription, "To the World's Greatest Violinist."

Heifetz, who had picked it from the tray, bowed and handed it across the table and said, "For you, Mischa."

Elman read it and said, "No, no," and handed it back. "Something for you, Jascha."

Thus they shilly-shallied back and forth until finally Heifetz was persuaded to open it. He drew out the letter and unfolded it. It began, "Dear Fritz."

1360—There is a legend which would have it that, when Jascha Heifetz made his triumphant New York debut, among the audience were the other violinist, Mischa Elman, and the distinguished pianist, Josef Hofmann. The hall was crowded and it was an evening in Spring. The concert progressed and the audience was spellbound by the genius of Heifetz. As the music went on Elman became increasingly nervous and fidgety, running his finger frequently around the inside of his collar and mopping at his forehead with a handkerchief. In the pause between two selections, he leaned over and whispered to Hofmann, "Awfully hot in here, isn't it?"

Hofmann smiled and whispered back, "Not for pianists."

1361—Mischa Elman, the violinist, takes delight in telling the following story.

"While visiting a friend of the family I was asked to play something to the assembled group of people. For an urchin of seven, as I was at that time, I flatter myself I rattled off Beethoven's 'Kreutzer Sonata' finely. The Sonata has in it several long and impressive rests. In one of these rests a motherly old lady leaned forward, patted my shoulder and said, 'Play something you know, dear.' "

1362—Jascha Heifetz arrived in great haste at Radio City, perilously near to being late for a radio concert with the NBC Symphony Orchestra. He hastened into the elevator carrying his violin in its case.

"You'll have to go in the freight elevator with that," said the operator.

"I have no time," said Heifetz, "I'm in a hurry."

"I don't care," said the operator. "All musicians with instruments have got to ride in the freight elevator."

"Look," said the exasperated musician, "I'm Jascha Heifetz."

"I don't care if you're Rubinoff," said the operator, "you've got to ride in the freight elevator."

1363—"Ole Bull (celebrated 18th Century Norwegian violinist) was a man of singular and beautiful simplicity of character. He spoke English with much expression and had quaint turns of dialect as original as they were unstudied. He was describing the grandeur of the hills and fiords of his native land and its deep forests resounding with musical cataracts when someone exclaimed: 'Did you play to them, Ole?'

" 'No,' he replied, 'I listened.' "

SEE ALSO
Conductors 1335

RELATED SUBJECTS
Music 1303–1306
Operas and Concerts 1341–1348

SINGERS

1366—Catherine II was treating her court to concerts by Catterina Gabrielli the celebrated Italian soprano. The Empress had asked the artist to come to St. Petersburg without stating any definite price. Gabrielli determined, however, that a royal patron should be royally charged; and when at the end of the season Catherine inquired of her entertainer what she was to be paid for her singing, she replied, "Five thousand ducats."

"Five thousand ducats!" the Empress exclaimed. "Why not one of my field marshals is paid as much as that."

"Well, then," retorted Gabrielli like a flash, "Your Majesty had better get one of your field marshals to sing for you."

1367—Samuel Foote once asked a man why he forever sang one tune.

"Because it haunts me," replied the other.

"No wonder," said Foote. "You continually murder it."

1368—During rehearsals of Verdi's great opera, "Otello," by an American opera company, the tenor, who was preparing for the chief role, was perplexed by certain instructions given him by the stage director. This dignitary insisted that at a certain moment, nearing a climax in the action, while the chorus was singing and while there was a rest of a matter of only a few bars in the tenor role, that he should go to the back of the stage and return again toward the footlights to resume singing. It required swift timing and was seemingly utterly senseless from the point of view of dramatic action. The tenor protested. The stage director would not yield. "It is the tradition of the part," he insisted.

"Why?"

"I don't know. It is the tradition. You must do it."

"Who created this role?"

"Tamagno."

Unable to do anything but accede, the tenor carried the incident in his memory. A year or so later, being in Italy, he sought out the great, aged tenor, Tamagno. And, being granted an interview, said:

"Maestro, I wish to ask you about a certain piece of business in the role of Otello."

The old man heard him out and was obviously puzzled. In an effort to recollect his motive, he peered for a time at the pages of the score.

"Yes, yes," he said at last, "it is very simple. Note that in the final passage Otello must sing a high B flat. So while the chorus was singing I went upstage to spit."

SEE ALSO   RELATED SUBJECTS
Eating 21   Music 1303–1306
Reputation 77   Operas and Concerts 1341–1348
Melancholy 368
Vanity 620
Fatness 689
Courtships 852
Operas 1346
Actors 1423

DANCERS

1371—Finley Peter Dunne, the "Mr. Dooley" of humorous fame, once went to see Isadora Duncan perform. The famous dancer wore very few clothes, and as a result of their lack, looked even plumper than usual. A floodlight threw calcium beams on her. As Dunne was leaving, one of the patronesses hailed him.

"Oh, Mr. Dunne," she twittered, "how did you enjoy the madame's dancing?"

"Immensely," said Dunne. "Made me think of Grant's Tomb in love."

RELATED SUBJECTS
Music 1303–1306
Operas and Concerts 1341

THEATRE AND FILM

PLAYWRIGHTS

1376—It is reported that Sam Goldwyn telephoned to George Bernard Shaw and attempted to drive a bargain for the film rights to some of his plays. Shaw's terms were stiff and Goldwyn endeavored to whittle them down by an appeal to the artist.

"Think of the millions of people who would get a chance to see your plays who would otherwise never see them. Think of the contribution it would be to art."

"The trouble is, Mr. Goldwyn," Shaw replied, "that you think of nothing but Art and I think of nothing but money."

1377—Sir Herbert Beerbohm Tree, to a would-be dramatist:
"My dear Sir: I have read your play. Oh, my dear Sir!
"Yours faithfully."

1378—"Not all your plays are successes, I suppose, Sir James," someone remarked to J. M. Barrie at a dinner party.
In the manner of one imparting a confidence, Barrie leaned toward him and said, "No, some Peter out and some Pan out."

1379—Clare Boothe's first produced play, "Abide with Me," was a failure. The playwright, however, was evidently possessed of some ebulliency on the occasion of its opening. Richard Watts, drama critic, reported, "One almost forgave 'Abide with Me' its faults when its lovely playwright, who must have been crouched in the wings for a sprinter's start as the final curtain mercifully descended, heard a cry of 'Author,' which was not audible in my vicinity, and arrived to accept the audience's applause just as the actors, who had a head start on her, were properly lined up and smoothed out to receive their customary adulation."

1380—Richard Brinsley Sheridan, threatening to cut his son Thomas off with a shilling, he immediately replied, "Ah father, but where will you borrow the shilling?"

1381—Boyer, a French dramatic author, had been fifty years writing without success. That he might prove whether his condemnation was not on account of the prejudice of the critics, he gave it to be understood that the new tragedy of "Agamemnon" was the production of a young man lately arrived at Paris. The piece was received with great applause, even by Racine himself, who was the great scourge of Boyer. The next night the tragedy was hissed, Boyer having made it known that he was the author.

1382—Oscar Wilde arrived at his club one evening, after witnessing a first production of a play that was a complete failure.

"Oscar, how did your play go tonight?" said a friend.

"Oh," was the lofty response, "the play was a great success but the audience was a failure."

1383—Cumberland, a third rate dramatist, was jealous of Sheridan's reputation and lost no occasion to talk him down. An acquaintance of Sheridan's, meeting him on the street one day, informed him that Cumberland was telling everyone how he had gone to see "The School for Scandal" and had thought it a very bad thing—couldn't see how people saw anything funny in it at all.

"Why, did he not laugh at my comedy?" asked Sheridan, pretending the deepest concern.

"No."

"Well then, I must say that is very ungrateful in Mr. Cumberland, for I laughed at his last tragedy until I almost split my sides."

1384—"When I wrote 'Major Barbara,' the characters were modelled on people I knew. The likenesses were unmistakable, and therefore I was anxious to make sure that no words used in the play could hurt the originals. I read the play to an old dear friend of the family. All went well till I came to the lines: 'Never call me Mother again.' 'Oh,' said she, 'you must not say that for those are the very words used by . . . (the character copied in the play), and used in tragic circumstances.'"

Shaw paused. Bridges opened his eyes, "remarkable coincidence," he said and closed his eyes again.

1385—A librettist accosted De Wolf Hopper at the stage entrance to Weber & Fields.

"I wish to explain the story of my new opera," he began. "The hero is stranded on a desert island, and the natives make him King. You see now the splendid beginning for complications."

"I do," said the comedian, "and I know them well; they are chiefly of a financial character, if memory serves me." And he fled.

SEE ALSO	RELATED SUBJECTS
Producers 1395	Plays 1386–1388
Audiences 1441	
Hollywood 1449	

PLAYS

1386—The play "Merrily We Roll Along," famous for its reverse sequence of events, was a succes d'èstime but was otherwise disappointing to its authors, George S. Kaufman and Moss Hart. Attempts were made to analyze the reason for the play's failure. According to Kaufman, the best diagnosis of the trouble was made by Herman Mankiewicz, who said, "Here we have this young man: a successful playwright, wealthy, honored, loved by beautiful women, the owner of yachts, sought out by everyone, and the problem is, how the Hell did the poor son-of-a-gun ever get himself into such a jam!"

1387—On the first night of the performance of one of Douglas Jerrold's pieces, a successful playwright rallied him on his nervousness.

"I," said this colleague, "never feel nervous on the first night of my pieces."

"Ah, my boy," Jerrold replied, "you are always certain of success. Your pieces have all been tried before."

1388—The influence of antiquity is perpetual. The art and literature of the ancient Greeks and Romans is evident in most of the things about us in modern everyday life. Many artists owe their great success to emulating the ancient classics, the masterpieces of many writers are based on the great dramas of Euripides, Sophocles and Aeschylus. Corneille notably patterned his plays on the Greek idea. His "Andromaque" is a well-known example. The classic basis of this play earned for him probably the highest praise ever accorded a dramatist. Napoleon, a great lover

of the classics, exclaimed after seeing "Andromaque,"
"If Corneille were alive I would make him King!"

SEE ALSO   RELATED SUBJECTS
Critics 1102, 1103   Playwrights 1376–1385
Playwrights 1378, 1382   Producers 1391–1397
Sin and Sinners 1647   Directors 1401–1403
                             Actors 1406–1431
                             Audiences 1436–1441

PRODUCERS

1391—When Gary Cooper had finished making a certain picture
for Samuel Goldwyn, another producer, Hunt Stromberg, exercised the option which he held on Cooper's
services. Goldwyn called the other producer on the
'phone, and in an aggrieved tone, said, "It isn't that I
mind your taking Cooper. But you could have been
nicer about it. You could at least have called me up and
said, 'Sam, I need Cooper right away, if it doesn't interfere with your plans.' Then, I'd have said, no."

1392—How Producer Gabriel Pascal acquired the film rights to
Bernard Shaw's plays—a mine of entertainment material
practically every producer in Hollywood has tried to buy
at one time or another—is an utterly implausible story.
In 1935, after spending six months in Hollywood doing
nothing, Pascal, who had made one successful picture in
England and a succession of shorts, left in disgust. He
arrived in London, and out of a clear sky called on Shaw,
whom he had never met, saying he wanted to produce
his plays. When Shaw asked how much capital he had
to do it with, Pascal replied: "Fifteen shillings and six-
pence—but I owe a pound."
Delighted as much with this effrontery as with Pascal's
obvious admiration for his work, Shaw gave him a pound
to pay his debts, and agreed to the experiment. The
successful "Pygmalion" was the result.

1393—Sam Goldwyn, impressed by the wide sale of Radcliffe
Hall's "The Well of Loneliness," expressed a desire to
purchase the film rights. "You can't film that," he was
advised. "It deals with Lesbians." "So all right," replied Goldwyn, "where they got Lesbians, we'll use
Austrians."

1394—To Billy Rose came a seedy looking individual with a
startling proposition.

"I'll do an act in your show that will be the greatest sensation ever presented. You can advertise it in advance, and get $100 a ticket. If you'll put $25,000 in escrow for my wife, I'll then commit suicide in the full view of your audience."

"It's a natural!" said Rose, simulating enthusiasm, "but just a minute. What will you do for an encore?"

1395—They say that Samuel Goldwyn read the first script submitted by a new writer attached to the studio and summoned the hopeful to his desk. "This is a perfect scenario," said Goldwyn. "It is the first time in my life that I've seen a perfect scenario. There's absolutely nothing wrong with it. I want you to have a hundred copies made so I can distribute them to all the other writers so that everybody should see a really perfect script. And hurry," he called as the thrilled and excited writer hastened out of the office, "before I start rewriting it."

1396—The film producer, Darryl Zanuck, of whom Eddie Cantor has said, "Zanuck is Goldwyn without the accent," once epitomized the Hollywood approach in speaking of "Les Misérables," which he was about to film, referring to it as "Lee's Miserables," depicting it as " 'I'm a Fugitive from a Chain Gang.' in costume."

1397—The following incident occurred at the Flea Show in Paris. One of the dear creatures which acted as coachman to the great flea-coach, managed to hop off his box, and elected a rather stout lady standing near, as his resting-place. The proprietor of the show, who had spent much time and patience upon the education of his insect, was in despair, and the lady was asked if she would mind making a search for the missing flea.

She accordingly retired to a private room, and in a few minutes returned triumphant, carefully holding the captive in the most approved flea-style. She handed him to the showman who started and changed color, and returning the flea to the lady remarked:

"Madame, this is not my flea!"

SEE ALSO	RELATED SUBJECTS
Parties 519	Plays 1386–1388
Authors 1177	Hollywood 1446–1449
Composers 1324	
Playwrights 1376	
Funerals 1776	

DIRECTORS

1401—John Barrymore once asked the great Russian director, Constantin Stanislavski, how he selected his artists. "I choose them by means of this," said Stanislavski, picking up a pin. "Now, you go into the next room."

Barrymore went out and in a moment Stanislavski said, "You may come in now. Please look for the pin."

The Russian watched as Barrymore picked up the glasses from the table, looked under them and lifted each plate. He felt along the surface of the tablecloth, lifted the corner, and there was the pin.

Stanislavski clapped his hands: "Very good—you are engaged! I can tell a real actor," he explained, "by the way he looks for a pin. If he prances around the room, striking attitudes, pretending to think very hard, looking in ridiculous places—exaggerating—then he is not good."

1402—One day at rehearsal Sir Herbert Tree asked a youthful actor to "step back a little." The player did so. Tree eyed him critically—and went on rehearsing. After a time he repeated his request: "A little further back." The youth obeyed. Surveying him, Tree went on with his work. Shortly afterwards he again asked him to step still further back.

"If I do," expostulated the youth, "I shall be right off the stage."

"Yes," said Tree, "that's right."

1403—This story concerns the Hollywood director, Joseph von Sternberg, who came to sword's points with Sam Jaffe when the actor was appearing in "The Scarlet Empress" under Von Sternberg's direction.

Mr. Jaffe deemed certain arbitrary instructions to be improper, and disputed the point.

"Mr. Jaffe," screamed Von Sternberg, "I am Von Sternberg, I have 10,000 followers."

"You're very fortunate," said Jaffe coldly, "Jesus Christ had only 12."

SEE ALSO	RELATED SUBJECTS
Actors 1425, 1426	Plays 1386–1388
	Actors 1406–1431

ACTORS

1406—Someone remarked to Adolph Menjou that the depredations of the draft were working havoc in the ranks of Hollywood's romantic leading men. "That is true," said

Menjou, "and it will be the first time that some of our leading ladies will be playing opposite men their own age."

1407—No actress could ever have enjoyed a more touching tribute than that once received by Helen Hayes when she was portraying the role of Mary of Scotland. As darkness was falling after the matinee one winter's afternoon, she encountered outside the stagedoor a small boy gazing at her adoringly. After several successive matinees he still appeared faithfully; then, one time he impulsively stepped forward thrusting something into her hand and fled down the street. Miss Hayes found herself holding a small box. Opening it she found a little gilded medal bearing the inscription, "Scholarship Medal, Public School 42, 1933."

1408—When Alfred Lunt and Lynn Fontanne, a notably devoted husband and wife, started rehearsing "At Mrs. Bean's," a play in which it was necessary for Miss Fontanne to strike Mr. Lunt in the face, she found she couldn't hit him. She pulled her hand back and let go—and then stopped dead before she struck. Her husband begged her to do it, but after 30 minutes she still couldn't. Finally Mr. Lunt shouted: "For God's sake, Lynn, you're the lousiest actress I've ever played opposite!"
The Fontanne hand made a direct hit. Mr. Lunt yelped with pain, then grinned. But when they put on the show he had to whisper, "Don't be lousy, dear," each time before she would hit him.

1409—A film salesman was trying to sell the latest Clark Gable picture to a cinema proprietor in the wilds of Venezuela. "Clark Gable is dead," he was told. "You recall the film 'Parnell'?"
"Yes. A box-office winner."
"Si, señor, but, the Gable he died in that."
"Look here, I don't . . ."
"I tried to show another Gable film after that," went on the Venezuelan. "And what happen? Hell broke loose. Señor, my clients see the Gable die in one picture. Cannot one believe one's own eyes? So far as this village is concerned, Gable is dead."

1410—Robert Palmer, the 18th Century actor, was in the early part of his life a bill-sticker, which circumstance was pretty generally known to the performers. One evening, being dressed for Sir Brilliant Fashion, he strutted into the green-room, with sparkling buckles on his shoes and and at his knees, and a brilliant ring on his finger. One of the company inquired if they were real. "I wear nothing but diamonds," replied Palmer. "I congratulate you," said John Bannister, "for I remember when you wore nothing but paste." This occasioned a war, which was heightened by Mrs. Jordan crying out—"Stick him against the wall, Bob—stick him against the wall."

1411—Miss Clara Morris told the following story of her own experience:

"Somewhere in the wide world there is an actor—and a good one—who never eats celery without thinking of me. It was years ago, when I was playing Camille. In the first scene, you will remember, the unfortunate Armand takes a rose from Camille as a token of love. We had almost reached that point, when, as I glanced down, I saw that the flower was missing from its accustomed place on my breast.

"What could I do? On the flower hung the strength of the scene. However, I continued my lines in an abstracted fashion, and began a still hunt for that rose or a substitute. My gaze wandered around the stage. On the dinner table was some celery. Moving slowly toward it, I grasped the celery and twisted the tops into a rose form. Then I began the fateful lines:

" 'Take this flower. The life of a camelia is short. If held and caressed it will fade in a morning or an evening.'

"Hardly able to control his laughter, Armand spoke his lines which ran: 'It is a cold, scentless flower. It is a strange flower.' I agreed with him."

1412—John Kemble was performing one of his favorite parts at some country theatre and was interrupted from time to time by the squalling of a child in the gallery, until at length, angered by this rival performance, Kemble walked with solemn steps to the front of the stage, and addressing the audience in his most tragic tones, said, "Ladies and gentlemen, unless the play is stopped, the child cannot possibly go on."

1413—A pushing young actor who was understudy in one of Mr. Barrie's plays found his opportunity one night through the illness of his principal. He accordingly flooded his managerial and influential acquaintances with telegrams announcing: "I play So-and-So's part tonight." Except that the theatre was comparatively empty this breathless disclosure produced no result, other than a telegram in reply from Mr. Barrie to this effect: "Thanks for the warning."

1414—When John Barrymore was playing Hamlet on Broadway, Jane Cowl attended one of the matinees. She was not inaudible while watching it, and the audience soon knew she was there. Barrymore became aware of her presence, also, but didn't acknowledge it until the end of the performance. In making his curtain speech he bowed in the direction of the famed lady's box. "And in conclusion," he said, "may I take this opportunity to thank Miss Cowl for the privilege of co-starring with her this afternoon."

1415—During a theatrical engagement at Manchester, Kemble and Lewis were walking one day along the street, when a chimney-sweeper and his boy came up. The boy stared at them with open mouth and exclaimed:
"They be play-actors."
"Hold your tongue, you dog," said the old sweep, "you don't know what you may come to yourself."

1416—Lillah McCarthy tells of Lord Lucas that, "He wanted me to play a season of Shakespeare and knew how much I wished it; and one day he came to the theatre with a cheque. 'Here's the money for Shakespeare. I've sold my pig-farm. I like his pearls better than my pigs!'"

1417—Beerbohm Tree was once trying to get a well-known actor back into his company. He invited the man to call and received him in his dressing room as he was making up.
"How much would you want to come back?" inquired Mr. Tree, busy with his paint pots. The actor named an exorbitant salary to which Tree replied as he went on making up:
"Don't slam the door when you go out, will you?"

1418—Sam Ward told this story. "I remember awaiting in Rachel's box at the Théatre Français, in the summer of 1855, the arrival of the great tragedienne, after the curtain had dropped upon her performance of Phèdre, the memory of which is still fresh with many now living. She hardly used a gesture or made a motion to depart from the statuesque repose of her inspired declamation.

It was Jules Janin who took me to her dressing room, who placed my hand upon her costume, the white chlamys, and called my attention to the fact that it was wringing-wet!"

1419—An extra came up to Helen Westley, elderly character actress, on a movie set. "Why, Miss Westley," she gushed, "what are you doing in this picture?"
"My dear," the reply sped back, "hadn't you heard? I furnish the sexagenarian appeal."

1420—Alfred Lunt and Lynn Fontanne made one movie while I was in Hollywood. When they were asked to see the rushes (uncut scenes in the picture) Lynn saw them alone and was horrified. She rushed home to her husband.
"Well?" said Alfred.
"I was awful," said Lynn wildly, "terrible, unbelievable. I can't go on with it."
"How was I?" asked her husband.
"Oh, charming, dear, perfectly wonderful, as you always are. You'll have to do a little something about your makeup, because you look as though you didn't have any lips. But Alfred, I can't go on with this. My voice sounds impossible and I haven't any eyes, and my face is entirely expressionless and I don't seem to know what to do with my hands and feet."
There was a long pause.
"Alfred," said Lynn, "I tell you I can't go on. What'll I do?"
"No lips, eh?" said Alfred.

1421—It was Dorothy Parker who commented acidly about the performance of a certain prominent American actress, saying, "She certainly ran the gamut of emotions from A to B."

1422—Someone remarked to Mrs. Siddons that applause was necessary to actors, as it gave them confidence. "More," replied the actress, "it gives us breath."

1423—At a dinner in Hollywood to celebrate his birthday, Charlie Chaplin entertained the guests throughout the evening by imitating people they knew: men, women and children, his chauffeur, his Jap servants, his secretaries. Finally he sang at the top of his voice an aria from an Italian Opera—sang it superbly. "Why Charlie, I never knew you could sing so beautifully," someone exclaimed. "I can't sing at all," Chaplin rejoined. "I was only imitating Caruso."

1424—Jacob Adler, the great actor of the Yiddish theatre, was reputed to have many progeny scattered along his trail, aside from the numerous family of distinguished actors who have descended from him. Not infrequently some claimant to his paternity would present himself. Once, while the great actor was in his dressing room, such a young man gained entrance to him and introduced himself, saying, "I'm your son." Adler peered intently at the youth for a moment. "So you are—so you are," he said, and turning to his valet he said, "Give the boy a pass."

1425—The late John Barrymore used to tell of the confusion that prevailed in an old stock company with which he had once played repertory. The vast number of plays, the frequency and inconsistency with which they were performed, rendered confusion more or less inevitable. One evening Barrymore found himself unable to remember his lines. Faking a piece of business, he sidled over into the wings and hastily called to the director, "What's the line, what's the line?"
The director sighed wearily and asked, "What's the play?"

1426—"Many are called, but few are chosen" might well be the motto emblazoned above the doors of the Hollywood casting directors.
One hopeful young actor was turned down time and again by the same company. Despairing, yet determined, he made a final effort. Approaching one film director, he said, "It's now or never, if you want me in one of your pictures. I now have many companies after me."
"You have?" asked the director, his interest aroused by this statement. "What companies?"
"Well," said the actor seriously, "there's the telephone company, the electric and gas companies, the milk company . . ."
The director laughed—the actor got a job.

1427—Roger Kemble, father of the famous Mrs. Siddons, had once expressly forbidden the young lady to marry an actor.
She defied this parental instruction, wherewith Kemble upbraided her not only for her disobedience but for

the aggravating circumstance that she had married undoubtedly the most incompetent member of his company.

"Exactly," replied the defiant bride. "Nobody can call him an actor."

1428—William Randolph Hearst, according to a legend, once invited Will Rogers to come to San Simeon for a week-end. Hearst had assembled a considerable company, and Rogers was the star guest whom Hearst did not fail to show off to his best advantage. A few days later Hearst received from Rogers a bill for several thousand dollars for services as a professional entertainer. He called Rogers on the phone and protested, saying, "I didn't engage you to come as an entertainer. I invited you as a guest."

Rogers snapped, "When people invite me as a guest, they invite Mrs. Rogers too. When they ask me to come alone, I go as a professional entertainer."

1429—Once in the dressing room of Katherine Cornell those old stagers, Mrs. Leslie Carter and Mrs. Patrick Campbell, chanced to meet. They were introduced as "surely being acquainted with one another."

"Honored. Honored," said Mrs. Campbell grandly, shaking Mrs. Carter's hand. Then turning to a by-stander she confided in a loud stage-whisper, "I thought she was dead."

1430—When someone was lamenting Samuel Foote's unlucky fate of being kicked in Dublin, Dr. Johnson said he was glad of it. "He is rising in the world," said he. "When he was in England, no one thought it worth while to kick him."

1431—At the finish of the filming of "Bill of Divorcement," Katherine Hepburn turned to John Barrymore and said, "Thank God, I don't have to act anymore with you!"

"Oh," he replied, "I didn't know you ever had, darling."

SEE ALSO
Reputation 76
Devotion 172
Eccentricity 207
Long-Windedness 360
Memory 373

RELATED SUBJECTS
Plays 1386–1388
Producers 1391–1397
Directors 1401–1403
Audiences 1436–1441

Rudeness 519
Shrewdness 527, 529
Fatness 685
Handicaps 702, 704
Introductions 791
Names 831
Women 843
Divorce 911
Babies 958
Directors 1401
Sermons 1549
Kings 1987
Parliament 1999

AUDIENCES

1436—When John Barrymore was playing "Redemption" in New York . . . he struggled against a particularly croupy audience. When it came to the scene where he, as a derelict, is being questioned by the prefect of police, and was asked if he couldn't say anything for himself, he waved his hand out toward the audience, and cried:

"Say anything! How can I say anything with that bunch of trained seals out there?"

1437—An old farmer went to the movies for the first time. He watched the proceedings with interest, especially one scene in which a group of girls started to undress to go swimming. During this process a train passed by and in the next scene they were shown in the water.

The old man had gone into the show early in the afternoon. Late that evening, an usher, seeing him still in his seat, came up to him and asked why he stayed through so many performances.

"Waal," drawled the old codger, "I figger that one of these times that train is goin' to be late."

1438—True or not, it is a good story. Orson Welles once lectured in a small Middle-Western town before an audience sparse almost to invisibility. He opened his remarks with a brief sketch of his career: "I'm a director of plays, a producer of plays. I'm an actor of the stage and motion pictures. I'm a writer and producer of motion pictures. I write, direct and act on the radio. I'm a magician and painter. I've published books. I play the violin and the piano." At this point he paused and surveyed his audience, saying, "Isn't it a pity there's so many of me and so few of you!"

1439—Rachel, the celebrated French actress, once remarked after an opening night at the theatre :

"Mon dieu! When I came out on the stage the audience simply sat there open mouthed."

"Oh, nonsense !" rudely interrupted a younger rival of hers : "They never all yawn at once."

1440—A person threw the head of a goose on the stage of the theatre. The manager, advancing to the front, said : "Gentlemen, if any one among you has lost his head, do not be uneasy, for I will restore it at the conclusion of the performance."

1441—After the première performance of "Arms and the Man," Bernard Shaw was called upon to take a bow. As he stepped forward upon the stage amidst the applause, a loud voice called from the balcony, "Come, come, Shaw, you know all this stuff is balderdash."

Shaw good-naturedly looked up toward the balcony and called back, "I quite agree with you, my friend, but who are you and I against so many ?"

SEE ALSO   RELATED SUBJECTS
Patriotism 396   Plays 1386–1388
Babies 960   Actors 1406–1431

HOLLYWOOD

1446—W. C. Fields has crowned perhaps all other estimates of Hollywood with one observation. Someone asked him whether he had ever had the D.T.'s since coming to Hollywood. "I don't know," said Fields, "I don't know. There's no way of telling where the D.T.'s leave off and Hollywood begins."

1447—James Thurber, the "New Yorker" cartoonist, attended one of Hollywood's super-colossal premieres. When they were leaving the theatre Thurber asked a writer friend what he thought of the picture.

"I thought it stank," replied the friend in no uncertain terms. "What did you think of it ?"

"I can't say I liked it that well," replied Thurber.

1448—Typical of Hollywood is the authentic story of the first effort made by the now prominent star, Roland Young, to get into the movies; or more accurately the movies' first effort to get him. Young became an unquestioned star of the legitimate stage over night with his success in the play, "The Last of Mrs. Cheney." The films purchased the story and desired to bring its celebrated leading man to Hollywood to appear in the screen version; but when Young arrived on the coast, he was sent back to New York. They decided he wasn't the type.

1449—The popular writer Edgar Wallace was once portraying to a friend the fabulous glories of the film industry. "I write a scenario in a couple of days and get a fortune for it. You ought to try it."

"It's too baffling for me," his friend said ruefully. "I was once asked to submit something to a film company. I sent them four scenarios—and got back nine."

SEE ALSO
Rough and Ready 507
Divorce 911
Producers 1396
Actors 1406

RELATED SUBJECTS
Producers 1391–1397
Directors 1401–1403
Actors 1406–1431

RELIGION AND MORALS

CHURCHMEN

1451—While Raphael was engaged in painting his celebrated frescoes, he was visited by two cardinals who began to criticize his work, and found fault without understanding it.

"The Apostle Paul has too red a face," said one.

"He blushes to see into whose hands the Church has fallen," answered the angry artist.

1452—Julian Huxley tells this: "I recall the story of the philosopher and the theologian. The two were engaged in disputation and the theologian used the old quip about a philosopher resembling a blind man, in a dark room, looking for a black cat—which wasn't there.

"'That may be,' said the philosopher, 'but a theologian would have found it.'"

1453—When the learned John Selden was a member of the Assembly of Divines at Westminster he delighted to puzzle them by curious quibbles. Once they were gravely engaged in determining the exact distance between Jerusalem and Jericho; and one of them, to prove it could not be great, observed, "that fish were carried from one place to the other." At which the resourceful Dr. Selden observed: "Perhaps it was salt fish?" This again threw the Assembly into confusion.

1454—The theologian, Leonard Bacon, was present at a religious conference. He had made a certain statement on the floor whereupon a member, opposed to his views, burst forth with the exclamation, "Why, I never heard of such a thing in all my life."

"Mr. Moderator," appealed Bacon, "I cannot allow my opponent's ignorance, however vast, to prejudice my knowledge, however small."

1455—Shortly before his death Chief Justice Melville Fuller presided at a church conference. During the progress of a heated debate a member arose and began a tirade against universities and education, thanking God that he had never been corrupted by contact with a college.

"Do I understand the speaker thanks God for his ignorance?" interrupted the Chief Justice.

"Well, yes," was the answer. "You can put it that way if you wish."

"All I can say then," said the Chief Justice, "is that the member has a great deal to thank God for."

1456—At a gathering in London, where a furious theological controversy occurred, Dean Swift lost his temper and boisterously asked a stranger who sat next to him: "On which side, sir, are you? Are you an atheist or a Deist?"
"Oh, neither, Sir," was the immediate reply;
"I am a dentist."

SEE ALSO
Eating 7
Authors 1172

RELATED SUBJECTS
Ministers 1461–1477
Priests 1481–1483
Rabbis 1486–1488
Bishops 1491–1498
Popes 1501–1504
Evangelists 1511–1516
Missionaries 1521
Churches 1526–1528
Church Services 1531–1538

MINISTERS

1461—Henry Ward Beecher asked Park Benjamin, the poet and humorist, why he never came to hear him preach. Benjamin replied, "Why, Beecher, the fact is, I have conscientious scruples against going to places of amusement on Sunday."

1462—John Wesley, in a considerable party, had been maintaining with great earnestness the doctrine of Vox populi vox Dei against his sister. At last the preacher, to put an end to the controversy, said, "I tell you, sister, the voice of the people is the voice of God."
"Yes," replied his sister mildly, "it cried: 'Crucify him! Crucify him!'"

1463—A young minister who was temporarily filling a city pulpit made the following request in his prayers: "May the brother who ministers to this flock be filled full of fresh veal and new zigor."

1464—"Can I lead a good Christian life in New York City on $15 a week?" a young man once asked Dr. S. Parkes Cadman.
"My boy," was the reply, "that's all you can do."

1465—"I am thankful that the Lord has opened my mouth to preach without any larning," said an illiterate preacher. "A similar event took place in Balaam's time," replied a gentleman present.

1466—John Wilkes was once asked by a Roman Catholic gentleman in a warm dispute upon religion: "Where was your religion before Luther?" "Did you wash your face this morning?" inquired the facetious alderman. "I did, sir." "Then pray where was your face before it was washed?"

1467—A Presbyterian minister of the early days settled near the headwaters of the Susquehanna. A good man, he was, but full of humor and ready with his repartee on all occasions.

Jack Rickitt, a quasi-parishioner, but who was more punctual at the river than at Church, presented the minister one Monday morning with a fine string of pickerel. The minister thanked him gravely for the gift.

"But parson," suggested Jack, still retaining the fish, "those fish were caught yesterday. Perhaps yer conscience won't let you eat 'em."

"Jack," replied the minister, stretching out his hands toward the string, "there's one thing I know—the pickerel were not to blame!"

1468—Sydney Smith, the clergyman, had a combat of wit with a friend. His defeated antagonist intending to cast a slur on Smith's vocation, fired back: "If I had a son who was an idiot, I would make him a parson."

"Your father was of a different opinion," was Sydney Smith's answering thrust.

1469—The Reverend Doctor Edgar DeWitt Jones propounded the specifications of a good minister. "He should get religion like a Methodist; experience it like a Baptist; be sure of it like a Disciple; stick to it like a Lutheran; pray for it like a Presbyterian; conciliate it like a Congregationalist; glorify it like a Jew; be proud of it like an Episcopalian; practice it like a Christian Scientist; propagate it like a Roman Catholic; work for it like a Salvation Army lassie; enjoy it like a colored man."

1470—Jerome D. Engel, the famous Baptist preacher, was once vacationing at a well-known shore resort. One of the local churches had expected to have its pulpit filled on

Sunday morning by a "supply" or visiting minister. At the last minute, the visitor was unable to appear, and the church found itself with no one to conduct services. The leaders of the church scurried around distractedly in search of a preacher, and were unable to find anyone. At last, chancing to hear of the presence in town of the eminent divine, one of the church members sought out Engel and begged for his services. Graciously, the minister consented. Delighted and relieved, the committeeman said, "You know, Dr. Engel, we'd have been willing to accept a poorer preacher, but it was impossible to find one."

1471—In the Southern states the church of the élite is generally the Episcopal. There is a legend concerning an eminent Episcopal divine who was once asked, after a dissertation, "Pastor, is it possible for a man to achieve salvation outside of the Episcopal church?"

The minister replied, "It is conceivable that such a possibility might exist. However, no gentleman would avail himself of it."

1472—Jerome D. Engel, the famous Southern Baptist divine, was strolling along the seawalk during a Church Convention at Charleston. He came upon an old colored man who was fishing from the pier. For some time Engel watched the Negro patiently waiting for a bite. At last he pulled in a fish of repulsive appearance, seeming to be something between a toad and a bullhead. Knowing little about so wordly a matter as fishing, Engel asked, "What kind of fish is that, George?"

"Dey calls it a Baptist fish," croaked the old man.

"A Baptist fish?" inquired Engel sceptically.

"Sho'." answered the fisherman, throwing his catch back into the sea. "Dey calls dem dat 'cause dey spoils so fast after dey is taken out of de water."

1473—George Ade, automobiling in Indiana, dined at a country hotel among a roomful of ministers. The ministers, who were holding a convention in the town, were much amused when Mr. Ade's identity was disclosed to them. One of them said during dinner: "How does a humorist of your stamp feel, sir, in such reverend company as this?"

"I feel," said Mr. Ade promptly, "like a lion in a den of Daniels."

1474—Reverend Henry Ward Beecher entered Plymouth Church one Sunday and found several letters awaiting him. He opened one and found it contained the single word "Fool." Quietly and with becoming seriousness he announced to the congregation the fact in these words:

"I have known many an instance of a man writing a letter and forgetting to sign his name, but this is the only instance I have ever known of a man signing his name and forgetting to write the letter."

1475—A new clergyman in town sought the services of the best local physician, a man irregular in his church attendance. The medical treatment was prolonged, and the young pastor, worried over the accumulating expense, spoke to the doctor about the matter of his bill.

"I'll tell you what I'll do, Pastor," said the doctor, "I hear you're a pretty good preacher and you seem to think I'm a fair doctor. We'll make a bargain. I'll do all I can to keep you out of Heaven, and you do all you can to keep me out of Hell, and it won't cost either of us a cent."

1476—Bursting with her news, Mrs. Meadows hurried to her neighbor's house.

"Have you heard, Mrs. Smith? The minister's son has decided to become a jockey. Of course you know that he was supposed to go to the Theological Seminary this year."

Mrs. Smith, more of the woman of the world than her friend, replied drily, "Well, I must say that he'll bring a lot more people to repentance that way than he would as a minister."

1477—Some years ago a theological tempest in a teapot raged over the issue of Fundamentalism versus Modernism. Dr. Harry Emerson Fosdick, of the Riverside Church in New York, was in the forefront of this fray.

There is a legend that, at this time, Dr. Fosdick was awakened in the small hours of the morning by the persistent ringing of his telephone. He climbed out of bed and hastened to answer it, and sleepily said, "Hello."

A voice came over the wire, saying, "Ish thish Mr. Foshdick?"

Dismayed the minister said, "Yes, this is Dr. Fosdick speaking."

"Dr. Harry Emerson Foshdick?"

"Yes, yes," was the impatient answer, "What is it you want?"

"Dr. Foshdick, I want to know the difference between Fundamentalism and Modernism."

Exasperated, Dr. Fosdick said, "Good Heavens, man, that's not something I can explain to you over the telephone, and obviously you're in no condition to hear. Come around to my study tomorrow and I'll be glad to answer your questions."

"But, Dr. Foshdick," insisted the voice, "I can't wait until tomorrow. I must know now."

Angrily Dr. Fosdick said, "Why can't you wait until tomorrow? Why do you have to know now?"

"Becaush," said the voice patiently, "tomorrow I won't give a damn."

SEE ALSO   RELATED SUBJECTS
Smoking 64   Churchmen 1451–1456
Boners 116   Church Services 1531–1538
Hypocrisy 302   Sermons 1541–1559
Laziness 327
Prejudice 449
Love 849   Golf 1862
Marriage 878   Political Parties 1907
Home Life 999   Poverty 2209
Sermons 1543, 1549   Salaries 2254
Miracles 1619   Horse 2287
Sin and Sinners 1647   Parrot 2292
Doctors 1671   Witnesses 2504, 2505
Deathbed Scenes 1772   Wills 2607

PRIESTS

1481—The Rev. Alexander Doyle of the Paulist Fathers is a clever speaker and a warm advocate of abstinence and tight-closed saloons for Sunday. Among his auditors was a country girl who was deeply impressed by the preaching of Father Doyle. She wrote home to her mother this bit of criticism.

"I never get tired of going to hear the sermons in the Paulist Church, Mother. Father Doyle is such a lovely preacher that you would think every word he said was true!"

1482—Curran said to Father O'Leary:

"Reverend Father, I wish you were St. Peter."

"Why," said the priest.

"Because, then you would have the keys of heaven, and could let me in."

"I had better have the keys," said Father O'Leary, "of another place, and then I could let you out."

1483—A new Protestant pastor had come to town and his clerical dress was not unlike that of a priest. He chanced to pass several little Catholic boys on the street, and a number of them tipped their hats and chorused, "Good evening, Father." No sooner had the minister passed than one of the boys turned on his companions in disgust, "Father! He's no father—he's got three kids!"

SEE ALSO
Vanity 628

RELATED SUBJECTS
Churchmen 1451–1456
Church Services 1531–1538
Sermons 1541–1559

RABBIS

1486—A place-hunter in Prussia, having asked Frederick the Great for the grant of some rich Protestant bishopric, the king expressed his regret that it was already given away, but broadly hinted that there was a Catholic abbacy at his disposal. The applicant managed to be converted in a week, and to be received into the bosom of the true church; after which he hastened to his friend, the king, and told him how his conscience had been enlightened. "Ah!" exclaimed Frederick, "how terribly unfortunate! I have given away the abbacy. But the chief rabbi is just dead, and the synagogue is at my disposal; suppose you were to turn Jew?"

1487—Applying for a post as keeper at the Bronx Zoo, a burly Irishman came to the question, "What is rabies and what can you do about it?"

The applicant wrote: "Rabies is Jewish priests, and you can't do anything about it."

1488—A certain Jewish man had left Pinsk to go to work in Minsk. For six months he had been away. He had a short vacation and was very anxious to get back home to see his wife and children. It was late on a Friday afternoon, however, and his friend said, "Look, you shouldn't travel on the Sabbath. It's against religion. Stay over with me until the Sabbath is over. Be my guest."

"No," said the other, "I'm anxious to get back to Pinsk. Six months I've been away."

"Six months," said his friend. "So what's another day? You shouldn't travel on the Sabbath. Stay with me. I've got a nice house. I'll give you nice Jewish meals."

After much argument, the man yielded, against his better judgment, and remained over the Sabbath. Even then his friend would not let him go and insisted on detaining him yet another day, entertaining him practically to exhaustion. At last he announced his departure.

"I can't stay another minute. I'm going right away."

"All right," said his host at last, and as his friend was about to leave the house he presented him with a bill for food and lodging. Outraged, the man cried, "What kind of a business is this! You make me stay against my will; you won't let me go. You insist that I be your guest. You keep me overtime—then you give me a bill! I won't pay it."

Equally firmly, his host insisted that he must pay. Finally he said, "All right. We'll consult the rabbi."

They sought out the rabbi. He heard the whole story, stroked his beard, and pored at length over the books of the Law. At last, after recapitulating the whole case, he delivered his verdict: "You must pay."

The victim flew into a rage. They thrashed the case back and forth many times. But the rabbi was adamant: "You must pay."

At last, weary and desirous only of getting to Pinsk, the man drew out his wallet and paid the money, demanding a receipted bill. His friend took the money, receipted the bill, and then handed the money back again, saying, "Forget it!"

"What!" screamed the other in despair. "You force me to be your guest; you won't take no for an answer; you keep me there; you give me a bill; you drag me to the rabbi; he tells me I must pay; I pay. And now you give me back the money. What is this?"

"Ah," said his friend, "I just wanted you to see what kind of a dope we have got for a rabbi in Minsk."

SEE ALSO   RELATED SUBJECTS
Wealth 2181   Churchmen 1451–1456

BISHOPS

1491—"Pat," casually asked the contractor of his workman, "didn't you once tell me that you had a brother who was a bishop?"

"Yes."

"And you are a bricklayer. It surely is a funny world. Things in life aren't divided equally, are they, Pat?"

"No, that they ain't, sor," said Pat as he proudly slapped the plaster along the line of bricks, "my poor brother couldn't do this to save his loife, sor."

1492—Somebody jested with a noted British jurist, Lord Salisbury, noting that a bishop was a man of greater authority than he. "A judge can do no more than say, 'You be hanged.' A bishop has the power to say, 'You be damned.'"

"That may be true," said Salisbury, "but when a judge says, 'You be hanged,' you are hanged!"

1493—Some years ago a person requested permission of the Bishop of Salisbury to fly from the top of the spire of that Cathedral. The good Bishop, with an anxious concern for the man's spiritual as well as temporal safety, told him he was very welcome to fly to the Church, but he would encourage no man to fly from it.

1494—When Archbishop Patrick J. Ryan of Philadelphia was a very young priest he was stationed at a Parish in St. Louis, where Archbishop Kendrick presided over the diocese. The latter lived in a very small, unpretentious house, scarcely in keeping with his position in the Church.

One day when Father Ryan was passing the house of the Archbishop, accompanied by a Chicago priest who was visiting St. Louis, he pointed out the house as the residence of the head of the local church. The Chicago priest said with surprise:

"Why, you should see the splendid residence we have in Chicago for our Archbishop!"

"Yes," said Father Ryan, "but you should see the splendid Archbishop we have in St. Louis for our residence."

1495—An eminent English Bishop, who had sojourned in America for some time, was speaking of his adoption of American slang. "I now say to my chauffeur, 'Step on the gas, George,' but I have not yet had the courage to say to the Archbishop of Canterbury, 'O.K., Chief.'"

1496—When the Reverend Whitefield became so popular a character it was agitated in the Privy Council that some method should be used to stop his preaching. Lord Chesterfield being present, turned on his heel and said: "Make him a bishop and you will silence him at once."

1497—One time Phillips Brooks was about to embark for Europe. A friend suggested jokingly that possibly he would bring a new religion back with him. He cautioned that if this was so, he should be careful, it might be difficult to get a new religion through the Customs House.
"I doubt it," said Bishop Brooks. "In all likelihood any new religion popular enough to import would have no duties attached to it."

1498—Bishop Manning of New York is fond of recalling the occasion upon which he was introduced in great dignity to a Negro congregation by its Negro pastor as, " a sounding brass and a tinkling cymbal."

SEE ALSO
Smoking 65
Profanity 67, 68
Memory 374
Pompousness 423
Marriage 877
Sermons 1553
Believers 1593
Hypochondriacs 1720
Stealing 2582

RELATED SUBJECTS
Churchmen 1451–1456

POPES

1501—Michelangelo, when painting in the Pope's chapel the picture of Hell and the souls of the damned, made one of the latter so exact a resemblance of a cardinal who was his enemy, that everyone immediately applied to Pope Clement, desiring it might be effaced; to which the latter replied, "You know that I have power to deliver a soul out of purgatory, but not out of Hell!"

1502—New made Popes were formerly seated on a chair with a hole in it, from whence they threw money to the people. The design of this delicate throne was to intimate to the newly elected Pope, that he was subject to the calls of nature like other men.

1503—When Sixtus the Fifth aspired to the Popedom he counterfeited old age for fifteen years. During the conclave assembled to elect a new Pope, he leaned upon a crutch and appeared remarkably infirm. His plan took so well that the Cardinals elected him, expecting that he would die soon. But shortly after his election he performed the "miracle" of his own cure.

1504—Goethe, walking through Rome with a friend, said to him, "There is not a relic of primitive Christianity here; and if Jesus Christ was to return to see what his deputy was about, he would run a fair chance of being crucified again."

SEE ALSO   RELATED SUBJECTS
Quick Thinking 483   Churchmen 1451–1456

EVANGELISTS

1511—One of the Lincoln stories has it that, during his 1846 campaign for Congress, he attended a preaching service of Peter Cartwright. The Evangelist called on all who wished to go to Heaven to stand up. All rose but Lincoln. The Evangelist called for all to rise who did not want to go to Hell. "I am grieved," said Cartwright, "to see Abe Lincoln sitting back there unmoved by these appeals. If he doesn't want to go to Heaven and doesn't want to escape Hell, will he tell us where he does want to go?"
Lincoln got up slowly and said, "I'm going to Congress."

1512—An evangelist was exhorting his hearers to flee from the wrath to come. "I warn you," he thundered, "that there will be weeping, and wailing and gnashing of teeth!"
At this moment an old woman in the gallery stood up. "Sir," she shouted, "I have no teeth."
"Madam," returned the evangelist, "teeth will be provided."

1513—An eloquent evangelist who was holding a meeting had been interrupted on several occasions by the departure of some one of the audience. He determined to stop it by making an example of the next person. Therefore, when a young man arose to depart in the middle of his sermon he said: "Young man, would you rather go to hell than listen to this sermon?"
The young man stopped midway up the aisle and turning slowly answered: "Well, to tell the truth, I don't know but I would."

1514—A traveling Negro evangelist was fond of making spectacular finales for his revival meetings. Coming to a church, he arranged for his usual climax by secreting in the rafters of the ceiling a small Negro boy with a caged dove. At the height of his sermon the parson would shout for the Holy Ghost to come down, whereupon the dove was to be released to fly about. The moment came, and fervent in his cry, the preacher called out, "Holy Ghost come down!" Nothing happened. Again he raised his arms heavenward and said, "Holy Ghost come down!" Nothing happened, and in the expectant hush the little Negro boy poked his head over the rafters and called down, "A yaller cat is dun et the Holy Ghost, shall I throw down de yaller cat?"

1515—That aggressive American revivalist, Dwight Moody, once passed through a large crowd in a Chicago railway station distributing tracts on temperance.

One of those to receive this material was a benign elderly gentleman who glanced at the paper in his hand and peered quizzically at Moody.

"Are you a reformed drunkard?" he asked.

"No, sir, I'm not!" cried Moody in indignation.

"Then," answered the old gentleman, "why don't you reform?"

1516—Billy Sunday, the rootin', tootin', sawdust-trail evangelist, was once interrupted in his harangue by a heckler, who shouted the question, then famous in all agnostic or atheistic circles, "Who was Cain's wife?"

Billy Sunday shot back the reply, "I respect any seeker of knowledge, but I want to warn you, young man, don't risk being lost to salvation by too much inquiring after other men's wives."

SEE ALSO   RELATED SUBJECTS
Conversions 1621   Revivals 1576–1578
                         Conversions 1621–1625

MISSIONARIES

1521—A missionary told how she was once describing the loving character of the Christians' God to a company of her Chinese sisters. As she went on in her holy enthusiasm, picturing God's real character as full of mercy to the sinful and the suffering, one of the Chinese women turned to her neighbor and said, "Haven't I often told you that there ought to be a God like that."

SEE ALSO
Long-Windedness 344

RELATED SUBJECTS
Conversions 1621–1625

CHURCHES

1526—Many years before the popularity of Florida as a winter resort, John D. Rockefeller, Sr., was in the habit of spending his winters at Augusta, Georgia.

While there he always attended the colored Baptist church on the first Sunday of his stay, and the white Episcopal and Methodist churches the following two Sundays.

The Methodist minister, intrigued by this invariable schedule, once asked the Baptist preacher if he knew why Mr. Rockefeller always visited his church first.

"Why, that's easy," replied the preacher. "You Methodists burn electricity, the Episcopalians use gas, but we'uns burn kerosene oil."

1527—There had been a series of severe electrical storms in Orange, New Jersey, and the vestrymen of a certain church in that town had discussed the advisability of placing lightning rods on the edifice. So they went to call on Thomas Edison, the inventor, to get his opinion.

"I think, sir," said their spokesman, "that lightning rods are a mighty good thing on a building. What do you think?"

"What sort of building is it?" asked Edison impatiently.

"A church."

"By all means put them on," said the great inventor. "You know Providence is absent-minded at times."

1528—Harpo Marx is not a religious man. He has never entered a synagogue but once since his Bar Mitzvah. On this occasion he entered a synagogue in search of his bootlegger. He got his pocket picked.

SEE ALSO
Prejudice 451
Poverty 2210
Salaries 2253

RELATED SUBJECTS
Churchmen 1451–1456
Church Services 1531–1538

CHURCH SERVICES

1531—One day the telephone in the office of the Rector of President Roosevelt's Washington church rang, and an eager voice said, "Tell me, do you expect the President to be in church this Sunday?"

"That," the Rector explained patiently, "I cannot promise.

However, God will be there and that will be incentive enough for a reasonably large attendance.

1532—Rebuking her small son for not going to church willingly, his mother said, "You go to the movies for entertainment and you go down to Freddie's house, and over to Tommie's house, and you have a nice time. Now don't you think it is only right that once a week you should go to God's House, just for one hour?"

The boy thought it over and said, "But, Mom, what would you think if you were invited to somebody's house and every time you went, the fellow was never there!"

1533—An extreme instance of tongue-twistedness is found in the case of the nervous and confused usher on Easter morning when the church was crowded to overflowing. Finding a lady somewhat disconcerted at being unable to occupy her usual place, he hastened up and said, "Mardon me, padam, but this pie is occupewd. May I sew you to another sheet?"

1534—In a small and impoverished Negro community, the church had no other hall to hold its services than a large room below a second-story dance hall with a wild reputation. Often, when evening service was being held, it was difficult for the preacher to make himself heard above the stomping and clatter from above. The building was ramshackle, and one night in the midst of a sermon a particularly vigorous jive was in progress above. There was the splintering of a plank, and looking upward in alarm, the parson saw, protruding through a hole that had given way in the ceiling, the solid and buxom leg of a Negress. In consternation, he at once called out, "Any man what raises his eyes to the ceiling De Lawd will strike blind!"

A hushed silence fell over the congregation, when the quavering voice of an aged Negro at the rear of the church was heard to remark, "Waal, I'll risk one eye on it anyhow."

1535—The noted Baptist preacher, Jerome D. Engel, was once annoyed by an old gentleman who fell asleep during his sermon on several consecutive Sundays. A small boy habitually accompanied the old gentleman and, after service one morning, Engel spoke to the boy in the vestry and said, "My lad, who's the elderly gentleman with whom you attend church?"

"Grandpa," was the reply.

"Well," promised Engel, "if you will only keep him awake during the sermon, I will give you a nickel each week." This seemed advantageous to the lad, and for the following two weeks the old gentleman listened attentively. But the third week, he once again dropped off soundly to sleep and Engel was vexed. Sending for the boy, he said, "Didn't you agree to keep him awake every week for a nickel?"

"Yes, sir," said the boy, "but now Grandpa gives me a dime not to disturb him."

1536—In a small Scottish church, a sexton was painstakingly pursuing his duties, seeing that everyone had his place and was properly quiet during the sermon.

Suddenly he spied an old Scotswoman with an ear trumpet. Being unfamiliar with this device, he hurried over to her and in a low tone said, "One toot and you're oot."

1537—In the later years of his ministry, the Southern preacher, Jerome D. Engel, became slightly hard of hearing. A legend has it that at one service during the announcement period, Engel informed the congregation about new hymnals which were being ordered and which were to be purchased individually by the congregation. When he had finished the announcement, the Deacon of the church arose to remind the audience that the following Sunday was the regular day for the baptism of infants. Engel, not hearing clearly and thinking the deacon had made reference to the books, hastily added, "All you who haven't any, can get as many as you want, by calling on me, at 75¢ a piece."

1538—A woman engaged an Irish maid from the city to serve at her country estate. The girl was a devout Catholic and suffered from the fact that the only church of any description within reach of her new place of employment was a Christian Science temple. Feeling the necessity to worship in somewise she at last attended services there. Upon her return her employer asked, "Well, Mary, how did you like the Christian Science services?"

"Faith," said Mary, "it was mighty quare. I went in and sat down and after a time a man on one side of the church got up and told what Mary Baker Eddy had done for him; then another man got up and told what Mary Baker Eddy had done for him. And next a woman in

front of me got up and told what Mary Baker Eddy had
done for her, and it went on until I couldn't stand it any
longer, and I got right up and told what Lydia E. Pinkham had done for me."

SEE ALSO   RELATED SUBJECTS
Hypocrisy 301   Sermons 1541–1559
                           Collections 1561–1569
                           Sunday School 1571
                           Revivals 1576–1578
                           Prayer 1606–1612

SERMONS

1541—The well-known and popular preacher, Charles Spurgeon,
    was admonishing a class of Divinity students on the im-
    portance of making the facial expressions harmonize
    with the speech in delivering sermons. "When you
    speak of Heaven," he said, "let your face light up and
    be irradiated with a Heavenly gleam. Let your eyes
    shine with reflected glory. And when you speak of Hell
    —well, then your every-day face will do."

1542—Mark Twain occasionally attended the services of Dr.
    Doane, later Bishop of Albany, but then Rector of an
    Episcopal church in Hartford. One Sunday morning
    Twain said to him at the end of the service, "Dr. Doane,
    I enjoyed your service this morning. I welcomed it like
    an old friend. I have, you know, a book at home con-
    taining every word of it."
    "You have not," said Dr. Doane indignantly.
    "I have so."
    "Well, you send that book to me. I'd like to see it."
    "I'll send it," promised Twain. The following day he sent
    Dr. Doane an unabridged dictionary.

1543—A visiting minister was eating breakfast with his host, be-
    fore the morning service at which he was to speak. He
    ate very little, explaining that it is not good for a
    preacher to eat heavily before a sermon. The housewife
    had prepared the meal with great care and felt some-
    what peeved at the apparent lack of appreciation of her
    cooking. She could not attend the service, as she had
    the dinner to prepare.
    When her husband got home she inquired:
    "Well, how was he?"

The husband, drawing a sigh, replied:
"He might just as well of et."

1544—When a Scotch minister told his neighbor that he had preached two hours and a half the day before, the neighbor said to him, "Why, minister, were you not tired to death?"

"Aw, na," said he, "I was as fresh as a rose, but it would have done your heart good to see how tired the congregation was."

1545—A minister named Craig purchased a whistle and when his hearers went to sleep, he emitted from it a very shrill sound. All were awake and sat up to hear him. "You are certainly smart specimens of humanity," said he, as he slowly gazed at his wondering people; "when I preach the gospel you go to sleep, when I play the fool you are wide awake."

1546—"I ought not to be surprised by anything at my time of life," said a well-known minister, "but one of my flock did manage to take my breath away. I was preaching about the Father's tender wisdom in caring for us all; illustrated by saying that the Father knows which of us grows best in sunlight and which of us must have shade. "You know you plant roses in the sunshine," I said, "and heliotrope and geraniums; but if you want your fuchsias to grow they must be kept in a shady nook." After the sermon, which I hoped would be a comforting one, a woman came up to me, her face glowing with pleasure that was evidently deep and true. "Oh, Dr. ——, I am so grateful for that sermon," she said, clasping my hand and shaking it warmly. My heart glowed for a moment, while I wondered what tender place in her heart and life I had touched. Only for a moment, though. "Yes," she went on fervently, "I never knew before what was the matter with my fuchsias."

1547—George Whitefield, the celebrated preacher, was on one occasion describing a blind man's approach unknowingly to the edge of a precipice.

"Tap, tap, went his stick, feeling the way. Shuffle, shuffle, came his feet. Rods of distance dwindled to yards, yards dwindled to inches. The last full step took him to the edge; his stick reached into vacancy and slipped from his hand; he moved forward to retrieve it; he lifted one

foot over vacancy"—and the skeptical, licentious Lord
Chesterfield, who was in the audience, leaped to his feet,
crying out: "My God! He's gone!"

1548—The celebrated preacher, Rowland Hill, was greatly annoyed whenever any noise diverted the attention of his
hearers from what he was saying. On one occasion, a
few days before his death, he was preaching to a
crowded congregation, and in the middle of his discourse
observed a commotion in the gallery.
"What's the matter there," he exclaimed. "The devil seems
to have got among you!"
A plain, country-looking man started to his feet, and addressing Mr. Hill in reply, said:
"No sir—it aren't the devil as is doing it! It's a fat lady
what's faint; and she is a very fat 'un, sir, as don't seem
likely to come to again in a hurry."
"Oh, that's it—is it?" observed Mr. Hill, drawing his hand
across his chin. "Then I beg the lady's pardon—and the
devil's too."

1549—Garrick said he would give a hundred guineas if he could
say "Oh!" as well as the Rev. Whitefield.

1550—Dr. South, when preaching before Charles II observed
that the monarch and his attendants began to nod; and
some of them soon after snored. On this he broke off
his sermon, and said, "Lord Lauderdale, let me entreat
you to rouse yourself; you snore so loud, that you will
awake the king."

1551—"My brethren," said the satirical Dean Swift in a sermon,
"there are three kinds of pride—of birth, of riches, and
of talent. I shall not speak of the latter, none of you being liable to that abominable vice."

1552—A somewhat self-satisfied and greatly inexperienced young
preacher one Sunday supplied the pulpit of a country
church. After services he asked one of the church fathers
what he thought of his sermon. "Now, I'll tell you,"
said the old man, "I'll put it in a sort of parable. I recollect Archie Tucker's first deer hunt. He was kind of
green. He followed the deer all right, but he followed
it all day in the wrong direction."

1553—A prominent bishop tells of the Sunday morning when he
was approached after the service by an old lady, who

said in a tone of appreciation, "Bishop, you'll never know what your service meant to me. It was just like water to a drowning man!"

1554—A certain minister recounted a harrowing experience which befell him during one of his sermons. Just as he was beginning his address, an elderly lady of stern mien marched down and seated herself directly beneath him in front of the pulpit. She opened up a little kit, assembled the various parts of a rather elaborate hearing mechanism and affixed it to her ears. After not more than 10 minutes of his discourse, she suddenly took off the ear-pieces, unscrewed the mechanism and packed it neatly away in its little box, and sat with her hands in her lap throughout the rest of the sermon.

1555—"I believe you have never heard me preach, Charles?" said Coleridge, referring to the days of his Unitarian ministry.

"Yes," retorted Lamb. "I-I never heard you do anything else."

1556—When the celebrated Reverend Whitefield preached before seamen in New York some two hundred years ago he used the following graphic description to describe the plight of sinners:

"Well, my boys, we have a clear sky, and are making fine headway over a smooth sea before a light breeze, and we shall soon lose sight of land. But what means this sudden lowering of the heavens, and that dark cloud arising from beneath the western horizon? Don't you hear distant thunder? Don't you see those flashes of lightning? There is a storm gathering! Every man to his duty! How the waves rise and dash against the ship! The air is dark! The tempest rages! Our masts are gone! The ship is on her beam ends! What next?"

At this point the congregation of tars arose as one man and shouted: "Take to the long boats!"

1557—It is told of John Wesley that when he saw some of his hearers asleep he stopped in his discourse and shouted: "Fire! Fire!"

The sleepers were alarmed, and waking up, cried out: "Where, sir, where?"

"In hell!" replied Wesley solemnly—"In hell for those who sleep under the preaching of the word."

1558—A Clergyman in a Lawrence church on a recent occasion discovered, after beginning the service, that he had forgotten his notes. As it was too late to send for them, he said to his audience, by way of apology, that this morning he should have to depend upon the Lord for what he might say but in the afternoon he would come better prepared.

1559—An admirer of a distinguished clergymen remarked in his praise: "President Holley was an excellent preacher—he never put any religion or politics in his sermon."

SEE ALSO   RELATED SUBJECTS
Liars 335   Speeches 756–782
Long-Windedness 342   Ministers 1461–1477
Handicaps 701   Church Services 1531–1538
Wife 932
Collections 1568

COLLECTIONS
1561—Andrew Carnegie told this story: One day he found himself in a sleepy little town in Georgia on a Sunday, and he determined to visit the colored church. When the plate was passed he dropped a fifty dollar banknote on it. The old man who passed the plate put it down at once, examined the note carefully on both sides, then counted the change in the plate. Then he marched solemnly to the front with the plate and whispered to the pastor, nodding first at the fifty dollar note and then at Mr. Carnegie. The minister put the plate on the pulpit, fingered the note, blinked once or twice and said: "Bre'ren, de Lawd hab be'n mighty good to us dis day. De collec'shun mounts to one dollar en twenty-fo cents, 'en ef de fifty dollar bill wha' dat man wid de grey ha'r 'en beard put in de plate, am good, we have fifty-one dollahs 'en twenty-fo' cents. Let us t'ank de Lawd, en pray dat it may be a good bill."

1562—Wishing to develop his son's character, a father once gave him a penny and a quarter as he was departing for church, and said, "Now, son, you put whichever one you want in the collection plate."
When the boy got back, his father asked which coin he had given. The young fellow said, "Well, just before they sent around the plate the preacher said, 'The Lord

loveth a cheerful giver,' and I knew I could be a lot more cheerful if I gave the penny, so I gave it."

1563—A young hopeful, setting out for Sunday School one morning, was given two nickels, one for the collection plate and one for himself. As he was rambling down the street he played with the coins. One of them slipped out of his hand, rolled away from him and disappeared irretrievably into the sewer. The youngster gazed ruefully down through the grate for a moment and then said, "Well, there goes the Lord's nickel."

1564—A very old lady and a very small boy were seated side by side in the pew of the church. As the collection plate was being passed the little boy noticed that the lady seemed to be fumbling fruitlessly in her purse.

Leaning toward her he whispered, "Here, you take my dime. I can hide under the seat."

1565—The Rev. Sydney Smith, preaching a charity sermon frequently repeated the assertion that, of all nations, Englishmen were most distinquished for generosity and the love of their species. The collection happened to be inferior to his expectations and he said that he had evidently made a great mistake, for that his expression should have been, that they were distinguished for the love of their specie.

1566—The Vicar of St. John's Church in Waterloo, England, contrived an original way of dispensing with annual Church bazaars. To all the members of his congregation he sent the following bill: "Bus fare . . . admission . . . wear and tear on clothes and tempers . . . tea . . . useless articles . . . total . . . Please remit."

The sums received were in excess of any previously raised.

1567—In the church meeting the suggestion had been made and well received that a drive be undertaken to raise money to buy a chandelier for the church. A crusty old elder, however, arose and said, "It's tomfoolery and extravagant frippery. It will not only cost money to buy the durn thing and install it, but next we'll have to hire somebody to play it."

1568—"Brudren," said a darky minister down South, "brudren, I'se got a five-dollar sermon, an a two-dollar sermon, an' a one-dollar sermon, an' I want dis here indelicate audience to take up a collection as to which one ob dem dey can afford to hear."

1569—The official board of the church had called a meeting in order to seek a means of raising funds for much-needed repairs. The little church was literally falling apart and the pastor, stirred by a very real emotion, having been connected with this parish for nearly twenty years, made a moving speech.

Great was his and the other members' surprise when the most miserly member of the board rose and offered to start the fund with a contribution of five dollars. As he spoke a bit of plaster fell and hit him on the head. A trifle dazed, he rose again and said, "Reckon I'd better make that fifty dollars."

From the back of the hall came a pleading voice. "Hit him again, Lord!"

SEE ALSO
Long-Windedness 344
Shrewdness 541
Stinginess 557
Collection 2179

RELATED SUBJECTS
Generosity 241–248
Stinginess 556–566
Church Services 1531–1538

SUNDAY SCHOOL

1571—"Which is the first and most important sacrament?" asked a Sunday-school teacher of a girl preparing for confirmation.

"Marriage," was the prompt response.

"No, baptism is the first and most important sacrament," the teacher corrected.

"Not in our family," said the pupil haughtily, "we are respectable."

SEE ALSO
Patriotism 401
Collections 1563
Fishing 1852

RELATED SUBJECTS
Church Services 1531–1538

REVIVALS

1576—At one time, Henry Ward Beecher used to amaze earnest inquirers at revival meetings by asking them, instead of the expected questions about their souls, how much exercise they took and whether their bowels moved regularly. He called this "clinical theology": it enabled him, as he said, to distinguish in his penitents between "dyspepsia and piety."

1577—Jerome D. Engel, when conducting one of his celebrated revivals in Philadelphia, stopped a small newsboy and asked him the way to the post-office.

"Down this street three squares and turn to the left."

"You seem a bright little fellow," said Engel, a man of considerable self-esteem. "Do you know who I am?"

"Naw."

"I am the famous preacher who is holding the revival over in the big tabernacle. If you will come to my meeting tonight I will show you the way to Heaven."

"Aw, go on," said the youngster, "you don't even know the way to the post-office."

1578—The Negro Baptist minister was exhorting his flock, "Come, my children. Get your sins washed away."

One of his congregation spoke up, "I already have. Over at the Methodist church."

"Brother Jones," sternly replied the minister, "you ain't been washed, you just been dry cleaned."

SEE ALSO	RELATED SUBJECTS
Hypocrisy 302	Evangelists 1511–1516
Evangelists 1514	Devout Persons 1601–1602
	Conversions 1621–1625

BIBLE

1581—A bigoted old churchgoer, firmly set in his notions, rebuffed his neighbor who was speaking of a new American version of the Bible. Said he, "If the King James version was good enough for St. Paul, it's good enough for me."

1582—The Rev. Dr. W. S. Rainsford once told of the futility of trying to comfort people with Bible texts.

"Whenever I tried to persuade an Irish member of my flock to pay more attention to his church duties, he would make the excuse that it took him all his time to earn a living, and he would touch my heart by his expatiation upon the difficulty of making money.

"But Patrick," I protested, "man does not live by bread alone."

"No, y'r Riverance," replied Patrick, "Sure, an' he needs a bit o' mate an' some vegetables as well!"

1583—Someone remarked in President Grant's presence that Sumner did not believe in the Bible. "Why should he?" asked the President, "he did not write it."

1584—On one occasion, when Mrs. William Gladstone was entertaining visitors, conversation turned on the Bible, and there was a lively argument on the meaning of a certain passage.

Presently one of the callers, hoping to end the discussion, remarked devoutly:

"There is One alone who knows all."

The cloud vanished from Mrs. Gladstone's face and she smiled sunnily as she said:

"Yes, and William will be down in a few minutes."

1585—Mark Twain was fond of telling the story of the small boy's account of Elijah in his less ingratiating mood.

"There was a prophet named Elijah. One day he was going up a mountainside. Some boys threw stones at him. He said, 'If you keep on throwing stones at me I'll set the bears on you and they'll eat you up.' And they did, and he did, and the bears did."

1586—Greatly distressed by the prevailing ignorance of the villagers in the small village in which she was vacationing, an old lady persuaded the schoolteacher to give some lessons to some of the more illiterate adults.

Meeting one of these pupils on the street one day she asked kindly, "Well, John, I guess you can read your Bible by this time."

"Bless your heart, ma'am," was the grateful reply, "I was out of the Bible and into the baseball news over a week ago."

SEE ALSO   RELATED SUBJECTS
Liars 335   Churchmen 1451–1456
Society 796   Church Services 1531–1538
School Classrooms 1053 Sermons 1541–1559
Rationing 2357

BELIEVERS

1591—Chateauneuf, keeper of the seals of Louis XIII, when a boy of only nine years old, was asked many questions by a bishop, and gave very prompt answers to them all. At length the prelate said, "I will give you an orange if you will tell me where God is."

"My lord," replied the boy, "I will give you two oranges if you will tell me where he is not."

1592—When John Jay was asked how it was possible for him to occupy his mind after his retirement from public life, he replied with a smile, "I have a long life to look back upon and an eternity to look forward to."

1593—Parson Paten was so much averse to the Athanasian Creed that he would never read it. Archbishop Secker having been informed of his recalcitrance, sent the archdeacon to ask him his reason. "I do not believe it," said the priest.

"But your metropolitan does," replied the archdeacon.

"It may be so," rejoined Mr. Paten, "and he can well afford it; he believes at the rate of seven thousand pounds a year, and I only at fifty."

1594—Four gentlemen—a Baptist, Presbyterian, Methodist and Roman Catholic—met by agreement to dine on fish. Soon as grace was said, the Catholic rose, armed with a knife and fork, and taking about one-third of the fish, including the head, removed it to his plate, saying with great satisfaction: "The Pope is the head of the church." Immediately the Methodist minister arose, and helping himself to about one third, embracing the tail, said: "The end crowns the work." The Presbyterian now thought it was time for him to move, and taking the remainder of the fish to his plate, exclaimed: "Truth lies between the two extremes."

Our Baptist brother had nothing before him but an empty plate, and the prospect of a slim dinner, so seizing a bowl of melted butter, he dashed it over them, exclaiming: "I baptize you all."

1595—Shortly before the death of Thoreau, a pious aunt visited him and asked, "Have you made your peace with God, Henry?"

"I don't know that we ever quarrelled," he replied.

1596—Abraham Lincoln once remarked to a friend that his religion was like that of an old man named Glenn in Indiana, whom he heard speak at a church meeting and who said: "When I do good I feel good; when I do bad, I feel bad; and that's my religion."

SEE ALSO
Football 1858
Stool Pigeons 2591

RELATED SUBJECTS
Devout Persons 1601–1602
Prayer 1606–1612
Miracles 1616–1619
Conversions 1621–1625
Bigotry 1626–1629
Superstition 1631–1636
Atheists and Agnostics 1651–1659

DEVOUT PERSONS

1601—Henry M. Stanley, the famous deliverer of Dr. Livingston from darkest Africa, one time came to Edison's laboratory to see the great inventor demonstrate his new invention, the phonograph.

Having heard the machine and been tremendously impressed by it, he asked, "Mr. Edison, if it were possible for you to hear the voice of any man whose fame is known in the history of the world, whose voice would you prefer to hear?"

"Napoleon," Edison answered without hesitation.

"No, no," said Stanley with an overtone of disapproval, "I should like to hear the voice of Our Savior."

"Oh, well," replied Edison slightly embarrassed by his guest's religious feeling, "You know I like a hustler."

1602—An ignorant coal miner, a devout man, was chided because he had not succeeded in converting his three sons. He defended himself with these words: "I tells 'em to pray and they won't pray, and I tells 'em again to pray and they won't pray, and I knocks 'em down and they won't pray."

SEE ALSO
Church Services 1538

RELATED SUBJECTS
Devotion 171–173
Believers 1591–1596
Prayer 1606–1612
Miracles 1616–1619
Conversions 1621–1625
Bigotry 1626–1629

PRAYER

1606—To a clergyman during the early war period Lincoln made a significant remark. "Let us have faith, Mr. President," the minister said with great solemnity, "that the Lord is on our side in this great struggle."

To which Lincoln quietly retorted, "I am not at all concerned about that, for I know that the Lord is always
on the side of the right; but it is my constant anxiety
and prayer, that I and this nation may be on the Lord's
side."

1607—A pious lady had prayed St. Raboni for the conversion of
her husband—a few days after, he died—whereupon the
widow exclaimed, "What a gracious saint is Raboni, he
even gives us more than we pray for."

1608—Bion was sailing in a vessel, when a great storm came on.
The mariners, who were wicked and dissolute fellows,
called upon the gods; but Bion said, "Peace; let them
not know you are here."

1609—After the capture of Ticonderoga, Ethan Allen, the American patriot, hurried home to his family in Bennington,
Vermont, and while there attended a Thanksgiving service at the Old First Church. Town history says that
during the long prayer in which the Rev. Mr. Dewey
was giving all the credit for the victory to the Lord,
Allen interrupted: "Parson Dewey, Parson Dewey!" At
the third call, the minister paused and opened his eyes.
"Please," said Allen, "mention to the Lord about my being
there."

1610—Dr. Franklin, when a child, found the long graces used by
his father before and after meals very tedious. One day,
after the winter's provisions had been salted: "I think,
father," said Benjamin, "if you were to say grace over
the whole cask, once for all, it would be a vast saving
of time."

1611—It was said that Oliver Cromwell, the English statesman
and soldier, usually said the following grace before
meals: "Some people have food but no appetite; others
have appetite, but no food. I have both. The Lord be
praised."

1612—The new preacher had finished his sermon in which he
had listed all the human wants that he thought the Lord
should gratify.
The deacon asked the old Negro janitor who had listened
patiently throughout this sermon, if he did not think the
minister had offered up a good prayer.
"Ah most suttinly does, boss. Why that man asked de

Lawd fo' things de othah preacher didn't even know
He had."

SEE ALSO   RELATED SUBJECTS
Shortness 694   Believers 1591–1596
Congress 1941   Devout Persons 1601–1602
Bosses 2234   Miracles 1616–1619
Civil War 2329

MIRACLES

1616—Caedmon was so unlettered that he had to retire for shame
from the Refectory at Whitley Abbey when the harp,
passing from hand to hand during dinner, approached
him with its implication that he must recite. "On one
of these occasions," as narrated by Bede, "it happened
to be Caedmon's turn to keep guard at the stable during the night and overcome with vexation, he quitted
the table and retired to his post of duty, where, laying
himself down, he fell into a sound slumber. In the midst
of his sleep, a stranger appeared to him, and, saluting
him by his name, said: 'Caedmon, sing me something.'
Caedmon answered: 'I know nothing to sing; for my
incapacity in this respect was the cause of my leaving
the hall to come hither.' 'Nay,' said the stranger, 'but
thou hast something to sing.' 'What must I sing?' said
Caedmon. 'Sing the Creation,' was the reply; and thereupon Caedmon began to sing verses which he had never
heard before.

"Caedmon then awoke, and he was not only able to repeat
the lines which he had made in his sleep, but he continued them in a strain of admirable versification. In
the morning he hastened to the town reeve, or bailiff of
Whitley, who carried him before the Abbess Hilda; and
there, in the presence of some of the learned men of the
place, he told his story, and they were all of the opinion
that he had received the gift of song from Heaven."

1617—On February 10, 1872 Mr. Wallace Wright publicly challenged Mrs. Mary Baker Eddy—

" 1st. To restore the dead to life again as she claims
she can.

" 2nd. To walk upon the water without the aid of
artificial means as she claims she can.

" 3rd. To live 24 hours without air, or 24 days without nourishment of any kind without its having
any effect upon her.

" 4th. To restore sight when the optic nerve has been destroyed.

" 5th. To set and heal a broken bone without artificial means."

Mr. Wright ended the controversy by the exultant announcement on Feb. 17 that his opponent and her Science were practically dead and buried.

1618—A Negro preacher addressed his flock with great earnestness on the subject of Miracles, as follows:

"My beloved, friends, de greatest ob all miracles was 'bout the loaves and fishes. Dey was 5000 loaves and 2000 fishes, and de twelve apostles had to eat 'em all. De miracle is dey didn't bust."

1619—John Wesley, the hymnist, was nominated a special person by divine fiat. When a baby, he was miraculously saved from his father's burning office. Just after his escape the roof fell in. This incident contributed so strongly to his later evangelism, giving him the conviction that he had been saved by God for a special mission, that he adopted a device found on some of the contemporary prints, of him, namely, a house in flames, with this motto from the prophet, "Is he not a brand plucked from the burning?"

SEE ALSO
Popes 1503
Boats 1816

RELATED SUBJECTS
Believers 1591–1596
Prayer 1606–1612
Superstition 1631–1636

CONVERSIONS

1621—During the Civil War the late Colonel Gabe Bouch organized a regiment which he controlled as a dictator.

"I am an humble servant of the Lord," said an itinerant evangelist who had wandered into camp one day," endeavoring to save the souls of the unfortunate. I have just left the camp of the Massachusetts, where I was instrumental in leading eight men into the paths of righteousness."

"Adjutant," thundered Colonel Bouch, after a moment's pause, "detail ten men for baptism. No d—d Massachusetts regiment shall beat mine for piety."

1622—George Cruikshank having become a teetotaller, showed all the vehement zeal of a convert. Douglas Jerrold, meeting him shortly after his conversion, exclaimed, "Now, George, remember that water is very good anywhere—except upon the brain."

1623—A woman was testifying of her conversion at a revival meeting. She said: "I was very foolish and vain. Worldly pleasures, and especially the fashions, were my only thought. I was fond of silks, satins, ribbons and laces. But, my friends, when I saw they were dragging me down to perdition I gave them all to my sister."

1624—A young man, who had formerly attended Dr. Bethune's meetings, after an absence of a few years called upon him and said: "Dr. Bethune, I have become a Christian since I saw you, and have joined the army of the Lord."

"I am very glad to hear it," said the doctor, and added, "With what denomination have you become connected?"

"The Baptists."

"Oh the Baptists," said Dr. Bethune. "Why they are not the army, but the navy of the Lord."

1625—A Methodist in America, bragging how well he had instructed some Indians in religion, asked one of them "if he had not found great comfort last Sunday, after receiving the sacrament."

"Aye, master," replied the savage, "but I wished it had been brandy."

SEE ALSO	RELATED SUBJECTS
Rabbis 1486	Evangelists 1511–1516
Devout Persons 1602	Revivals 1576–1578
Jail 2563	Miracles 1616–1619

BIGOTRY

1626—"What did the Puritans come to this country for?" asked a teacher in a class of American history.

"To worship in their own way, and make other people do the same," was the reply.

1627—The Young Men's Christian Association appointed a committee to go to President Lincoln to protest his appointment of the Rev. Mr. Shrigley as hospital chaplain in the army. When they first approached the President, mentioning Mr. Shrigley's name, he misunderstood them and thought that they had come to praise his choice, and said:

"Oh yes, I have sent it to the senate. His testimonials are

highly satisfactory, and the appointment will no doubt
be confirmed at an early date."

Hastily the committee spokesman protested:

"But, sir, we have come not to ask for the appointment, but
to solicit you to withdraw the nomination, on the
ground that Mr. Shrigley is not evangelical in his senti-
ments."

"Ah!" said the President, "that alters the case. On what
point of doctrine is the gentleman unsound?"

"He does not believe in endless punishment," was the
reply.

"Yes," added another member of the committee, "he believes that even the rebels themselves will finally be
saved; and it will never do to have a man with such
views hospital chaplain."

The President was silent for a moment. Then, regarding
the expectant faces about him, he said with emphasis:
"If that be so, gentlemen, and there be any way under
heaven whereby the rebels can be saved, then let the man
be appointed!"

1628—There are few more tragic records of the struggle of the
human mind and spirit against bigotry than this text of
Galileo's recantation before the "Holy Inquisition."

"But because I have been enjoined by this Holy Office
altogether to abandon the false opinion which maintains
that the sun is the center and immovable, and forbidden
to hold, defend, or teach the said false doctrine in any
manner, and after it had been signified to me that the
said doctrine is repugnant with the Holy Scripture . . .
I abjure, curse, and detest the said heresies and errors
. . . and I swear that I will never more in future say or
assert anything verbally, or in writing, which may give
rise to a similar suspicion of me."

1629—In connection with the destruction of the 700,000 manuscript volumes of the Alexandrian Library, the Caliph
Omar said:

"Either these books conform to the Koran or they do not.
If they do, they are not needed; if they do not, they are
positively harmful. Therefore, let them be destroyed."

SEE ALSO   RELATED SUBJECTS
Courage 153   Hypocrisy 301–303
Bible 1581   Prejudice 441–452
                            Tolerance 601–603

Devout Persons 1601–1602
Superstition 1631–1636
Censors 2351–2355

SUPERSTITION

1631—Coleridge, when asked by a lady if he believed in ghosts, replied, "No, madam, I have seen too many to believe in them."

1632—Carefully explaining the correct procedure in serving meals, the wealthy society lady ended her little lecture to the new maid by saying, "Now, Mary, don't forget. You always serve from the left and take the plates from the right."
"I won't forget, Ma'am," answered the girl in a conciliating tone of voice, "but what's the matter? Superstitious or something?"

1633—Lincoln told this story: a balloon ascension occurred in New Orleans before the war, and after sailing in the air for several hours the aeronaut, who was arrayed in silks and spangles like a circus performer, descended in a cotton field where a gang of slaves were at work. The frightened Negroes took to the woods—all but one venerable darky, who was rheumatic and could not run, and who, as the resplendent aeronaut approached, having apparently just dropped from heaven, said "Good-mornin', Massa Jesus; how's yo' pa?"

1634—When the first telephone line was put in for King Ibn Saud in Arabia, Moslem religious leaders protested against such innovations and works of the Devil from the land of the Infidel. Ibn Saud listened to their complaint, and gave judgment: "If the telephone is really a work of the Devil, the holy words of the Koran will not pass over it; if the holy words do pass over it, it assuredly cannot be the work of the Devil. So we will appoint two mullahs, one to sit in the Palace and one in the telephone exchange, and they are to take turns reading a passage from the Holy Book, and we will see." By this test the religious leaders were convinced.

1635—A snake having twined itself round a key, which was declared by the seers to be a portent, Leotychidas remarked: "It would have been more of a portent if the key had twined itself round a snake."

1636—General Emilio Mola, second in command with the Spanish fascists, was killed in an airplane crash. When peasants picked him up, they found he was in his stocking-feet. A brother officer explained that a Gypsy had once told the General he would die with his boots on, and he therefore always took his shoes off when in an airplane.

SEE ALSO
Dictators 2001
Judges 2492

RELATED SUBJECTS
Prejudice 441–452
Stupidity 576–583
Devout Persons 1601–1602
Bigotry 1626–1629

PROHIBITIONS AND RESTRICTIONS

1641—Here we have just another proof that most conceptions of personal morality depend largely upon whose ox is being gored. As the Negro parson was preaching fervently against all the common sins, ranging from murder to simple crapshooting, a devout old Negress swayed and rocked in her pew, murmuring, "Amen—Amen. Praise God!" at each prohibition. Then the parson started on the subject of snuff dipping, at which the pious old Negress sat bolt upright and muttered to herself, "Now he done stop preachin' and took to meddlin'."

1642—A little lesson in morality was imparted to the youngster who asked his father, "What is a 'necessary evil?' "
"One that we like so much we don't want to abolish it," replied his parent.

SEE ALSO
Behavior 1
Drinking 45
Tolerance 602
Censors 2355

RELATED SUBJECTS
Drinking 36–55
Smoking 61–65
Profanity 66–68
Gambling 71–74
Ministers 1461–1477
Sermons 1541–1559
Bigotry 1626–1629
Sin and Sinners 1646–1647
Censors 2351–2355
Laws 2596–2599

SIN AND SINNERS

1646—An old Negro preacher, wearied of the many complaints he heard about the temptations placed in the paths of members of his congregation by Satan: "Folks is all de time making out dat Satan is runnin' after them fo' to tempt them. De truth is, dere is so many people pulling at the Debil's coattails, he ain't got de time to chase nobody."

1647—In the days of the great Edwin Booth most ministers considered it a sin to attend theatrical performances. However, one clergyman, anxious to see the great actor perform, sent Mr. Booth a letter asking if he might be permitted to enter the theatre by a private door as he did not wish anyone to see him going into such a place.

"Sir," was Booth's reply, "there is no door in my theatre through which God cannot see."

SEE ALSO	RELATED SUBJECTS
Drinking 36	Drinking 36–55
Conscience 146	Smoking 61–65
Hypocrisy 302	Profanity 66–68
Vanity 628	Gambling 71–74
Ministers 1464	Conscience 146–147
Chiseling 2128	Hypocrisy 301–303
	Conversions 1621–1625
	Prohibitions and Restrictions 1641–1642

ATHEISTS AND AGNOSTICS

1651—The noted agnostic, Colonel Robert Ingersoll, during a visit with Henry Ward Beecher, noted a beautiful globe portraying the constellations and stars of the heavens. "This is just what I've been looking for," he said after examining it. "Who made it?"

"Who made it?" repeated Beecher in simulated astonishment. "Why Colonel, nobody made it; it just happened."

1652—Someone once charged David Hume, the agnostic, with being inconsistent because he went to hear the orthodox, Scotch minister, John Brown. Hume replied, "I don't believe all that he says, but he does. And once a week I like to hear a man who believes what he says."

1653—A Portuguese sculptor, upon his death bed, had a crucifix placed before his eyes by a confessor, who said, "Behold that God whom you have so much offended. Do you recollect him now?"

"Alas! Yes, Father," replied the dying man, "it was I who made him."

1654—When Phillips Brooks was recovering from an illness, and was denying himself to all visitors, Robert G. Ingersoll, the agnostic, called. The bishop received him at once.

"I appreciate this very much," said Mr. Ingersoll, "but why do you see me when you deny yourself to your friends?"

"It is this way," said the bishop, "I feel confident of seeing my friends in the next world, but this may be my last chance of seeing you."

1655—Once, while addressing an open-air meeting, an atheist asked Bishop Carpenter if he believed that Jonah was swallowed by the whale.

"When I get to heaven I will ask Jonah," said his lordship.

"But supposing," the other persisted, "he is not there?"

"Then you will have to ask him," was the quick retort.

1656—The late Dr. Jowett, the famous master of Balliol College, Oxford, was met one day in the "quad" by an undergraduate who informed him that he, for his part, could find no positive evidence of the existence of God.

"Well, Mr. B.," said Dr. Jowett tartly, "if you do not find a God by five o'clock this afternoon, you will leave this college!"

1657—One day, when D'Alembert and Condorcet were dining with Voltaire, they proposed to converse of atheism, but Voltaire stopped them at once. "Wait," said he, "till my servants have withdrawn. I do not wish to have my throat cut tonight."

1658—During the riots of 1780 most persons in London, in order to save their houses from being burnt or pulled down, wrote on their doors, "No Popery!" Old Grimaldi, to avoid all mistakes, wrote on his, "No Religion!"

1659—The little Louis Napoleon did not respond with particular susceptibility to his religious education. In the course of it, he stumbled upon one of the puzzling problems which is remarked upon by many young theological students.

His instructor had portrayed with great melodrama the anguish and suffering of Christ. Louis manifested little reaction.

"Aren't you grieved," demanded his teacher, "to think how these wicked men behaved to our Lord?"

"Well," objected Louis, "if He was all powerful, why did He let them?"

SEE ALSO
Shrewdness 538
Libraries 1226
Churchmen 1456
Evangelists 1516

RELATED SUBJECTS
Cynicism 166–170
Believers 1591–1596

PAGAN GODS

1661—According to a story told by Roy Chapman Andrews, the famous explorer, the Living Buddha of Mongolia, a personage only a stage less exalted than the Great Lama of Tibet, was a man of original ideas. One of the regular ceremonies of his office was the laying on of hands to many worshippers and lesser priests who came daily for his blessing. The Buddha conceived a mass blessing. He had a small American Delco generator in his palace. This he rigged up with a wire stretching down a long areaway. The many pilgrims would line up clutching the wire and each received a memorable blessing as the Living Buddha threw the switch by his throne.

Dr. Andrews was invited to partake of the blessing, which courtesy he could not refuse. He reports that the shock nearly knocked him over.

SEE ALSO
Buying and Selling
2066

RELATED SUBJECTS
Believers 1591–1596
Superstition 1631–1636

DOCTORS

1666—Dr. Samuel Garth, the celebrated physician of Pope's time, loved wine to excess. At a favorite club of which he was a member, he once remained to drink to a late hour. A companion said to him, "Really, Garth, you ought to quit drinking and hurry off to your patients."

"It is no great matter," replied Garth, "whether I see them tonight or not; for nine of them have such bad constitutions that all the physicians in the world can't save them; and the other six have such good constitutions, that all the physicians in the world can't kill them."

1667—A certain person coming to a doctor said, "Sir, when I awake from sleep I have a dizziness for half an hour, and then I feel all right."

"Get up after the half-hour," the physician replied.

1668—Senator Beveridge told this story: "I once saw two famous physicians introduced at a reception. They were deservedly famous, but they were of opposing schools; and the regular, as he shook the other by the hand, said loudly:

"I am glad to meet you as a gentleman, sir, though I can't admit that you are a physician."

"And I," said the homeopathist smiling faintly, "am glad to meet you as a physician, although I can't admit you are a gentleman."

1669—Whistler had a French poodle of which he was extravagantly fond. The poodle was seized with an infection of the throat, and Whistler had the audacity to send for the great throat specialist Sir Morell Mackenzie. Sir Morell, when he saw that he had been called in to treat a dog, didn't like it much, it was plain. But he said nothing. He prescribed, pocketed a big fee, and drove away. The next day he sent post-haste to Whistler, and Whistler, thinking he was summoned on some matter connected with his beloved dog, dropped his work and rushed like the wind to Mackenzie's. On his arrival Sir

Morell said gravely: "How do you do, Mr. Whistler? I wanted to see you about having my front door painted."

1670—Professor Charles A. Beard relates this story:

A young doctor returned to the village of his birth and called upon the old family physician.

"I suppose that you intend to specialize," remarked the elder.

"Oh, yes," replied the youth, "in the diseases of the nose; for the ears and throat are too complicated to be combined with the nose for purposes of study and treatment."

Thereupon the family physician inquired: "Which nostril are you concentrating on?"

1671—Stephen Leacock tells this story: "Years ago when I first got my Ph.D. degree, I was inordinately proud of it and used to sign myself 'Dr. Leacock' in season and out. On a trip to the Orient I put my name down that way on the passenger list of the liner. I was just getting my things straight in my cabin when a steward knocked and said: 'Are you Dr. Leacock?' 'Yes,' I answered. 'Well, the captain's compliments, doctor, and will you please come and have a look at the second stewardess's leg?'

I was off like a shot, realizing the obligations of a medical shot. But I had no luck. Another fellow got there ahead of me. He was a Doctor of Divinity."

1672—Before Oliver Wendell Holmes was a writer, he practiced medicine, and taught anatomy at Harvard and Dartmouth. As a practitioner he was not successful, for people were a bit doubtful about the flippant youth, who posted the following sign above his office door: "Small fevers gratefully received."

1673—A doctor was aroused in the middle of the night by a phone call from a man to whose family he had not had occasion to render medical services for some time. "Doctor," said the excited man, "please come over right away. My wife is in great pain and I'm sure it's appendicitis." The doctor had been sleepily mulling over the medical history of the family and said, "Well now, it probably isn't anything like that. I'll come around first thing in the morning. Don't worry. Probably just indigestion."

"But, doctor, you've got to come. I'm positive it's appendicitis," protested the alarmed husband.

"Oh come, Mr. Johnson," the doctor said, somewhat irritably, "I took out your wife's appendix almost two years ago. You know as well as I do that she hasn't got another one."

"That's all right," said the husband, "but I've got another wife."

1674—The patient was lying on the stretcher waiting to be pushed into the operating room. "I'm so nervous," he remarked to a sympathetic young woman standing by. "This is my first operation."

"So am I," said the young lady, "my husband is the doctor and it is his first too."

1675—"I don't understand it," the doctor said to the patient who was still complaining. "Have you carried out all my instructions."

"All but one, doctor. I am not able to take that two mile walk every morning that you suggested. I get too dizzy."

"Dizzy?" asked the doctor. "What do you mean?"

"You see," said his patient, "I forgot to tell you. I'm a lighthouse keeper."

1676—Robert Smith, brother of Sydney Smith, and an ex-Advocate-General, on one occasion engaged in an argument with a physician over the relative merits of their respective professions.

"I don't say that all lawyers are crooks," said the doctor, "but you'll have to admit that your profession doesn't make angels of men."

"No," retorted Smith, "you doctors certainly have the best of us there."

1677—Alexandre Dumas, the French novelist, being the guest one day of Dr. Gistal, an eminent doctor of Marseilles, was asked by his host after dinner to enrich his album with one of his witty improvisations.

"Certainly," replied Dumas with a smile, and drawing out his pencil he wrote under the eyes of the doctor, the following lines:

"Since Dr. Gistal came to our town,
    To cure diseases casual and hereditary,
The hospital has been pulled down"—

"You flatterer!" exclaimed the doctor, mightily pleased. But the poet went on—

"And we have made a larger cemetery."

1678—A physician was talking over some of his cases with a layman friend. A bit maliciously the friend remarked, "Say, doctor, I hear that that man you treated for a liver ailment died of a heart attack."

Outraged at this slur against his professional skill, the doctor shouted, "See here, my good man, when I treat someone for liver trouble, he dies of liver trouble."

1679—A patient going to a doctor for his first visit was asked, "And whom did you consult before coming to me?"

"Only the village druggist," was the answer.

"And what sort of foolish advice did that numbskull give you?" said the doctor, his tone and manner denoting his contempt for the advice of the layman.

"Oh," replied his patient, with no malice aforethought, "he told me to come and see you."

SEE ALSO
Eating 22
Gambling 72
Gratitude 264
Long-Windedness 362
Melancholy 366, 367
Handicaps 706
Births 1015
Scientists 1122
Authors 1212
Painting 1272, 1289
Instrumentalists 1356
Ministers 1475

RELATED SUBJECTS
Scientists 1116–1122
Doctors' Fees 1681
Psychiatrists 1686–1687
Hospitals 1691
Dentists 1696–1697

Sickness 1704
Hypochondriacs 1718, 1719
Medicines 1728
Prisoners 2366
Lawyers 2531

DOCTORS' FEES

1681—"I reckon you get paid right handsome for looking after the rich Johnson boy," observed the cleaning woman to the doctor.

"Why, yes. I get pretty good fees," he replied, somewhat amused. "Why do you ask?"

"I just hope you won't forget that it was my boy what threw the brick that hit him."

RELATED SUBJECTS
Doctors 1666–1679

PSYCHIATRISTS

1686—A Jewish mother was much distressed over the problem of her young son who was afraid to eat the popular dish known as kreplach. She took the boy to a psychiatrist for consultation. After hearing the case, the doctor said, "Now, madam, this is very simple. Take the boy home, take him out in the kitchen, and show him the ingredients that go into the dish. And then, show him how kreplach is made. This should probably eliminate the condition."

Hopefully the mother followed his advice. On the kitchen table she put out a small square of dough beside which was a small mound of prepared chopped meat. "Now," she said, "there's nothing here you should mind." The lad beamed and nodded encouragingly. The mother then put the meat in the center of the dough and folded over one corner. The boy smiled and all seemed to be going well. She folded over the second corner and the third. The boy was nodding and the experiment seemed to be progressing most favorably. Then she folded over the fourth and final corner; whereupon the boy groaned and muttered, "Oi, kreplach!"

1687—A man came to a psychiatrist and proceeded to unfold before the doctor his life story, covering his childhood experiences, his emotional life, his eating habits, his vocational problems, and everything else he could think of. "Well," said the doctor, "it doesn't seem to me as though there were anything wrong with you. You seem as sane as I am."

"But, doctor," protested the patient, a note of horror creeping into his voice, "it's these butterflies. I can't stand them. They're all over me."

"For Heaven's sake," cried the doctor, recoiling, "don't brush them off on me!"

SEE ALSO   RELATED SUBJECTS
Students 1036   Eccentricity 196–209
                         Doctors 1666–1679

HOSPITALS

1691—In West Virginia a contest was once held for a name for a new county hospital. The first prize was a free appendectomy.

SEE ALSO   RELATED SUBJECTS
Doctors 1674   Doctors 1666–1679
                         Sickness 1701–1707
                         Diseases 1721

DENTISTS

1696—After the war, General Pershing found himself in need of dental care. Following the advice of his dentist, he had a number of teeth removed. Great was his indignation when he learned that these teeth were being sold as souvenirs under the name, "Famous General's Teeth."

He hurriedly sent out his aides to round up the molars. There is no record of what he said when they returned with a total of 175 teeth, all purported to be his.

1697—A patient called his dentist for an appointment. "So sorry," said the dentist, "not today. I have eighteen cavities to fill." Whereupon he hung up the phone, picked up his golf bag and departed from his office.

SEE ALSO   RELATED SUBJECTS
Churchmen 1456   Doctors 1666–1679

SICKNESS

1701—C. R. W. Nevinson, English painter, tells one of the finest of all sick-bed stories: "Then came pleurisy, culminating in pneumonia that nearly ended my life. The telephone was at my bedside, and in order that I should not be disturbed we were supposed to be cut off from all incoming calls. One night, however, when the night nurse had gone out of the room the bell rang. Instinctively I reached out my hand.

" 'Yes,' I quavered.

" ' "Daily Blank" speakin',' announced a very Cockney voice. 'Is 'e gone yet?'

"It hurt me to laugh and I maintained my gravity by thinking they should not have left it to the office boy.

" 'No,' I said. 'He's still with us.'

"I then said that the patient had expressed a desire that certain matters should be remembered in his obituary notice, and I dictated a paragraph which the voice assured me it had taken down. I wished him good-bye.

" 'Good-bye,' said the voice. 'An' if 'e goes within the next hour give's a scoop will yer?'

"I promised to do my best in difficult circumstances, and rang off."

1702—The steward attempted to encourage the suffering passenger. "Don't be downhearted, nobody's ever died of seasickness."

"Oh," moaned the sufferer, "how can you be so cruel! Only the hope of death has kept me alive so far."

1703—"Could there be anything worse," an ailing friend once wrote complainingly to Mark Twain, "than having a toothache and an earache at the same time?"
Mark Twain wrote back: "Rheumatism and St. Vitus' Dance."

1704—Looking down at the sick man, the doctor decided to tell him the truth.
"I feel that I should tell you. You are a very sick man. I'm sure that you would want to know the facts. Now—is there anyone you would like to see?"
Bending down toward his patient, the doctor heard him feebly answer, "Yes."
"Who is it?"
In a slightly stronger tone the sufferer said, "Another doctor."

1705—Demetrius would at times tarry from business to attend to pleasure. On such occasions he usually feigned indisposition. His father, coming to visit him, saw a beautiful young lady retire from his chamber. On his entering, Demetrius said, "Sir, the fever has left me."
"I met it at the door," replied the father.

1706—The old-timer had been sick in bed for weeks. The local doctors had been unable to help or to diagnose. The old codger insisted that he didn't need anybody's help, but specialists were called in over his protests. When they had gone, his friends and relatives asked the old man what they had said.
"Told you I was all right," he said triumphantly. "Them gentlemen used a lot of big words I couldn't understand but they finally said, 'Well, no use worrying about it or arguing over it. The autopsy will soon give us the answer.'"

1707—Abraham Lincoln was once confined to the White House with a bad cold. A congressman, who had called to express his sympathy, was interrupted in the middle of his solemn words by the President, who said laughingly, "Well—I expect colds." And looking down at his large feet he continued, "There's so much of me on the ground, you know."

SEE ALSO
Doctors 1674
Office Seekers 1967
Stocks 2147

RELATED SUBJECTS
Doctors 1666–1679
Hospitals 1691
Poor Health 1711–1712
Hypochondriacs 1716–1720
Diseases 1721
Medicines 1726–1731
Death 1746–1749

POOR HEALTH

1711—Daniel Webster described in this way his last interview with John Adams: "While I was with him and conversing on the common topics of the day, someone, a friend of his, came in and made particular inquiry of his health. John Adams answered, 'I inhabit a weak, frail, decayed tenement; battered by the winds and broken in upon by the storms, and, from all I can learn, the landlord does not intend to repair.'"

1712—It is related that during the Civil War Senator Douglas was approached by a constituent, at a time when the most momentous battles were being fought, when the very fate of the Union was hanging in the balance.

"Oh, Mr. Douglas!" exclaimed this constituent, "I am so glad to see you! Tell me—is there—have you any news?"

"Thank you!" answered Senator Douglas gravely. "Thank you—I am feeling much better!"

SEE ALSO
Drinking 42
Congress 1947

RELATED SUBJECTS
Sickness 1701–1707
Hypochondriacs 1716–1720
Diseases 1721

HYPOCHONDRIACS

1716—Hypochondriacs should never go to medical lectures. Invariably they become afflicted with symptoms of any disease they hear about. One such man, having returned from a lecture on diseases of the kidney, immediately called upon his doctor.

The doctor attempted to explain that in that particular disease there were no pains or discomfort of any kind.

"I knew it," gasped the hypochondriac. "My symptoms exactly."

1717—"When I meet a man whose name I cannot remember," Disraeli said, "I give myself two minutes, then if it is a hopeless case, I always say, 'And how is the old complaint?' "

1718—A lady much afflicted with nervous complaints went to consult the celebrated surgeon Dr. Abernethy (18th Century). The rough and caustic manner in which he catechised her, so discomposed the fair one's weak spirits, that she was thrown into a fit of hysterics. On parting, she put the usual fee into his hands in the form of a sovereign and a shilling. Dr. Abernethy pocketed the sovereign with one hand, and with the other presented the shilling to her, saying gravely, "Here, madam, take this shilling, go to the next toy-shop, buy a skipping-rope, and use it every day; it will do you more good than all my prescriptions."

1719—A lady who went to consult the blunt Dr. Abernethy, began a description of her complaint thus: "Whenever I lift my arm, it pains me exceedingly."
"Why, then, madam," said the doctor impatiently, "you are a great fool for lifting it."

1720—A certain Archbishop, getting along in years, had been worried for some time that he would fall a victim to a paralytic stroke. One evening, while playing chess with a very charming young lady, he suddenly became very agitated, and feeling that his presentiment had been fulfilled, he fell back in his chair, murmuring, "Your move."
Alarmed, his partner hurried to his side. "Are you ill?" she asked.
"It has come," the Archbishop replied, "at last it has come, my right side is paralyzed."
"How can you be so sure?"
"I have been pinching my leg," weakly said the Archbishop, "and there is absolutely no feeling."
"Oh," said the charming young lady, blushing profusely, "Your Grace, I do beg your pardon, but it was my leg you were pinching."

RELATED SUBJECTS
Imagination 306
Pessimism 411
Sickness 1701–1707
Poor Health 1711–1712

DISEASES

1721—The founder of Washington's famous Smithsonian Institution, James Smithson, was long troubled by an obscure illness which none of the many doctors consulted were able to diagnose.

"I earnestly desire," he remarked one time, "that you perform an autopsy to discover what is the matter with me, for I am dying to know what my ailment is."

SEE ALSO
Painting 1272

RELATED SUBJECTS
Doctors 1666–1679
Hospitals 1691
Sickness 1701–1707
Medicines 1726–1731

MEDICINES

1726—An old lady, on her way to a summer resort, kept pestering the conductor to tell her when they would reach Ellenville.

Finally, harried by her constant questioning, he pleaded with her to bother him no more, that he would tell her as soon as they reached the town. Becoming busy with all his duties, the train reached and passed Ellenville with the conductor forgetting all about the old lady. Suddenly recollecting her anxiety about the place, he backed up the train and as it pulled into the little station, he hurried out and told the woman, "Here you are now —in Ellenville. I'll help you with your baggage."

"Oh, thank you," replied the dear old lady. "Never mind. I'm not getting off here. My daughter just told me that when I got to Ellenville, it would be just about time to take another of my pills."

1727—Many years ago an English sailor who had broken his leg was advised to send to the Royal Society an account of the remarkable manner in which he had healed the fracture. He did so. His story was that, having fractured the limb by falling from the top of a mast, he had dressed it with nothing but tar and oakum, which had proved so wonderfully efficacious that in three days he was able to walk just as well as before the accident. This remarkable story naturally caused some excitement among the members of the society. No one had previously suspected tar and oakum of possessing such miraculous healing powers. Several letters accordingly passed between the Royal Society and the humble sailor, who continued to assert most solemnly that his broken leg had been treated with tar and oakum, and with these two applications only. The Society might have remained puzzled for an indefinite period had not the man remarked in a postscript to his last letter:

"I forgot to inform your honors, by the way, that the leg was a wooden one."

1728—"Pray Dr. Abernethy, what is the cure for gout?" asked an indolent, luxurious citizen of the famous doctor.
"Live on sixpence a day, and earn it!" was the pithy answer.

1729—When one of Dr. Chapman's patients revolted at a monstrous dose of medicine, and said: "Why, doctor, you don't mean such a dose as this for gentlemen?"
The doctor replied: "Oh no, but for 'working' men."

1730—"Now be sure," the farmer's wife cautioned the druggist, "to label them bottles plain; which one is for the horse, and which one is for my husband. I don't want nothing to happen to that horse before Spring plowing!"

1731—A man, having hurt his forehead, was advised to rub it with brandy. Some days after, being asked if he had done so, he answered, "I have tried several times, but can never get the glass higher than my mouth."

SEE ALSO
Drinking 43
Melancholy 367
Handwriting 733
Hypochondriacs 1718
Deathbed Scenes 1770

RELATED SUBJECTS
Doctors 1666–1679
Hospitals 1721
Sickness 1701–1707
Diseases 1721

ACCIDENTS

1736—"Rastus," said his friend who had been reading in the paper of a number of fatal accidents, "if you had to take your choice 'twixt one or 'tother, which would you ruther be in, a collision or an explosion?"
"Man—a collision," said Rastus.
"How come?"
"Why man, if you's in a collision thar you is, but if you's in an explosion whar is you?"

RELATED SUBJECTS
Injury 1741
Accidental Death 1751

INJURY

1741—An enthusiastic lady told a group of friends in delight of
the opportunity she had had to apply the knowledge she
had acquired in her First Aid class. "It was wonderful,"
she said, "it was so fortunate that I had had the training.
I was crossing Fifth Avenue at 57th Street and heard a
crash behind me. I turned around and saw a poor man
who had been struck by a taxicab. He had a compound
fracture of the leg, was bleeding terribly, was unconscious and seemed to have a fractured skull. Then all my
First Aid came back to me; and I stooped right down
and put my head between my legs to keep myself from
fainting!"

RELATED SUBJECTS
Accidents 1736
Accidental Death 1751

DEATH

1746—One day when the Sultan was in his palace at Damascus
a beautiful youth who was his favorite rushed into his
presence, crying out in great agitation that he must fly
at once to Baghdad, and imploring leave to borrow His
Majesty's swiftest horse.

The Sultan asked why he was in such haste to go to
Baghdad. "Because," the youth answered, "as I passed
through the garden of the Palace just now, Death was
standing there, and when he saw me he stretched out his
arms as if to threaten me, and I must lose no time in
escaping from him."

The young man was given leave to take the Sultan's horse
and fly; and when he was gone the Sultan went down
indignantly into the garden, and found Death still there.
"How dare you make threatening gestures at my favorite?" he cried; but Death, astonished, answered:
"I assure Your Majesty I did not threaten him. I only
threw up my arms in surprise at seeing him here, because I have a tryst with him tonight in Baghdad."

1747—Mark Twain, being a celebrity, turned the famous erroneous announcement of his death into a well-known quip.

More difficult was the situation of the obscure man whose death was mistakenly noted in his local paper. The "corpse" hastened to the editor to protest. "I'm awfully sorry," the editor replied. "And it's too late to do much about it. The best thing I can do for you is to put you in the "Birth Column" tomorrow morning, and give you a fresh start."

1748—It is recorded that Xerxes, the King of Persia, who had gathered vast forces at the Hellespont for the invasion of Greece, caused a lofty seat to be set up on a hill from which he could survey them. "But when he saw," says Herodotus, "the whole Hellespont hidden by his ships, and all the shores and plains of Abydos thronged with men, Xerxes first declared himself happy, and presently he fell a-weeping. . . . 'For,' he said, 'I was moved to compassion when I considered the shortness of all human life, seeing that of all this multitude of men not one will be alive a hundred years hence.' "

1749—A philosopher who went to call on a sick friend, was told at the door:
"He is already departed."
"Well, tell him I called," replied the philosopher.

SEE ALSO	RELATED SUBJECTS
Absent-Mindedness 86	Hospitals 1691
Brevity 131	Sickness 1701–1707
Cheerfulness 143	Diseases 1721
Cowardice 157	Accidental Death 1751
Extravagance 232	Natural Death 1756–1757
Quick Thinking 482	Deathbed Scenes 1761–1775
Stinginess 564	Funerals 1776–1778
Husband 916	
School Classrooms 1052	
Literature 1162	Funerals 1778
Composers 1316	Kings 1976
Producers 1394	Collection 2178
Prayer 1607	Bankruptcy 2198
Superstition 1636	Begging 2217
Diseases 1721	Horse 2288

ACCIDENTAL DEATH

1751—The new foreman was puzzling over the formal papers which had to be filled out explaining the details of the

casualty in which Murphy, one of his workmen, had lost
his life by falling from a high scaffold. At last he managed to complete all of the task except for one more
unfilled line which seemed to stump him. Finally, lick-
ing his pencil, he applied himself firmly to the section
headed, "Remarks," and wrote, "He didn't make none."

RELATED SUBJECTS
Accidents 1736
Injury 1741
Death 1746–1749

NATURAL DEATH

1756—"Scrope Davies," said Lord Byron, "is a wit and a man of
the world and feels as much as such a character can do."
Davies was a great gambler and was always backing
horses, and when at Cambridge, as a student, he had a
peculiar habit of attempting to cut his throat after every
Newmarket meeting when he lost. Indeed, so frequently
did he amuse himself in this way that on one occasion
the doctor who was sent for declined to hasten himself
when he heard it was Scrope's throat that he was required to attend to, saying: "There is no danger of him,
I have sewn him up six times already."
Scrope Davies was enabled to survive this little peculiarity
for over forty years and died a natural death in Paris.

1757—Sir Samuel Garth, the London doctor, lay dying. The presence of officious friends troubled him; and, when he saw
his doctors consulting together, he raised his head from
his pillow, and said with a smile, "Dear gentlemen, let
me die a natural death." After he had received extreme
unction, a friend approached him, and asked how he was
feeling. "I am going on my journey," was the answer;
"They (pointing to the doctors) have greased my boots
already."

SEE ALSO   RELATED SUBJECTS
Insurance 2136   Sickness 1701–1707
                        Diseases 1721
                        Death 1746–1749
                        Accidental Death 1751
                        Deathbed Scenes 1761–1775

DEATHBED SCENES

1761—During his last illness a number of Pennsylvania politicians called upon Thaddeus Stevens to pay their respects and in the course of conversation one of them remarked on his appearance.

"Ah, gentlemen," he said, "it is not my appearance that I am concerned about just now, but my disappearance."

1762—Shortly before his death, Judge John Marshall Harlan of the U. S. Supreme Court became partly conscious and spoke his farewell words to those who were at his bedside: "Goodbye, I am sorry to have kept you all waiting so long."

1763—An old French countess, of the most exquisite politeness, was about to breathe her last, when she received a call from an acquaintance ignorant of her mortal illness. The answer sent down from the chamber of the departing sufferer was eminently unique.

"The Countess de Rouen sends her compliments to Madame de Calais, but begs to be excused, as she is engaged in dying."

1764—A few hours before his death, Marcel Proust asked his servant to bring to his bed a certain page from his manuscript wherein the death agony of one of his characters was described—because "I have several retouchings to make here, now that I find myself in the same predicament."

He wrote like a maniac to the end.

1765—Three days before Blake's death he was working on the "Ancient of Days." "He sat bolstered up in bed, and tinted it with his choicest colors, and in his happiest style. He touched and retouched it—held it at arm's length, and then threw it from him, exclaiming: "There! That will do! I cannot mend it." He saw his wife in tears . . . "Stay, Kate!" cried Blake. "Keep just as you are—I will draw your portrait—for you have ever been an angel to me." And so he did—and it was his last work.

1766—Dr. Arne, the Eighteenth Century English composer, died as he had lived. His intimate friend, Vernon, the favorite singing actor of Drury Lane Theatre described his end:

"I was talking on the subject of music with the doctor, who suffered much from exhaustion, when in attempting to illustrate what he had advanced, he in a very feeble and tremulous voice sang part of an air, during which he became progressively more faint until he breathed his last! Making, as our immortal Shakespeare expresses it, 'a swan-like end, fading in music.' "

1767—When Curran, the witty English lawyer of the 18th Century, lay on his deathbed, he was told by his physician that he coughed rather easier than before. "In faith, so I think I ought, for I have been practicing all night."

1768—When Lord Holland was on his deathbed, his friend George Selwyn called to inquire how his Lordship was, and left his card. This was taken to Lord Holland, who said: "If Mr. Selwyn calls again, show him into my room. If I am alive, I shall be glad to see him. If I am dead I am sure he will be delighted to see me."

1769—Louis XIV lingered in a prolonged deathbed agony, during the whole of which, the courtiers of his chamber were required to be in attendance. After some days of his slow decease, the King opened his eyes and remarked faintly, "Gentlemen, I must apologize for being such an unconscionable time dying."

1770—When John Donne, the English poet, was dying the great physician Doctor Simon Faxe told him he might be restored "by cordials and drinking milk twenty days together"; but the Dean loathed milk and "passionately refused to drink it." Upon the doctor's insisting, he did try it for ten days, then said he would rather die than continue since he didn't fear death.

1771—Scrope Davies, the witty gambler and friend of Byron, was lying on his deathbed. He had seriously taken leave of his physician who told him that he could not live beyond eight o'clock next morning. Exerting the small strength left to him he called the doctor back. "Doctor," he whispered, "I'll bet you five guineas I live till nine."

1772—A clergyman came to a man near to death and said: "Dear friend, do you know who died to save you?"
"Oh, meenister, meenister," said the dying man, "is this a time for conundrums?"

1773—Alonzo Cano, a Spanish artist, when a priest presented to him a crucifix badly executed, turned his eyes away and refused to look at it, but when one of good workmanship was brought to him, he devoutly embraced it and expired.

1774—When the chieftain Rob Roy Macgregor was on his deathbed, a gentleman whom he had reason to consider as an enemy came to see him. On being requested to admit the visitor to his bedside he said, "No enemy shall see Rob Roy in the posture of defeat. Raise me up, put on my clothes, buckle on my arms, then admit him." He was obeyed: the guest was received with cold civility by the dying man, and in a short time departed. "Now," said Rob Roy—"now help me to bed, and call in the piper." The piper appeared; Rob Roy shook hands with him, and desired him to play "Cha tuile mi tuileadgh" and not to cease while he continued to breathe. He soon expired, with the "voice of war" pealing around him.

1775—A moving example of deserted genius was the poet, Heinrich Heine. When the great German lyricist lay on his mattress deathbed in a poverty-ridden Parisian garret, all had forsaken him except his friend, Hector Berlioz, the composer. Moved by this sole demonstration of loyalty the dying poet commented bitterly, "I always thought you were an original, Berlioz."

SEE ALSO	RELATED SUBJECTS
Vanity 614	Sickness 1701–1707
Generosity 244	Diseases 1721
Atheists 1653	Death 1746–1749
Natural Death 1757	Natural Death 1756–1757

FUNERALS

1776—Charles Dillingham and Florenz Ziegfeld, both eminent producers and both now deceased, were pall-bearers at the funeral of the great escape artist, Houdini. As they lifted the beautiful and heavy casket to their shoulders, Dillingham whispered to Ziegfeld, "Suppose he isn't here."

1777—A Chinese servant asked permission of his master to attend the funeral of a friend, also Chinese. The man gave his permission and jokingly added, "I suppose you will follow the old Chinese custom of putting food on the grave."
"Yes, sir," was the answer.

"And," still laughing, the man said, "when do you suppose the food will be eaten?"

The man was somewhat shaken out of his Occidental complacency when his servant replied, "As soon, sir, as the friend you buried last week will smell the flowers you put on his grave."

1778—Lord Chesterfield, a little before his death, was so infirm, whenever he went out in his coach the horses were generally led step by step. In this situation he was one morning met by an acquaintance, who congratulated his lordship on being able to take the air. "I thank you kindly sir," says his lordship; "but I do not come out so much for the air, as for the benefit of rehearsing my funeral."

SEE ALSO   RELATED SUBJECTS
Boners 117   Death 1746–1749
Devotion 172   Accidental Death 1751
Stinginess 562   Natural Death 1756–1757
Vanity 621, 623
Wife 929
Civilians in War 2339
Lawyers 2528

LONGEVITY

1781—Fontenelle was continually being told by his doctors that what he liked to eat was bad for him. Toward the end of his life, one warned him that he must give up coffee, explaining at great length in the most appalling medical terms, that it was a slow poison and would eventually ruin his system. In a tone of deep conviction the nonagenarian replied, "Doctor, I am inclined to agree with you that it is a slow poison—very slow, for I have been drinking it for the past 80 years." Coffee-lovers may derive some comfort from the fact that Fontenelle came within a month of living to be a hundred years old.

1782—Until Joseph Chamberlain, British Prime Minister, was seventy, he seemed to hold the secret of perpetual youth. Someone asked him what the secret of his good health was. He smiled and said, "Never walk if you can drive; and of two cigars always choose the longest and the strongest."

RELATED SUBJECTS
Age 671–678
Insurance 2136–2140

RECREATION AND SPORTS

RELAXATION

1786—When Maxim Gorky visited America he was taken to Coney Island by friends who wanted him to behold this huge playground swarming with holiday throngs. They took him through the crowded concessions, where he saw one dizzy contraption after another, swinging people through the air, swirling them in eccentric curves, shooting them down breathtaking inclines. They took him underground and overground, into bewildering mazes, museums of freaks, palaces of jugglers, theatres of dancing ladies and living statuary. They were giving Maxim Gorky the time of his life! Finally, at the end of what may have seemed to them a perfect day, they asked him how he had liked it. He was silent for a moment. Then he said, very simply, "What a sad people you must be!"

RELATED SUBJECTS
Diligence 176–177
Laziness 326–327

TRAVEL

1791—One day in the Yosemite Valley, a traveller was told that there was an old man in the office of the hotel who in 1851 had been one of the company that had discovered the Yosemite. Eagerly he seized the opportunity of finding out what it was like to be the first of civilized men to behold one of nature's most marvellous works. "It must have been wonderful," he said, "to have the Valley burst suddenly upon you."

The old man spat over the edge of the veranda and looked reflective for a moment. "Well," he said, "I'll tell ye. If I'd ha' knowed it was going to be so famous I'd ha' looked at it."

1792—A tourist journeyed by camel to see the great Pyramids. He was swept away by the beauty of the desert night and the work-a-day world seemed to fade away from his

313

remembrance. After absorbing all the glamour of the
experience and desiring to preserve every detail of the
dream-like world in which he found himself, he re-
mounted his steed, at the same time asking his Arab
guide, "What is the name of my camel?"

"Greta Garbo," replied the guide.

1793—There is the story of a Harvard man who spent some days
in Egypt, and enjoyed during that time the services of a
French-speaking native guide and courier. As they
parted, the guide requested, "Sire, teach me words of
English with which I may attract your countrymen."
The Harvard man did so.

Some time later, he returned to Egypt, looked up his guide,
and said, "How did you make out with the English I
taught you?"

"Sire," said the guide, "some there were who smiled and
came with me, others there were who were angered and
turned away."

The phrase he had been taught was, "To Hell with Yale!"

1794—In the days of the Underground Railway many Southern
Negroes conceived of Canada, the ultimate objective of
most runaway slaves, as a kind of free Paradise. Old
Uncle Jake had the notion that he would like to get
there. He asked a friend how one might get to Canada,
and was told that if he were to travel far enough all the
way up the length of the Mississippi he could get there.
The old Negro had no geographic sense, but he had a
considerable desire for liberty. Sneaking off early one
morning, he took his battered rowboat and headed up-
stream, rowing as vigorously and intently as he could.
The current was swift and the old man, working feverishly without looking to the right or the left, barely held
his own and, by the end of the day, actually lost some
six or twelve feet of distance. At this time, he was
aroused from his intense concentration by an acquaintance who hailed him from the shore, "What you doin'
out there in that boat, Jake?"

"Fo' de Lord's sake," exclaimed Jake. "Who on earth
knows me way up here in Canada!"

1795—The poet, John Godfrey Saxe, had his bag packed for a
trip when a friend encountered him and asked, "Where
are you going?"

"To Boston, Deo volente."

"What route is that?" his acquaintance asked.

"By way of Providence, of course," replied Saxe.

1796—Texas is a big state. Easterners so far into the Middle West as Chicago have a lot to learn about it. An instance is the Chicago firm that sent a wire to its traveling representative in El Paso, saying that as long as he was in Texas anyway, he might as well clear up a little affair in Texarkana. The salesman wired back: "Be cheaper send man from Chicago. Closer than I am."

Astonished, his home office checked with the map and sent out a man from Chicago.

SEE ALSO
Eating 9
Reputation 77
Curiosity 161
Exaggeration 223
Stupidity 576, 577, 582
Universities 1021
Porter 1806
Presidents 1939

RELATED SUBJECTS
Explorers 1141–1142
Trains 1801–1802
Porters 1806
Autos 1811
Boats 1816

TRAINS

1801—One time Winston Churchill almost missed a train and Mrs. Churchill was alarmed. Sir Edward Marsh, Churchill's private secretary, tried to calm her by saying, "Winston is such a sportsman, he always gives the train a chance to get away."

1802—Mrs. Theodore Roosevelt, the younger, after having been absent from home for several days, wired her husband to meet her at a certain station. Hurrying to be on time, Colonel Ted arrived at the station just in time to see the train whizz through at a great speed. Somewhat bewildered, he stared at the speeding cars and was more astonished to see his wife standing on the very back platform frantically waving an important looking envelope in her hand. Spying him, she threw it at him, and, the train rounding a corner, she disappeared from sight.

Scrambling about in the bushes into which the envelope had fallen, the Colonel finally found it and quickly opened it. He was amused and somewhat relieved to read:

"Dear Ted: This train doesn't stop here."

SEE ALSO   RELATED SUBJECTS
Absent-Mindedness 81   Travel 1791–1796
Exaggeration 221   Porters 1806
Practical Joking 431
Medicines 1726
Public Relations 2111
Debt 2172

PORTERS

1806—A gentleman, considerably inexperienced in travel, had made a transcontinental touring trip. As he was about to disembark he was in some doubt as to what sum he should give the Pullman porter who had catered to him throughout most of the journey. "Sam," he asked, "what's the average tip you get?" "Five dollars," replied Sam. Whereupon he was presented with that sum. Overcome and embarrassed, Sam shuffled his feet for a moment, and then said, "Well, Boss, Ah reckon Ah ought to tell you that so far you is de fust one what's come up to the average."

RELATED SUBJECTS
Travel 1791–1796
Trains 1801–1802
Servants 2276–2283

AUTOS

1811—An old mountaineer was on his way to the town. He decided to use the new highway that had just been completed. Just as he was about to steer his horse onto the road, an automobile whizzed by. The old man had never before seen one of these new-fangled machines. Open-mouthed he stared after it. Scarcely a minute passed and, following in close pursuit, came a motorcycle cop. The old man was astounded. Muttering to himself he said, "Well, by gol! Who'da thunk that thing could have a colt?"

SEE ALSO   RELATED SUBJECTS
Chiseling 2126   Travel 1791–1796
Machinery 2272
Rationing 2356

BOATS

1816—An old lady on a sinking ship was told that they had no
other hope but to trust in Providence.
"Has it come to that?" said she.

SEE ALSO
Accuracy 92
Prayer 1608
Sickness 1702
Parrot 2293

SPORTS

BASEBALL

1821—The New York Yankees were playing an exhibition game
with a Texas University. The college team was doing
very well in holding the New York team to a close score.
Then Lou Gehrig came to bat. There were two runners
on base. It was three and two for Gehrig, when suddenly, the pitcher threw one right down the slot.
Gehrig swatted and the ball sailed clean over the park and
disappeared from sight. The college catcher raged up to
the pitcher.
"Why didn't you watch your signals," he stormed. "You
might have known that guy would slap it a mile."
"Yes," the pitcher said with a sigh of contentment, "I
know. But I got to thinking. I knew I'd never pitch a
Big League game and I knew I'd probably never get to
see a game at the Yankee Stadium. And I sure did want
to see Gehrig bust just one!"

1822—Woodrow Wilson was a lifelong baseball fan. During the
harassing and anguished days of the War the only
chance he had to attend the sport was the occasion of a
Red Cross benefit game played in Washington.
Returning from this, he found one of his advisers, Mr.
Garfield, waiting with troubling news about a coal short-
age.
"Oh hang it all, Garfield," said the President, "I've just
been to a ball-game and I wish I could say, three strikes
and out to this job."

1823—A baseball game was being held for a charity affair. The
committee could only find eight men who were available
to play. Seeking to make up the team, they persuaded

an old fellow who had never played before to fill in. His first time up at bat he smacked the ball and hit it over the fence of the ball park. His teammates cheered, and they and the spectators together kept yelling at the man to run. "Why, shucks," said he, "what's the use of running. I'll buy another ball for you."

1824—Now a member of a minor league team, a former big time baseball player, was regaling his teammates with stories of his former prowess.

"Was I fast! Lissen, you guys, when I played for the Giants, every time I hit one of my many home runs I reached first base before the spectators could hear the crack of the bat. Then when I rounded second, the second baseman usually said something that made me sore, so I slapped the third baseman in the catcher's mouth. Not bad, eh?"

SEE ALSO　　　　　RELATED SUBJECTS
Zanies 643　　　　　Football 1856–1858
Bible 1586　　　　　Golf 1861–1869

BILLIARDS

1826—Finding no other means of recreation in the small town in which he was stranded, the travelling salesman wandered into the local poolroom.

Indicating his desire to play a game, he was shown to the only table in the place and was given a set of balls of the same uniform, dirty-gray color.

"Hey," he said to the proprietor, "how do you expect me to play with these. I can't tell the red from the white."

"Oh, that's all right. You'll get to know them by their shape."

1827—A farmer, from way back in the country, came into town one day with his pockets fairly well lined from the sale of his crops. Seeking to appear worldly, he walked into a saloon and gaming house over the entrance to which was a great sign proclaiming, BILLIARDS.

Strolling up to the bar with a simulated air of assurance the farmer slapped a coin on the counter and said, "Gimme a glass of them there billiards."

The barkeeper took a long look at him and, sizing up the situation, made no comment. Going into the none too immaculate kitchen behind the bar he came forth with a large, foamy glass of dark and dangerous dishwater which he shoved across the counter to his customer. The farmer, with his eyes slightly popping, drank it down in one long draught. Banging the glass back down on the counter he wiped his mouth and said, "Waal, efen I warn't an old and hardened billiard drinker, I'd 'a said that there was dishwater!"

BULL FIGHTING

1831—At a party in Paris, the American bullfighter, Sidney Franklin, was cornered by a dowager who took him severely to task for the alleged cruelty of his art. She would have none of his careful explanations, but pattered on endlessly about the "poor, helpless bulls." After ten minutes of this, Franklin came to the limit of his patience.

"Madam," he said, "I can't agree with you. I have killed many bulls, but I have always spared them the ultimate cruelty—not one did I ever bore to death!"

SEE ALSO
Prize Fighting 1886

CARD PLAYING

1836—You can't beat Texas! A supercilious and wealthy New Yorker asked the desk clerk in his hotel if there were not a card game which he could get into.

"There is a poker game now going on in Room 600," said the clerk, "but you'd better look out. They play for mighty high stakes."

The New Yorker sniffed at the implication and went to seek the game. Entering the room he found a table surrounded by grim-faced, flinty-eyed Texans, methodically sorting and handling their cards. Stepping up brashly, the New Yorker drew out a hundred-dollar bill from his pocket and threw it on the table, saying, "I hear you boys play for big money. Well, give me chips for that." No one said a word. The dealer motioned him to a chair, looked him coldly in the eye and deliberately pushed across the table at him—one white chip.

1837—Horne Took, the sly wit, being asked by George III whether he played at cards, replied, "I cannot, Your Majesty, tell a king from a knave."

1838—A bridge expert was being harassed by many questions from the hopeful bridge player. "And do tell me, Mr. Jacoby, how would you have played the hand, under the same circumstances."

"Under an assumed name, Madam," said Mr. Jacoby tersely, and made a quick exit.

1839—Dr. Parr was a constant and conscientious whist player. Nothing annoyed him more than to have as his partner one who could not match his skill at the game. One evening he was coupled with just such a player. As the evening wore on, he became increasingly disgusted. When his hostess came to the table and asked how the game was going, Dr. Parr exploded, "As well as could be expected, Madam, considering that I have three adversaries."

1840—The following is without a doubt a nice description of a "friendly" game of bridge:

The old quarrel between North and South has spread out to include East and West, and is now called contract bridge.

SEE ALSO   RELATED SUBJECTS
Gambling 74   Gambling 71–74

DANCING

1841—There is a legend of doubtful authenticity about Tommy Hitchcock, who, at a certain dance, was paired off for one number with a young woman to whom he had not been formally introduced. Slightly apologetic he said, "I'm afraid I am not dancing very well this evening; I'm a little stiff from polo." His partner answered coldly, "It doesn't make any difference to me where you come from."

SEE ALSO   RELATED SUBJECTS
Beauty 666   Parties 741–746
Church Services 1534   Dancers 1371

FISHING

1846—"Uncle" Joe Cannon, the late Speaker of the House, was once telling Chauncey Depew, in somewhat lurid terms, about a fish he had nearly caught.

"About the size of a whale, wasn't it?" asked Depew.

"I was baitin' with whales," said "Uncle" Joe.

1847—Daniel Webster liked to commune with plain people whom he encountered. On one of his fishing excursions he wanted to try a certain brook and he drove to the house of a certain Mr. Baker whom he knew nearby, and asked permission to leave his horse a few hours. Mr. Baker volunteered to go with Webster and show him just where the people usually fished at that brook. The old man pointed out the spot. The ground was very muddy —Mr. Webster sank in half-way up his leg. Said he, "Rather miry here, Mr. Baker."

Mr. Baker answered, "Yes, I know it, and that's the worst on't."

The mosquitoes began to bite annoyingly. With the hand that was not holding his fishing rod Webster was busy all the time slapping and scratching. Said Webster, "These mosquitoes are pretty thick and hungry."

Baker answered, "Yes, I know it. That's the worst on't."

Now the heat in the damp, low ground became intense. Mr. Webster wiped his forehead and rested. Then he said, "It's very hot down in these bushes, Mr. Baker."

And Baker answered, "Yes, I know it. That's the worst on't."

Webster resumed his fishing and after an hour's struggle with the heat, the bushes, the mire and the mosquitoes Webster said, "There seem to be no fish here, Mr. Baker."

Came the answer, "Yes, I know it. That's the worst on't."

1848—Mark Twain, according to one story, was returning from a trip to the Maine woods. Chumming up in the smoking car with a homespun New Englander occupying the same seat, Mark said, "Stranger, it's the closed season for fishing up here, but, just between you and me, I've got two hundred pounds of the finest rock bass, out there in the baggage car, that you ever laid eyes on."

"Waal," drawled Mark's new acquaintance, "that's interestin', but d'ye know who I am?"

"Not guilty," replied Mark. "Who are you?"

"Waal," came the reply, "I'm the State Game Warden."

Quoth Mark: "Now doesn't that beat the Dutch? Say, d'ye know who I am, Warden? I'm the damnedest liar in the United States!"

1849—Anyone who is discouraged at the lack of results being yielded by his efforts should take heart with the point of view of the country lad who hailed the city fisherman by the creek and asked, "How many fish yer got, Mister?"

"None yet," he was told.

"That ain't bad," replied the boy, "there was a feller fished here for two weeks and he didn't get any more than you got in half an hour."

1850—A seasoned old fisherman found his neighbor on the bank of the stream one day to be a rank greenhorn at the art of angling. This personage fished for some hours doing practically everything wrong. Notwithstanding this, from the sheer operation of the law of averages, the beginner finally got a bite. Feverishly he reeled and reeled and reeled until at last, some miracle having saved his line, he had wound his small catch all the way up to the tip of his pole. Overcome with the excitement of it all, he turned to the experienced fisherman and said, "Now what shall I do? Now what shall I do?"

"Looks to me," said the old-timer laconically, "as though there was nothing left for you to do except climb up the pole and git him."

1851—For the first time in their long married life, Mrs. Smith had persuaded her husband to take her fishing with him.

Seated by the side of the stream, Mr. Smith was silently doing his best to make a catch. The guide with them was also engrossed only in the business at hand. But Mrs. Smith kept chattering away, asking all the questions she could think of.

Suddenly she spied a strip of oily water, seeming to cross the lake like a broad smooth street.

"Oh, guide, guide, what's that streak over there?"

"Where, ma'am?" asked the guide, endeavoring to bait a hook.

"Right over there. What is it?"

"Why that, ma'am," drawled the guide, "that's just where the road went across the ice last winter."

1852—During the course of the Sunday School session, the teacher called upon one of the pupils to recite some parables. "Do you know the parables, Johnnie?" she asked.

"Yes, ma'am."

"Well, I want you to tell us about the one that you like the best."

"That's easy, ma'am, I like the one where somebody loafs and fishes."

1853—An old colored man was sitting by the side of a stream patiently waiting for a bite. A youngster, ambling along the banks, stopped to watch him.

"Say, uncle, how many you caught?"

"Well, sonny, ef I ketch dis heah one I'm after, and two mo', I'll have three."

1854—Mr. Jones and Mr. Glover were lunching together. As their various friends passed the table, Mr. Jones would stop them and, in glowing terms, describe his success on his recent fishing trip.

Glover, amused by the enthusiastic Mr. Jones, finally said, "Say, I notice that in telling about that fish you changed the size of it for each different listener."

"Yes, sure, I never tell a man more than I think he will believe."

SEE ALSO
Drinking 49
Profanity 67
Gratitude 263
Ministers 1467
Freedom 2038

RELATED SUBJECTS
Hunting 1876–1879

FOOTBALL

1856—Coach Dana X. Bible of Texas A. and M. College delivered perhaps the quietest, shortest, most effective pep talk in recent football history. His team had been badly trounced in the first half of one of their big games. The interval between halves was one of silence and gloom in which the coach said nothing. At last, as the team prepared to go out again on the field, he looked them over slowly and deliberately and said, "Well, girls, shall we go?"

They won the game.

1857—The football game between Notre Dame and Yale was in full swing. The score was tied. The spectators were yelling wildly; the players were grimly determined that their side would win.

About the middle of the third quarter time was called at the request of the Yale center. Walking up to the referee he said, "Look here, Mr. Referee, I don't like to complain but every time we get tangled up in a scrimmage play that big Irish center bites me. What do you think I should do about it?"

"Well," snapped the referee, "the only thing I advise is that you play him only on Fridays."

1858—In Belfast they still tell you about the football game that took place between the 100 percent Catholics and 100 percent Protestants. A Limey attended that game, and when the Catholics made a skillful play he applauded and when the Protestants in their turn scored he again joined in the shouting. At this point an Irishman jabbed the Limey in the back and said:

"My God, man, haven't you got any religion at all?"

SEE ALSO   RELATED SUBJECTS
Marriage 883   Baseball 1821–1824
Newspapers 1247   Golf 1861–1869

GOLF

1861—Don Marquis, author and playwright, once had a bet on with an expert golfer. The stakes were five dollars a hole and in the bargain, Don Marquis gave the expert two strokes.

Before starting the game, the expert turned to Marquis, just before teeing off for his first drive, and said, "Now where do I get my two strokes?"

"I don't care where you take the second," said Don Marquis, "but the first has to be a stroke of apoplexy."

1862—A certain preacher was chagrined by the fact that one of his friends and golfing companions invariably beat him. His companion, an older man, said, "Don't take it too hard. You win in the end. You'll probably be burying me one of these days."

"I know," said the preacher, "but even then it will be your hole."

1863—Real devotees of the game of golf are fanatics of a peculiar breed. There was the case of such a man, who returned home after a long day on the links. His wife greeted him, and observed that their young son, William, had come in only a moment before. "He says he's been caddying for you all day."

"Is that so?" replied the sportsman. "Somehow I thought that boy seemed mighty familiar."

1864—The late Justice McKenna, of the United States Supreme Court, was an earnest but poor golfer. Deciding that his game might be improved, he hired an instructor to teach him the finer points.

One day, while practicing on a golf course near Washington, he missed, teeing off. He tried three or four times, but each time his club hit several inches behind the ball. His instructor watched silently. Finally the Justice, becoming disgusted, glared at the still stationary ball and muttered, "Tut—tut!"

Gravely the instructor walked toward him—"Sir," he said, "you'll never learn to play golf with them words."

1865—Searching frantically for almost an hour, two novices at the game of golf attempted to find their balls which they had driven into the rough.

About to give up they were approached by a sweet old lady who had been watching them sympathetically. "I don't wish to interfere, gentlemen, but would it be cheating if I were to tell you where the balls are?"

1866—A foursome at golf were going around on a course which had as its hazard a deep ravine. Three of them were caught and two of them decided to forfeit the hole rather than take a chance on having too many strokes chalked up against them. The other decided to take his chances.

He disappeared into the ravine and the others gathered around to watch his progress. Finally the ball appeared and bounced up onto the green.

"How many strokes?" asked one.

"Three."

"But we heard six."

"Three of them were echoes."

1867—The golfer, annoyed at the loss of his ball, started to scold his caddie for not having been more careful in watching its flight.

Replying thoughtlessly, attempting to excuse himself, the caddie said, "Well, sir, it don't usually go anywhere, so it sort of took me unprepared like."

1868—A couple of day laborers, on their way home from work, stopped to watch a game of golf. They saw a golfer drive his ball into the rough; watched as he toiled to extricate himself. Then he got into a sand trap and labored, throwing up huge clouds of sand, to get himself out of his difficulty.

Finally, after getting on the green, he managed to putt the ball into the cup. One of the laborers, a burly Irishman, had been watching all this with a most sympathetic eye. Unable to repress his verbal sympathy, he said, "Now, mister, yez arre in a helluva fix!"

1869—A new member of a golf club was led to the first tee. Surrounded by grinning spectators he teed off and, with an almost miraculous drive, landed the ball in the first hole. Noticing no sign of anything from his watchers, who were in fact struck speechless by this feat, he marched off to the second tee. Taking his stance he again drove at the ball, and again it went into the cup.

Waving his club as though in near disappointment he said, "Gosh, I sure thought I'd missed it that time."

SEE ALSO   RELATED SUBJECTS
Stinginess 565   Baseball 1821–1824
Dentists 1697   Football 1856–1858

HORSE RACING

1871—"I thought you were sick yesterday," the employer said to the clerk.

"Yes, sir, I was," replied Jones.

"Well," retorted his employer, "you certainly didn't look very sick when I saw you at the races yesterday afternoon."

"I didn't? You should have seen me after the end of the fourth race."

1872—Leaning from her window one fine Spring morning, a woman noticed a poorly dressed man standing in front of a vacant store located just under the window. She noticed that, in passing, many people stopped to give the man money. Impressed and sympathetic, the woman put a two-dollar bill in an envelope, scribbled on a piece of paper, "Godspeed," and tossed it down to him.

A few days later, she saw the man again. This time he was walking back and forth in front of the building where she lived and looking perplexedly up at her window. As she walked out of her house, he came up to her and said, "Say, lady, I've been looking for you. Here's your $52. 'Godspeed' won at twenty-six to one."

SEE ALSO
Gambling 72
Liars 333
Ministers 1476
Natural Death 1756

RELATED SUBJECTS
Gambling 71–74
Horses 2286–2288

HUNTING

1876—A Californian went out to follow up a grizzly bear and was gone three days. Then he turned up without his game. "Lost the trail, Bill, I suppose," said one of his cronies.

"Naw, I kept on the trail all right."

"Then what's the matter?"

"Waal, the footprints was getting too fresh, so I quit."

1877—An old hunter was holding his usual court before a group of summer visitors in the small town. "How many bears did you kill?" asked one of them.

"Oh, 'bout a hundred."

"Say, you must have had plenty narrow escapes."

"Young man," replied the old-timer, "if thar was any narrer escapes, 'twas the bears had 'em."

1878—An eager sportsman accosted one of the natives in the small Maine town where he was spending his vacation. "Is there much good hunting around here?" he asked eagerly.

The native glanced around him for a minute then said, "Well, sure, there's plenty huntin', but damned little findin'."

1879—A cowboy from one of the many dude ranches in the Rockies was spending his day off doing a little hunting. Sighting an eagle, he took aim and brought the bird down. He scrambled down the crag and retrieved his game. As he slung the bird over his shoulder he saw one of the customers from the dude ranch approaching him.

"I say," said the Easterner in a patronizing sort of tone, "I was watching you. You should have saved that shot, Why the fall alone would have killed the eagle."

SEE ALSO
Exaggeration 225
Gratitude 262
Sermons 1552

RELATED SUBJECTS
Fishing 1846–1854

MISCELLANEOUS CONTESTS

1881—There is a legend of an Indian chief who was wont to try the strength of his youths by making them run in a single effort as far up the side of a mountain as each could reach by his main strength. On an appointed day, four left at daybreak. The first returned with a branch of spruce, indicating the height to which he had attained. The second bore a twig of pine. The third brought an Alpine shrub. But it was by the light of the moon that the fourth made his way back. Then he came, worn and exhausted, and his feet were torn by the rocks.

"What did you bring, and how high did you ascend?" asked the chief.

"Sire," he replied, "where I went there was neither spruce nor pine to shelter me from the sun, nor flower to cheer my path, but only rocks and snow and barren land. My feet are torn, and I am exhausted, and I have come late, but—."

And as a wonderful light came into his eyes, the young brave added:

"I saw the sea."

1882—A dinner in honor of the winning members of the track meet was being held at the local hotel. Various honors were given them in the form of medals and blue ribbons. Each presentation was accompanied by a toast. Toward the end of the evening the prize honor of all, a beautiful silver cup, was awarded the young man who had won the gruelling mile run, the major event of the meet.

The boy accepted the cup and a toast was proposed amid shouts of "Speech! Speech!"

He won more than the ordinary cheers and shouts of the crowd when he said:

"Gentlemen, I have won this cup by the use of my legs. I trust I may never lose the use of my legs by the use of this cup."

1883—Mr. Block was always annoying the members of his local club with stories of his great physical prowess. One day a new member, already tired of the boasting and blustering, determined to quash him once and for all.

"Block," said the new member, "I'll bet you that I can wheel something in a wheelbarrow from this clubhouse to the gate, and you can't wheel it back."

Mr. Block looked the newcomer over carefully. Not an impressive looking man, small and puny. He could think of nothing that this man could do that he couldn't top. "O.K.," he said, "I'll take you up on that."

The newcomer smiled blandly. A wheelbarrow was brought to the clubhouse steps.

Rubbing his hands in great glee, the new member grasped the handles of the barrow, motioned to Block and said, "All right, get in."

PRIZE FIGHTING

1886—Jack Johnson, the Negro heavyweight champion, who became a prominent figure in Mexico, was scheduled to face barehanded a bull in the ring. Some days later he was asked how it had gone.

He wrinkled up his brow, rolled his eyes and boomed: "Ah sure wuz scared. Ah'd rather fight a hundred men than one bull any day."

1887—John L. Sullivan was once interviewed by a reporter who asked him why he had never become a boxing instructor.

"Well, son, I tried it once," said the famous fighter. "A husky young man took one lesson from me and went home a little the worse for wear. When he came around the second time he said, 'Mr. Sullivan, it was my idea to learn enough about boxing from you to be able to lick a certain young fellow I've got it in for. But I've changed my mind. If it's all the same to you, Mr. Sullivan, I'll just send this fellow down here to take the rest of my lessons for me.'"

SWIMMING

1891—Bernard Shaw was enjoying a swim in a pool during a stay in South Africa; so were some boys who knew nothing of the august author. One small boy was "dared" by his playmates to "duck the old man" for a shilling. He accepted, but when he was close to his victim, panic seized him. Shaw turned, saw the youngster, and asked him what he wanted. In halting accents, the boy revealed the plot and the shilling bet.

"Well," said Shaw, looking sternly at the youngster, "if you wait a moment while I get my breath, I'll let you push my head under water."

He did, and the small boy swam back triumphantly to collect his shilling.

1892—The greatest and most mysterious of all Shelley's preoc-
cupations was with water, boats and swimming. He was
apparently fascinated by water as a great element, and
time and again prophesied his death by drowning. But
it was typical of Shelley's humorless absolutism where
his fancy was involved that he was without fear in the
business, and never troubled to learn either to navigate
or to swim.
  In 1816 the friendship that sprang up with Byron at
Geneva was based partly on mutual literary admiration,
and partly on their common love of boating. Byron
knew something of sailing and navigation, and they took
a trip together around the lake in an open boat. They
nearly foundered in a sudden storm one night. After
Byron had got the sail down and while the water poured
in and the wind roared in the darkness, they sat in furious argument, Byron, proud of his power as a swimmer,
declaring that he would save Shelley when they sank,
Shelley equally determined that he would not be saved.

1893—Although unable to swim, Shelley was forever invading
pools and streams . . . One day when Trelawney, a
powerful swimmer, jumped into a deep pool in the Arno,
Shelley immediately jumped in after him and lay "like a
conger eel" on the bottom till Trelawney fished him up
with some difficulty, Shelley protesting as soon as he
could breathe that truth lay always "at the bottom of the
well" and that "in another minute I should have found
it."

1894—Impressing upon his class an admiration for notable feats
of physical prowess the teacher related the exploit of a
vigorous man who swam three times across a broad
river, in the morning, before breakfast.
  There was a giggle from one of the youngsters in the class.
"Well," said the teacher with some irritation, "what is it
that seems to be so amusing? I see nothing amusing."
"It's only this, sir," replied the pupil. "I was wondering
why he didn't make it four times and get back on the
side where he left his clothes."

1895—A certain American soldier, attached to one of the American
Tank Units fighting with the British in the Libyan campaign, had been carried by the exigencies of the service
many miles deep into the heart of the desert with his
comrades. This outpost of the Front had been quiet for

days. The soldier found himself one afternoon with a few hours' leave.

It was with some surprise that his commanding officer spotted the man striding purposefully across the sands clad in his bathing trunks.

"Murphy!" shouted the officer in some astonishment. "Where in blazes do you think you're going?"

"Why, sir," said the soldier, "I just thought while I had a couple of hours off I'd take a dip in the surf."

"Are you crazy?" demanded the officer. "The ocean is 500 miles from here!"

"Beautiful big beach, isn't it?" said the soldier.

SEE ALSO
Fatness 688

GOVERNMENT AND RULERS

POLITICS

1896—There is a story how Eyre, the surveyor, called upon his friend and neighbor, Lord Lyndhurst, the Chancellor of England. "I find," said he, "your lordship has changed your politics."

"Yes," said Lord Lyndhurst, "and is ready to change them again if you will make it worth his while."

1897—President Wilson had been asked to receive a group of Irish-American leaders who wished to present a paper. He had consented to do so, with the proviso that Daniel F. Cohalan should not accompany them. During the War Cohalan had been a great disturber. Nevertheless the committee had shown up, headed by Cohalan. Tumulty was urging the President to relent. "Oh, Governor," he pleaded, "this will make a terrible impression on his followers." Cohalan was an influential political leader.

The President took out his watch. "That's just what I wanted it to do, Tumulty; but I think it will make a good impression on decent people."

1898—The following is a statement attributed to the late G. K. Chesterton:

"The mere proposal to set the politician to watch the capitalist has been disturbed by the rather disconcerting discovery that they are both the same man. We are past the point where being a capitalist is the only way of becoming a politician, and we are dangerously near the point where being a politician is much the quickest way of becoming a capitalist."

1899—In Washington, during the career of the notorious Huey Long, a political follower of the Louisiana senator was pleading with him to procure him the nomination, which would be equivalent to election, for representative from a certain Louisiana district.

"I can't do that," Long said. "It's all your own fault. Even I couldn't get you elected. Not after that story about the hotel episode in New Orleans."

"That story is a damned lie!" cried the aspiring politician. "Why there isn't even any Hotel Episode in New Orleans."

1900—When Oliver Cromwell first coined his money, an old cavalier looking on one of the new pieces, read this inscription on one side: "God is with us,"—on the other— "the Commonwealth of England." "I see," said he, "that God and the Commonwealth are on different sides."

1901—A New Jersey Congressman once brought two citizens of that state to visit the President. Seeking to impress Lincoln, he introduced them as being "among the weightiest men in southern New Jersey."

Upon their departure, Lincoln said to one of his aides who was standing by, "I wonder that end of the state didn't tip up when they got off it."

SEE ALSO	RELATED SUBJECTS
Cynicism 170	Political Parties 1906–1907
Discretion 181	Campaigning 1911–1920
Quick Thinking 485	Elections 1921
Rough and Ready	Public Officers 1926
503, 504	
Stupidity 581	
Births 1012	
Explorers 1142	
Cabinet Members 1951	

POLITICAL PARTIES

1906—Thaddeus Stevens, once going into the room of the Committee on Elections of which he was a member, found a hearing going on. He asked one of his Republican colleagues what was the point in the case. "There isn't much point to it," was the answer. "They are both damned scoundrels."

"Well," said Stevens, "which is the Republican damned scoundrel? I want to go for the Republican damned scoundrel."

1907—Senator George W. Norris had made a speech in Norfolk, Nebraska, the night before and was taking a walk after breakfast when he noticed some men hitching a horse in a livery stable across the street. One of them recognized him and crossed over hurriedly introducing himself as a preacher in a place twelve miles away, in haste to get home to deliver his sermon.

The preacher wanted to shake his hand. "I have followed your record in Congress," he said, "and I came down to your meeting last night to hear you talk. Mr. Norris, I am so anxious to have you succeed that every night on bended knees I ask God to guard and protect you and see that you are elected to the Senate in order that your activities may have a wider scope. Why, I get so enthusiastic that I almost feel as though I ought to vote for you myself!"

"Well, my good friend, if that's the way you feel about it, why don't you vote for me?"

"Oh, Mr. Norris, I never could do that. I am a Democrat."

SEE ALSO   RELATED SUBJECTS
Campaigning 1911   Politics 1896–1901
                      Campaigning 1911–1920
                      Elections 1921
                      Office Seekers 1966–1970

CAMPAIGNING

1911—Once Theodore Roosevelt was making a political speech during one of his campaigns, when a heckler interrupted him from the large crowd with a repeated and slightly inebriated cry, "I am a Democrat."

Roosevelt was generally a dangerous man to heckle. Pausing in his speech and smiling with oriental unction, he leaned forward and said, "May I ask the gentleman why he is a Democrat?"

The voice replied, "My grandfather was a Democrat, my father was a Democrat, and I am a Democrat."

Roosevelt said, "My friend, suppose your grandfather had been a jackass, and your father had been a jackass, what would you be?"

Instantly the reply came back, "A Republican!"

1912—Sam Houston, when running for Governor of Texas, overlooked no prospective voters. He went around to most of the farmhouses and personally harangued the inmates, getting their promises to vote for him.

At one such farmhouse he had gotten the farmer's promise of a vote, and seeing the lanky son of the house pass by, sized him up as another prospective supporter.

"Son," he said to the boy, "you look old enough to vote; how old are you?"

"Waal, I was 21 last April, but I didn't bow my head when dad ast the blessin', so he sot me back two years . . . so now I can't vote."

1913—A candidate for a minor county office had depicted himself as a true man of the people. A delegation once called on him at his country home. The candidate received them in his shirtsleeves and with a pitchfork in his hand. Saying that he was busy, he consented to talk with them if they would conduct the little meeting in the barn, where he had some hay to pitch into the loft. They all trotted down to the barn but found no hay there.

"Hiram," asked the candidate of his hired man, "where's the hay?"

"Sorry, sir," was the man's reply, "I ain't had time yet to throw it back since you threw it up for yesterday's delegation."

1914—"Fellow-citizens," said the candidate, "I have fought against the Indians. I have often had no bed but the battlefield, and no canopy but the sky. I have marched over the frozen ground till every step has been marked with blood."

His story told well, till a dried-up looking voter came to the front.

"Did you say yer'd fought for the Union?"

"Yes!" replied the candidate.

"And agin the Indians?"

"Yes, many a time."

"And that you had slept on the ground with only the sky for a kiver?"

"Certainly."

"And that your feet bled in marching over the frozen ground?"

"That they did," cried the exultant candidate.

"Then I'll be darned if you hain't done enough for your country. Go home and rest. I'll vote for the other fellow."

1915—The political speaker found himself repeatedly interrupted by a heckler who shouted, "Liar!" again and again during his discourse. His patience exhausted, the speaker at last said, "If the gentleman will be good enough to tell us his name as well as his calling, we shall be pleased to hear from him."

1916—To the revilings of a local Conservative, a Liberal candidate for a parliamentary vacancy in Surrey replied, "The gentleman taunts me with not having been born in this district as he was. Let me tell the gentleman that my only excuse is that I am a Lancashire man from choice, while he is one by necessity. If there is any difference between us, it is that I came into this country with my pants on, while the gentleman came into it with his off."

1917—When Mr. Thomas Sheridan, son of the celebrated Richard Brinsley Sheridan, was a candidate for the representation of a Cornish borough, he told his father, that if he succeeded, he should place a label on his forehead with the words "to let," and side with the party that made the best offer.

"Right, Tom," said the father, "but don't forget to add the word 'unfurnished.'"

1918—On one occasion Lord Macaulay had an unpleasant experience at Edinburgh. He was re-contesting a seat in that constituency, and was standing side by side with his opponent on the balcony one evening, when he was suddenly struck by a dead cat. The member of the audience who threw the animal at once apologized and said that he had intended it for his opponent.

"Well," said Macaulay, "I wish you had meant it for me and struck him."

1919—Political orators are not known for their gentle remarks when attacking an opponent. A particularly vicious example of this is the remark made by John Randolph about Edward Livingston.

"He is a man of splendid abilities, but utterly corrupt. Like a rotten mackerel by moonlight, he shines and stinks."

1920—Shortly after his entrance into political life Disraeli stood for a certain Middlesex borough in the Conservative interest. It was a "personally conducted" canvass, and, among others, the future Prime Minister solicited the vote and interest of a well-to-do but somewhat irascible farmer, who was supposed to be rather doubtful in his political convictions.

"Vote for you!" he shouted when Mr. Disraeli made known the object of his call. "Why, I'd vote for the devil sooner."

"Oh, quite so!" said Mr. Disraeli, suavely, "but in event of your friend not standing, may I hope for your interest?"

SEE ALSO	RELATED SUBJECTS
Generosity 245	Speeches 756–782
Lateness 322	Politics 1896–1901
Rough and Ready 501	Political Parties 1906–1907
Beauty 667	Elections 1921
Introductions 786	Public Offices 1926
Evangelists 1511	

ELECTIONS

1921—There is the story of a Yankee farmer who promised his vote to the Democratic candidate for Selectman and ten minutes later promised it to the Republican nominee. To his wife's rebuke he replied cannily:

"Did you notice how pleased each of the candidates were?"

"Yes."

"Well, I pleased them both, and on election day I'll please myself, and then we shall all be pleased together."

SEE ALSO	RELATED SUBJECTS
Prejudice 445	Politics 1896–1901
	Political Parties 1906–1907
	Campaigning 1911–1920
	Public Offices 1926

PUBLIC OFFICES

1926—The typically parlimentary mind suffers considerably from the necessity of departing from orderly procedure. This was clearly demonstrated in the meeting of the Town Council of a small city on the West Coast. The session was interrupted by a mild earthquake shock, and all present hastened out of the building to safety. The clerk found himself severely perplexed by the problem of concluding his formal minutes of the meeting in the proper manner. After mulling over the problem for a considerable length of time, he was inspired to the following conclusion, "On motion of the City Hall, the Council adjourned."

SEE ALSO   RELATED SUBJECTS
Wealth 2187   Politics 1896–1901
                     Campaigning 1911–1920
                     Elections 1921
                     Presidents 1931–1940
                     Congress 1941–1948
                     Cabinet Members 1951–1953
                     Governors 1956
                     Mayors 1961
                     Office Seekers 1966–1970
                     Judges 2486–2497

PRESIDENTS

1931—Lincoln was once asked if he did not find the office of the Presidency with all its attendant ceremonies rather tiresome at times.

Lincoln replied, "Yes, sometimes. In fact, I feel sometimes like a man who was ridden out of town on a rail, and said: 'If it wasn't for the honor of the thing, I'd rather walk!'"

1932—On the reception of the news of the death of Washington, Napoleon addressed the following letter to the consular guard and the army:

"Washington is dead! That great man who fought against tyranny, and consolidated his country's freedom. His memory will be always dear to Frenchmen, and to all free men in both worlds—but especially to the French soldiers, who, like him and the American soldiers, have struggled for liberty and equality. The First Consul, therefore, orders that for ten days black crêpe shall be suspended from all the flags and standards of the Republic."

1933—John Bach McMaster, the historian, told this story of Abraham Lincoln.

When he was a very small boy he was taken to a reception at the White House. The guests were lined up and led past the President under the watchful eyes of the ushers. No one was allowed to come very close or to shake his hand. One old man, who had come a long distance just for this occasion, was very disappointed at not having shaken hands with the President. Just before leaving the line the old-timer waved his hat at the President and shouted, "Mr. President, I'm from up in York state where we believe that God Almighty and Abraham Lincoln are going to save this country."

Jovially the President waved back at him. "My friend, you're half right," was his reply.

1934—During the first year of the war Peter Harvey, the pompous friend and biographer of Daniel Webster, went to Washington, and on his return was asked how he liked President Lincoln.

"Well," he said, "Mr. Lincoln is a very singular man. I went in to see him, and told him that I'd been an intimate personal friend of Daniel Webster; that I had talked with him so much on the affairs of the country that I felt perfectly competent to tell him what Mr. Webster would advise in the present crisis; and thereupon I talked to Mr. Lincoln for two solid hours, telling him just what he should do and what he should not do; and would you believe it, sir, when I got through, all Mr. Lincoln said was, as he clapped his hand on my leg, "Mr. Harvey, what tremendous great calves you have got!"

1935—Jefferson Davis insisted on being recognized by his official title as commander or President in the regular negotiation with the U. S. Government. This Mr. Lincoln would not consent to.

Mr. Hunte thereupon referred to the correspondence between King Charles the First and his Parliament as a precedent for a negotiation between a constitutional ruler and rebels. Mr. Lincoln's face then wore that indescribable expression which generally preceded his hardest hits, and he remarked: "Upon questions of history, I must refer you to Mr. Seward for he is posted in such things, and I don't profess to be; but my only distinct recollection of the matter is that Charles lost his head."

1936—The last story of Calvin Coolidge's occupancy of the White House concerns the Hoover inauguration. It had poured rain. As he and Mrs. Coolidge were leaving Washington by train he watched the rain spattering on the window for a little while and remarked, "A lot of people got wet today, all right."

1937—When Lincoln was criticized by a deputation sent to call on him he said, "Gentlemen, suppose all the property

you were worth was in gold, and you had put it in the
hands of Blondin to carry across Niagara River on a
rope. Would you shake the cable and keep shouting—
'Blondin, stoop a little more—go a little faster—lean a
little more to the north—lean a little more to the south?'
No, you would hold your breath as well as your tongue,
and keep your hands off until he was safe over. The
Government is carrying an immense weight. Untold
treasures are in our hands. We are doing the very best
we can. Don't badger us. Keep quiet, and we will get
you safe across."

1938—A newspaper correspondent visited Coolidge at Plymouth,
watched the automobiles rolling by, and said:
"It must make you proud to see all these people coming by
here, merely to look at you sitting on the porch. It shows
that although you are an ex-President you are not forgotten. Just look at the number of those cars."
"Not as many as yesterday," replied Mr. Coolidge. "There
were 163 then."

1939—When Mrs. Calvin Coolidge went abroad after her husband's death she feared there would be an unnecessary
fuss made over the wife of an ex-President. But the
friend with whom she was travelling said, "Don't worry.
In the little places where we'll be stopping they don't
know one President of the United States from another.
People won't bother you." And no one did—until in a
small Italian town they received word that reservations
had been made for them in the next town. This sounded
ominous. When they reached the hotel in question they
were received pompously by the manager. Bowing pro-
foundly, he said, "We are proud to welcome the wife of
the great President of the United States. Will you register, Mrs. Lincoln?"

1940—"I think the White House should set an example of a
standard of decent living for those who have to work
in somebody else's house," Mrs. Roosevelt explained,
as she planned to make the servants' quarters "humanly
livable." The kitchens had not previously been improved
in a quarter of a century. Even the upper servants who
do no basement or kitchen work, felt the impact of Mrs.
Roosevelt's improvements of the working conditions of
White House servants. One of the oldest Negro door-
men, who had served the White House for administra-

tion after administration, suddenly spoke one day for himself and his fellows. An old friend of the Roosevelts was departing after a few days' visit. She commented on the courtesy and graciousness of the colored servants in the White House. He thanked her with the proper dignity. She said she had always loved to visit the White House, but she was not sure she would like it so much again, after the Roosevelts left.

The liveried man dropped his dignity and her bags, turned, and exclaimed, "Oh, Ma'am, I don't know what we'll do without Mrs. Roosevelt here!"

SEE ALSO
Ambition 96
Boners 107, 109
Brevity 133
Economy 211, 212
Honesty 292
Kindness 314
Modesty 381, 383, 384
Prejudice 441
Homeliness 652
Tallness 696
Talking 813
Friendship 867
Church Services 1531
Prayer 1606
Baseball 1822

RELATED SUBJECTS
Politics 1896–1901
Campaigning 1911–1920
Elections 1921
Office Seekers 1966–1970
United States 2031–2032

Congress 1943, 1948
Freedom 2037
Taxes 2191
Civil War 2326
Detectives 2557
Stealing 2589

CONGRESS

1941—When Edward Everett Hale was Chaplain of the Senate, someone asked him, "Do you pray for the senators, Dr. Hale?" "No, I look at the senators and pray for the country," he replied.

1942—Laboulaye said, in one of his lectures, that Jefferson, who had become so completely imbued with French ideas as even to admire the unicameral system of legislation, one day visited Washington at Mount Vernon, and, in the course of the conversation that ensued, the comparative excellence of the two systems came up for consideration. After much had been said on both sides, finally, at the tea-table, Washington turning sharply to Jefferson, said, "You, sir, have just demonstrated the superior excellence of the bicameral system, by your own hand."

"I! How is that?" said Jefferson.

"You have poured your tea from your cup out into the saucer to cool. We want the bicameral system to cool things. A measure originates in one house, and in heat is passed. The other house will serve as a wonderful cooler; and, by the time it is debated and modified by various amendments there, it is much more likely to become an equitable law! No, we can't get along without the saucer in our system."

1943—Fiume was said by Colonel House to have been one of the causes of the United States Senate's rejection of the Treaty of Versailles. One day at his apartment in New York, several years after the Peace Conference, while I was discussing with the Texan the sabotage of the pact at Washington, the Colonel spun this amusing yarn:

"When Mr. Wilson told me of his decision to oppose the cession of the Adriatic port to the Italians, I said: 'Mr. President, aren't you afraid the Senate is going to be highly displeased when it hears about Fiume?'

"The President replied: 'I suppose it will, as soon as it learns where Fiume is!'

"Somehow or other, that aspersion of the Senate's geographical knowledge," House continued, "got back to Washington. Lodge & Co. never forgave it!"

1944—The late Senator Henry Cabot Lodge was talking about the ineffectiveness of most Congressional investigating committees.

"Some of them," he observed, "remind me of Si Hoskins. Si got a job at shooting muskrats, for muskrats overran a mill-owner's dam. There, in the lovely Spring weather, Si sat on the grassy bank, his gun on his knee. Finding him one morning, I said: 'What are you doing, Sir?'

'I'm paid to shoot the muskrats, sir. They're underminin' the dam.'

'There goes one now!' said I. 'Shoot, man! Why don't you shoot?'

"Si puffed a tranquil cloud from his pipe and said: 'Do you think I want to lose my job?'"

1945—Once the House was making an effort to secure a quorum, and, as is usually done in such cases, telegrams were sent to members who were absent. One man, who was delayed by a flood on the railroad, telegraphed Thomas B. Reed, Speaker of the House, saying:

"Wash-out on line; can't come."

Reed telegraphed back: "Buy another shirt and come on next train."

1946—"Congress is so strange," commented Boris Marshalov, a Russian actor and dramatic coach, after a visit to the spectators' gallery of the House of Representatives. "A man gets up to speak and says nothing. Nobody listens —and then everybody disagrees."

1947—The nervous condition resulting from high tension in our national capital in war time is indicated by the case of the weary Congressman who paused in the drugstore of his hotel and asked for a box of aspirin tablets. "Sorry, sir," said the clerk. "We're all out of everything for headaches."

1948—Ward Lamon told this story of President Lincoln, whom he found one day in a particularly gloomy frame of mind Lamon said, "The President remarked, as I came in, 'I fear I have made Senator Wade of Ohio my enemy for life.'

" 'How?' I asked.

" 'Well,' continued the President, 'Wade was here just now urging me to dismiss Grant and in response to something he said, I remarked: 'Senator, that reminds me of a story.'

" 'What did Wade say?' inquired Lamon of the President.

" 'He said in a petulant way, the President responded: 'It is with you, sir, all story, story! You are the father of every military blunder that has been made during the war. You are on your road to hell, sir, with this government, by your obstinacy, and you are not a mile off this minute.'

" 'What did you say then?'

" 'I good naturedly said to him,' the President responded, 'Senator, that is just about from here to the Capitol, is it not?' He was very angry, grabbed up his hat and cane, and went away.' "

SEE ALSO

Boners 108

Gentlemanliness 255

Liars 333

Long-Windedness 346, 347, 351

RELATED SUBJECTS

Politics 1896–1901

Political Parties 1906–1907

Campaigning 1911–1920

Elections 1921

Parliament 1996–2000

Politeness 420
Prejudice 441
Quick Thinking 471
Rough and Ready 496, 497
Shortness 692
Evangelists 1511
Poor Health 1712
Political Parties 1906
Army 2402

CABINET.MEMBERS

1951—When Attorney-General Bates resigned in 1864, the Cabinet was left without a Southern member. A few days before the meeting of the Supreme Court, which then met in December, Mr. Lincoln sent for Titian G. Coffey, and said: "My Cabinet has shrunk up North, and I must find a Southern man. I suppose if the twelve apostles were to be chosen nowadays, the interests of locality would have to be heeded."

1952—Lincoln received many complaints because of the stern dictatorial methods employed by the Secretary of War, Stanton. He finally silenced them by saying:

"We may have to treat Stanton as they are sometimes obliged to treat a Methodist minister I know out West. He gets wrought up to so high a pitch of excitement in his prayers and exhortations that they put bricks in his pockets to keep him down. But I guess we'll let him jump awhile first."

1953—When former Prime Minister Menzies of Australia was sworn into office, various representatives of the press were on hand to interview him. The reporter from the radical press said, somewhat bluntly, "I suppose, Mr. Prime Minister, that you will consult the powerful interests that control you in choosing your Cabinet?"

"Young man," snapped the Prime Minister, "keep my wife's name out of this."

SEE ALSO
Drinking 37
Ambition 96
Modesty 384
Diplomats 2022

RELATED SUBJECTS
Politics 1896–1901
Public Offices 1926
Presidents 1931–1940

GOVERNORS

1956—A certain Colonel on the staff of the Governor died suddenly. Many applicants for his position were clamoring to be heard. Before even the funeral had taken place, one of these managed to detain the Governor for a moment, asking, "Would you object to my taking the place of the Colonel?"

"Not at all," snapped the Governor. "Speak to the undertaker."

SEE ALSO	RELATED SUBJECTS
Drinking 54	Politics 1896–1901
Generosity 243	Political Parties 1906–1907
Politeness 417	Campaigning 1911–1920
Quick Thinking 484	Elections 1921
Rough and Ready 502	
Civil War 2326	
Jail 2561	

MAYORS

1961—A mayor of a city in southern Italy, in an address of welcome to the King of Italy, said: "We welcome you in the name of our five thousand inhabitants, three thousand of whom are in America."

SEE ALSO	RELATED SUBJECTS
Boners 112	Politics 1896–1901
Laws 2597	Political Parties 1906–1907
	Campaigning 1911–1920
	Elections 1921

OFFICE SEEKERS

1966—One time, Abraham Lincoln drawled, he read a story of a certain King who wanted to go hunting, and asked the Court Minister if it would rain. The Minister told him the weather would be fair. Setting out, the royal party met a farmer riding a jackass. He warned the King it was going to rain. The King laughed, went on, and no sooner got started hunting than a heavy downpour drenched him and his party. He went back, threw out the Minister, and called for the farmer.

"Tell me how you knew it would rain."

"I did not know, Your Majesty. It's not me, it's my jackass. He puts his ear forward when it's going to be wet."

The King sent the farmer away, had the jackass brought and put in place of the Minister.

"It was here," said Lincoln, "that the King made a great mistake."

"How so?" asked some of the audience?

"Why, ever since that time, every jackass wants an office. Gentlemen, leave your credentials with me and when the war is over you'll hear from me."

1967—A Commissioner to the Hawaiian Islands was to be appointed, and eight applicants had filed their papers, when a delegation from the South appeared at the White House on behalf of a ninth. Not only was their man fit— so the delegation urged—but was also in bad health, and a residence in that balmy climate would be of great benefit to him.

President Lincoln was rather impatient that day, and before the members of the delegation had fairly started in, suddenly closed the interview with this remark:

"Gentlemen, I am sorry to say that there are eight other applicants for that place, and they are all 'sicker'n your man.'"

1968—An old acquaintance of President Lincoln visited him in Washington. Lincoln desired to give him a place. Thus encouraged, the visitor, who was an honest man but wholly inexperienced in public affairs or business, asked for a high office, Superintendent of the Mint.

The President was aghast, and said:

"Good gracious! Why didn't he ask to be Secretary of the Treasury, and have done with it?"

Afterward, he said: "Well, now, I never thought Mr. —— had anything more than average ability, when we were young men together. But, then, I suppose he thought the same thing about me, and—here I am!"

1969—To someone who wanted an appointment which was already filled, Lincoln sent the following telegram:

"What nation do you desire General Allen to be made quarter-master-general of? This nation already has a quarter-master-general.—A. Lincoln."

1970—Master (Goeffrey) Chaucer was a man of law, for he had studied at the Temple, probably about the time when he is said to have cudgelled a friar in Fleet Street; he was a soldier, and had been taken captive in the wars; he was a courtier and an ambassador, and had negotiated a royal marriage. There was probably ground, therefore, for supposing that were he given an office of profit under the Crown he would take his pleasure and leave the duties to be performed by others, as was not uncommon in those days. Wherefore he was bound down to this close bargain: "That the said Goeffrey write with his own hand the rolls touching the same office, and continually reside there, and do and execute all things pertaining to the said office in his own proper person, and not by his substitute."

SEE ALSO
Rabbis 1486

RELATED SUBJECTS
Politics 1896–1901
Public Offices 1926
Presidents 1931–1940

KINGS AND EMPERORS

1971—The late King George the Fifth, in his domestic setting, was quite an average husband and family head. When, on social occasions, he would talk too long to someone or express himself too rashly, Queen Mary would prod him gently with her umbrella and murmur, "Now, George." Also when palace guests would admire the Cloisonné, the Wedgwood, the Chippendales, etc., the King would always refer to his wife, saying, "Now, May, you know about this."

1972—It is reported that King Victor Emanuel, when asked what he thought of the African campaign, replied very enthusiastically: "If Italy wins, I shall be King of Ethiopia; if the Ethiopians win, why then I shall be King of Italy again."

1973—It is said that the late King George the Fifth and the Princess Victoria, his sister, were accustomed to have a brief chat on the telephone at the same hour every morning. Their conversations were of a personal, highly informal, and often joking sort. One morning when her phone rang at the accustomed time, the Princess picked up the instrument and said, "Hello, you old fool."
The voice of the operator broke in, saying, "I beg your pardon, Your Royal Highness, His Majesty is not yet on the line."

1974—In the work of James I entitled "True Law of Free Monarchies," is laid down, "That a free Monarchy is one in which the Monarch is perfectly free to do as he pleases."

1975—James Brevoort, the correspondent of Washington Irving, wrote from Paris of the unceremonious manner in which the Chamber of Deputies legislated General Lafayette out of his great office. Louis Philippe attempted to smooth matters by offering him the title of Honorary Commander-in-Chief of the National Guard for life, to which the veteran hero of two hemispheres replied: "How would Your Majesty be pleased with the title of Honorary King of the French?"

1976—Peter the Great was so much affected by the death of Peter, his son by Catherine I, that he shut himself up at Peterhof, intending to starve himself to death; and forbade every person, of whatever description, under pain of death, to disturb his retirement. The senate assembled on this desperate resolution of the prince, and Dolgorouki undertook to drive him from it. He went and knocked at the door of the room where Peter was shut up. "Whoever you be," cried the Czar with a terrible voice, "fly off, or I will open the door and knock out your brains."

"Open, I say," replied Dolgorouki in a firm tone, "it is a deputy from the senate come to ask you whom you wish to have named as emperor in your room, since you have resigned."

Peter, struck with the courageous zeal of Dolgorouki, opened, embraced his faithful courtier, yielded to his councils, and resumed the reins of government.

1977—Alexander III (of Russia), the grandson of Nicholas I, begged his son Nicholas II to continue the good work his great-grandfather had initiated in setting the principle of primogeniture firmly on its feet. At long last they had managed to maintain it unbroken for a second generation, twice in succession handing on the throne from father to son. "Now remember," Alexander III enjoined his son, "that when I pass the scepter to you on my death, you are not to let it pass out of your hands except to your eldest son on your death. Remember! No brothers! No women! No uncles! Always the eldest son. Is that clear?"

"Yes, Papa."

"Promise me."

"Yes, Papa."

1978—Louis Napoleon was present at the opening of the Chambers, and remarked afterwards, very seriously: "There's no doubt, Papa, you made a very fine speech."

"Well, Louis," returned Napoleon the Third, "when you grow up, it will be your job to make the speeches."

"But then what will you do?" asked Louis innocently.

1979—At a dinner during the First World War the German Kaiser was being discussed. Opinions differed about him. Some of the diners attacked him savagely. Others insisted he was a fine man despite his shortcomings. J. M. Barrie, the playwright, listened in silence, then without looking up from his plate, remarked dryly, "He is an infernal scoundrel but that is his only fault."

1980—The first Napoleon, dining at a table full of monarchs, when he heard one of them deferentially alluding to the Bonaparte family as being very old and noble, exclaimed, "Pish! My nobility dates from the day of Marengo!"

1981—The Duke of York meeting King Charles the Second, attended only by two persons, expressed his surprise that the King should so expose himself. "No man," replied the Monarch, "will take away my life to make you King."

1982—Nicholas II at the moment was playing tennis at Peterhof. When the Emperor was handed a telegram he had two tennis balls in his left hand, the racket raised, ready to serve, in his right. He took the telegram with the right hand raising racket and telegram to his eyes, reading: "Russian Fleet annihilated at Shushima Stop Nearly all our ships sunk."

The Czar shoved the telegram into his trouser pocket. "Thirty-fifteen," he said, and served.

1983—James I would say to the lords of his council, when they sat upon any great matter, and came to him from council, "Well, you have sat, but what have you hatched?"

1984—One day in a gathering of family and friends, Napoleon the Third observed, "We are a mixed lot here. We represent all parties. Conneau there is a republican, and always was. Madam Lebreton is an orleanist. The Empress is a legitimist, and I am a socialist, as we all know."

"But, in that case," spoke up little Louis Napoleon, "who are the Bonapartists?"

The Emperor put an arm around him, "You are the Bonapartist, dear child."

1985—Seeing his young grandson deeply engrossed in his studies, the late King George V of England stopped to see what was interesting the child.

"And who are you studying about now?" he asked, giving the youngster a friendly pat on the head.

"About Peter Warbeck," was the reply.

"And who was he?"

"Oh," answered the boy, "he's just someone who pretended he was the son of a king. But he wasn't really; he was the son of respectable parents."

1986—Suetonius relates how at a royal feast the Roman emperor Caligula suddenly burst out in uproarious laughter. He laughed and laughed, and the rest of the company, in order to be polite and save their lives, laughed with him. The fun-smitten host at length fell back in his chair exhausted, and a guest near his chair respectfully inquired the reason for his merriment. The jovial monarch with a wave of his fat hand over the crowded banquet-hall, replied: "Nothing, but that upon a single nod of my head, you would all have your throats cut."

1987—Benjamin Constant had such a command of language, that when he chanced to displease his audience by an expression, he would go on substituting synonyms till he suited them. For example; "I am anxious to spare the Crown" —a murmur; "the Monarch"—the murmurs continued; "the Constitutional King"—the murmurs are hushed.

1988—Disraeli, in conversation with a friend, disclosed the secret of his ascendancy in royal favor. "When talking with the Queen," he said, "I observe a simple rule of conduct; I never deny; I never contradict; I sometimes forget."

1989—When Charles V retired in weariness from the greatest throne in the world to the solitude of the monastery at Yuste, he occupied his leisure for some weeks in trying to regulate two clocks. It proved very difficult. One day, it is recorded, he turned to his assistant and said: "To think that I attempted to force the reason and conscience of thousands of men into one mould, and I cannot make two clocks agree!"

1990—Disraeli, explaining his popularity with the queen said, "Gladstone speaks to the queen as if she were a public department. I treat her with the knowledge that she is a woman."

1991—A gentleman begging the Duke of Buckingham to employ his interest for him at Court, added, that he had nobody to depend upon but God and his Grace. Then said the Duke: "Your condition is desperate; you could not have named two beings who have less interest at Court."

1992—A German prince in a dream saw three rats, one fat, another lean, and a third blind. He sent for a learned Bohemian gipsy to interpret the dream.

"The fat rat," she answered, "is your prime minister, the lean rat is your people, and the blind rat is yourself."

1993—When Napoleon, after a series of victories, came to visit annexed Belgium, he found, on entering Ghent, a triumphal arch erected by the Guild of Butchers. It was inscribed:

"The little butchers of Ghent to Napoleon the great (butcher)."

SEE ALSO
Flattery 236
Long-Windedness 348
Melancholy 368
Quick Thinking 482, 483
Rough and Ready 498, 506
Shortness 691
Divorce 910
Small Children 967
Teachers 1056
Erudition 1076
Learned Men 1088
Scientists 1116
Plays 1388

RELATED SUBJECTS
Parliament 1996–2000
Dictators 2001–2011
Equality 2046
Revolutions 2061–2064
War 2316–2323

Death 1748
Card Playing 1837
Dictators 2008
Diplomats 2024
Freedom 2042
Revolutions 2061
Officers 2413, 2425
Stealing 2587

PARLIAMENT

1996—One night Burke severely attacked some acts of the Government. George Onslow arose and haughtily said that he must call the honorable member to a sense of his duty, and that no man should be suffered in his presence to insult the sovereign.

Burke, in reply, gravely addressed the Speaker: "Sir, the honorable member has exhibited much ardor but little discrimination. He should know that, however, I may reverence the king, I am not at all bound, nor at all inclined to extend that reverence to his ministers. I may honor his majesty, but, sir, I can see no possible reason for honoring," and he glanced round the treasury bench at Mr. Onslow and the other ministers, "his majesty's man-servant, and maid-servant, his ox, and his ass!"

1997—During one of his much admired debates in Parliament, Sheridan was annoyed by the persistence of a well-meaning fellow, who kept punctuating, by the exclamation, "Hear, Hear!", almost all of his most telling remarks.

In the course of discussion, Sheridan took occasion to describe a political enemy as, "wishing to play the rogue but having only sense enough to act the fool. Where," he cried forcefully, "where shall we find a more foolish knave or a more knavish fool than he?"

"Hear! Hear!" was the annoying response.

Sheridan swung about and thanked him forthwith, sitting down amid a general roar of laughter.

1998—A young peer once asked Disraeli what course of study he had best take to qualify himself for speaking so as to gain the ear of the House of Lords.

"Have you a graveyard near your house?" asked Disraeli.

"Yes," was the reply.

"Then," said Disraeli, "I should recommend you to visit it early of a morning and practice upon the tombstones."

1999—A nobleman wished Garrick to be a candidate for the representation of a borough in Parliament. "No, my lord," said the actor, "I would rather play the part of a great man on the stage than the part of a fool in Parliament."

2000—At one time the House of Commons had sat in a long and ineffectual session. Mr. Papham, speaker of the House of Commons, was summoned by Queen Elizabeth, who said to him, "Now, Mr. Speaker, what has passed in the Commons' House?"

He replied, "If it please Your Majesty—seven weeks."

SEE ALSO
Liars 334
Long-Windedness 345,
 349
Patriotism 402
Age 675
Speeches 766, 767
Campaigning 1916
Freedom 2039
War 2318
Stealing 2581

RELATED SUBJECTS
Politics 1896–1901
Congress 1941–1948
Kings and Emperors 1971–1993

DICTATORS

2001—Adolf Hitler is known to frequent astrologers, sooth-sayers and others of that ilk. A certain astrologer was asked by him, "On what day will I die?"

After peering over his charts, the astrologer announced, "You will die on a Jewish Holiday."

Much perturbed, Hitler demanded, "Which one?"

"I do not know," replied the astrologer.

Hitler became very angry, "You must know," he shouted, "I insist upon the truth."

"I do not know," persisted the astrologer, "because any day you die will be a Jewish Holiday."

2002—When that late and noble statesman, Neville Chamberlain, was about to depart from the fatal Munich Conference, Herr Hitler said to him, "Mr. Chamberlain, vud you be so kind as to gif me your umbrella for a keepsake?"

"No, no," said Chamberlain, "I can't do that."

"But, Mr. Chamberlain, it vud mean so much to me. I request it of you. Please!"

"I'm sorry I can't oblige you," said Chamberlain.

Hitler flew into a rage. "I insist!" he screamed, stamping on the Prime Minister's foot.

"No," said Chamberlain firmly, "It's impossible. You see—the umbrella is mine."

2003—According to a story circulating in Rome, Mussolini dies and goes to Paradise, where he is greeted warmly by Napoleon. "God will be here in a few minutes," says Napoleon. "Since you are new here, you should probably be warned that we rise when he enters."

"What! I get up? Don't forget that I am the Duce."

"I am Caesar," states a voice. "Yet I have the manners to rise."

"Not I!" says Mussolini. The argument is becoming warm
when Machiavelli approaches.

"Peace, friends," he exclaims. "I will arrange everything."

Three solemn knocks announce the coming of God.

"Attention!" thunders Machiavelli. "Here comes the
photographer!"

Whereupon Mussolini hops to his feet, folds his arms,
sticks out his chin and chest.

Peace reigns.

2004—Sir Oswald Moseley, one time leader of the British Fascist
movement, had once staged a most effective setting for
his rabble-rousing. In a concentration of spotlights he
marched stiffly up to the platform accompanied by an
escort of Black Shirts and faced the audience. Solemnly,
in a hush of silence, he raised his right arm high in the
Fascist salute. From the balcony issued a shrill voice,
"Yes, Oswald, you may leave the room!"

2005—In the days of Mussolini's higher prestige, it is said that he
was once stranded in a small town due to the breaking
down of his automobile. He went into a local cinema.
When his picture appeared on the screen everyone rose
but he remained seated. The manager of the theatre
came forward, tapped him on the shoulder, whispering
in his ear, "I feel the same way but you'd better stand
up. It's safer."

2006—Calamy, the celebrated Presbyterian minister, on one occasion objected to Cromwell assuming the supreme power
as Protector, as being in his opinion, both unlawful and
impracticable. Cromwell observed: he "cared little
about the lawfulness; but why may I ask you is it
impracticable?"

"Oh!" observed the divine, "it is impracticable inasmuch
as it is against the voice of the people; you will have nine
in ten against you."

"Very well, sir," replied Cromwell, "but what if I should
disarm the nine and put the sword into the tenth man's
hand: would that not do the business, think you?"

The events which succeeded proved that Cromwell not
only entertained the opinion he thus expressed, but that
he also acted upon it.

2007—Frank Gannett, American newspaper publisher, spent three
hours one afternoon in No. 10 Downing Street, where

Prime Minister Stanley Baldwin cocked his feet on an old-fashioned roll-top desk, smoked pipe after pipe, and opened his mind to Gannett. Baldwin had already announced in the House of Commons that the frontier of Britain was on the Rhine.

"What do you intend to do about that man across the Rhine?" Gannett asked.

"If a python gets out of a cage," replied Baldwin, "one man would be a fool to try alone to get him back. But several men can get him back without much trouble. No; we are not going to tackle him alone."

2008—King Victor Emmanuel of Italy has long been known as the very silent partner in the management of his country. One day the King and Mussolini were walking about the palace gardens discussing affairs of state. The King dropped his handkerchief. Mussolini, still mindful of the fact that the code of behavior called for him to pick it up, was just about to stoop for it when the King stopped him.

"Permit me," he said. "This is about the only thing you have been letting me put my nose into these days."

2009—In Italy the underground wiseacres are asking, "What's the difference between Christianity and Fascism?"

The answer is, "In Christianity one man sacrifices himself for all. Under Fascism all men sacrifice themselves for one."

2010—Mussolini died and went to Heaven. He received a tremendous ovation. Millions of angels sang and praised him. He was given a crown and put on a great throne. Looking around he was surprised to notice that his crown and his throne were both bigger than those of God the Father. Even he was unprepared for this. "How is it?" he asked of God.

"You are greater than I," said God respectfully. "I gave your people one day of fasting a week. You have given them seven. I gave them faith. You have taken it away."

2011—In the year when the 20th anniversary of Fascism was "celebrated," a stranger was riding through the streets of Naples in a carriage. They passed a bakery and he saw a great mob of people storming the place. He asked the driver about it and the cabby, afraid to speak, said that it was a film being made. Not much farther along another mob of people was seen outside a grocery. "What's that?" asked the stranger.

"The second scene," said the driver.

Further along a similar mob was besieging a butcher. Without waiting to be asked, the cab driver said, "This is the third scene."

"What's the name of this picture, anyway?" asked the passenger.

"Twenty years after," said the driver.

SEE ALSO	RELATED SUBJECTS
Absent-Mindedness 88	Kings and Emperors 1971–1993
Rudeness 520	Freedom 2036–2042
Mathematicians 1148	Revolutions 2061–2064
Kings 1972	War 2316–2323
Civilians in War 2334, 2344	

INTERNATIONAL RELATIONS

2016—According to F. W. Wile, "It was the President himself (Wilson) who told us of one of his conversations with Signor Orlando about Fiume. The Italian premier argued that, as the population, language and institutions of the city were overwhelmingly Italian, Italy's claim to the city was indisputable.

" 'Well, Mr. Prime Minister,' rejoined Mr. Wilson, 'I hope you won't press that point with respect to New York City, or you might feel like claiming a sizable piece of Manhattan Island.' "

SEE ALSO	RELATED SUBJECTS
Honor 297	Diplomats 2021–2027
Dictators 2002, 2007	War 2316–2323

DIPLOMATS

2021—According to diplomatic procedure, the representative of a foreign country, before being actually presented to the President, always exchanges with him the text of the speeches.

On one such occasion this formality never reached its ordinary climax. Instead of stiltedly repeating the already familiar words, President Roosevelt greeted the foreign diplomat with, "Now, Mr. Minister, I've read your re-

marks and you've read mine, so suppose we dispense
with the speeches and have a friendly chat."

2022—After the Russo-Japanese War, Admiral Togo, Commander of the victorious Japanese fleet, visited the
United States and was cordially received. A state dinner
was tendered him at which it fell to the lot of William
Jennings Bryan, then Secretary of State, to propose a
toast to Togo. Bryan, a staunch Prohibitionist, would
not touch champagne, and it was feared that some diplomatic impasse might arise from the difficulty. Bryan,
however, rose at the proper time, picked up his glass of
water and said, "Admiral Togo has won a great victory
on water, therefore I will toast him in water. When
Admiral Togo wins a victory on champagne, I will toast
him in champagne."

2023—When Lady Baldwin of Bewdley visited Manhattan with
her husband (Stanley Baldwin) last summer, she wanted
to see the General Motors Futurama at the New York
World's Fair, but did not want to stand in line. So
Earl Baldwin telephoned the British Consulate; the
Consulate called the British Embassy in Washington;
the Embassy cabled the Foreign Office in London; the
Foreign Office appealed to Ambassador Joe Kennedy.
Resourceful Joe sent a cable direct to General Motors'
Building at the Fair. A press agent there called Lady
Baldwin at the Waldorf (cost, 5 cents), told her to come
right out, he'd see that she was well taken care of.

2024—Henry VIII, in a spell of temper against his rival
Francis I, King of France, commissioned a clergyman
named Bonner to deliver an insolent and threatening
message to the French court. The clergyman realized it
would be a risky job and protested that he could never
hope to get back to England alive if he dared to talk to
the French king in the manner Henry VIII wished.
"Don't worry about that," said the monarch soothingly.
"If the King of France puts you to death, I will cut off
the heads of all the Frenchmen I can get my hands on."
"That may be, your majesty," replied Bonner, tapping his
head: "but of all the heads in England, there is none that
fits my shoulders as well as this one does."

2025—Among the guests at a luncheon, was the wife of the
Finance Minister of one of the neutral countries. Her

gown was very décolleté but nature had not endowed her with the necessary charms to wear such a garment. German Foreign Minister Rantzau gazed at her and then murmured, "She is just like her husband, an uncovered deficit."

2026—When James B. Reynolds was Assistant Secretary of the the Treasury, Senator Root sent for Mr. Reynolds one day to discuss with him some matter concerning a trade conference in Paris which Mr. Reynolds had been selected to attend.

"I suppose," said Mr. Root, "you speak French?"

"Well, yes," responded Mr. Reynolds. "I know a little French. I have no trouble to make the waiters and the cab drivers understand me."

"I see," said Mr. Root. "But, Mr. Reynolds, suppose there should be no waiters and cab drivers at the conference?"

2027—The famous Marshal Villars, having given some offense to the mistress and ministers of Louis XIV, occasion was soon found to send him on very dangerous service in Germany. When coming to take his farewell of the king, the marshal thus expressed himself:

"Sire, I leave your Majesty surrounded by my enemies, while I go to be surrounded by yours."

SEE ALSO	RELATED SUBJECTS
Long-Windedness 350	Tact 586–591
Quick Thinking 474	International Relations 2016
Congress 1943	

UNITED STATES

2031—Judge T. Lyle Dickey of Illinois related that when the excitement over the Kansas-Nebraska bill first broke out, he was with Lincoln and several friends attending court. One evening several persons, including himself and Lincoln, were discussing the slavery question. Judge Dickey contended that slavery was an institution which the Constitution recognized, and which could not be disturbed. Lincoln argued that ultimately slavery must become extinct. "After a while," said Judge Dickey, "we went upstairs to bed. There were two beds in our room, and I remember that Lincoln sat up in his nightshirt on the edge of the bed arguing the point with me. At last we went to sleep. Early in the morning I woke up and there was Lincoln half sitting up in bed. "Dickey," said he, "I tell you this nation cannot exist half slave and half free."

"Oh, Lincoln," said I, "go to sleep."

2032—Cobden used to tell the following anecdote: "When in America I asked an enthusiastic young lady why her country could not rest satisfied with the immense unoccupied territories it already possessed, but must ever be hankering after the lands of its neighbors; when her somewhat remarkable reply was:

"Oh, the propensity is a very bad one, I admit, but we came honestly by it, for we inherited it from England."

RELATED SUBJECTS
Presidents 1931–1940
Freedom 2036–2042
Equality 2046

FREEDOM

2036—"You do not know what you are advising us to do," replied the Spartans to a Persian envoy who urged them to submit to Xerxes, "for you know what it is to be a slave, but the sweetness of freedom you have never tasted. If you felt it, you would tell us to fight for it, not with spears only, but with axes."

2037—When the Emancipation Proclamation was taken to Lincoln by Secretary Seward, for the President's signature, Lincoln took a pen, dipped it in ink, moved his hand to the place for the signature, held it a moment, then removed his hand and dropped the pen. After a little hesitation, he again took up the pen and went through the same movement as before. Lincoln then turned to Seward and said:

"I have been shaking hands since nine o'clock this morning, and my right arm is almost paralyzed. If my name ever goes into history, it will be for this act, and my whole soul is in it. If my hand trembles when I sign the Proclamation, all who examine the document hereafter will say: 'He hesitated.'"

2038—At a little stream on the Swiss frontier, a Swiss and a Nazi were fishing from the opposite sides of the water. Great success had attended the Swiss, and he had a handsome

string to show for his efforts; whereas the Nazi had not
had so much as a nibble.

"Why is it," called the German across the water, "that you
have so much better luck? Are we not using the same
bait?"

"Well," said the Swiss, "on this side the fish aren't afraid
to open their mouths."

2039—On August 1, 1836, the British Parliament abolished
slavery in the West Indies, but the decree was not to go
into effect for a year. On July 31, 1837, a year later,
twenty thousand slaves came together in Jamaica. They
put on white robes, and at eleven o'clock at night they
all knelt down, and with faces turned upward they
waited for an hour. As the clock struck twelve the
twenty thousand former slaves rose up and shouted
joyously:

"We are free! We are free!"

2040—Years ago there was an insurrection in Massachusetts.
There were thousands of men in arms against the State
authorities. One of the leaders, Luke Shay, spoke thus
at Springfield:

"My boys," said he, "they talk to you about liberty; they
tell you that liberty means the right to do what you have
a mind to. That is not liberty. Liberty is the right to
make other folks do what you want to have them do."

2041—Harold Laski has this story to tell: I discussed recently
with a Hindu I knew—a man of great culture—the
question of Indian Independence. "If England were to
withdraw from India," I said, "wouldn't the country
relapse into a state of anarchy—much like what it was
in the 18th Century when Clive and Hastings laid the
foundations of the British Raj?"

My friend assented sadly, "Yes, I suppose you are right."

"And that would be followed by a tyranny, or several
tyrannies, would it not?"

"Yes, probably."

"And then the pendulum would swing back to anarchy
again?"

"Yes," he said, "yes, I am afraid it would!" Then, after
a long pause, he added, "but it will be our tyranny and
our anarchy!"

2042—Having been subordinated and suppressed for eighteen
years, Catherine the Great revelled in doing what she

pleased. "O Freedom," she wrote, "The soul of all things; without thee there is no life." But when the miners and other serfs of the land rebelled, she decided that freedom was too precious to be scattered around, and she wrote to Vyazemsky, who had quelled the revolt with cannon: "The Russian Empire is so vast that any other form of government than that of an autocratic emperor would be detrimental, for every other form fulfills itself more slowly and embodies passions which dissipate its strength."

SEE ALSO
Courage 152
Shrewdness 535
Engagement 857
Presidents 1932
Kings 1974

RELATED SUBJECTS
Equality 2046
Woman's Suffrage 2051-2052
Revolutions 2061-2064

EQUALITY

2046—The liberal historian Mrs. Catherine Macaulay used to debate with Doctor Johnson the question of social equality. One day at dinner in her house the Doctor put on a grave face and said, "Madam, your arguments have converted me to your way of thinking. I am convinced that all mankind should stand upon an equal footing; and, to give you proof, Madam, that I am in earnest, here is a very sensible, civil, well-behaved fellow-citizen— your footman; I desire that he may be allowed to sit down and dine with us." This proposition the hostess of course indignantly rejected, much to the Doctor's amusement. Later, he said, reporting his victory from his arm-chair, "I thus showed her the absurdity of her levelling doctrine. She has never liked me since. Your levellers wish to level down as far as themselves; but they cannot bear levelling up to themselves."

RELATED SUBJECTS
Freedom 2036-2042
Woman's Suffrage 2051-2052
Socialism 2056-2057
Revolutions 2061-2064

WOMAN'S SUFFRAGE

2051—Among the ardent feminists arrested during the suffragette movement in England was an elderly crusader, often in jail for the Cause, and a young thing sentenced for the first time and taking it very hard. They were assigned to adjoining cells. Anon the older woman heard the younger sobbing. She rapped energetically on the dividing wall, and called:

"There, there, dear, don't cry! Put your trust in God— She will protect you!"

2052—One evening when Lloyd George was addressing a meeting of hostile suffragettes, one woman, in an ugly mood, rose and said, "If you were my husband I would give you poison."

Lloyd George, noted for his ready wit, snapped back, "My dear lady, if I were your husband I would take the poison."

RELATED SUBJECTS
Women 841–843
Equality 2046

SOCIALISM

2056—One rainy day, standing at a window with Sidney Webb (Lord Passfield), I asked him how the Socialists were going to bring about all these great changes. He pointed to the rain, gentle, steady, incessant, and said in a voice no less gentle: "I want the Socialists to work like that: without noise, without fuss." And then (using another simile): "Under the earth are the burrows of the moles; we must work as they work, unobtrusively, slowly and gradually undermining the existing system until, one day, it subsides."

2057—Andrew Carnegie was once visited by a socialist who preached to him eloquently the injustice of one man possessing so much money. He preached a more equitable distribution of wealth. Carnegie cut the matter short by asking his secretary for a generalized statement of his many possessions and holdings, at the same time looking up the figures on world population in his almanac. He figured for a moment on his desk pad and then instructed his secretary, "Give this gentleman 16¢. That's his share of my wealth."

RELATED SUBJECTS
Freedom 2036–2042
Equality 2046

Revolutions 2061–2064
Wealth 2181–2187

REVOLUTIONS

2061—On the afternoon of July 14, 1789, the Duc de La Rochefoucauld-Liancourt brought to King Louis XVI at Versailles the news of the capture of the Bastille. The King exclaimed, "Why, this is a revolt!"
"No, sire," replied the Duke, "it is a revolution."

2062—The character of the natural revolutionary is typified by the Irishman who was cast ashore upon a beach after a shipwreck. Weak and exhausted from his struggle with the waves, the castaway staggered along the sands until he encountered a man. "What place is this?"
He was answered. "Is there a government here?" he asked next.
"Of course," was the reply.
"Then—I'm agin it!"

2063—During the time of the French Revolution, when the months in France were named Thermidor, Floreal, Nivose, etc.—Sheridan proposed to extend the innovation to the English language, beginning with January, as—"Freezy, Sneezy, Breezy, Wheezy, Showery, Lowery, Flowery, Bowery, Snowy, Flowy, Blowy, Glowy."

2064—A man living in a village outside Paris during the Revolution met a friend fresh from the city and asked what was happening. "It's awful," was the reply, "they're cutting off heads by the thousand."
"Good Heavens! Surely not heads," he cried. "Why, I'm a hatter!"

SEE ALSO
Shrewdness 538
Authors 1197

RELATED SUBJECTS
Kings and Emperors 1971–1993
Dictators 2001–2011
Freedom 2036–2042
Equality 2046
Socialism 2056–2057
War 2316–2323
Civil War 2326–2329

BUSINESS, INDUSTRY AND POSSESSIONS

BUYING AND SELLING

2066—Among the Romans, the deity who presided over commerce and banking was Mercury, who, by a strange association, was also the god of thieves and of orators. The Romans, who looked upon merchants with contempt, fancied there was a resemblance between theft and merchandising and they easily found a figurative connection between theft and eloquence; hence, thieves, merchants, and orators, were placed under the superintendence of the same deity. On the seventeenth of May, in each year, the merchants held a public festival, and walked in procession to the temple of Mercury, for the purpose, as the satirist said, of begging pardon of that deity for all the lying and cheating they had found it convenient to practice, in the way of business, during the preceding year.

2067—One time in Mexico, Carleton Beals had fallen into the habit of buying two oranges from an orange woman near his house. One day, when he was planning to give a party, he undertook to buy her entire stock of four dozen oranges.

Severely she said, "Here are your two," and handed him his usual purchase.

"But this time I want to buy all the rest of them."

"Why," she said, outraged, "you can't. What do you think I would do all the rest of the day with no oranges to sell!"

SEE ALSO
Shrewdness 526, 536
Practical Joking 434
Clothing 718

RELATED SUBJECTS
Stores 2071–2072
Bargaining 2076–2082
Price 2086
Salesmen 2091–2097
Advertising 2101–2108
Competition 2116
Credit 2166–2167
Businessmen 2236–2237

STORES

2071—A certain flower store in New York has a sign on its walls, saying, "Kindly desist from telling us to make up your order 'nice, nice, nice.' You worry yourself and the sales help needlessly. You must realize it is a great strain on the salesmen to be told to 'make it nice' by one customer after another. Your order will be carefully executed without unnecessary reminders."

2072—The story is told of an ingenious young man who desired to present his sweetheart with a gift. He decided that perfume would be appropriate, but he did not know the name of the brand she used, and was too shy to ask her. He solved the problem by taking her little pet dog for a walk. Snatching the animal into a store, he proceeded to instruct the astonished clerk to wave the stoppers of a large number of perfumes under the nose of the rather indifferent dog. At last came a perfume which caused the animal to jump up excitedly and wag its tail. On this evidence he bought his gift which turned out to be right.

SEE ALSO
Honesty 290
Quick Thinking 492
Names 831, 834
Congress 1947
Advertising 2105
Collection 2178
Bosses 2231

RELATED SUBJECTS
Buying and Selling 2066-2067
Price 2086
Advertising 2101-2108

BARGAINING

2076—Georges Clemenceau, "The Tiger" of France, told this story:

"One day in a little village in the East Indies, I noticed a little statuette, and said to the dealer, 'I like your statuette. How much is it?'

" 'Because it's you,' he answered, '75 rupees.'

" 'Because it's you,' I answered, 'I offer you 45 rupees.'

"He raised his hands to heaven.

" 'Forty-five rupees! You're making fun of me! What if anyone happened to hear of it?'

" 'Forty-five rupees,' I said.

"Then he made a fine gesture of indignation. 'Impossible! I'd rather give it to you.'

" 'Agreed!' I took the statuette, stuffed it into my pocket,
and said, 'You are extraordinarily kind, and I thank you.
But it is quite evident that this gift can only come from
a friend to a friend. Consequently you won't take it
amiss if I in turn make you a gift.'

" 'Naturally not.'

" 'Well, here are 45 rupees to use in good works.'

"He took them and we parted, enchanted with each other."

2077—Shrewd bargaining is typified by the woman who entered
one of the large department stores of New York and
ordered a yard of silk which had been priced at 35¢ a
yard. After her purchase, there was left a remnant of one
and a half yards, and the clerk suggested that she take
it also. "What do you want for it?" she asked. "Oh,
20¢," replied the clerk. "All right," said his customer,
"I'll take it and you can keep the yard you just cut off."

2078—William F. Hallstead of Scranton was General Manager
of the Delaware, Lackawanna Railway. One day a
Lackawanna County farmer walked into his office and
bluntly asked for a pass to New York and return. Mr.
Hallstead, who knew the old fellow very well, said:
"Look here, Silas, suppose I should drop in on you some
day and ask you to hitch up and drive me to Honesdale
and return, what would you think of me?"

The old farmer thought for a moment, and in a slow
drawl, replied, "Waal, I think it would be gol darn
cheeky; but Mr. Hallstead, suppose I was driving to
Honesdale anyway, and you asked me for a ride, what
would you think of me if I refused?"

Mr. Hallstead saw the point and Silas got the pass.

2079—An English firm cabled Edison and offered him "Thirty
thousand" for one of his patents.

"Too cheap, Edison," said a friend.

"Too cheap?" repeated Edison. "The thing isn't worth half
of that."

His friends induced him to cable back: "It is yours."

Within a fortnight he received a draft for one hundred and
fifty thousand dollars. It had turned out, of course, that
the English firm had meant the amount in pounds.

Edison wanted to cable that some mistake had occurred,
but his friends intervened.

"Well," he said, "it beats me."

2080—It happened on one of those downtown Manhattan streets where the cloak-and-suiters rush out and seize the passers-by by the arm. "Look," said one of them eagerly to the man he had seized, "a fine suit; the best; nice cut; fine quality materials. To you, $15." "No," said the customer, trying to break from him. "Look," said the clothier, dragging his victim a little closer to the shop, "a very special cut, with cuffs even; the last suit. To you, special, $12." "No," said the man, trying to pull free. "An opportunity that shouldn't be passed up," continued the salesman, "Look, because it's early, to start the day right, the first sale—$8."

"Nothing doing," snarled the customer. "My God," wailed the proprietor, throwing his hands up into the air, "such a person. To make the thing right, to start the day; I start something, I should finish it. I'm giving it to you for nothing." "Not without two pair of pants!" said the customer.

2081—At one time the great copper magnate, Fritz Augustus Heinze, struggled bitterly with John D. Ryan, head of Standard Oil's copper holdings, for control of rich copper deposits at Butte, Montana.

The transaction had nearly stalled when the two men at last met face to face in secrecy, and conferred privately for many hours far into the night. Negotiations broke down again at a point when they were a half million dollars apart in their ideas and it seemed as though a real impasse had been reached. No other channels of negotiation were left open. Abruptly one of them said, "All right, let's toss a coin to see which one gives up the half million."

Probably never before or since has this much money fallen with the fall of a coin.

2082—Soon after Sir William Johnson had been appointed superintendent of Indian affairs in America he wrote to England for some suits of clothes richly laced. When they arrived Hendrick, king of the Mohawk nation, was present and particularly admired them. In a few succeeding days Hendrick called on Sir William and acquainted him that he had had a dream. On Sir William's enquiring what it was, he told him that he had dreamed that he had given him one of those fine suits he had lately received. Sir William took the hint and immediately presented him with one of the richest suits. The Indian chief, highly pleased with the generosity of Sir William, retired. Some time after this, Sir William happening to be in company with Hendrick, told him that he had also had a dream. Hendrick being very solicitous to know what it was, Sir William informed him, that he had dreamed that he (Hendrick) had made him a present of a particular tract of land (the most valuable on the Mohawk River) of about 5,000 acres. Hendrick presented him with the land immediately, remarking shrewdly: "Now, Sir William, I will never dream with you again. You dream too hard for me."

SEE ALSO	RELATED SUBJECTS
Playwrights 1376	Honesty 286–294
Church Services 1535	Shrewdness 526–541
Horses 2286	Buying and Selling 2066–2067
	Competition 2116
	Chiseling and Swindling 2121–2132

PRICE
2086—Walking in the country, Douglas Jerrold, plucking a buttercup, was wont to say, "If it cost a shilling a root, how beautiful it would be!"

SEE ALSO	RELATED SUBJECTS
Inventors 1126	Economy 211–213
Painting 1273, 1276, 1282	Buying and Selling 2066–2067
Bargaining 2080	Stores 2071–2072
Public Relations 2112	Bargaining 2076–2082
Machinery 2272	

SALESMEN
2091—James H. Rand, of Remington, Rand, Inc. was, at the outset of his career, a salesman for a bank-equipment firm. Frank A. Munsey, the eccentric publisher and financier, was about to open banks in Baltimore and Washington. Rand called upon Munsey to sell him equipment, and the publisher cross-questioned him minutely as to the merits and demerits, desirability and undesirability of all types of equipment. Finally he said, "All right, I'll give you a letter to my Washington manager. You can go to him for the order."
Delighted, Rand took the letter and hastened to Washington. He talked to Munsey's manager and got an order

for $25,000 worth of equipment. In his zeal he forgot all about the letter and did not even present it. Back in New York several days later, Rand suddenly found the letter in his pocket. Curious, he opened it. Munsey's instructions to his manager had been, "Learn all you can from this man, but don't buy anything from him if you can help it."

2092—The traveling salesman was anxious to gain admission to the office of a prominent industrialist, the establishing of business relations with whom would be the highlight of his whole trip. But the man in question was difficult to see. Entering his outer office, he gave his card to the secretary. It was taken within and, through the partly opened door, the salesman saw the executive tear it in half and throw it into the waste basket. The secretary returned meanwhile and stated that her employer would not see him. "May I have my card back?" asked the salesman. Slightly embarrassed, the secretary reported to her superior who sent her back out again with a nickel and a message that he was sorry, but the card had been destroyed. More than equal to the occasion, the salesman drew another card from his wallet and gave it to the girl. "Take this back to him," he said, "and tell him I sell two cards for a nickel."
He got his interview and he got his order.

2093—The executive was taken down a peg.
"You may well feel proud of yourself, young fellow," he said to the life insurance agent, "I've refused to see seven insurance men today."
"I know," said the agent, "I'm them."

2094—"We need to have the whole place re-equipped all over electrically," said the office manager to his boss.
"Send for Markman of our sales force," snapped the boss. "He hasn't done anything but wire the house since he's been on the road."

2095—The sales manager was delivering a terrific dressing down to one of his salesmen. He became so abusive in his anger that the culprit protested, saying, "Don't talk to me that way. I take orders from no one."
"That's what I'm raising Hell about," snapped the manager.

2096—An advertising salesman arrived at a large Chicago hotel and took a room. He carried with him only a small grip and the hotel porter asked for the tags for his trunks.

"I have none," said the salesman.

"Why, I understood you was a salesman," said the porter.

"That's right, I am. But I don't need any trunks. I sell brains."

The porter scratched his head and said, "Well, sir, Boss, you is the first traveling salesman what's ever come here without no samples."

2097—"I owe my success as a salesman," said the speaker, addressing the gathering of young men being trained for this profession, "to the first five words which I invariably utter when a woman opens the door, 'Miss, may I speak to your mother?'"

SEE ALSO   RELATED SUBJECTS
Travel 1796   Buying and Selling 2066–2067
Real Estate 2141   Bargaining 2076–2082
                            Competition 2116
                            Insurance 2136–2140
                            Real Estate 2141–2142

ADVERTISING

2101—During Mark Twain's days as a newspaperman, he was editor of a small Missouri newspaper. One day he got a letter from a subscriber, stating that he had found a spider in his paper, and asking if this was an omen of good or bad luck.

Twain wrote: "Finding a spider in your paper is neither good luck nor bad. The spider was merely looking over our paper to see which merchant was not advertising so that he could go to that store, spin his web across the door and lead a life of undisturbed peace ever afterward."

2102—The famous tenor, Giovanni Martinelli, was once asked if he smoked. "Tobacco! I would not think of it!" said the singer. "But," said one of the reporters, "didn't you once endorse a cigarette and say that it did not irritate your throat." "Of course I endorsed it, and it is true that the cigarettes did not hurt my throat. I never smoked them."

2103—"This," said the manager of the store, "is an inferior grade of shoe. I'm an honorable business man and I refuse to pass it off as anything better. Put it in the window and mark it—'A Shoe Fit for a Queen.' A Queen does not have to do much walking."

2104—One of the great press agents was the late Dexter Fellows who functioned in that capacity for Ringling Brothers and Barnum and Bailey. He knew he had the greatest show on earth. He once entered a newspaper office in the Mid-West and announced without preliminaries, "I am Dexter Fellows of the circus."

"What circus?" someone asked.

"Good Lord, man," he said, with all the horror of sacrilege on his face, "if you were in London and heard a man say, 'God Save the King,' would you interrupt him and ask what king?"

2105—Unique in the entire field of advertising is S. Klein, celebrated New York dress merchant. Klein advertises only occasionally to announce, in connection with holidays or other special days, that his store will be closed, in order to keep immense crowds from being disappointed and needlessly cluttering up Union Square. He dares not advertise in any other way for, on the one or two times in the past when he attempted to do so, the result was an actual riot in Union Square, with cordons of police and fleets of squad cars required to restore peace.

2106—From the Lost and Found Column of a Nashville paper: Bird or Hat:—Flew in or blew in out of car passing Dannaker's Service Station, Franklin Road. It's sorta round with green and red polka dot quills or feathers in it. If you've lost a hat or a bird, drive by and see it— it's funny.

2107—When the famous Pre-Raphaelite painter Burne-Jones visited the U. S. he one day received a circular letter from a firm engaged in the sale of dried fruit, inviting him to compete for a prize to be given for the best design to be used in advertising their wares. Only one prize, the circular stated, was to be given, and all unsuccessful drawings were to become the property of the firm.

After reading the circular, and not to be outdone by the audacious request, Sir Philip sat down and wrote the following letter in reply:

"Manager, Dried Fruit Company:

"Dear Sir: I am offering a prize of fifty cents for the best specimen of dried fruit, and should be glad to have you take part in the competition. Twelve dozen boxes of each kind of fruit should be sent for examination, and all fruit that is not adjudged worthy of the prize will remain the property of the undersigned."

2108—A certain small boy had been steeped in radio advertising, comic strip promotions, and general conversations on the subject of vitamins. His mother one day offered him some little candies. "These are good," the child said. "What vitamins do they have?"

"Oh, none in particular," replied his mother.

The child was astonished. "Do you mean to say they're just for fun?" he asked.

SEE ALSO	RELATED SUBJECTS
Talking 810	Buying and Selling 2066–2067
Newspapers 1236	Stores 2071–2072
Salesmen 2096	Public Relations 2111–2112
Chiseling 2122	Competition 2116
Evidence 2521	

PUBLIC RELATIONS

2111—In one of his political speeches in the early days of the N.R.A., Hugh "Ironpants" Johnson revived a story which probably dates from the days of Chauncey Depew and Rufus Choate, demonstrating the usual futility of letters of complaint.

It concerns the case of the man who was tormented by bedbugs in his sleeping car and who wrote an indignant letter about the matter to the general passenger agent of the railroad.

He was cautioned by his friends that he would probably not receive so much as a reply, and his satisfaction was great when, in due course, he received an apologetic letter assuring him that such a thing could never happen again. His elation was quashed a moment later, however, by the discovery of the inter-office memo which had inadvertently been inserted with the letter and which said tersely, "Send this s.o.b. the bug letter."

2112—Seeking to establish closer ties with its consumers, a gas and light company in a small town held a party at which its customers were addressed by a member of the firm, who made a gallant effort to extol the virtues of the company, and, telling of its use to the community, he said, "Think of all the good this company has done. If I may be permitted a pun, it may well be said, 'Honor the Light Brigade.'"

From the audience a raucous voice called out, "Oh what a charge they made."

SEE ALSO   RELATED SUBJECTS
Police 2551   Speeches 756–782
                      Advertising 2101–2108

COMPETITION

2116—A young and conscientious fellow ran a newsstand in front of a bank. One day a friend of his stopped by and asked him for a loan of five dollars.

"Sorry," said the young man, "I'm afraid I couldn't do that. You see I have an agreement with the bank."

"You—an agreement with the bank. What do you mean?"

"Well, you see, it's this way. I don't give loans. The bank doesn't sell newspapers. It's a perfect agreement. I'm sorry, but I'm bound."

SEE ALSO   RELATED SUBJECTS
Chiseling 2131, 2132   Ambition 96–97
                            Diligence 176–177
                            Quick Thinking 471–492
                            Bargaining 2076–2082
                            Salesmen 2091–2097
                            Advertising 2101–2108
                            Chiseling and Swindling 2121–
                               2132

CHISELING AND SWINDLING

2121—Colonel Putnam told the story of an Indian upon the Connecticut River who called at a tavern in the fall of the year for a dram of rum. The landlord charged him two coppers for it. The next spring, at the same house, he called for another, and had to pay three coppers.

"How is this, landlord—last fall you asked but two coppers for a glass of rum; now you ask three?"

"Oh," says the landlord, "it costs me a great deal to keep a head of rum over the winter—as much as to keep a horse over the winter."

"I can't see that," says the Indian. "He won't eat so much hay—maybe he drink as much water."

2122—A farmer advertised a "frog farm" for sale, claiming that he had a pond that was thoroughly stocked with fine bull-frogs. A prospective buyer appeared and was taken late one warm evening to the pond that he might hear the frogs. The "music" made so favorable an impression on the buyer that the sale was made. Soon afterward the purchaser proceeded to drain the pond in order to catch and market the frogs. To his surprise, when the water was drained out of the pond, he found that all the noise had been made by one old bull-frog.

2123—A poor Irishman applied to one of the overseers of the poor for relief.

"Och, yer honor," said he, "sure I'd be starved long since, but for me cat."

"But for what?" asked the astonished interrogator.

"My cat," rejoined the Irishman.

"Your cat—how so?"

"Sure, yer honor, I sold her eleven times for sixpence a time, and she was always home before I could get there meself."

2124—In the days before gold coins were withdrawn from circulation, they were invariably an object of interest to small boys, not to mention adults. A paternal gentleman making a purchase in the store of little Abie's father permitted the child to hold in his hand and examine a shiny five-dollar gold piece. To his consternation, as very young children will do, the child popped the small coin into his mouth and swallowed it. "Do not worry. Do not worry," said the proprietor, "I'll take him into the back and hold him up by the heels and shake him." The store owner was gone for some little time. At last he appeared apologetically with some change, and said, "Too bad we couldn't have worked quicker. Here's two dollars and fifty cents. Abie has digested the rest."

2125—The folly which is ineradicable from human nature is neatly summed up by the case of the middle aged school teacher who invested her life savings in a business enterprise which had been elaborately explained to her by a swindler. When her investment had disappeared and the wonderful dream was shattered, she went to the office of the Better Business Bureau, which was able at once to confirm her darkest fears. "Why on earth," asked the man, "didn't you come to us first? Didn't you know about the Better Business Bureau?"

"Oh, yes," said she sadly, "I've always known about you. But I didn't come because I was afraid you'd tell me not to do it."

2126—Not all inhabitants of the Tobacco Road region of Georgia are as indigent as the Lester family. Witness the case of the motorist who had become bogged down in the sticky clay of an unpaved Georgia road, and had paid $10 to be pulled out by a Georgia cracker with a team of mules. "I should think," said the motorist, just about to get into his car to continue, "that you would be pulling people out of this stuff day and night."

"Nope," drawled the mule driver, "at night's when we tote the water for the roads."

2127—A lesson well learned is demonstrated by the remarks made by a man who had, at one time in the past, lost a great deal of money in a gold mine speculation. When asked by a friend to define the term, "bonanza," he said, "A bonanza is a hole in the ground owned by a champion liar."

2128—Farmer Jones had a very beautiful horse of which he was very proud. One day he drove him into town and carefully tied the animal to the hitching post in front of the local tavern. Two thieves, hurrying through the town, happened to spy the horse and decided to steal it. Realizing that the horse was much too fine and valuable an animal to be stolen in the ordinary manner, they decided on a stratagem to carry out their plan.

One of them hurriedly untied the horse and rode swiftly away. The other remained by the post.

The farmer finally emerged from the tavern. Seeing that his horse was not where he had left him he was just about to shout when the thief walked up to him. In a sad, low tone he said, "Sir, I am your horse. Years ago I sinned and for my sins I was punished. I was changed into a horse. Today my sentence is over, and I can be released if you will be so kind."

The farmer, amazed yet touched by this story, sent the man away wishing him luck in his new life.

Several weeks later Farmer Jones went to a fair in a neighboring town. Great was his surprise to see his own horse for sale there. Gazing long at the animal to make sure that his eyes did not deceive him, he walked over and whispering in the horse's ear said, "So—you've sinned again."

2129—A man whom Dr. Johnson reproved for following a useless and demoralizing business, said: "You know, doctor, that I must live."

Dr. Johnson replied: that "he did not see the least necessity for that."

2130—Whether Laurie Marks, the New York gambler, implicated in the swindle once practiced on the Bank of Liverpool, really did commit suicide by jumping overboard from a steamer, was under discussion by a group of police officials. Ex-Inspector Byrnes, who had known Marks well, had the following to say:

"Marks is not dead. He is too much of a gambler for anything like suicide, and if a search were made for him he would be found in some of the great cities. Marks would as soon think of suicide as of going into hiding in a village or backwoods community. Once when he was seriously ill Marks refused to go to a quiet resort, saying he preferred to go to some place where things were moving and sandwiches were $2 apiece, for then he would know he had a chance to get somebody else's money."

2131—A certain merchant prince was raising his small son with an eye to equipping him for the harsh realities and cut-throat competition of the world. As one object lesson he put the youngster on a high mantelpiece and coaxed him to jump into his arms. The boy did this repeatedly until he had built up a certain confidence. On the last jump the father stepped aside and the child crashed to the floor. Lifting up the whimpering youngster the father said, "Now then, let that be a lesson to you. Never trust anyone—not even your own father."

2132—Cornelius Vanderbilt wrote the following letter to certain business rivals:

Gentlemen:

You have undertaken to cheat me. I will not sue you, for law takes too long. I will ruin you.

                     Sincerely yours,

                       Cornelius Vanderbilt

SEE ALSO
Wealth 2185

RELATED SUBJECTS
Greed 271–276
Honesty 286–294
Liars 331–336
Stinginess 556–566
Bargaining 2076–2082
Competition 2116

INSURANCE

2136—The life insurance office was taken aback by the old man of 97 years, who wished to take out a policy. His application was turned down. Whereupon the old gentleman said with annoyance, "You folks are making a big mistake. If you look over your statistics you'll find that mighty few men die after they're 97."

2137—Insurance agents are sometimes faced with difficult problems when the answer to the required questions put to applicants for insurance touch upon sensitivities or family scandals.

In one such instance the consummation of a deal was held up for a long time by the refusal of the prospective insured to give the cause of his father's death. After much wheedling the agent extracted from his client the information that the father had been hanged, but could not induce him to state this on the insurance blank.

"All right," said the agent, "we'll put it this way."

And in the troublesome blank he wrote: "Fell from scaffold; death instantaneous."

The problem was solved.

2138—Fire insurance is a more delicate legal problem than life insurance, as it is somewhat easier to set fire to your barn than to cut your own throat to collect for it.

A certain merchant heavily insured his warehouse. As he signed the papers concluding the deal, he said in a tone of jocularity, "Now if this warehouse were to burn down tonight, how much would I get?"

"No less than 10 years," said the agent grimly.

2139—When an insurance adjuster returned from investigating a blaze, his boss asked what had caused the fire.

"Friction," the investigator replied tersely.

"Something rubbing together, eh?"

"Yeah," the adjuster added, "the fire was caused by rubbing a $3,000 insurance policy against a $2,000 house."

2140—A hearing was being held to determine whether or not it was, as some seemed to think, an incendiary fire. The adjuster was questioning some of the villagers attempting to find out if the fire had been started for the purpose of collecting insurance. One of those under questioning was an old man, deaf as a post. Unable to hear the questions being fired at him, he turned to his wife, a puzzled look on his face.

At the top of her voice she shouted, "What the man wants to know is was the Jobson's fire kotched er was it sot?"

SEE ALSO
Salesmen 2093

RELATED SUBJECTS
Longevity 1781–1782
Salesmen 2091–2097

REAL ESTATE

2141—Groucho Marx, after much evasion, finally succumbed to the blandishments of a realtor who wanted to show him a palatial ocean-front estate which was for sale. The salesman drove the comedian up the mile-long, beautifully landscaped approach, escorted him through the house, the stables, the gardens, the kennels, babbling of the wonders of this dream palace by the sea. Groucho patiently plodded after him, nodding gravely, apparently much impressed. Finally he was ushered out on the flagged terrace and the salesman waved proudly toward the broad expanse of the Pacific.

"Now what do you think?" he challenged.

"I don't care for it," replied Groucho thoughtfully and he waved in turn at the view. "Take away the ocean and what have you got?"

2142—An artist who wanted a home among the Taconic Hills of Vermont was talking the matter over with a farmer who allowed that he had a house for sale. "I must have a good view," said the artist. "Is there a good view?"

"Well," drawled the farmer, "from the front porch yuh kin see Ed Snow's barn, but beyond that there ain't nuthin' but a bunch of mountains."

RELATED SUBJECTS
Buying and Selling 2141–2142
Salesmen 2091–2097

FINANCE AND WEALTH

SEE ALSO
Universities 1018
Painting 1264
Politics 1898
Lawyers' Fees 2543

STOCKS AND BONDS

2146—During the hectic days following the crash of 1929, many discussions of the whys and wherefores were overheard along Wall Street. One of the more honest and direct explanations of his plight was the following:

"I hear that you lost quite a lot of money in the crash. Were you a bull or a bear?"

"Neither, just a plain, simple jackass."

2147—A stock broker, suffering a slight nervous breakdown from the constant pressure of fluctuating business, was taken to a hospital to rest.

While more or less in a daze, he overheard his nurse say, as she handed the patient's chart to the doctor, "Temperature today, 102."

Weakly the broker raised his head and said, "When it reaches 102½, sell," then wearily fell back against his pillow.

SEE ALSO
Gossip 822

RELATED SUBJECTS
Buying and Selling 2066–2067
Wealth 2181–2187
Bankruptcy 2196–2198
Businessmen 2236–2237

BANKS

2151—The Hon. Hugh McCulloch, Secretary of the Treasury during Lincoln's second term, was once announced with a delegation of New York bankers. As the party filed into the room he preceded them and said to the President, in a low voice:

"These gentlemen from New York have come on to see the Secretary of the Treasury about our new loan. As bankers they are obliged to hold our national securities. I can vouch for their patriotism and loyalty, for, as the good Book says, 'Where the treasure is, there will the heart be also.'"

To which Lincoln quickly replied: "There is another text,
Mr. McCulloch I remember, that might equally apply,
'Where the carcass is there will the eagles be gathered
together.' "

2152—Judge Giles Baker of a Pennsylvania county was likewise
cashier of his home bank. A man presented a check one
day for payment. He was a stranger. His evidence of
identification was not satisfactory to the cashier.

"Why, Judge," said the man, "I've known you to sentence
men to be hanged on no better evidence than this !"

"Very likely," replied the judge. "But when it comes to
letting go of cold cash we have to be mighty careful."

2153—Upon being questioned as to the occupation of his father,
the young man replied, "He cleans out the bank."

"Janitor or president?" was the final question.

2154—Pausing for a moment before completing the transaction
before him, the teller in the bank peered at the young
lady and asked, "I'm sure that this check is all right,
but could you show me some positive identification?"

The young lady seemed about to turn away; then, in a
faltering tone, she said, "I have a mole on my thigh just
above the knee."

2155—A young bride walked into a bank to cash a check. She
was somewhat taken aback when the clerk informed her
that the check would have to be indorsed by her before
it could be cashed.

"Why, it's a good check. My husband sent it to me. He's
away on business."

"Yes, madam, it's perfectly all right. But, please sign it on
the back so that your husband will know that you got
the money."

The bride walked to the writing desk, seemed to be lost in
deep contemplation for a moment, and then returned to
the teller's window and handed the check to him.

Great was his surprise when he saw scrawled across the
back of the check: "Your loving wife, Ethel."

2156—Returning home one evening a father was accosted by his
daughter in the hallway of their home.

Indignantly the daughter said, "Father, why in the world
did you tell me to put my money in such a bank? Why
it's absolutely on the rocks."

"What," said her father, "why that's one of the strongest banks in the country. What do you mean by such a statement?"

Waving a check in the air, his daughter replied, "Look at this. It's my check for $25.00 and it was returned today by the bank and marked 'No Funds.'"

2157—A stranger in Chicago, a New Yorker, stopped a little boy and asked him the way to the Fifth National Bank, adding, "Direct me there, son, and I'll give you a dollar."

Suppressing a grin, the boy replied: "O.K., boss, just follow me."

About half a block farther, the boy stopped and pointed to the building nearest them. "Here you are, sir."

The man, chagrined by his gullibility, handed the boy the dollar but couldn't help saying, "That certainly was an easily earned dollar."

"That's right," said the boy, "but don't forget that bank directors in Chicago are highly paid."

2158—A man working as a teller in a bank bumped into an old friend of his one day.

Seeing that the bank teller seemed very preoccupied, the friend said, "What is the matter with you?"

"Well, there is a lot of trouble down at the bank. We are going through a complete reorganization."

"Why?"

"It seems that we had more vice-presidents than depositors," replied the bank teller as he walked away.

SEE ALSO
Exaggeration 222
Extravagance 231
Hypocrisy 302
Buying and Selling 2066
Salesmen 2091
Competition 2116
Loans 2162
Collection 2176
Bankruptcy 2196
Bosses 2233
Stealing 2583

RELATED SUBJECTS
Loans 2161–2164
Credit 2166–2167
Debt 2171–2174
Wealth 2181–2187

LOANS

2161—According to Cicero, "When Cato was asked what was the most profitable feature of an estate, he replied: 'Raising cattle successfully.' What next to that? 'Raising cattle with fair success.' And next? 'Raising cattle with but slight success.' And fourth? 'Raising crops.' And when his questioner said, 'How about money-lending?' Cato replied: 'How about murder?'"

2162—It is said that Henry Clay once asked the Riggs Bank for a $250 loan on his personal note. There was no reflection upon his credit, the bank replied, but it was a necessary formality in connection with this particular institution to have an indorser.

Clay happened upon Daniel Webster and asked him if he would be kind enough to indorse for him.

"Certainly," said Webster, "but look here, I need some money myself. Why not make the note for $500 and you and I will split it."

This was done, and to this day the note is in the Riggs bank, unpaid.

2163—Having persuaded Benjamin Franklin to lend him $50, his "poor relation" asked for a sheet of paper in order to give him a note for the sum.

"What," said Franklin, "do you want to waste my stationery as well as my money?"

2164—The famous French satirical writer, Voltaire, was worth $500,000 at the age of 40. But he did not earn his money from books. He made most of it by lending money to needy noblemen. He would lend an heir to an estate a large sum on condition that he would pay him 10% interest on the amount as long as both of them lived. The heir would be neither required nor allowed to pay off the principal; and the agreement ended only when Voltaire died. Voltaire picked only younger men and, because of his tubercular appearance, had no difficulty in getting clients. It is said that when a prospective buyer hesitated, the satirist would cough in a way that always closed the deal.

RELATED SUBJECTS
Borrowing 121–126
Banks 2151–2158
Credit 2166–2167
Debt 2171–2174
Collection 2176–2179

CREDIT

2166—The Vicar of Sheffield, the Rev. Dr. Sutton, once said to the late Dr. Peech, a veterinary surgeon:

"Mr. Peech, how is it that you have not called upon me for your account?"

"Oh," said Dr. Peech, "I never ask a gentleman for money.

"Indeed," said the Vicar, "then how do you get it if he doesn't pay?"

"Why," replied Dr. Peech, "after a certain time I conclude he is not a gentleman, and then I ask him."

2167—Those who believe in a strictly cash business have as their shining example the small son of a mountaineer, who was accosted by a revenuer.

"Where's your pappy?" asked the officer.

"Pappy's up at the still."

"Where's your mother?"

"She's up at the still too."

"I'll give you a dollar," said the officer, "if you'll take me up there."

"All right," said the boy, "give me the dollar."

"I'll give it to you when we get back," said the officer.

"No sir, mister, give it to me now," insisted the boy. "You ain't a-comin' back."

SEE ALSO	RELATED SUBJECTS
Salaries 2252	Buying and Selling 2066–2067
	Banks 2151–2158
	Loans 2161–2164
	Debt 2171–2174
	Wealth 2181–2187
	Salaries 2251–2254

DEBT

2171—A friend once observed to Sheridan, "Being of an illustrious Irish family, it is strange that your name has not an O prefixed to it."

"True," replied Sheridan, "no family has a better right to it. We owe everybody."

2172—The train came to a sudden stop. People started to look out of the window and then, hurriedly dropped back into their seats as they saw that the cause of the stop was a hold-up.

The robbers came through the train ruthlessly stripping the money, jewels and valuables from the passengers.

One man seemed to become more and more nervous as the bandits approached the seat where he sat with his friend. Finally, drawing a ten-dollar bill from his pocket he leaned toward his friend and said, "Here, Jerry. Here's the ten dollars I owe you."

2173—Charles Fox, the English Statesman, once received a severe reprehension from his father who asked him how it was possible for him to sleep, or enjoy any of the comforts of life, when he thought about the immense sums he owed. "Your lordship need not be in the least surprised," answered Charles; "your astonishment ought to be how my creditors can sleep."

2174—Richard Brinsley Sheridan, the playwright, wit and spendthrift, being dunned by a tailor to pay at least the interest on his bill, answered: "It is not my interest to pay the principal, nor my principle to pay the interest."

SEE ALSO
Borrowing 122

RELATED SUBJECTS
Borrowing 121–126
Banks 2151–2158
Loans 2161–2164
Credit 2171–2174
Collection 2176–2179
Taxes 2191–2194
Bankruptcy 2196–2198

COLLECTION

2176—A meeting of bank directors included J. Edward Simmons and Russell Sage. In the course of a general conversation Mr. Simmons remarked:
"Money isn't everything—is it, Mr. Sage?"
"No," replied Mr. Sage thoughtfully, "the work of collecting it is very important."

2177—A new technique of collection was practiced by the man who called up his debtor and demanded payment of a long outstanding account.
"I can't give it to you now," was the answer, as usual.
"Give it to me now," replied his ingenious creditor, "or I'll tell all your other creditors you've paid me."

2178—A Canadian butcher, many of whose customers' accounts were in bad standing, put a sign in his window: "This business will soon close because of bad debts. Names and amounts will be posted here."

The business is now thriving.

2179—Benjamin Franklin, noted for so many different things, was also known as one of the best money raisers of his generation. He set forth his principles on this subject thus:

"First, call upon all those whom you know will give something; next apply to those you are uncertain whether they will give or not, and finally to those you are sure will give nothing, for in some of these you may be mistaken."

SEE ALSO
Debt 2174

RELATED SUBJECTS
Banks 2151–2158
Loans 2161–2164
Debt 2171–2174
Taxes 2191–2194
Bankruptcy 2196–2198

WEALTH

2181—One day a rich but miserly Chassid came to a Rabbi. The Rabbi led him to the window. "Look out there," he said, "and tell me what you see."

"People," answered the rich man.

Then the Rabbi led him to a mirror, "What do you see now?" he asked.

"I see myself," answered the Chassid.

Then the Rabbi said, "Behold—in the window there is glass and the mirror there is glass. But the glass of the mirror is covered with a little silver, and no sooner is a little silver added then you cease to see others and see only yourself."

2182—Some years ago while Baron Rothschild and a nobleman friend were taking a pleasure trip along the Rhine a young lad on the boat noticed the end of a silk handkerchief sticking out of Rothschild's pocket. With visions of the fabulous value of a Rothschild handkerchief he took the end of the handkerchief and gently tugged at it. At this point the nobleman turned to the Baron and whispered: "Baron, that boy beside you is taking your handkerchief."

"Let him alone," said the Baron. "We all had to start small."

2183—For a certain invention the Western Union Company offered Thomas Edison one hundred thousand dollars. He could not grasp the idea of such a sum, and wouldn't take the money. "Safer with you," he said. "Give me six thousand dollars a year for seventeen years."

2184—Julius Rosenwald, the Chicago multi-millionaire, who once said, "I never could understand the popular belief that because a man makes a lot of money he has a lot of brains"—was fond of telling the following story: "A certain man won a million dollars on number 14. When asked how he had figured it out, he said: 'I had a dream. One night I saw in my dream a great big 9, and next I saw a 6, so I used my brains and figured that 9 and 6 is 14.'"

2185—The usual group of respected citizens were assembled to address the graduating class of the local high school. One of them, a self-styled, self-made millionaire, began and ended his speech by saying, "And all my success in life I owe to one thing; pluck, pluck, pluck."

A voice from the back of the auditorium, emanating from a bored but eager graduate said, to the somewhat disconcerted speaker, "We know, sir, but how about telling us something about how and whom to pluck?"

2186—Dr. Johnson, being asked by a young nobleman what had become of the gallantry and military spirit of the old English nobility, replied, "Why, my lord, I'll tell you what has become of it: it has gone into the city to look after a fortune."

2187—Certain government officials approached President Lincoln with the request that they be given control over funds now in the hands of other branches of the governmental set-up.

Lincoln answered them with this story:

"You are very much like a man in Illinois whose cabin was burned down, and, according to the kindly custom of early days in the West, his neighbors all contributed something to start him again. In his case they had been so liberal that he soon found himself better off than before the fire, and got proud. One day a neighbor brought him a bag of oats, but the fellow refused it with scorn, and said, 'I am not taking oats now; I take nothing but money.'"

SEE ALSO
Economy 213
Extravagance 232
Stinginess 558, 559,
    560, 566
Vanity 611
Composers 1312
Socialism 2057
Loans 2164
Taxes 2191

RELATED SUBJECTS
Economy 211-213
Greed 271-276
Buying and Selling 2066-2067
Stocks and Bonds 2146-2147
Banks 2151-2158
Credit 2166-2167
Taxes 2191-2194
Bankruptcy 2196-2198
Businessmen 2236-2237

TAXES

2191—President Roosevelt has frequently been a guest, in years past, on the Nourmahal, luxurious yacht belonging to Vincent Astor. He was once invited to take a winter cruise.

"Oh, don't put that big thing in commission just for me," he protested.

"Mr. President, the Nourmahal is in commission all year round," said its owner.

"Well," rejoined the President, "I guess we'll have to raise taxes on the rich again."

2192—A New York man received from the Bureau of Internal Revenue a "Second Notice" that his tax payment was overdue, and carrying with it dire threats as to what would be done if it was not immediately forthcoming. Hastening to the Collector's office, the man paid up and said, "I would have paid this before but I didn't get your first notice."

"Oh," replied the clerk, "we've run out of first notices, and besides, we find that the second notices are a lot more effective."

2193—A commentary on the artist and society is found in the incident of Joseph Conrad and the offer of knighthood that was sent him in a long blue official envelope, bearing the legend "On His Majesty's Service."

For weeks this lay untouched on Conrad's desk. At last the Prime Minister sent a messenger to see what had happened. Conrad, it transpired, had been afraid to open it. He thought it was the income tax.

2194—Theodore Hook, the English poet, was entertaining a party at his cottage at Fulham with comic song improvisations, when in the middle of it his servant entered with,

"Please, sir, here's Mr. Winter, the tax-collector; he says
he has called for taxes." Hook would not be interrupted,
but went on at the pianoforte, as if nothing had hap-
pened, with the following stanza:—
"Here comes Mr. Winter, collector of taxes.
I advise you to pay him whatever he axes:
Excuses won't do; he stands no sort of flummery.
Though Winter his name is, his presence is summary."

SEE ALSO	RELATED SUBJECTS
Babies 962	Wealth 2181–2187
Critics 1105	Laws 2596–2599
Bishops 1497	

BANKRUPTCY

2196—The following note was found among the effects of a businessman after his death. He had long been known for
his frequent lapses into bankruptcy.
"I hereby name the following six bankers to be my pall-
bearers. Since they have carried me for so long during
my lifetime, they might as well finish the job now."

2197—Forced into bankruptcy for the fifth time, the merchant
was going over his accounts with his lawyer and accountant.
"It looks pretty bad this time," said the accountant, "can't
see how you will be able to pay more than 4 cents on a
dollar."
"What," retorted the merchant, "I've always paid ten cents
on the dollar. And I'm going to do it this time too. Yes,
sir, even if I have to take it out of my own pocket."

2198—Abraham Ibn Ezra was an old Hebrew scholar who lived
centuries ago. He was known far and wide as a most
unlucky man. Everything he did seemed doomed to
failure. In fact, so perverse was his fortune, he once
remarked jestingly that should he go into the shroud
business, mankind would suddenly cease to die.

SEE ALSO	RELATED SUBJECTS
Farmers 2312	Economy 211–213
	Extravagance 231–232
	Credit 2166–2167
	Debt 2171–2174
	Poverty 2201–2211

POVERTY

2201—When Abraham Lincoln once was asked to tell the story of his life, he replied: "It is contained in one line of Gray's 'Elegy in a Country Churchyard': 'The short and simple annals of the poor.' "

2202—In December 1846, Edgar Allan Poe, being in the direst need, inserted a notice in "The Express":

"We regret to learn that Edgar A. Poe and his wife are both dangerously ill with the consumption, and that the hand of misfortune lies heavy upon their temporal affairs. We are sorry to mention the fact that they are so far reduced as to be hardly able to obtain the necessities of life. This is indeed a hard lot, and we hope the friends and admirers of Mr. Poe will come promptly to his assistance in his bitterest hour of need."

2203—When Mark Twain was a young and struggling newspaper writer in San Francisco, a lady of his acquaintance saw him one day with a cigar-box under his arm looking in a shop window. "Mr. Clemens," she said, "I always see you with a cigar-box under your arm. I am afraid you are smoking too much." "It isn't that," said Mark. "I'm moving again."

2204—During his early newspaper days in Chicago, George Ade was accustomed to pawn a large old-fashioned gold watch every Monday morning, to tide him over that trying period between weekly pay checks.

Many years later, when he had become nationally known and had attained a certain degree of affluence, Ade met his old pawnbroker friend on the street.

"Why, George," asked the old pawnbroker, "what happened to you? I haven't seen you in years. Did you lose your watch?"

2205—C. R. W. Nevinson tells this story: "One day he (Henri Matisse) wanted to do a lithograph. I offered him all my chalk and stones, but he would have none of them. He got some lithographic paper, broke one of my lithographic chalks in half, and left himself with only about an inch and a quarter of grease to draw with. When I protested and pressed him to take a box, he assured me it was unnecessary and much too expensive a gift, a comment on the wonderful French economy and the appalling poverty he must have suffered in his early days."

2206—At one time Pablo Picasso was so poor that he and Max Jacob occupied the same bed in turns. Jacob, who besides being a cultivated poet, was an impoverished novelty-shop clerk, slept at night while Picasso worked. When Jacob got up in the morning to let Picasso go to bed, the floor would be carpeted with drawings, which Jacob had to walk on and from which his footprints later had to be cleaned by art experts, since every early Picasso fragment eventually became so valuable that it could be sold.

2207—Hogarth, the celebrated engraver, died, as he had for the greater part of his life lived, in the greatest poverty. Within a few days of his dissolution, bailiffs were sent to seize the bed on which he lay, for a small debt which he was unable to discharge. "Spare me," said the expiring artist, "my bed for a little while—only until I can find another in the grave."

2208—A New York firm applied to Lincoln, some years before he was President, for information as to the financial standing of one of his neighbors. Here was the answer:
"Yours of the 10th received. First of all he has a wife and baby; together they ought to be worth $500,000 to any man. Secondly, he has an office in which there is a table worth $1.50 and three chairs worth, say, $1.00. Last of all, there is in one corner a large rat hole, which will bear looking into.
Respectfully
A. Lincoln"

2209—A certain clergyman in charge of a poor church habitually suffered financial difficulties and was constantly appealing to his bishop for help. The bishop, losing patience, finally chided the man for making so many appeals. Not long after, the bishop received a wire from the clergyman, which said, "This is not an appeal. It is a report. I have no pants!"

2210—One of the saddest announcements ever seen, was that posted before the Negro church, saying, "Next Saturday night the annual Baptist strawberry festival will be held. On account of the depression, prunes will be served."

2211—On August 24, 1770, Chatterton's landlady, a Mrs. Angel, sack-maker, No. 4 Brook Street, Holborn, aware of his desperate condition, offered him a good dinner which he

proudly refused. The following morning he failed to
respond to a knock on the door of the garret where he
lived. The door was broken down, the room was found
strewn with bits of paper, fragments of Chatterton's
manuscripts and letters which he had carefully destroyed, and himself dead, having taken arsenic, aged
seventeen years, nine months and a few days.

SEE ALSO
Pride 457
Inventors 1126
Painting 1282
Ministers 1464
Deathbed Scenes 1775

RELATED SUBJECTS
Debt 2171-2174
Wealth 2181-2187
Bankruptcy 2196-2198
Begging 2216-2219
Employment and Work 2226-2228

BEGGING

2216—Thackeray tells of an Irishwoman begging alms from him,
who, when she saw him put his hand in his pocket, cried
out:
"May the blessing of God follow you all your life !" But
when he only pulled out his snuff box, immediately
added: "and never overtake ye."

2217—A beggar, who was daily stationed near the office of a
wealthy businessman, had received from him a dime a
day over a long period of time. Business took the businessman out of town for a month. When he had returned he passed the beggar, who said to him with a
slight tone of reproach, "You owe me $3.00."

2218—Boswell observing to Johnson that there was no instance
of a beggar dying for want in the streets of Scotland, "I
believe, sir, you are very right," says Johnson; "but this
does not arise from the want of beggars, but the impossibility of starving a Scotsman."

2219—Leigh Richmond when traveling in Ireland, passed a man
who was a painful spectacle of squalor and raggedness.
His heart smote him, and he turned back and said to
him:
"If you are in want, my friend, why don't you beg?"
"And sure, isn't it begging I am, your honor?"
"You didn't say a word."
"Ov coorse not, your honor; but see how the skin is
speakin' through the holes of me trousers, and the bones
crying out through me skin ! Look at me sunken cheeks,

and the famine that is starin' in me eyes! Isn't it begging that I am with a hundred tongues?"

SEE ALSO
Generosity 241
Honesty 286
Shrewdness 533

RELATED SUBJECTS
Borrowing 121–126
Poverty 2201–2211

STATISTICS

2221—In the course of a Parliamentary debate, an opponent of Disraeli's government was supporting his arguments and charges with a ponderous and bewildering barrage of statistics. Instead of scurrying around for similar ammunition to refute these arguments, Disraeli rose and commented drily, "Gentlemen, there are three kinds of lies—lies, damned lies, and statistics."

2222—Louis Sterne of London tells this story of his father Simon Sterne who, while dining with Chauncey Depew and Edward Atkinson, was appealed to by the latter:
"Now, Sterne, you can bear me out in this; you know," (quoting certain statistics) "and that figures never lie."
"Never," said Mr. Sterne gravely, "except when liars figure."

SEE ALSO
Insurance 2136

RELATED SUBJECTS
Accuracy 91–92
Mathematicians 1146–1154
Efficiency 2266–2270

EMPLOYMENT AND WORK

2226—An enterprising American telephone engineer established somewhere in Panama a unique business, a four-leaf clover farm. The conditions were ideal and he raised fine, large clovers which he was able to market in a variety of ways for a variety of purposes, to florists, manufacturers of novelties, etc. At the height of his success, all of his employees, a group of Panamanian girls, confronted him with an unprecedented labor problem. They had no objections to the wages or the hours, they just seemed to have nothing to do with the money. Perplexed in the extreme, their employer racked his brains until he hit upon a brilliant solution. He sent for a Sears-Roebuck catalog and put it in the hands of the girls, explaining to them how they could come into possession of the many fabulous articles pictured therein. His problem was solved.

2227—A butter-fingered man who had been suffering from a long siege of unemployment at last found a job in a china-ware house. He had been at work only a few days when he smashed a large vase. He was summoned to the manager's office and told by that dignitary that he would have to have money deducted from his wages every week until the vase was paid for.

"How much did it cost?" asked the culprit.

"Three hundred dollars," said the manager.

"Oh, that's wonderful," he said, "I'm so happy. At last I've got a steady job!"

2228—In Paris a young man named Arsène hanged himself at his master's home. He left a memorandum bewailing his hard lot, and beseeching his parents to erect a simple tombstone to his memory with the inscription:

"Born to be a man—died a grocery clerk."

SEE ALSO
Lateness 321
Laziness 326
Learned Men 1084
Bishops 1491
Banks 2153
Machinery 2271

RELATED SUBJECTS
Bosses and Executives 2231-2235
Hiring and Firing 2246-2249
Salaries 2251-2254
Working Conditions 2256
Servants 2276-2283
Waiters 2306-2308
Farmers and Farming 2311-2313

BOSSES AND EXECUTIVES

2231—Ira Hirschmann, the department store executive, once visited a department store in a medium sized Mid-Western city. The manager of the store was a bustling little man filled with self-importance and a belief in himself as a modern high-pressure executive. "One of the things I pride myself on," he explained, "is the morale of the personnel in this store. I keep them up on their toes all the time with inspiring slogans. You'd be surprised how it works. Now the slogan this week is one I thought up myself. 'If a thing is worth doing, it's worth doing at all.'"

2232—That celebrated newspaper publisher, James Gordon Bennett, was a man of harsh principles; and most especially was he intolerant of drinking. One time one of his pressmen turned up, after a spree, with a conspicuous black eye. Bennett happened to enter the pressroom and, fearful of being spotted and asked for an explanation, the culprit hastily smeared printer's ink over his face, and applied himself to his tasks. "Who's that fellow?" Bennett demanded, noting the grimy workman. "What are you paying him?" he asked next. The foreman told him. "Double it!" ordered Bennett. "He's obviously doing more work than anyone else in the place."

2233—The owner of a fruit and vegetable store employed a boy whose duty it was to be on hand at 3 o'clock every morning to deal with the truck farmers. The proprietor did not arrive until opening time. For the sake of checking up he unexpectedly came to his shop one night, and at 3 o'clock the boy had not arrived; 3:05 and the boy had not yet come. A moment or so later the boy hastened in. "So," bellowed his employer, "Banker's hours!"

2234—Grover Whalen, during his administration of the World Fair, was known for his inaccessibility. The story is told of one man, who, after repeated rebuffs, stormed past the receptionist one morning. The astonished girl called out, 'You can't speak to Mr. Whalen." The visitor paused in his advance long enough to say, "Young lady, I talk with God twice a day and He listens to me. I can certainly talk to Grover Whalen." He got his interview.

2235—Into the office of one of his subordinate executives came Edward H. Harriman, the railroad king. His unexpected entrance caught the man tilted back in his chair with his feet on his desk. The executive hastily straightened up, fearing a possible scene, and with visions of being fired on the spot. With relief he heard Harriman say, "I'm glad you take time to think."

SEE ALSO
Lateness 321
Long-Windedness 341
Quick Thinking 472, 475
Newspapers 1247, 1248
Horse Racing 1871
Bargaining 2078
Insurance 2093
Salesmen 2095

RELATED SUBJECTS
Employment and Work 2226–2228
Businessmen 2236–2237
Hiring and Firing 2246–2249

Banks 2158
Hiring 2246
Working Conditions 2256
Efficiency 2267, 2268

BUSINESSMEN

2236—Soon after Colbert came into the management of the finances of France, he sent for the principal merchants of that kingdom; and in order to ingratiate himself with them, and to acquire their confidence, he asked what he could do for them. They unanimously answered:
"Pray, sir, do nothing! Laissez nous faire. Let us do for ourselves."

2237—Napoleon openly expressed his aversion to commerce and those engaged in it. When a deputation of businessmen came out from Antwerp to welcome him on his approach to that city, he met them with the words: "I don't like merchants! A merchant is a man who would sell his country for a shilling."

SEE ALSO
Reputation 76
Quick Thinking 473
Inventors 1127
Churches 1526
Revolutions 2064

RELATED SUBJECTS
Buying and Selling 2066–2067
Stocks and Bonds 2146–2147
Banks 2151–2158
Wealth 2181–2187
Bosses and Executives 2231–2235
Partnerships 2241–2242

PARTNERSHIPS

2241—The father of the Marx Brothers was a tailor who operated, at one time, a business in Queens. Marx was a much liked and very nice man, but the suits he made did not always fit. He entered, therefore, into a partnership with a very skilful Negro tailor under the firm name of "Marx and Washington."

2242—"Oi, Sam," said one business man to his partner as they were about to enter the ocean at Coney Island on the afternoon they had decided to take off, "we forgot to close the safe!"
"What does it matter?" asked his partner. "We're both here, ain't we?"

RELATED SUBJECTS
Businessmen 2236–2237

HIRING AND FIRING

2246—The Irish foreman on the construction job was new to his post of dignity. One of his first acts was the discharge of one of his erstwhile fellow-workers. Asked why he had fired the man, he said, "I fired him not because I had anything against him, but because I had the authority."

2247—A personnel manager found himself confronted with a real problem. He had explained to the applicant that he could not place him because the firm was overstaffed. "That's all right," said the job seeker. "The little bit of work I would do wouldn't be noticed."

2248—So great has been the demand for typists in the many war bureaus of Washington, that the legend has come into existence that the following test is now the standard by which applicants for such positions are hired: the girl is shown into a room containing three objects, a washing machine, a typewriter and a machine-gun; if she can identify the typewriter, she's hired.

2249—Mark Twain was always impressed by the story of an industrious boy who became a millionaire. One of the things which remained in his mind was the fact that the boy had gotten his big chance by being noticed by a big business man while in the act of picking up a pin from the sidewalk.

When Mark Twain went to look for a job he deliberately went to the street in front of an office window and began to pick up some pins which he had surreptitiously strewn about. After a while he did succeed in attracting the attention of one of the men in the office. He came out into the street and, instead of the expected praise at such industry, Twain was astonished to hear the man say, "Here you, haven't you anything better to do than pick up pins in the street? You must be an utterly idle and worthless fool."

SEE ALSO	RELATED SUBJECTS
Inventors 1129	Employment and Work 2226–2228
Authors 1180	Bosses and Executives 2231–2235
Servants 2276	Servants 2276–2283
Juries 2516	

SALARIES

2251—A young man, employed at a very modest salary by a bank, began conspicuously to lead a rather lavish life, dressing flashily, buying a car, and otherwise giving evidence of sudden wealth. Finally the personnel manager felt called upon to speak about the matter and asked, "How is it that you, who are only receiving a salary of $20 a week, can spend what must certainly be $75 or more dollars a week." "Why, it's simple," the clerk replied unabashed, "there are more than 200 employees here and every pay-day I raffle off my salary at 50¢ a ticket."

2252—A group of newspapermen were talking about the various has-beens that they had known. One old-timer topped off this session by telling them about a once prominent Chicago newspaperman whom he had met just recently.

"I ran into him the other day and he looked fit to bust. I asked him what the trouble was. 'Why,' says he, 'I've just been offered a job in St. Joe, Mo. And am I insulted!'

" 'Insulted? Why should that be an insult?' I asked.

" 'It's the salary, it's the salary,' he shouts. 'They offered me $12 a week.'

"Well I didn't want to insult him further by suggesting that he hadn't earned even that much in a long time so I just said: 'Well, that's better than nothing.'

" 'The hell it is,' said the one time big shot. 'Why, I can borrow more than that right here in Chicago.' "

2253—The colored sexton of a wealthy church had a very stylish mulatto wife. Finding his domestic income not quite equal to his expenses, he decided to apply for an increase in salary. So he wrote a letter to the committee in charge with this explanation at the close: "It's mighty hard to keep a sealskin wife on a muskrat salary."

2254—At a meeting of the church board the minister announced that he had had a "call" to go to another parish.

After wishing him well in his new field, one of the deacons asked how much salary he was to get.

"Three hundred dollars," the minister replied.

"That's fine," said the deacon, "I don't blame you for going. But, Parson, don't you think you should be a bit more exact in your language. That isn't a 'call,' that's a 'raise.' "

SEE ALSO
Quick Thinking 472
Shrewdness 529
Marriage 888
Singers 1366
Bosses 2232

RELATED SUBJECTS
Employment and Work 2226–2228
Bosses and Executives 2231–2235
Working Conditions 2256

Servants 2279
Farmers 2312
Soldiers 2432

WORKING CONDITIONS

2256—A well-meaning employer desired to introduce a new spirit
into his plant. He called his employees together, and
said, "Whenever I come into the shop I want to see
every man cheerfully at work. I am placing a box here
and I should like anyone who has any suggestions as to
how this may be brought about more efficiently to just
put it in here."
The next day he saw a slip of paper in the box; took it out
and looked at it. It said, "Take the rubber heels off your
shoes."

SEE ALSO   RELATED SUBJECTS
Kindness 311   Employment and Work 2226–2228
Horses 2288   Bosses and Executives 2231–2235
                           Hiring and Firing 2246–2249
                           Salaries 2251–2254

MANUFACTURING

2261—Alfred O. Tate was riding one afternoon through central
Jersey when Edison pointed from a ridge to a lovely
valley through which a stream meandered.
"Tate," said Edison, "see that valley?"
"It's a beautiful valley," Tate replied.
"Well," said the inventor, "I'm going to make it more
beautiful. I'm going to dot it with factories."

SEE ALSO   RELATED SUBJECTS
Efficiency 2266   Employment and Work 2226–2228
                           Businessmen 2236–2237
                           Efficiency 2266–2270
                           Machinery 2271–2272

EFFICIENCY

2266—A New Yorker on one of the Ford Motor Company's tours
of inspection for visitors lagged behind the party at one
point and found himself alone with Henry Ford. Ford
nodded to him; then, pointing to a completed automobile, said, "There are exactly 4719 parts in that car."
Greatly struck with Ford's grasp of affairs—and with his
own—the visitor, talking subsequently with one of the

company's engineers, asked him lightly if it were true that such-and-such a model had exactly 4719 parts. "I'm sure I don't know," the engineer said, "I can't think of a more useless piece of information."

2267—One of Chauncey Depew's stories:
Some years ago, a few days after I had sailed for Europe, a man went into my office and said:
"I want to see Chauncey Depew."
"He has gone to Europe," my colored porter told him.
"Well, I want to see his secretary."
"He has also gone to Europe."
"Then I want to see Cornelius Vanderbilt."
"He is in Newport."
"Oh, I guess I want to see W. K. Vanderbilt."
"He is also in Newport."
"You don't tell me. Well, may I see the first vice-president?"
"He is at Albany."
"How about the second vice-president?"
"He is out of town."
"Is the third vice-president in?"
"No, he is in Europe."
"Is the superintendent in?"
"No, he is up the road somewhere."
"How about the general passenger agent?"
"He has gone to Cape May."
"Who in thunder is running this road, anyway?"
"I guess it do be running itself."

2268—An assistant rushed into William S. Knudsen's office one day, very upset because a certain report was missing. How could they act?
"There are two kinds of reports," Knudsen said calmly. "One says you can't do it. The other says it has been done. The first kind is no good. The second kind you don't need."

2269—When Charles M. Schwab had not yet become a great man in his own right in the field of steel, he worked for Andrew Carnegie.
The little Scotchman taught him the hard lesson of the commercial world, that one day's laurels are of little use on the next.
"All records broken yesterday," Schwab wired to his chief.

In reply to which, Carnegie telegraphed, "What have you done today?"

2270—A sage bit of advice is contained in a rebuke delivered to no less a personage than William Jeffers, head of the Union Pacific Railway, by one of his employees.

Jeffers was traveling in his official car. At a certain stop, the engineer dismounted from his cab and came into the president's car and asked him a question concerning some details of their immediate route. Being preoccupied with some papers before him, Jeffers absently gave an obviously erroneous reply. Angrily the engineer snorted, "That doesn't make sense. Don't ever get so busy that you haven't time to think." Whereupon he turned and strode back to the cab.

SEE ALSO	RELATED SUBJECTS
Procrastination 461	Diligence 176–177
	Employment and Work 2226–2228
	Bosses and Executives 2231–2235
	Machinery 2271–2272

MACHINERY

2271—The economic fallacy of unemployment arising from machinery is well illustrated by the two workmen who watched with awe the performance of a huge steam shovel which took up many tons of earth in one bite. Said one of them, "If it wasn't for that blasted scoop, five hundred of us might be working with shovels." "Yes," was the reply of the other, "and if it wasn't for our shovels, a million of us might be working with spoons."

2272—The value of specialized training is exemplified in this little episode.

The car simply would not run. The mechanic was called in, lifted the hood, reached inside, gave a twist of the wrist to a little mechanism—and all was well.

"What do I owe you?"

"One dollar and ten cents," said the mechanic.

"Great Heavens!" remonstrated the car owner. "It seems like an awful lot for just twisting a little gadget. How do you itemize it?"

"Well," said the mechanic, "for twisting the little gadget—10¢. For knowing which little gadget to twist—$1.00."

RELATED SUBJECTS
Inventors 1126–1131
Manufacturing 2261
Efficiency 2266–2270

SERVANTS

2276—Lord St. John being some time ago in want of a servant, an
   Irishman offered his service, but being asked what
   countryman he was, answered: an Englishman.
   "Where were you born?" said his Lordship.
   "In Ireland an' plaze your worship," said the man.
   "How then can you be an Englishman?" said his Lordship.
   "My lord," replied the man, "'sposen I was born in a
   stable, that's no razen I should be a horse."

2277—William K. Vanderbilt was fond of telling the following
   story on himself. He once observed to his valet that a
   towel which he was using did not seem clean. The man
   replied that the towels had been done by the regular
   laundry. "But," Vanderbilt said, "this one smells like
   dead fish."
   "Well, sir," replied his man, "perhaps you have used it
   previously."

2278—Marshal Turenne had chosen for his valet the stoutest
   grenadier in the army, who frequently fought with
   another of his domestics, named Stephen. One day the
   marshal stooped down to look out of a window, with one
   of his hands upon his back. His valet, coming into the
   room, gave his master a furious blow upon his back. As
   the marshal turned, the valet fell upon his knees in
   despair, begging for mercy, for he "thought it was
   Stephen."
   "Well," said the marshal, rubbing the pained part, "if it
   had been Stephen you ought not to have struck so hard,"
   and he said no more on the subject.

2279—Mrs. William Dean Howells, wife of the noted novelist,
   had hired a girl to do the housework. Several weeks
   passed and from seeing her master constantly about the
   house, the girl received an erroneous impression.
   "Excuse me, Mrs. Howells," she said to her mistress one
   day, "but I would like to say something."
   "Well, Mary?"
   The girl blushed and fumbled with her apron: "Well, you
   pay me four dollars a week——"

"I really can't pay you any more," interrupted Mrs. Howells apologetically.

"It's not that," hastily answered the girl, "but I am willing to take three till Mr. Howells lands a job."

2280—The hostess had the additional problem of breaking in a new maid just before a big party. She cautioned, winding up her instructions about dress, "Don't wear any jewelry."

"I don't have any, ma'am," answered the maid, "but thanks for the warning."

2281—A married couple, returning from Europe, became interested in an attractive red-cheeked Finnish girl in the steerage. They found that she was coming to America to look for work and decided to offer employment. "Can you cook?" they asked. "No," said the girl, "I can't cook. My mother always did the cooking."

"Well," they said, "then you can do the housework."

"No," said she, "I don't know how. My oldest sister always did the housework."

"Well, then we could let you take care of the children."

"No, I couldn't do that. My youngest sister always took care of the children."

"Well can you do the sewing?"

"No," said the girl, "my aunt always did the sewing."

"What can you do?" cried the despairing couple.

The girl was quite bright and cheerful as she volunteered, "I can milk reindeer."

2282—Entering the kitchen one evening the lady of the house was amazed to see her cook, who was going home for the night, packing some empty grapefruit hulls into her black bag. Completely mystified at this procedure and curious to find out the reason for it she asked, "Mandy, why in the world do you take the trouble to carry home those empty grapefruits?"

"Well, ma'am, Ah admit they ain't any use to me—but they sure does make my garbage look stylish."

2283—The Count de Mirabeau, brother of the celebrated orator, one morning called his valet to him: "You are faithful," said he, "you are zealous; in short—I am satisfied with your services, but I give you your dismissal."

"On what account?" naturally inquired the valet.

"Notwithstanding our agreement, you get drunk on the **same** days as I do," said Mirabeau.

"It is not my fault," replied the valet, "you get drunk every day."

SEE ALSO
Old Maids 873
Husband 917
Wife 930
Scientists 1122
Superstition 1632
Funerals 1777
Equality 2046

RELATED SUBJECTS
Banquets and Dinners 751–753
Home Life 996–1001
Porters 1806
Employment and Work 2226–2228
Salaries 2251–2254
Working Conditions 2256
Waiters 2306–2308

PROPERTY
SEE ALSO
Cheerfulness 143
Presidents 1937
Dictators 2002

HORSES

2286—Abraham Lincoln, after a friendly contest of wits on the subject of horses, agreed to a horse trade with a certain judge, sealing the bargain by saying:

"Well, look here, Judge! I'll tell you what I'll do. I'll make a horse trade with you, only it must be upon these stipulations: neither party shall see the other's horse until it is produced here in the courtyard of the hotel and both parties must trade horses. If either party backs out of the agreement, he does so under a forfeiture of twenty-five dollars."

It was agreed. Lincoln and the judge parted to find their animals. The news of the trade got around and quite a crowd collected to see the fun. Great was the laughter when the judge appeared with an incredible looking animal; skinny, blind and scarcely able to walk. But the laughter turned to uproarious shouts when Lincoln strode upon the scene with a carpenter's saw-horse on his shoulders. Putting the saw-horse down, Lincoln surveyed the scene for a moment and, spying the judge's horse, said with a note of disgust, "Well, Judge, this is the first time I ever got the worst of it in a horse trade."

2287—Henry Ward Beecher, the famous preacher, was once contemplating buying a horse. After looking over many of them, the owner of the stables finally burst out into praise of one particularly fine animal.

"Now here's a horse that's really sound. He can go any gait. He stands without hitching; works any place you put him; goes when you want him to and stops the minute you say 'Whoa.' He is perfectly gentle, yet full of spirits. He has no bad traits, doesn't kick, doesn't bite. Comes when you call him and doesn't run off when he sees something strange."

With a wistful look in his eye, Mr. Beecher sighed, "If only that horse were a member of my church."

2288—Two staunch friends of a lifetime, Moe and Abe, were walking down the street. They discussed every phase of life together from politics to personal affairs. They were discussing the hereafter and made one of those agreements that whichever should die first should communicate with the other if possible.

Little more than a year later Abe passed away. Moe was downcast and had all but forgotten their agreement. It chanced that he was passing down the street one day when a sorrowful voice suddenly said, "Moe, Moe." He paused and looked around. There was no one in sight. He thought it must have been an illusion. He was about to move on when once again the voice cried, "Moe." He looked about once more. There was no living thing in sight except a horse hitched to an ice wagon. He stared at the animal and the horse, to his astonishment, said, "Yes, Moe, it's me—Abe."

"Abe," cried Moe in horror, "a horse you come back?"

"Yes, Moe."

"But, Abe, what kind of a life is it? How are they treating you?"

"Oi, it's terrible," said the horse. "All day long pulling a heavy wagon in the hot sun and the driver he beats me. He doesn't give me water."

"This is terrible," said Moe, "I'll speak to the man. I'll tell him you're my friend. He shouldn't treat you so."

"Moe, Moe," said the horse in great alarm, "don't say nothing to him, please! He finds out I can talk, he'll make me yell 'Ice!'"

SEE ALSO	RELATED SUBJECTS
Zanies 643	Horse Racing 1871–1872
Civilians in War 2346	Farmers and Farming 2311–2313
Officers 2415	
Marches 2456	
Hanging 2566	

PARROTS

2291—Pat was wandering around a pet shop one day. Coming to a cage which housed a large, green parrot, he put his hand in to pet it. The bird turned quickly and cackled, "Hello. Hello. Who are you?"

Startled, Pat drew back. Hastily he tipped his hat and said, "Excuse me, sor, I thought ye was a burrd."

2292—A certain old maid had a parrot which swore vigorously. She was used to the bird, but was in the habit of covering its cage every Sunday in order that it might remain silent on that day. It chanced on a Monday morning, after the cover had been removed, that the old lady saw the minister come up the walk to pay a call. Hastily she replaced the cover on the cage; hearing the parrot observe as she moved towards the door, "This has been a damn short week!"

2293—In the days of luxurious trans-Atlantic travel, shipboard entertainments frequently drew upon the professional talents to be found in the passenger list. On one occasion, the program followed up the performance of a remarkable parrot with a brief demonstration by a traveling magician. The parrot's cage had been shoved to one side of the stage when the magician came on for his act. Holding up a pack of cards, the man covered it with a handkerchief, waved his wand, and the cards disappeared. The parrot, looking on from the wings, cocked its head to one side. Next the magician took a book, covered it with a scarf, waved his wand, and the book disappeared. The parrot meditatively scratched its head with its claw. Taking a cloak, the magician threw it over a chair, waved his wand, and the chair disappeared. The parrot hopped up and down on its perch in the growing excitement. In the next moment the ship was struck by a submerged iceberg; split in two, the lights were extinguished, there were screams and cries, and shortly thereafter nothing was left on the black night sea save the parrot clinging to a piece of driftwood, bobbing up and down on the waters. The bird looked about at the dreary scene for a moment, and then said, "Marvelous! Marvelous!"

HOTELS AND RESTAURANTS

2296—A man walked into a hotel and asked for a room.

"On the American Plan or the Japanese Plan?" asked the clerk.

"What's the difference?"

"The American Plan is with cross ventilation. The Japanese Plan is with double-cross ventilation."

2297—A certain cafeteria in New York city caused much pleasure to many of its patrons by prominently displaying on its walls, the motto, "Courteous and Efficient Self-Service."

2298—A certain lodging-house in the south of Italy had the Russian writer Maxim Gorky as its guest some years ago. He complained to the landlady "the morning after the night before" that his bed was infested by vermin. The landlady indignantly remonstrated: "No, sir, we haven't one single bug in the house."

"No, madam," Gorky agreed amiably, "they are all married and have large families too."

2299—A game of poker at Delmonico's had lasted well into the night when one of the party, the late Colonel John R. Fellows, ordered a plate of sandwiches. The familiar dainty triangle variety was served and disappeared instantly. A hungry shout went up for more.

"More sandwiches, waiter," said Fellows.

"Yes, sir! How many, sir?" returned the waiter.

"Well," said Fellows, with a calculating air, "judging by the size of your sandwiches and the size of this bill, I should say about $2,000 worth."

2300—Mr. Disraeli said he did not remember a certain inn, upon which the owner assured him that he must be mistaken. "You must remember the house, sir; there was a very handsome bar-maid there—monstrous fine gal—you must have been in the King's Arms, sir."

"Perhaps," said Disraeli, "if I had been in her arms I might have remembered it."

2301—For a laconic philosophy it is hard to match the case of the man who checked into a hotel in a small Mid-Western city and went up to his room. Later in the evening he came down, his suitcase in his hand, and checked out.

"What's the trouble, sir?" asked the clerk, slightly puzzled. "Don't you find the room satisfactory?"

"The room is all right," said the man, "except for one thing. It's on fire."

2302—In a gloomy and depressed state Eugene Field wandered into a restaurant. A busy waiter hastened up and reeled

off at high speed a long line of dishes on the present
menu. Field gazed up in melancholy and said, "Friend,
I want none of these things. All I want is an orange and
a few kind words."

SEE ALSO   RELATED SUBJECTS
Eating 17, 23   Eating 6–23
Absent-Mindedness 83   Banquets and Dinners 751–753
Eccentricity 196   Businessmen 2236–2237
Prejudice 448   Waiters 2306–2308
Shrewdness 531
Fatness 684
Authors 1169
Instrumentalists 1354
Politics 1899
Chiseling 2121

WAITERS

2306—Robert Louis Stevenson, in the days of his residence in
San Francisco, took a friend to a restaurant in which, he
said, the waiters would never admit that there was anything lacking from the bill of fare. "They'll take your
order for a slice of the moon," said he, "and go away as
if to fetch it, and come back to tell you they're just out
of it."

The two men seated themselves and the waiter came up.
"A double order of broiled Behemoth," said Stevenson.
"Will you have it rare or well done?" asked the waiter.
"Rare," said Stevenson.

In a few moments, the waiter had returned: "I'm very
sorry, sir," he began . . .
"What!" interrupted Stevenson in a tone of annoyance.
"No more Behemoth?"
"Oh, no, sir," said the waiter hastily, then lowering his
voice. "I have some more, sir," he explained, "but the
truth is I would not bring it to you as it is not quite
fresh."

2307—Bishop Brewster of Connecticut, while visiting some
friends, tucked his napkin in his collar to avoid the juice
of grapefruit at breakfast. He laughed as he did so, and
said it reminded him of a man he knew who rushed into a
restaurant and, seating himself at a table, proceeded to
tuck his napkin under his chin. He called a waiter and
said, "Can I get lunch here?"

"Yes," replied the waiter in a dignified manner, "but not a shampoo."

2308—Into a restaurant walked a wag in search of breakfast. The Negro girl who was waiting upon the tables came forward to take his order.

"I want ham and eggs," said the gentleman, "but I want the eggs eliminated."

"Yes, sir," said the waitress disappearing into the kitchen. She was back again in due time with a plate of ham with regulation fried eggs.

"Waitress," said the customer, "I told you I wanted the eggs eliminated."

"Yassuh, boss," she said, "I'se sorry, but de truf is dat no-count cook has done drapped de eliminator and busted de handle right off."

SEE ALSO
Eating 13
Absent-Mindedness 85
Stealing 2584

RELATED SUBJECTS
Eating 6–23
Banquets and Dinners 751–753
Servants 2276–2283
Hotels and Restaurants 2296–2302

FARMERS AND FARMING

2311—"You have no complaint," a city man said to a farmer, "you have your own milk, butter, eggs, meat, and vegetables. With enough to eat and a place to sleep what more do you want?"

"Well," said the farmer, "you come around a few months from now and you'll see the fattest, sleekest, nakedest farmer you ever saw."

2312—Ranches in some parts of the West are by no means always a paying proposition. At such a place a traveler stopped, seeking a night's lodging. Discussing with his host hard times in general, the stranger asked, "How in the world do you manage to make enough on this place to run it?" His host pointed toward his hired man at the far end of the table.

"You see that feller. Well, he works for me and I can't pay him. In two more years he gits the ranch. Then I'm goin' to work for him till I git it back!"

2313—The Department of Agriculture is the constant recipient of queries and pleas for advice from householders with small lawns and gardens as well as from farmers. The story is told about the man who had fought a losing battle against dandelions on his lawns. He wrote to the Department complaining how much he loved his lawn and begging them to help him save it. In due course, the Department of Agriculture replied with the practical suggestion that he learn to love the dandelions too.

SEE ALSO
Diligence 176
Endurance 216
Gratitude 265
Home Life 997
Hospitality 1007
Audiences 1437
Billiards 1827
Chiseling 2128
Loans 2161

RELATED SUBJECTS
Employment and Work 2226–2228
Horses 2286–2288

WAR AND THE MILITARY

WAR

2316—Jean Gabin, the film-actor, upon his arrival in New York recently, was asked what was the French attitude toward the British.

"We are both pro- and anti-British," he said. "Those who are pro-British say each night in their prayers, 'Please, God, let the gallant British win quickly.' Those who are anti-British say each night in their prayers, 'Please, God, let the dirty British win right away.'".

2317—According to one story, Marshal Foch's chauffeur was constantly besieged by journalists and plain information-seekers with the question, "When is the war going to end? What do you hear?"

The chauffeur put off his questioners, saying, "As soon as I hear the Marshal say anything, I will tell you." At last he said, "The Marshal spoke today."

"Well," they demanded, "what did he say?"

"He said, 'Well, Pierre, what do you think? When is the war going to end?'"

2318—Mr. Pitt, speaking in the House of Commons of the glorious war preceding that in which England lost the colonies called it "The last war." Several members cried out: "The last but one!" He took no notice, and soon, after repeating the mistake, was interrupted by a general cry of "The last war but one!"

"I mean, sir," said Pitt, turning to the speaker, and raising his voice, "I mean, the last war that Britons would wish to remember."

2319—Bronislaw Malinowski says, "I once talked to an old cannibal who, hearing of the Great War raging then in Europe, was most curious to know how we Europeans managed to eat such enormous quantities of human flesh. When I told him that Europeans do not eat their slain foes, he looked at me in shocked horror and asked what sort of barbarians we were, to kill without any real object."

2320—In 1918 Premier Georges Clemenceau of France made the observation, "War is too important to leave to the Generals."

2321—In Italy it is whispered that a new technique for the fairy tale has come into existence. The old formula began, "Once upon a time." Now it begins, "The General Headquarters of the Armed Forces communicates."

2322—The Italians say among themselves, "In the First World War we prepared, fought, and made the Armistice. This time we made the Armistice (with France), fought, and now we are preparing."

2323—Lillah McCarthy went to stay with H. G. Wells in Essex. England also was now at war (1914).

"His face, generally so mobile, had become rigid and the playful look stern. I tried to distract him: 'No, Lillah,' he said, 'no, I can't get away from the war. The world is falling to pieces. I can do nothing but think, think.'"

SEE ALSO
Greed 274
Kings 1972

RELATED SUBJECTS
Courage 151–153
Cowardice 156–160
Patriotism 396–407
Dueling 801–803
Death 1746–1749
Kings and Emperors 1971–1993
Dictators 2001–2011
International Relations 2016
Revolutions 2061–2064
Civil War 2326–2329
Civilians in War 2331–2346
Battles 2371–2385
Strategy 2386–2393
Army and Navy 2401–2404
Officers 2406–2427
Soldiers and Sailors 2430–2437

CIVIL WAR

2326—During nullification in South Carolina, after President Jackson's proclamation, the governor of Virginia sent a request to the President, in case it became necessary to send United States troops down South, not to send them through that State. If he did they would have to pass over the Governor's dead body.

The President received the message and replied: "If it becomes necessary for the United States troops to go to South Carolina, I, as commander-in-chief of the army, will be at their head. I will march them by the shortest route. They may pass through Virginia; but if the governor makes it necessary to pass over his dead body, it will be found that I will have previously taken off both ears."

2327—Richmond fell. Lincoln himself entered the city on foot, accompanied only by a few officers and a squad of sailors who had rowed him ashore from the flotilla in the James River, a Negro picked up on the way serving as a guide. Never had the world seen a more modest conqueror and a less characteristic triumphal procession—no army with banners and drums, only a throng of those who had been slaves hastily run together, escorting the victorious chief into the capital of the vanquished foe. We are told that they pressed around him, kissed his hands and his garments and shouted and danced with joy, while tears ran down the President's care-furrowed cheeks.

2328—Near the end of the Civil War, when the Confederate forces were falling back on Richmond, an old Negro asked by his mistress for encouraging news, replied:
"Well, missy, due to de lie of de land where dey's fightin', dem Yankees is retreatin' forward, while we is advancin' backwards."

2329—The prayer of a Unitarian preacher in Massachusetts during the Civil War:
"Oh, God, we pray thee to bless the rebels. Bless their hearts with sincere repentance. Bless their armies with defeat. Bless their social condition by emancipation."

RELATED SUBJECTS
Revolutions 2061–2064
War 2316–2323

CIVILIANS IN WAR

2331—Louis Fischer, editor and correspondent, tells the story that at a dinner-party in England, the guests were discussing the fact that cigarettes were worse since the War started and the transportation, food, and indeed everything was worse.
"Only the people are better," someone observed.

2332—During a public "reception," a farmer from one of the border counties of Virginia told President Lincoln, that the Union soldiers, in passing his farm, had helped themselves not only to hay, but to his horse, and he hoped the President would urge the proper officer to consider his claim immediately.

Mr. Lincoln said that this reminded him of an old acquaintance of his, "Jack" Chase, a lumberman on the Illinois, a steady, sober man and the best raftsman on the river. It was quite a trick to take the logs over the rapids; but he was skilful with a raft and always kept her straight in the channel. Finally a steamer was put on, and Jack was made captain of her. He always used to take the wheel, going through the rapids. One day, when the boat was plunging and wallowing along the boiling current, and Jack's utmost vigilance was being exercised to keep her in the narrow channel, a boy pulled his coat-tail and hailed him with:

"Say, Mr. Captain! I wish you would just stop your boat a minute—I've lost my apple overboard!"

2333—President Lincoln was bothered to death by those persons who boisterously demanded that the War be pushed vigorously; also, those who shouted their advice and opinions into his weary ears, but who never suggested anything practical. These fellows were not in the army, nor did they ever take any interest, in a personal way, in military affairs, except when engaged in dodging drafts.

"That reminds me," remarked Mr. Lincoln one day, "of a farmer who lost his way on the Western frontier. Night came on, and the embarrassments of his position were increased by a furious tempest which suddenly burst upon him. To add to his discomfort, his horse had given out, leaving him exposed to all the dangers of the pitiless storm.

"The peals of thunder were terrific, the frequent flashes of lightning affording the only guide on the road as he resolutely trudged onward, leading his jaded steed. The earth seemed fairly to tremble beneath him in the war of elements. One bolt threw him suddenly upon his knees.

"Our traveler was not a prayerful man, but finding himself involuntarily brought to an attitude of devotion, he addressed himself to the Throne of Grace in the following prayer for his deliverance:

"'O God! hear my prayer this time, for Thou knowest it

is not often that I call upon Thee. And, O Lord! if it is all the same to Thee, give us a little more light and a little less noise.'

"I wish," the President said, sadly, "there was a stronger disposition manifested on the part of our civilian warriors to unite in suppressing the rebellion, and a little less noise as to how and by whom the chief executive office shall be administered."

2334—At a particularly loud clap of thunder, a lady walking along a London street involuntarily and visibly started. "It's all right, Lidy," said a passing urchin.

"It ain't 'itler, it's Gawd."

2335—In occupied France a Frenchman, walking down the street in Paris, saw another Frenchman in altercation with a Storm Trooper. The Frenchman knocked the Trooper down and, as he got up again, the second Frenchman rushed over, joined the fray and knocked him down a second time. Reinforcements suddenly arrived and the two Frenchmen were overpowered and taken before a Military Judge. The first culprit explained the nature of his quarrel and the reason for his blow.

"But why," asked the judge of the second man, "did you get into this? It was no quarrel of yours."

"I know," he replied, "but when I saw him knock him down, for a moment I thought it was the beginning."

2336—When the disasters of the Franco-Prussian War were falling thickly, and the iron band was closing around Paris, word came that Victor Hugo was coming to the city. He came at the very moment that the investment was complete, with the last train, the last breath of free air. On the way he had seen the Germans, seen villages burned with petroleum, and he came to imprison himself in Paris. A memorable ovation was given him by the people, and they never forgot his voluntary sharing of their sufferings.

2337—Harvey Klemmer tells this story: "Just before leaving England, I met a Cockney who had been buried beneath the ruins of his fish-and-chip shop. Fish-and-chips are not my idea of the proper food for building morale. However, there was nothing wrong with the morale of this chap. When the rescue workers dug him out of the remains of his little business—which by now consisted of a potpourri of fish, fat, bricks and plaster—he dusted himself off, drew himself up to his full five feet seven and spat into the wreckage.

'To 'ell with 'itler.' "

2338—An old watchman in a London warehouse was a bit perturbed because his son wouldn't take cover in the air raids. He went into the street and gave the lad a cuff on the ear.

"Get the hell inside," he said, "and let that shrapnel fall down."

2339—At the outbreak of the Franco-Prussian War one patriotic Parisian cabman, after driving a Prussian attaché to the station to join his regiment, refused to take any fare. "A man does not pay for being driven to his own funeral. So, adieu, monsieur."

2340—One night, at the beginning of the World War, Picasso and Gertrude Stein were taking a walk when they saw a camouflaged truck for the first time. He was amazed by its resemblance to cubist art, and, in the tone of a man who has just been plagiarized, said, "Why, it is we who invented that!" Later, when a new field uniform for the French army was being discussed, he told Cocteau: "If they want to make an army invisible at a distance, all they have to do is dress the men as harlequins."

2341—The many persons who have taken First Aid courses in the present War will be interested in the case of an inquisitive elderly lady who bent solicitously over a wounded soldier whose head was swathed with bandages. "Are you wounded in the head, my boy?" she asked.

"No, ma'am," said the victim feebly, "I was shot in the foot and the bandages slipped up."

2342—Harvey Klemmer tells of how, "One of the London wardens, a slim, elderly man, directed the work of removing the bodies.

" 'They got my house last night,' he said simply.

"I heard from one of the other wardens that, while this man was working on a job, someone came running to tell him his own house, a few streets away, had been hit. The house and all of his belongings had been destroyed; his wife and children, fortunately, had gone to a nearby shelter. I asked the man what he would do if he could lay his hands on the airman who had dropped the bomb.

He gulped a couple of times and I waited eagerly to hear what sort of punishment he would be prepared to mete out.

" 'Well,' he said slowly, 'I don't think I would give him a cup of tea.'

"That is the nearest thing to recrimination I have heard in England."

2343—An American, who had gone to England to carry out certain duties in connection with the War, was wearied by a seemingly interminable season of fog and rain. One day he glanced out of his window at the barrage balloons which could be seen mistily at their cable ends in the sky and asked, "Why don't they just cut the ropes on those things and let the place sink!"

2344—In Amsterdam, Nazi officers walking through the streets became conscious that many of the Dutch were hailing one another as they passed with the salute, "Heil, Rembrandt!" which they suspected to be a deeply subversive travesty of the required, "Heil, Hitler."

"Why do you say this?" demanded a German officer, accosting a Netherlander.

"You see," replied the man blandly, "we too have a great painter."

2345—During the First World War, the Germans entered and occupied a small Belgian town. Seeking to keep the occupants of the town under control, an officer of the German army called all the citizens to the town hall and insisted that they all take the oath of allegiance to the German Emperor.

One particularly truculent and obstinate inhabitant refused to be intimidated, and kept boasting of the brave defense the Belgians put up against the superior German force.

Finally, the German officer lost all patience:

"Take this oath of allegiance or you'll be shot!"

Faced with this alternative, the man gave in and took the oath.

"That's the spirit," said the German, "now you may come and go as you please. You are one of us."

With a sly grin on his face, the Belgian turned and said, "Say, didn't those Belgians give us a hell of a fight?"

2346—During the American Revolution, the soldiers sometimes had great difficulty getting horses. An officer was sent out to make the rounds in the Virginia countryside and confiscate all the horses he saw.

He came up to a fine, old mansion and, seeing a plow team down in the field, rang the bell and asked to see the mistress.

"Madam," he said to the dignified elderly woman who received him in the fine, old drawing-room, "I have come to claim your horses in the name of the government."

"Sir," was the answer, "you cannot have them. I need them for the spring plowing."

"I am sorry, madam. Those are the orders of my chief."

"And who is your chief?" she demanded.

"General George Washington, commander-in-chief of the American army."

"You go back and tell General George Washington that his mother says he cannot have her horses," replied the woman, a smile softening her hitherto stern features.

SEE ALSO
Patriotism 398
Hiring 2248
War 2320

RELATED SUBJECTS
Courage 151–153
Patriotism 396–407
Censors 2351–2355
Rationing 2356–2358
Refugees 2361

CENSORS

2351—According to John Gunther, an American journalist in Japan wrote to a friend and added the note, "Don't know if this will ever arrive because the Japanese censor may open it." A few days afterward, he received a note from the Japanese post office, saying, "The statement in your letter is not correct. We do not open letters."

2352—A young lady received a letter from her soldier sweetheart from "Somewhere in the Pacific Area." Upon opening the envelope she found, instead of a letter, a thin strip of paper bearing the brief message, "Your boy friend still loves you, but he talks too much, (signed) Censor."

2353—The book of Helvetius "De l'Esprit" and Voltaire's poem of "La Pucelle d'Orleans" were prohibited in Switzerland at the same time. A magistrate of Berne, after a strict search for these two works, wrote the Senate: "We have not found in the whole province either wit or maid."

2354—The French Ambassador to Spain complimented Cervantes on the great reputation he had acquired by his "Don Quixote." Cervantes whispered in his ear, "Had it not been for the Inquisition, I should have made my book much more entertaining."

2355—A grim lesson for the exponents of bigoted censorship is contained in the characteristic American-press-agent-story of how the famous picture "September Morn" was popularized.

An art dealer, stuck with a formidable surplus of this lithograph of a nude girl, consulted a well-known press agent, Harry Reichenbach. Reichenbach had many of the pictures placed in the shop window. He then hired a crowd of small children and grouped them around the front of the store. Next, he phoned to Anthony Comstock and hysterically demanded that he come and witness the sordid exhibition of vice and corruption. Comstock came and immediately opened one of his inimitable litigations. In consequence of the publicity resulting from this it might be said that Comstock "sold" 7,000,000 copies of this picture.

SEE ALSO
Authors 1199
Painting 1270

RELATED SUBJECTS
Prohibitions and Restrictions 1641–1642
Civilians in War 2331–2346
Laws 2596–2599

RATIONING

2356—A motorist driving through the back country of Vermont stopped at a little gas station and asked for a tankful. He remarked casually to the proprietor, "I guess you fellows are all pretty sore at Leon Henderson?" "Leon Henderson?" said the old timer. "Who's he?" The motorist, looking at him for a moment and then thinking quickly said, "Do you sell tires?" "Sure," the proprietor said, "you want some?" The motorist said, "I'll take four," paid his money and drove hastily away thanking Providence.

2357—A small boy, keenly aware of the transportation problems created by rationing, was looking at a book of Bible illustrations. One of these depicted the Prophet Elijah ascending to Heaven in a chariot of fire. He noted the halo above the Prophet's head and cried, "Oh, Mother! Look, he's carrying an extra tire!"

2358—"Does anyone here," asked the teacher of the Night School for Adult Education, administering a vocabulary test, "know the meaning of ratiocination?"

"I know," said the young stenographer in the class. "It's what they're doing to sugar."

> RELATED SUBJECTS
> Patriotism 396–407
> Civilians in War 2331–2346
> Laws 2596–2599

REFUGEES

2361—Many and devious have been the devices employed by refugees seeking to escape from occupied France. It is reported from hitherto unreliable sources, that such a man threw himself upon the mercy of the proprietor of a small traveling menagerie. "I'm afraid to disguise you as an employee," said the man. "You might be discovered too easily. It happens that our gorilla died a little over a week ago and we preserved his hide, thinking that we might recoup the loss by having it stuffed some day. If you want to put it on, you can travel with us in the cage."

Faced by his desperate need, the refugee did so. And whenever the menagerie was on exhibition he put on as good a show as he could manage.

One night when no one was around, he was horror struck to discover that the bars had become loosened between his own and the adjoining cage on the same truck. One of them had fallen out, and through the opening came his neighbor, the lion. As the animal slunk toward him the "gorilla" cringed in the corner and began to cry, "Help! Help!" "Shut up, you damn fool!" growled the lion, "you aren't the only refugee."

> RELATED SUBJECTS
> Endurance 216
> Poverty 2201–2211
> Civilians in War 2331–2346

PRISONERS

2366—Some of the Nazi airmen invite mistreatment by their belligerent attitude. There is the case of a wounded Nazi airman who panned English doctors, bemoaning the fact

that he had no good German doctors to fix him up. In
the middle of his tirade he had the misfortune to faint.
"Don't worry," the doctors told him when he came to.
"You'll be all right. The chances are that you will have
better manners, too, now that you've got a couple of
pints of good Jewish blood in you."

RELATED SUBJECTS
War 2316–2323
Battles 2371–2385
Soldiers and Sailors 2430–2437

BATTLES

2371—During the Revolutionary War, an Irishman in the American service, having come by surprise on a small party of
Hessians who were foraging, seized their arms which
they had laid aside. He then presented his musket, and
with threats drove them before him into the American
camp, where the singularity of the exploit occasioning
some wonder, he was brought with his prisoners before
General Washington who asked him how he had taken
them.
"By God, general," said he, "I surrounded them."

2372—General Winfield Scott said that during the War of 1812,
before an action began between the two opposing armies,
it was customary for the respective commanders to ride
forward accompanied by their staffs, and formally salute
each other. Each then returned to his own lines, and the
battle opened.
This custom is well illustrated by the anecdote told by
Fournier:
"Lord Hay at the Battle of Fontenay, 1745, called out:
'Gentlemen of the French Guard, fire first.'
"To which the Comte d'Auteroches replied:
"'Monsieur, we never fire first; please to fire yourselves.'"

2373—A Confederate soldier was seen by General Lee, who met
him retiring from the front with what Lee considered
unbecoming haste. Lee said to him, "Why don't you go
back to the front? That's the place where a soldier
should be when a battle is going on."
The reply was, "General, I have been there, and I give
you my word of honor it is not a place where any self-
respecting man would care to be."

2374—When General O'Kelly was introduced to Louis XVI soon after the Battle of Fontenay, his Majesty observed that Clare's regiment behaved very well in that engagement. "Sure," said the general, "they behaved very well, it is true—many of them were wounded, but my regiment behaved better for we were all killed."

2375—This is Winston Churchill's story.

"All was excitement and hustle at Abassiyeh Barracks (Cairo). Two squadrons of the 21st Lancers had already started up the Nile. The other two were to leave the next morning. Altogether seven additional officers from other cavalry regiments had been attached to the 21st to bring them up to full war-strength. . . . A troop had been reserved for me in one of the leading squadrons. But the delay and uncertainties about my coming had given this to another. Second Lieutenant Robert Grenfell had succeeded in obtaining this vacancy. He had gone off in the highest spirits. At the base everyone believed that we should be too late for the battle. Perhaps the first two squadrons might get up in time, but no one could tell. 'Fancy how lucky I am,' wrote Grenfell to his family. 'Here I have got the troop that would have been Winston's, and we are to be the first to start.' Chance is unceasingly at work in our lives, but we cannot always see its workings sharply and clearly defined. As it turned out, this troop was practically cut to pieces in the charge which the regiment made in the battle of September 2, and its brave young leader was killed."

2376—Almost everybody thought that Marshal Joffre had won the first battle of the Marne, but some refused to agree. One day a newspaperman appealed to Joffre: "Will you tell me who did win the battle of the Marne?"

"I can't answer that," said the Marshal. "But I can tell you that if the battle of the Marne had been lost the blame would have been on me."

2377—It is notorious (says Marmontel in his incomparable biography) that with much nobleness and dignity of soul, Marshal Saxe was fond of mirth and jollity. By taste, as well as by system, he loved merriment in his armies, stating that the French never did so well as when they were led on gayly, and what they most feared in war, was weary inactivity. He had always a comic opera in

his camp. It was at the theatre that he gave the order
of battle: and on these occasions, the principal actress
used to come forward and say—"Gentlemen, tomorrow
there will be no play on account of the battle the Marshal
gives; after tomorrow the 'Cock of the Village, with the
Merry Intrigues, etc.'"

2378—When Sir John Steel, the sculptor, had the Duke of Wellington sitting for a statue, he wanted to get him to look
warlike. All his efforts were in vain, however, for Wellington seemed, judging by his face, never to have heard
of Waterloo or Talavera.

At last Sir John lost patience, somewhat.

"As I am going to make the statue of Your Grace," he said,
"can you not tell me what you were doing before, say,
the battle of Salamanca? Were you not galloping about
the fields, cheering on your men to deeds of valor by
word and action?"

"Bah!" said the Duke scornfully. "If you really want to
model me as I was on the morning of Salamanca, then
do me crawling along a ditch on my stomach, with a
telescope in my hand."

2379—One day Chauncey Depew met a soldier who had been
wounded in the face. He was a Union Man and Depew
asked him in which battle he had been injured.

"In the last battle of Bull Run, sir," he replied.

"But how could you get hit in the face at Bull Run?"

"Well, sir," said the man, half apologetically, "after I had
run a mile or two I got careless and looked back."

2380—The Duke of Anjou, afterwards Henri III, besieged
Rochelle, the bulwark of the Calvinists. Near the
counterscarp was a mill which the besieged had no time
to fortify. They threw in a handful of troops in the day,
and at night commonly withdrew this small garrison,
leaving behind only one man. The Duke made the necessary dispositions for carrying this post; and advanced by
moonlight, with a small detachment and two culverins.

A single soldier had the guard this night and upon him the
whole defence depended. This brave man remained firm
and undismayed. He kept up, alone, a brisk fire upon
the assailants; and varying continually the tones of his
voice, he made them suppose that the besieged were in
great numbers. From the ramparts of the town they
called out to encourage this surprising commandant.

They exhorted the garrison to remain firm, and assured them of immediate success; till at length the soldier, seeing his little post upon the point of being carried, asked quarter for himself and comrades which was instantly granted. He then laid down his arms, and revealed the whole garrison in his own person.

2381—The Duke of Marlborough, observing a soldier leaning pensively on the butt of his firelock, just after the battle of Blenheim, accosted him thus:

"Why so sad, my friend, after so glorious a victory?"

"It may be glorious, your grace, but I am thinking that all the blood I have spilt this day has only earned me fourpence."

2382—The Swiss always will honor the memory of their national hero Arnold von Winkelried. When at the battle of Sempach in 1397 he saw that his countrymen could not attack the Austrians because the latter, being completely armed and dismounted to form closed ranks, presented an iron front of lances and pikes, he addressed them as follows:

"Friends, I am going to lay down my life to procure you victory. All I have to recommend to you is to provide for my family. Follow me and imitate my example."

With these words he arranged them in the form of a triangle, of which he himself occupied the point, and in this manner advanced towards the enemy. When close up to them, he seized as many of the pikes as he could lay hold of, and then falling on the ground, opened to those who followed him a way for piercing into this thick battalion. The Austrians, once broken, were defeated. The weight of their arms proved fatal to them.

2383—After a long period of inactivity among the Northern armies, a telegram came to President Lincoln informing him that General Burnside was believed to be in great peril at Cumberland Gap and that much firing had been heard in the vicinity of Knoxville. Great was the surprise of those about him when Lincoln calmly remarked that he was glad of it.

Seeing the astonishment in their faces, Lincoln said:

"Well, you see, it reminds me of Mistress Sallie Ward, a neighbor of mine, who had a very large family. Occasionally one of her numerous progeny would be heard crying in some out-of-the-way place, upon which Mrs.

Ward would exclaim, 'There's one of my children not
dead yet.' "

2384—A General rides forward. "I have the honor, your Imperial
Highness, to announce a great victory."
"Very well. Go and congratulate your troops."
"There are none left."

2385—A Turkish pasha is surveying the field with his glass. An
aide-de-camp rides up. "All our artillery has been captured."
The pasha strokes his beard philosophically and says, "Fortunately it was not paid for."

SEE ALSO   RELATED SUBJECTS
Cowardice 156, 159   Courage 151–153
Exaggeration 226   Cowardice 156–160
Officers 2423, 2426,   Death 1746–1749
    2427   War 2316–2323
                              Prisoners 2366
                              Strategy 2386–2393
                              Army and Navy 2401–2404
                              Officers 2406–2427
                              Soldiers and Sailors 2430–2437

STRATEGY

2386—Toward the end of the Civil War, in 1865, fears were felt
by the North that Johnson might break through to join
General Lee and thereby crush the Northern Armies
under Grant. A Congressman, representing the anxious
House, was sent to discuss the matter with the President,
whereupon the following conversation ensued:
"They are becoming anxious, some of them in the House,
about the situation," said the Congressman. "Have you
received anything lately? Aren't you afraid Grant is
making a mistake in not moving?"
Seeming to move entirely away from the subject at hand
the President asked, "Do you remember that Baptist
revival in Springfield, in such a year?"
Puzzled, the Congressman said, "I do not recall it."
The President continued, "Well, Bill, a hardened sinner,
was converted. Upon an appointed day the minister
baptized the converts in a small stream. After Bill had
been plunged under once, he asked the preacher to baptize him again; the latter replied it was unnecessary.
Bill, however, urged the matter, and he was accordingly

put under for the second time. As he came up, he again asked, as a particular favor, that he might be baptized just once more. The minister, a little angered, answered that he had already been under once more than the other converts. Still Bill pleaded, and the preacher put him under for the third time. As Bill came up puffing and blowing, he shook the water from his hair and exclaimed: 'There! I'll be blowed if the devil can get hold of me now.' "

The President went on in explanation of his story, "General Grant is very much like Bill. He is determined on making sure of the thing, and will not move until he has."

2387—After Lee had taken Harper's Ferry, the President, realizing how great a calamity it was to the Northern arms, determined, if possible, to fix the responsibility. Halleck was summoned, but did not know where the blame lay. "Very well," said Lincoln, "I'll ask General Schenck." The latter could throw no light upon the question further than to say he was not to blame. Milroy was the next to be called to the presence of the commander-in-chief, and to enter a plea of "not guilty." Hooker was next given a hearing, and "Fighting Joe" made an emphatic disclaimer of all responsibility. Then the President assembled the four in his room, and said: "Gentlemen, Harper's Ferry was surrendered, and none of you, it seems, is responsible. I am very anxious to discover who is." After striding across the room several times, the President suddenly threw up his bowed head and exclaimed, "I have it! I know who is responsible." "Who, Mr. President; who is it?" anxiously inquired the distinguished quartet. "Gentlemen," said the President, "General Lee is the man."

2388—President Lincoln one day remarked to a number of personal friends who had called upon him at the White House:

"General McClellan's tardiness and unwillingness to fight the enemy or follow up advantages gained, reminds me of a man back in Illinois who knew a few law phrases but whose lawyer lacked aggressiveness. The man finally lost all patience and springing to his feet vociferated: 'Why don't you go at him with a fi. fa., a demurrer, a capias, a surrebutter, or a ne exeat, or something; or a nundam pactum or a non est?'

"I wish McClellan would go at the enemy with something

—I don't care what. General McClellan is a pleasant and scholarly gentleman. He is an admirable engineer, but he seems to have a special talent for a stationary engine."

2380—In the first December of the first World War Admiral Beatty received a radiogram from Sir George Warrender from his ship: "Scarborough being shelled. I am proceeding toward Hull." Lord Beatty replied: "Are you? I am going to Scarborough."

2390—The Norwegian king, Harold Hardrada, who lost his life in the battle of Stamford Bridge in 1066, fought for some time under the banner of the Byzantine emperors. On one of his expeditions to Sicily, he came with his army to a populous town, to which he laid siege. The walls, however, were so strong, that he began to doubt whether it would be possible to make a breach in them; and the burghers had plenty of provisions, and everything which they needed for their defence. Harold, therefore, ordered his fowlers to catch the small birds that nested in the town, and flew to the forest during the day in quest of food. He then caused splinters of inflammable wood, smeared with wax and sulphur, to be fastened on their backs and enkindled. The birds, when set at liberty, flew immediately to the town to revisit their young and their nests on the roofs of the houses, which were thatched with reeds and straw. The fire fell from the birds on the thatch, and although each bore but a small quantity, their number was so great that one house after another began to burn, until the whole town was in flames. The inhabitants then came out and implored mercy, and Harold thus got possession of the town.

2391—When even the great patience of Lincoln had been exhausted by the "waiting campaign" of McClellan, he placed Hooker in command of the Army. In order to create the impression of immense and vigorous activity, General Hooker reported his movements in a dispatch headed "Headquarters in the Saddle." "The trouble with Hooker," Lincoln remarked, "is that he's got his headquarters where his hindquarters ought to be."

2392—Stories concerning the clashes between Lincoln and the inadequate General McClellan are common. Lincoln deemed it necessary for McClellan to report frequently and the General chaffed at this. One time he sent the President the following telegram from the field:

President Abraham Lincoln,
Washington, D. C.
Have just captured six cows. What shall we do with
them?
George B. McClellan

Lincoln promptly wired:
Gen. George B. McClellan
Army of the Potomac
As to six cows captured—milk them.
A. Lincoln.

2393—President Lincoln once wrote to General McClellan, when
the latter was in command of the army. General Mc-
Clellan, as is well known, conducted a waiting campaign,
being so careful not to make any mistakes that he made
very little headway. President Lincoln sent this brief
but exceedingly pertinent letter:
"My dear McClellan: If you don't want to use the army I
should like to borrow it for a while.
Yours respectfully,
A. Lincoln."

RELATED SUBJECTS
Quick Thinking 471–492
Shrewdness 526–541
War 2316–2323
Battles 2371–2385
Officers 2406–2427

ARMISTICE

2396—When the German delegation came to Marshal Foch at the
end of the War to ask for armistice terms, the Frenchman picked up a paper from his desk and read a set of
conditions. "But—there must be some mistake," the
leader of the German officers stammered in dismay.
"These are terms which no civilized nation could impose
on another!"
"I am very glad to hear you say so," replied Foch gravely.
"No, gentlemen, these are not our terms. They are the
terms imposed on Lille by the German commander when
that city surrendered."

2397—After the surrender of Lee to Grant at Appomatox Court
House, the Union soldiers began, without orders, to
salute the latter with cannon; but General Grant directed

the firing to cease, lest it should wound the feelings of the prisoners, who, he said, were still their countrymen.

RELATED SUBJECTS
War 2316–2323
Battles 2371–2385

ARMY AND NAVY

2401—Nearly all great scientific discoveries have been combated and misunderstood, even by great men. Admiral Sir Charles Napier fiercely opposed the introduction of steam power into the royal navy, and one day exclaimed in the House of Commons: "Mr. Speaker, when we enter her Majesty's naval service and face the chances of war, we go prepared to be hacked in pieces by cutlasses, to be riddled with bullets, or to be blown to bits by shot and shell; but, Mr. Speaker, we do not go prepared to be boiled alive!"

2402—General Washington seldom indulged in a joke or sarcasm, but when he did, he always made a decided hit. It is related that he was present in Congress during the debate on the establishment of the Federal Army, when a member offered a resolution limiting the army to three thousand men. Upon this Washington suggested to a member an amendment providing that no enemy should ever invade the country with more than two thousand soldiers. The laughter which ensued smothered the resolution completely.

2403—One day Lincoln and some of his friends were discussing the amount of manpower involved in the Civil War. Someone asked him how many men the Confederates had in the field. Lincoln astonished them by saying, "Twelve hundred thousand, according to the best authority."

"Yes, sir," repeated Lincoln, "twelve hundred thousand— no doubt of it. You see, all of our generals, when they get whipped, say the enemy outnumbers them from three or five to one, and I must believe them. We have four hundred thousand men in the field, and three times four make twelve. Don't you see it?"

2404—Following the battle of Antietam, the army under the command of McClellan lay unaccountably idle. President Lincoln accompanied by a friend, Mr. O. M. Hatch of Illinois, went to visit the camp.

They stood on a hill overlooking the vast army of tents.
Turning to his friend, Lincoln said:
"Hatch, Hatch, what is all this?"
"Why," said Hatch, "that is the Army of the Potomac."
"No, Hatch, no," said Lincoln, "that is General McClellan's
bodyguard."

SEE ALSO
Discretion 182
Conversions 1624

RELATED SUBJECTS
War 2316–2323
Battles 2371–2385
Officers 2406–2427
Soldiers and Sailors 2430–2437
Discipline 2441–2442
Regulations 2446
Camp 2451
Marches 2456
Drill 2461–2462
K. P. 2466

OFFICERS

2406—General Grant once expressed his contempt for a certain
officer. Another General protested that the man in question had been through 10 campaigns. "General," said
Grant, "so has that mule yonder, but he's still a jackass."

2407—Once, during the War, Barnum brought his show to Washington and invited President Lincoln to come and see its
wonders.
The President noted all the exhibitions with appropriate
remarks and, when shown the midgets, General Tom
Thumb and Admiral Nutt, remarked to Barnum, "You
have some pretty small generals, but I think I can beat
you."

2408—When George V was Prince of Wales, he held the rank
of Lieutenant in the Marines. One day on the afterdeck
of a battleship he was conducting drill under the super-
vision of a senior officer. The deck had been cleared even
of its quadrails. The Prince was not well versed in drill
and his superior was clearly put out at his awkwardness
and slowness of command. At last the squad was marching full on for the stern and the unguarded edge and it
seemed as though the Prince had either forgotten the
command to stop, or face about, or else failed to realize
the situation. Sputtering with wrath, the officer snapped,

as the men neared the edge, "God Almighty, Sir, can't you at least say Good-bye to your men!"

2409—Stonewall Jackson sent the following telegram to the War Department at Richmond: "Send me more men and fewer questions."

2410—A French field-marshal who had attained that rank by court favor, not by valor, going one evening to the opera, forcibly took possession of the box of a respectable Abbé, who for this outrage brought a suit. The Abbé thus addressed the court: "I do not come here to complain of Admiral Suffrein who took so many ships in the East Indies; I do not come to complain of Count de Grasse who fought so nobly in the west; I do not come to complain of the Duke de Crébillon who took Minorca; but I come to complain of Marshal B—— who took my box at the Opera, and never took anything else."

2411—An officer, having had some trouble with General Sherman, being very angry, presented himself before Lincoln who was visiting the camp, and said: "Mr. President, I have a cause of grievance. This morning I went to General Sherman and he threatened to shoot me."

"Threatened to shoot you?" asked Lincoln. "Well," (in a stage whisper) "if I were you I would keep away from him; if he threatens to shoot, I would not trust him, for I believe he would do it."

2412—A group of high-ranking officers, on a tour of inspection, were being conducted through the trenches. They were led by a captain. He turned to the general behind him and said in a hoarse whisper, "We are now in the third line trenches."

The general turned to the officer behind him, repeated the information, which went in a whisper all the way down the line.

A moment later the captain turned again and said, "We are now in the second line trenches."

The general relayed the information again, and again the whisper went all the way down the line.

A moment later the captain said, "We are now in the front line trenches."

The whisper was sent backward.

"Now," whispered the general, "where is the enemy?"

"About a quarter of a mile away," said the captain.

"A quarter of a mile!" said the general. "Then why are we whispering?"

"Because I have laryngitis," said the captain.

2413—Napoleon often resorted to a species of charlatanism to augment the enthusiasm of his troops. He would say to one of his aides-de-camp, "Ascertain from the colonel of such a regiment, whether he has in his corps a man, who has served in the campaigns of Italy, or the campaigns of Egypt. Ascertain his name, where he was born, the particulars of his family, and what he has done. Learn his number in the ranks, and to what company he belongs, and furnish me with the information."

On the day of the review Napoleon, at a single glance, could spot the man who had been described to him. He would go up to him as if he recognized him, address him by his name, and say—"Oh! so you are here! You are a brave fellow—I saw you at Aboukir—How is your old father? What! Have you not got the cross? Stay, I will give it you."

Then the delighted soldiers would say to each other, "You see the Emperor knows us all; he knows our families; he knows where we have served." What a stimulus this was to soldiers whom he succeeded in persuading that they would all, sooner or later, become marshals of the Empire.

2414—"Do you know General A——?" queried President Lincoln one day to a friend who had "dropped in" at the White House.

"Certainly; but you are not wasting any time thinking about him, are you?" was the rejoinder.

"You wrong him," responded the President, "he is a really great man—a philosopher."

"How do you make that out? He isn't worth the powder and ball necessary to kill him—so I have heard military men say," the friend remarked.

"He is a mighty thinker," the President returned, "because he has mastered that ancient and wise admonition, 'know thyself.' He has formed an intimate acquaintance with himself, knows as well for what he is fitted and unfitted as any man living. Without doubt he is a remarkable man. This War has not produced another like him. Greatly to my relief, and to the interests of the country, he has resigned. The country should express its gratitude in some substantial way."

2415—When President Lincoln heard of the Confederate raid at Fairfax, in which a brigader-general and a number of valuable horses were captured, he gravely observed:

"Well, I am sorry for the horses."

"Sorry for the horses, Mr. President!" exclaimed the Secretary of War, raising his spectacles and throwing himself back in his chair in astonishment.

"Yes," replied Lincoln, "I can make a brigadier-general in five minutes, but it is not easy to replace a hundred and ten horses."

2416—"General Grant is a drunkard," asserted powerful and influential politicians to President Lincoln, "he is not himself half the time; he can't be relied upon, and it is a shame to have such a man in command of an army."

"So Grant gets drunk, does he?" queried Lincoln.

"Yes, he does, and I can prove it," was the reply.

"Well," returned Lincoln, with the faintest suspicion of a twinkle in his eyes, "you needn't waste your time getting proof; you just find out, to oblige me, what brand of whiskey Grant drinks because I want to send a barrel of it to each one of my generals."

2417—When in Washington Lieutenant de Tessan, aide to Marshal Joffre and Colonel Fabry, was approached by a pretty girl who said: "And did you kill a German soldier?"

"Yes."

"With what hand did you do it?"

"With this right hand."

The pretty American girl seized his right hand and kissed it. At this Colonel Fabry said: "Heavens, man, why didn't you tell her that you bit him to death?"

2418—A woman once approached Lincoln rather imperiously. "Mr. President," she said very theatrically, "you must give me a colonel's commission for my son. Sir, I demand it, not as a favor but as a right. Sir, my grandfather fought at Lexington. Sir, my uncle was the only man that did not run away at Bladensburg. Sir, my father fought at New Orleans, and my husband was killed at Monterey."

"I guess, madam," answered Lincoln dryly, "your family has done enough for the country. It is time to give somebody else a chance."

2419—On one occasion a friend burst into Lincoln's room to tell him that a brigadier-general and twelve army mules had been carried off by a Confederate raid.

"How unfortunate! Those mules cost us two hundred dollars apiece!" was the President's reply.

2420—No figure of a popular hero in American public life probably was ever as much kissed as Richard Pearson Hobson who had distinguished himself in the Spanish American War. At a big function in Chicago, two pretty young cousins stood on tip-toe and kissed him. This started the ball rolling, and all the young ladies present, enamoured of the brave young Lieutenant, lined up to kiss him too. Count was kept up to one hundred and then given up. The audience stood by and rooted, calling out, "Good for number 76!" and other helpful comments. The kissing went on for 36 minutes with an average of five a minute. The publicity arising from this incident led to its repetition in every city to which the hero toured. He collected some 10,000 or more in all. A caramel was put on the market, called "Hobson's Kisses."

2421—Peter Heine, a Dutchman, from a cabin-boy rose to the rank of Admiral. He was killed in action at the moment his fleet triumphed over that of Spain.

The States-General sent a deputation to his mother, at Delft, to condole with her on the loss of her son. The simple old woman, who still remained in her original obscurity, answered:

"I always foretold that Peter would perish like the miserable wretch that he was. He loved nothing but rambling about from one country to another, and now he has received the reward of his folly!"

2422—At a council of Generals early in the Civil War one remarked that a certain Major was wounded and would not be able to perform a duty assigned to him.

"Wounded!" said Jackson. "If it really is so, I think it must have been by an accidental discharge of his duty."

2423—When the English fleet was bearing down upon the French off Trafalgar, a sailor who was devoutly kneeling at the side of a gun was asked by an officer if he was afraid. "Afraid!" replied the tar. "No! I was only praying that the enemy's shot might be distributed in the same proportion as the prize money, the greatest part among the officers."

2424—In camp the soldiers were awaiting imminent transfer to the fighting front. In the dusk one of the soldiers called out to a khaki clad figure only dimly seen: "Hey, buddy, got a match?"

A lighted match was forthcoming, and by its light, as he started to thank the other for the courtesy, the private was horrified to see the markings of a general.

"I beg your pardon, sir," he said, saluting smartly, "I didn't see that you were a general."

"That's all right, son," said the general benignly. "Just thank God I wasn't a second lieutenant."

2425—During the First World War an American officer was reconnoitering in the war zone. A young pleasant-looking chap in the uniform of a British subaltern came toward him.

"Who are you?" the American challenged.

"The Prince of Wales," the young man said mildly, continuing on his way.

"Oh, yeah," was the sarcastic rejoinder of the American. "And I'm the King of England."

Several nights later at a Red Cross hut the two men met again. Great was the chagrin of the American to find that the young man was actually the Prince of Wales. He was still more embarrassed when the Prince, grinning widely, waved to him from across the room and called out cheerily, "Hello there, dad!"

2426—Major-Gen. Smedley Butler used to tell the story of a doughboy who, during a battle in Flanders, suffered shell shock. He started running towards the rear. After some time he was stopped by an officer.

"Here, don't you know that there's a big battle going on up at the front?" he asked.

"Y-y-yes, I-I-I know," stuttered the frightened soldier.

"Then what are you doing here?"

The doughboy did not answer and cast his eyes down abashed.

"Why don't you answer?" roared the officer. "Do you know who I am?"

The doughboy shook his head feebly.

"I am your general," snapped the officer.

"Great guns! Am I that far back?" exclaimed the soldier and fainted away.

2427—A soldier, telling his mother of the terrible fire, was asked by her why he did not get behind a tree.

"Tree?" said he. "Why, there weren't enough for the officers."

SEE ALSO
Cowardice 156
Honor 297
Stubbornness 571
Scientists 1116
Conversions 1621
Superstition 1636
Dentists 1696
War 2320
Battles 2376
Strategy 2388, 2389

RELATED SUBJECTS
War 2316–2323
Strategy 2386–2393
Army and Navy 2401–2404
Soldiers and Sailors 2430–2437
Discipline 2441–2442

Army 2404
Marches 2456
K. P. 2466

SOLDIERS AND SAILORS

2430—Vice-President Henry A. Wallace, in his famous speech on "The Century of the Common Man" told the following story of heroism and courage:

"The American people have always had guts and always will have. You know the story of bomber pilot Dixon and radioman Gene Aldrich and ordnanceman Tony Pastula—the story which Americans will be telling their children for generations to illustrate man's ability to master any fate. These men lived for 34 days on the open sea in a rubber life raft, 8 feet by 4 feet, with no food but that which they took from the sea and the air with one pocket knife and a pistol. And yet they lived it through and came at last to the beach of an island they did not know. In spite of their suffering and weakness, they stood like men, with no weapon left to protect themselves, and no shoes on their feet or clothes on their backs, and walked in military file because, they said, 'If there were Japs, we didn't want to be crawling.'"

2431—During the heroic defence of the Bataan Peninsula, one of the commanding officers lined up a company of his men and asked for a volunteer for a mission of the utmost peril. Anyone willing to serve was instructed to step forward two paces from the line.

He glanced for a second at a memorandum in his hand and, looking up, was shocked and disappointed to see the ranks unbroken.

"What," he said unbelievingly, "not a single man!"

"You do not understand, sir," said an aide at his elbow, "the whole line has stepped forward two paces."

2432—A profound philosophy of life is reflected in the reply of the sailor who, when asked what he had done with his pay, said, "Part went for liquor and part for women. The rest I spent foolishly."

2433—Shortly after the Revolutionary War Benedict Arnold was presented at Court in London. While the king was conversing with him, Lord Balcarass, a stately old nobleman, who had fought under Gen. Burgoyne in the campaigns of America, was presented. The King introduced them with: "Lord Balcarass—General Arnold."

"What, Sire," said the haughty old earl, drawing up his lofty form, "the traitor Arnold!" and refused to give him his hand.

The consequence was a challenge from Arnold. They met, and it was arranged that the parties should fire together. At the signal Arnold fired. Lord Balcarass, however, throwing down his pistol, turned on his heel, and was walking away, when Arnold called after him:

"Why don't you fire, my Lord?"

"Sir," said the Earl, "I will leave that to the executioner."

2434—Two young girls were watching a shipload of marines depart for places unknown. Wistfully they watched the ship as it rapidly disappeared from sight.

"Ain't it a shame," mourned one of them, "that those handsome marines have to go way off to China or somewhere. What will they ever do there?"

"What will they do?" rejoined the more worldly of the two. "Have you ever had a date with a marine?"

2435—A group of soldiers were discussing the many things they would do when they were discharged from the army.

"First thing I'm goin' to do when I get out of this army," said one disgruntled individual, "is bust that sergeant right on the nose."

"Oh, yeah," retorted a nearby comrade, "that's what you think. You're goin' to wait right in line and take your turn, just like all the rest of us."

2436—They tell the tale of an American lady of notable good works, much esteemed by the French, who, at the end of June, 1918, visited one of the field-hospitals behind Degoutte's Sixth French Army. Degoutte was fighting on the face of the Marne salient, and the 2d American Division, then in action around the Bois de Belleau, north-west of Chateau Thierry, was under his orders. It happened that occasional casualties of the Marine Brigade of the 2d American Division, wounded toward the flank where Degoutte's own horizon-blue infantry joined on, were picked up by French stretcher-bearers and evacuated to French hospitals. And this lady, looking down a long, crowded ward, saw on a pillow a face unlike the fiercely whiskered Gallic heads there displayed in rows. She went to it.

"Oh," she said, "surely you are an American!"

"No, ma'am," the casualty answered. "I'm a Marine."

2437—During the traitor Arnold's predatory operations in Virginia in 1781, he took an American captain prisoner. After some general conversation, he asked the captain "what he thought the Americans would do with him if they caught him." The captain declined at first giving him an answer, but upon being repeatedly urged, he said: "Why, sir, if I must answer the question, you will excuse my telling you the truth; if my countrymen should catch you, I believe they would first cut off your lame leg which was wounded in the cause of freedom and virtue at Quebec, and bury it with the honors of war, and afterwards hang the remainder of your body on a gibbet."

SEE ALSO
Boners 116
Courage 151
Cowardice 159
Patriotism 407
Age 678
Sermons 1556
Medicines 1727
Deathbed Scenes 1774
Civilians in War 2341
Censors 2352
Battles 2377, 2379, 2381
Trials 2479

RELATED SUBJECTS
Courage 151–153
Patriotism 396–407
Death 1746–1749
War 2316–2323
Prisoners 2366
Battles 2371–2385
Army and Navy 2401–2404
Officers 2406–2427
Discipline 2441–2442

DISCIPLINE

2441—A telegram from one of his generals was on Lincoln's desk while an old man was pleading for a pardon for his son. Lincoln turned to him gently but firmly, "I am sorry, I can do nothing for you," he said with finality. "Listen to this telegram I received from General Butler yesterday : 'President Lincoln, I pray you not to interfere with the courts-martial of the army. You will destroy all discipline among our soldiers.' "

Greatly affected by the hopeless despair on the old man's face, Lincoln said, "By jingo! Butler or no Butler, here goes!"

The old man read, "Job Smith is not to be shot until further orders from me—Abraham Lincoln." He expressed disappointment. "Why, I thought it was a pardon! You may order him to be shot next week."

"My old friend," the President replied, "I see you are not very well acquainted with me. If your son never dies till orders come from me to shoot him, he will live to be a great deal older than Methuselah."

2442—During the Black Hawk War, Captain Abe Lincoln was one of the first of his company to be arraigned for unmilitary conduct. Contrary to the rules he fired a gun "within the limits" and had his sword taken from him. The next infringement of rules was by some of the men who stole a quantity of liquor, drank it, and became unfit for duty, straggling out of the ranks the next day, and not getting together again until late at night.

For allowing this lawlessness the captain was condemned to wear a wooden sword for two days.

SEE ALSO   RELATED SUBJECTS
Cowardice 160   Army and Navy 2401–2404
                           Officers 2406–2427
                           Soldiers and Sailors 2430–2437
                           Regulations 2446
                           Drill 2461–2462
                           K. P. 2466

REGULATIONS

2446—Strange things happen in military circles. An army officer was given the task of preparing a factual report on heavy ordnance. Partly because he was pressed for time and partly because the facts were there, arranged in their best way, he copied pretty much verbatim the article on the subject in the Encyclopedia Britannica, and turned it over to his superiors. Not long thereafter, he received, along with all his other brother officers, a mimeographed copy of his report from the War Department in an envelope heavily sealed and labeled, "Extremely Confidential."

RELATED SUBJECTS
Discipline 2441–2442

CAMP

2451—A Negro sentry, but recently inducted into the service and slightly bewildered by the many formalities required to be learned in so short a time, startled a number of his superior officers while serving his sentry duty, by hailing them with the challenge, "Halt! Look who's here!"

RELATED SUBJECTS
Army and Navy 2401–2404
Officers 2406–2427
Soldiers and Sailors 2430–2437
Discipline 2441–2442
Regulations 2446
Marches 2456
Drill 2461–2462
K. P. 2466

MARCHES

2456—A green young lieutenant was assigned to a new detachment. He was a very small and helpless looking individual, and when he first appeared before his company there were many audible comments made about his apparent ineptness. From the rear of the ranks a voice boomed, "And a little child shall lead them." There was a roar of laughter.

Seemingly undisturbed the lieutenant finished the business of the day. Next day there appeared a notice on the bulletin board: "Company A will take a 25 mile hike today with full packs. And a little child shall lead them . . . on a damned big horse."

RELATED SUBJECTS
Army and Navy 2401–2404
Officers 2406–2427
Soldiers and Sailors 2430–2437
Camp 2451
Drill 2461–2462

DRILL

2461—In the course of the Black Hawk Indian War, Abraham Lincoln was Captain of a company. He was inexperienced in the formalities of drill and manoeuvre, and made many blunders in his orders. His native ingenuity often enabled him to get out of difficulties, as in the instance when, marching with a front of more than 20 men, he came to a fence with only a narrow gate offering passage into the next field. "I could not, for the life of me," he said, "remember the proper word of command for the getting my company endwise so that it could get through the gate. So as we came near I said, 'This company is dismissed for two minutes, when it will fall in again on the other side of the gate.'"

2462—A sergeant cannot always be blamed for his tough treatment of rookie soldiers. There is the story of the sergeant who was training a bunch of recruits on a rifle range. At a hundred yards the order to fire was given. After the smoke had cleared away, the target was revealed as smooth and untouched. The sergeant gave the order to move up to fifty yards. Again the firing order was given. And still the target was untouched. They moved up to twenty-five yards—with the same results. Ordering the troops into closed ranks, the sergeant, red faced and seemingly about to burst, bellowed:
"Fix bayonets and charge!"

RELATED SUBJECTS
Army and Navy 2401–2404
Soldiers and Sailors 2430–2437
Camp 2451
Marches 2456

K. P.

2466—The late Smedley D. Butler, always an impulsive man, was generally careful of the welfare of his men. One time in France he encountered two soldiers emerging from the kitchen with a large soup kettle. "Let me taste that," he ordered. "But Gen—. . . ." "No buts! Give me a spoon." Taking a taste, the General sputtered, "You don't call that soup, do you?" "No, sir," replied the soldier, "I was trying to tell you, sir, its dishwater."

RELATED SUBJECTS
Army and Navy 2401–2404
Soldiers and Sailors 2430–2437
Discipline 2441–2442
Camp 2451

LAW AND JUSTICE

COURTS

2471—Chief Justice Fuller was practicing before Judge Mac-
Arthur of the Supreme Court of Illinois in Chicago. In
his speech before the Judge he pleaded his client's ignorance of an offense he had committed.

The Judge said, "Every man is supposed to know the law,
Mr. Fuller."

"I am aware of that," responded Mr. Fuller. "Every shoemaker, tailor, mechanic and illiterate laborer is presumed
to know the law. Yes, every man is presumed to know it,
except the judges of the Supreme Court, and we have a
Court of Appeals to correct their mistakes."

2472—The highly nervous young lawyer stepped up to plead his
case before the Court. It was in New York City. He laid
his coat and hat on the bench and stood before the Judge.
"Is this the first time you've practiced in this Court?"

"Yes, your Honor," replied the lawyer, feeling nervous and
afraid he had already committed some breach of precedent.

"Then get your hat and coat and put them where you can
keep an eye on them."

2473—There seems to be enough evidence to prove that, even if
Abe Lincoln had never been President of the United
States, he still would have become immortal—as a story
teller. Here is another example of his talents in that
direction as related by a court clerk:

"I was never fined but once for contempt of court. Davis
fined me five dollars. Mr. Lincoln had just come in, and
leaning over my desk had told me a story so irresistibly
funny that I broke out into a loud laugh. The Judge
called me to order, saying, 'This must be stopped. Mr.
Lincoln, you are constantly disturbing this court with
your stories.' Then to me: 'You may fine yourself five
dollars.' I apologized but told the Judge the story was
worth the money. In a few minutes the Judge called me
to him. 'What was that story Lincoln told you?' he

441

asked. I told him, and he laughed aloud in spite of himself. 'Remit your fine,' he ordered."

RELATED SUBJECTS
Trials 2476–2485
Judges 2486–2497
Witnesses 2501–2506
Juries 2511–2517
Evidence 2521–2523
Lawyers 2526–2537
Criminals 2571
Laws 2596–2599
Justice 2601

TRIALS

2476—When Thaddeus Stevens was a young lawyer he once had a case before a bad-tempered judge of an obscure Pennsylvania court. Under what he considered a very erroneous ruling it was decided against him; thereupon he threw down his books and picked up his hat in a state of indignation, scattering imprecations all around him. The judge assumed an air of offended majesty, and asked Thaddeus Stevens if he meant to express his "contempt for this court?" Stevens turned to him very politely, made a respectful bow and feigned amazement. "Express my contempt for this court? No sir; I am trying to conceal it, your honor," adding as he turned to leave, "but I find it damned hard to do it."

2477—A Chinese thus describes a trial in the English law courts: "One man is quite silent, another talks all the time, and twelve men condemn the man who has not said a word."

2478—"I feel very strongly on this subject and must deal severely with you," began the Judge, in his address to Sam, who was in court on a charge of wife desertion.
"But, Boss, you don't understand," protested the Negro. "You don't know my old woman. I ain't no deserter. I'se a refugee!"

2479—A sentry near one of the army camps on Long Island was bitten by a valuable dog from one of the neighboring estates, and in self-defense drove his bayonet into the animal. The owner brought charges against him to retrieve its value and the evidence showed that the sentry had not been badly bitten.

"Why did you not knock the dog with the butt end of your rifle?" asked the judge.

The sentry clinched his case by replying, "Why didn't he bite me with his tail?"

2480—A deaf man went to law with another deaf man, and the judge was much deafer than either. One of them asserted that the other owed him five months' rent, and the other said that his opponent had been grinding corn at night to avoid the tax. The judge looked at them and said, "Why are you quarreling? She is your mother; you must both support her."

2481—One of Winston Churchill's favorite stories is of the Earl of Birkenhead as a young barrister. He had gotten into a heated controversy with the Judge over some aspect of a case. Their remarks grew more and more heated and personal. At last the Judge said, "Young man, you are extremely offensive." "Yes," said the Earl, "we both are. But I am trying to be, and you can't help it."

2482—When the celebrated Dunning, afterward Lord Ashburton, was "stating law" to a jury in court Lord Mansfield interrupted him by saying, "If that be law, I'll go home and burn my books."

"My lord," replied Dunning, "you had better go home and read them."

2483—Once opposing counsel objected to a juror on the ground that he knew Mr. Lincoln, and as this was a reflection upon the honor of a lawyer, Judge Davis promptly overruled the objection. But when Lincoln, following the example of his adversary examined two or three of the jury and found that they knew his opponent, the Judge, interfered. "Now, Mr. Lincoln," he observed severely, "you are wasting time. The mere fact that a juror knows your opponent does not disqualify him."

"No, Your Honor," responded Lincoln dryly, "but I am afraid some of the gentlemen may not know him which would place me at a disadvantage."

2484—Thelwall, about to be tried for treason, wrote to Lord Erskine, the following laconic epistle: "I shall plead my own cause."

To which Erskine as laconically replied: "You'll be hanged if you do."

Mr. Thelwall wittily rejoined: "Then if I do, I'll be hanged."

2485—Knowing his client to be innocent, the defense lawyer rested his case in the assurance that all would be well.

Great was his astonishment when the justice of the court pronounced the man guilty, and imposed a fine of fifty dollars and a jail sentence.

The lawyer deliberately turned his chair so that his back was to the bench. "Fine me too," he said in a loud voice.

"Why?" asked the justice.

"For contempt."

Bewildered, the justice said, "Contempt? But you haven't said a word."

"Exactly. My contempt is silent."

SEE ALSO
Reputation 78
Absent-Mindedness 89
Laziness 327
Long-Windedness
   352, 355
Wife 933
Erudition 1072
Stealing 2589

RELATED SUBJECTS
Courts 2471–2473
Judges 2486–2497
Witnesses 2501–2506
Juries 2511–2517
Evidence 2521–2523
Lawyers 2526–2537

JUDGES

2486—A certain judge in the mining territory of Nevada had a reputation for probity. In keeping with this opinion, he opened a mining claim case one morning with the following words to the court: "Gentlemen, this court has received from the plaintiff in this case a check for $10,000. He has received from the defendant a check for $15,000. The court has returned $5,000 to the defendant and will now try the case on its merits."

2487—The late Max Steuer, the prominent lawyer, was compelled to apologize to the court one day. With stately dignity he rose in his place and, bowing to the judge, said: "Your Honor is right and I am wrong, as your Honor generally is."

There was a dazed look in the judge's eyes. He hardly knew whether to feel pleased or fine the lawyer for contempt of court.

2488—"This hurts me more than it does you," remarked the Magistrate, as he fined his daughter $10.00 for speeding and $3.00 for running past a red light, and then dug into his pocket for the fines.

2489—Judge Jeffries, reprimanding a criminal, called him a scoundrel. The prisoner hotly retorted: "Sir, I am not as big a scoundrel as your honor—" here the culprit stopped to look at the apoplectic judge, but hurriedly added— "takes me to be."

"Put your words closer together," muttered the judge.

2490—Judge Jeffries, of notorious memory, pointing with his cane to a man who was about to be tried, said: "There is a rogue at the end of my cane."

The man to whom he pointed, looking at him, said: "At which end, my Lord?"

2491—Aristides being judge between two private persons, one of them declared that his adversary had greatly injured Aristides. "Relate rather," said he, "what wrong he has done you, for it is your cause not mine that I now sit judge of."

2492—Lord Mansfield chanced to be in one of the counties on the circuit when a poor woman was indicted for witchcraft. The inhabitants of the place were exasperated against her. Some witnesses deposed that they had seen her walk in the air; and with her feet upward and her head downward. Lord Mansfield heard the evidence with great tranquility, and perceiving the temper of the people, whom it would not have been prudent to irritate, he thus addressed them:

"I do not doubt that this woman has walked in the air with her feet upward, since you have all seen it; but she has the honor to be born in England as well as you and I, and consequently cannot be judged but by the laws of the country, nor punished but in proportion as she has violated them. Now, I know not one law that forbids walking in the air with the feet upward. We all have a right to it with impunity; I see no reason, therefore, for this prosecution, and this poor woman may return home when she pleases."

2493—Nobody was more witty or more bitter than Lord Ellenborough. A young lawyer, trembling with fear, rose to make his first speech, and began: "My Lord, my unfortunate client—my Lord, my unfortunate client—my Lord——"

"Go on, sir, go on!" said Lord Ellenborough, "as far as you have proceeded hitherto, the court is entirely with you."

2494—In the traffic court of one of our large Mid-Western cities, a young lady was brought before the Judge to answer a ticket given her for driving through a red light. She explained to his Honor that she was a school teacher and requested an immediate disposal of her case in order that she might hasten away to her classes. A wild gleam came into the Judge's eye. "You're a school teacher, eh?" said he. "Madam, I shall realize my lifelong ambition. I've waited years to have a school teacher in this court. Sit down at that table and write 'I went through a red light' five hundred times!"

2495—Lincoln's guileless exterior concealed a great fund of shrewdness and common sense about ordinary matters, as well as genius in the higher realms.

"I remember once," writes Whitney, "that while several of us lawyers were together, including Judge Davis, Lincoln suddenly asked a novel question regarding court practice, addressed to no one particularly, to which the judge, who was in the habit certainly of appropriating his full share of any conversation, replied, stating what he understood the practice should be. Lincoln thereat laughed and said: "I asked that question, hoping that you would answer. I have that very question to present to the court in the morning, and I am glad to find out that the court is on my side."

2496—Shortly after Charles Evans Hughes became Chief Justice of the Supreme Court in 1930, he was much acclaimed for the liberalism of his maiden opinion which confirmed the right of citizens in California to hoist a red flag. Shortly thereafter, F. W. Wile, the newspaper man, encountered Hughes at a garden party at the estate of Secretary Stimson. He inquired how Hughes was reacting to the plaudits received for having blossomed out as a liberal.

"Wile," said Hughes, "I blossomed out a long time ago. But the trouble is, it never bore fruit."

2497—A judge, noted for his gentleness to defendants, asked the contrite and broken man before him, "Have you ever been sentenced to imprisonment?"

"No, your Honor," said the prisoner and burst into tears.

"There, there, don't cry," said the judge kindly. "You're going to be now."

SEE ALSO
Drinking 40
Long-Windedness
353, 354
Modesty 385
Bishops 1492
Banks 2152
Courts 2472
Lawyers 2526
Hanging 2568

RELATED SUBJECTS
Courts 2471–2473
Trials 2476–2485

WITNESSES

2501—Two friendly enemies were involved in a lawsuit. The issue at stake was small, but each was determined to win.

The day of the trial arrived. Mr. Johnson, the party of the first part, came into the courtroom surrounded by a covey of witnesses for his side of the case.

A few minutes later, Logan, the other man involved, entered. Looking about, he spied Johnson with the witnesses.

"Good Lord, Johnson, are these your witnesses?"

"They certainly are."

"Well, in that case, I give up. You win! I've used these witnesses twice myself."

2502—It is extraordinary to watch the occasional results of the fact that the prisoner before the bar is concerned only and strictly with the question of his guilt on the count charged and none other.

A peculiarly brazen piece of testimony was once given by a defendant under the charge of Samuel Leibowitz. The issue at stake was the question of a frame-up. The great criminal lawyer was frank in his examination of the witness as to his general character.

He questioned him thus:

Q. What is your occupation?
A. Professional pickpocket
Q. How long have you been a professional pickpocket?
A. Twenty-four years.
Q. If acquitted in this case, what will your occupation be in the future?
A. Professional pickpocket.

He was acquitted.

2503—This same character was one of Leibowitz's first cash clients. When he had come to the lawyer he had flashed a hundred dollar bill and handed it over as a retainer. He insisted that he had been framed.

"This guy says he felt my hand in his pocket. He's a liar. I've been a pickpocket for 24 years and no man ever felt my mitt in his kick."

When the client departed after this first interview, Leibowitz felt for the precious hundred dollar bill. No bill. He hunted through all his pockets, and was in the act of crawling under the desk when his client walked back in. "I told you it was a frame-up," said the man, "I want you to have your heart in this case. You can see for yourself the guy's a liar."

Wherewith he once again paid the hundred dollars.

2504—The Reverend Matthew Wilks, the celebrated London preacher, got caught in a shower in Billingsgate where there were a number of women dealing in fish; they were using the most profane and vulgar language.

"Don't you think," said Mr. Wilks with the greatest deliberation and solemnity, "I shall appear as a swift witness against you in the day of judgment?"

"I presume so," said one, "for the biggest rogue always turns State's evidence."

2505—In a Kansas court a witness, a tall awkward fellow, was called to testify. The counsel for the defense said to him, "Now, sir, stand up and tell your story like a preacher." "No sir!" roared the judge. "None of that; I want you to tell the truth!"

2506—Samuel Leibowitz once discredited a witness whose testimony had a critical bearing on the case at hand. The person in question was a lug of the dese, dem, and dose variety. On two occasions, in the course of a long testimony, the witness popped out with most unusual phrases, one of them, "I heard a weird, uncanny sound, a gasp, a cackle," and the other, "He was all a-flutter." Leibowitz insisted that nothing but the work of a coach or an animal trainer could have put such phrases in the witness's mouth. He was thus able to demonstrate perjury and the repeating of a prepared story.

SEE ALSO   RELATED SUBJECTS
Evidence 2522   Courts 2471–2473

Trials 2476–2485
Evidence 2521–2523

JURIES

2511—"It's a hundred dollars in your pocket," whispered the defendant's lawyer to the juror, "if you can bring about a verdict of manslaughter in the second degree." Such proved to be the verdict and the lawyer thanked the juror warmly as he paid him the money.

"Yes," said the juror, "it was tough work, but I got there after a while. All the rest wanted acquittal."

2512—The coroner's jury was pretty thoroughly baffled as to the cause of death in a certain case. Unable to come to any conclusion, they at last officially termed the case, "An act of God under very suspicious circumstances."

2513—The fifth day drew to its close with the twelfth juryman still unconvinced. The court was impatient.

"Well, gentlemen," said the court officer entering the jury room, "shall I, as usual, order twelve dinners?"

"Make it," said the foreman, "eleven dinners and one bale of hay."

2514—"Look here," said one of the jurymen, after they had retired, "if I understand aright, the plaintiff doesn't ask damages for blighted affections or anything of that sort, but only wants to get back what he's spent on presents, pleasure trips, and so forth."

"That is so," agreed the foreman.

"Well then, I vote we don't give him a penny," said the other hastily. "If all the fun he had with that girl didn't cover the amount he expended it must be his own fault. Gentlemen, I courted that girl once myself."

2515—John Scott Eldon, Lord Chancellor of England, was in court in York, one day when the Justice had spoken for over two hours and then observed, "there are only eleven jurymen in the box. Where is the twelfth?"

"Please you, my lord," said one of the jurors, "he had to go away on some business, but he has left his verdict with me."

2516—Annoyed by the long delay in settling what seemed to him to be a very plain case, the judge said, "I hereby discharge this jury."

One juryman, feeling that his personal integrity was at stake, exclaimed: "You can't do that."

"And why not?" asked the judge sternly.

"Because you didn't hire me," said the juror, pointing toward the defense lawyer. "I'm working for that man there."

2517—The community was shocked by a killing in its midst, doubly shocked because of the fact that the killer was one of the most popular and well-liked men in the town.

Realizing that the evidence against him was conclusive, the man entered his plea of guilty. No means of saving him from the electric chair could be seen.

But the jurors, all friends of his, determined to save him in spite of his plea of guilty. When, at the conclusion of the case, they were asked to give their verdict, it was "Not Guilty."

"Now how in the world," said the judge, "can you bring in such a verdict when the defendant pled guilty?"

"Well, your Honor," said the foreman of the jury, "the defendant is such a liar that we can't believe him, even under oath."

SEE ALSO   RELATED SUBJECTS
Trials 2483   Courts 2471–2473
Hanging 2567   Trials 2476–2485

EVIDENCE

2521—Justice John M. Harlan once explained the intricacies of evidence to a young man. "Usually in conflicting evidence one statement is far more probable than the other, so that we can decide easily which to believe. It is like the boy and the house-hunter. A house-hunter getting off the train at a suburban station, said to a lad, 'My boy, I'm looking for Mr. Smithson's new block of semi-detached cottages. How far are they from here?' 'About twenty minutes walk,' the boy replied. 'Twenty minutes!' exclaimed the house hunter, 'nonsense, the advertisement says five.' 'Well,' said the boy, 'you can believe me or you can believe the advertisement, but I ain't trying to make a sale.'"

2522—In a case tried by the famous criminal lawyer, Samuel Leibowitz, the determining evidence was that of an alleged eye-witness to the crime, one Brecht, who claimed to have been at the scene in the legitimate capacity of a seller of Eskimo Pies. Shortly after this testimony had been given, Leibowitz sent out and had brought in to him some 20 Eskimo Pies, which he blandly distributed to the judge, the jurymen, and others before the bar. The ice cream was eaten with appreciation and pleasure by all in the presence of the witness who, still on the stand, was unaware of the significance of what was going on. By his failure to identify the objects being eaten, their wrappers; and his inability to explain how the pies had been kept from melting when he was selling them, Leibowitz proved the perjury and fraudulent pretensions of the witness and won his case.

2523—In a certain murder case the alibi of the defendant was that he had been working in a fish-market at 114th St. and Lexington Avenue. The prosecutor compelled the witness to identify a large number of fish which were brought in in a basket. The witness was wrong on every identification.

Samuel Leibowitz, however, summing up for the defense, obtained an acquittal by the following ingenious device.

Said he, addressing the jurors, "I want you, Mr. Rabinowitz, and you, Mr. Epstein, and you, Mr. Goldfogel, and you, Mr. Ginsberg, to explain to your fellow jurymen the fraud which has been perpetrated on my client. You see through it; they do not. Was there in all that array of fish a single pike, or pickerel, or any other fish that can be made into gefülte fish? There was not. My client told you that he worked in a store at 114th St. and Lexington Avenue. The prosecutor knows that is a Jewish neighborhood, and he did not show a single fish that makes gefülte fish. What a travesty on justice! My client is an Italian who works in a Jewish fish-market, and they try him on Christian fish!"

RELATED SUBJECTS
Courts 2471–2473
Trials 2476–2485
Witnesses 2501–2506

LAWYERS

2526—A lawyer from Wyoming, with the picturesqueness of a cowboy and an even more picturesque method of speech, was arguing a case before the Supreme Court while Justice Holmes still was on the bench, and despite

a most impassioned appeal to the Court, full of the
language of the frontier, he lost. As he concluded,
Holmes, who sat on the right of Hughes, leaned over
and in one of his loud, hoarse whispers said:
"Can't we hear that old bird again?"
The clerk of the Court heard the remark and afterward
advised the cowboy that, if he applied for a rehearing, it
might be granted. This was done. In the rehearing, the
lawyer opened his appeal to the Court with these words.
"I come to you as John the Baptist saying: 'Repent ye,
repent ye.'"
Whereupon Justice McReynolds, who was enjoying the
performance almost as much as Justice Holmes, leaned
forward and said: "But are you not aware of what
happened to John the Baptist?"
"Yes, I am quite aware," was the immediate response.
"He lost his head through the influence of a harlot. But
I know the Supreme Court would not be so influenced."

2527—A man came to Newark, N. J. one day and asked a landlord
to direct him to a first-rate lawyer.
"Well," said the landlord, "if, you have a good cause, go to
Frelinghuysen; he is an honest lawyer and never under-
takes any other kind: but if you want a keen, sharp
lawyer, who sticks at nothing, go to lawyer So-and-so."
He watched the stranger and he went straight to So-and-so.

2528—A Dublin attorney died in poverty and many barristers of
the city subscribed to a fund for his funeral. Toler, later
Lord Chief Justice of Orbury, was approached for a
shilling. "Only a shilling?" said Toler. "Only a shilling
to bury an attorney? Here's a guinea; go and bury 20 of
them."

2529—A blacksmith failed in business and a friend, to enable him
to start once more, loaned him some iron which a
creditor attached at the forge. The friend sued in trover
for his iron. Rufus Choate, the well-known lawyer, appeared for him and pictured the cruelty of the sheriff's
proceeding as follows: "He arrested the arm of industry
as it fell towards the anvil; he put out the breath of his
bellows. Like pirates in a gale at sea, his enemies swept
everything by the board, leaving him, gentlemen of the
jury, not so much as a horseshoe to nail upon his door
post to keep the witches off."
The tears came into the blacksmith's eyes at this affecting

description. One of his friends, noticing them, said to him, "Why, Tom, what's the matter with you? What are you crying about?"

"I had no idea I had been so much abused," said the blacksmith, weeping bitterly.

2530—A certain lawyer had his portrait done in his favorite attitude, standing with one hand in his pocket. His friends thought it was an excellent picture of him. An old farmer remarked that the portrait would have looked much more like the lawyer if it had represented him with his hand in another man's pocket instead of his own.

2531—A lawyer and physician having a dispute about precedence, referred it to Diogenes, who gave it in favor of the lawyer in these terms: "Let the thief go before and the executioner follow."

2532—A lawyer, when pleading the cause of an infant, took the child in his arms and presented it to the jury suffused with tears. This had a great effect, but the opposing counsel asked the child what made him cry. "He pinched me," said the little innocent.

2533—Joseph Choate was one of the most accomplished lawyers who ever practiced in this country. At one time in the New York courts, his opponent was a Westchester County attorney, representing a client from White Plains. Having a weak case, the latter fell back in his plea to the jury upon the effort to belittle the opposing attorney, and cautioned the jury not to be hoodwinked by Choate's "Chesterfieldian urbanity."

Choate, in due time, acknowledged this by briefly admonishing the jury not to be too greatly influenced by "my opponent's Westchesterfieldian suburbanity."

2534—When Samuel Leibowitz graduated from Cornell Law School he consulted the Dean as to whether or not he should become a criminal lawyer.

"Not that, Sam. Anything but that," said the Dean.

2535—A stranger, arriving in a small New England town, approached the first native he saw and asked:

"Have you a criminal lawyer in this town?"

"Well," replied the native cautiously, "we think we have, but so far we can't prove it on him."

2536—When Lincoln was practicing law, with his partner, Mr. Herndon, in Springfield, Ill., he was approached by a

would-be client who wished to press a claim which involved several hundred dollars.

Before taking the case Lincoln investigated and found that
if his client won it would ruin a widow and her six
children.

He wrote the following letter refusing to take up the case:
"We shall not take your case, though we can doubtless
gain it for you. Some things that are right legally are
not right morally. But we will give you some advice for
which we will charge nothing. We advise a sprightly,
energetic man like you to try your hand at making six
hundred dollars in some other way."

2537—Justice Benjamin Cardozo did not like Washington and
frequently lamented, during the sessions of the Supreme
Court, that he could not return to New York.

At a dinner party where he had been expressing this
sentiment the discussion later turned to fur coats. "I
won a fur coat case in New York once," said Cardozo.
"My client was so overjoyed when we won that she
threw her arms around my neck and kissed me."

Seth Richardson, Assistant Attorney General, retorted,
"Well, Mr. Justice, in view of the type of practice you
had, I don't wonder you want to return to New York."

SEE ALSO
Honesty 294
Long-Windedness
353, 354, 356
Memory 371
Shrewdness 528
Tolerance 601
Erudition 1074
Doctors 1676
Office Seekers 1970
Courts 2472
Judges 2493
Evidence 2523

RELATED SUBJECTS
Speeches 756–782
Courts 2471–2473
Trials 2476–2485
Witnesses 2501–2506
Juries 2511–2517
Evidence 2521–2523
Lawyers' Fees 2541–2545
Criminals 2571
Laws 2596–2599

LAWYERS' FEES

2541—"How can I ever show my appreciation?" gushed a woman
to Clarence Darrow, after he had solved her legal
troubles.

"My dear woman," replied Darrow, "ever since the
Phoenicians invented money there has been only one
answer to that question."

2542—Lincoln was a poor money-maker. Daniel Webster, who sent him a case, was amazed at the smallness of his bill, and his fellow-lawyers looked upon his charges as very low. This was his only fault in their eyes. Once, when another lawyer collected $250 for their joint services he refused to accept his share until the fee had been reduced to what he considered fair proportions and the over-charge had been returned to the client. When the presiding judge of the circuit heard of this, he indignantly exclaimed, "Lincoln, your picayune charges will impoverish the bar."

2543—One of the best trust stories I know had the late John G. Johnson, Philadelphia corporation lawyer, for its hero. Johnson was retained, among others, by E. H. Harriman, one of those "malefactors of great wealth" whom T. R. was fond of berating. There came a time when Johnson's counsel was urgently required in connection with one of the Napoleonic railroad mergers which Harriman specialized in sponsoring. So a cable of prodigious length was dispatched to Johnson, narrating in minutest detail exactly what the project was. The point on which the railroad magnate and his associates needed guidance was whether the merger could be accomplished without subjecting its authors to Federal prosecution under the Sherman Anti-Trust Act. Harriman requested Johnson to spare no words or expense in cabling his opinion, as the deal depended on it. An answer came within twenty-four hours. It was four words long. It read "Merger possible; conviction certain." Someone told me that Johnson rendered Harriman a bill of $100,000 for that opinion—$25,000 a word.

2544—It was a common thing for Lincoln to discourage unnecessary lawsuits, and consequently he was continually sacrificing opportunities to make money. One man who asked him to bring suit for $2.50 against a debtor would not be put off in his passion for revenge. His counsel therefore gravely demanded ten dollars as a retainer. Half of this he gave to the poor defendant, who therefore confessed judgment and paid the $2.50. Thus the suit was ended to the entire satisfaction of the angry creditor.

2545—A young Jewish lawyer asked the eminent Joseph Choate if he thought $500 would be too large a fee in his first important case.

"You should make it $5,000, young man," said Choate, "in view of the great amount of effort and the importance of the issues involved."

"Almost thou persuadeth me to be a Christian!" the young Hebrew exclaimed.

SEE ALSO   RELATED SUBJECTS
Quick Thinking 486   Lawyers 2526–2537

LAW ENFORCEMENT

2546—The story is told of Bill MacDonald, an early Captain of the Texas Rangers. He received a request that a company of Rangers come to a nearby town to suppress a riot. He showed up himself, unaccompanied. The citizens' committee were disappointed and said, "We wanted a company, not one Ranger."

"Well, you ain't got but one mob, have you?"

2547—Robert Burns had a collie named Thurlow. When he was a Revenue officer he used to encourage Thurlow, who was well known throughout the countryside, to run a quarter of a mile or so ahead of him, that the moonshiners might be warned of his approach.

2548—During Prohibition a malicious person directed the Revenue officers to a man in whose cellar, they said, would be found a large cache of liquor. Swooping down upon the residence, they found nothing except the slightly incriminating presence of a hundred or more empty whiskey bottles.

"How did these get here?" they demanded of the owner.

"I certainly don't know," replied the man innocently, "I never bought an empty whiskey bottle in my life."

SEE ALSO   RELATED SUBJECTS
Shrewdness 535   Prohibitions and Restrictions
Vanity 625   1641–1642
Credit 2167   Courts 2471–2473
                        Police 2551–2552
                        Detectives 2556–2557
                        Jail 2561–2563
                        Hanging 2566–2568
                        Criminals 2571
                        Laws 2596–2599
                        Justice 2601

POLICE

2551—A policeman's life is sometimes a happy one. This is indicated by the floor-walker who threw up his job and entered the police force. When asked why, he said, "Well, the pay and the hours are all right, but the best thing is that the customer is always wrong."

2552—In New York City recently a Police car cruising along the street received the following radio call.

"Calling Car 13. Car 13. Go to Third Avenue and 14th Street. Nude woman running down the street. That is all."

There was a pause. Then came the afterthought. "All other cars stay on your beats. That is all."

SEE ALSO	RELATED SUBJECTS
Prejudice 447	Law Enforcement 2546–2548
Shrewdness 537	Detectives 2556–2557
	Jail 2561–2563
	Criminals 2571

DETECTIVES

2556—The French are lovers of ratiocination. Accordingly there are to be found in that nation, many admirers of the works of Conan Doyle. Sir Arthur had once taxied from the station to his hotel in Paris, and as he left the cab the driver said, "Merci, Monsieur Conan Doyle."

"How did you know who I am?" asked Doyle curiously.

The taximan explained, "There was a notice in the paper that you were arriving in Paris from the South of France. I knew from your general appearance that you were an Englishman. It is evident that your hair was last cut by a barber of the South of France. By these indications I knew you." "This is extraordinary. You had no other evidence to go upon?" asked Doyle. "Nothing except," said the driver, "the fact that your name is on your luggage."

2557—Edith Bolling Wilson tells the following story: "Writing the words 'Secret Service' recalls the funny idea of my colored Susan when the President (Woodrow Wilson) used to come to see me before we were married. She always announced with ceremony: 'The President and his Silver Service.' But when I told her it was not 'Silver' Service but 'Secret' Service, she amended it to

'The President and his Secretive Servants,' and beyond that she refused to budge!"

RELATED SUBJECTS
Police 2551–2552
Criminals 2571

JAIL

2561—In the first days of his governorship of the State of New York, Al Smith spoke to the assembled inmates of Sing Sing. Not until he had already risen to his feet did he realize that he did not know how to address this particular audience. "My fellow citizens," he said, almost without thinking, but then stopped, remembering that the citizenship of those there imprisoned was forfeited. Embarrassed he said, "My fellow convicts," and that too did not seem to be the mot juste. Giving the thing up as hopeless he launched once and for all into the sentence, "Well, in any case, I'm glad to see so many of you here."

2562—In an English act of Parliament there was a law passed for rebuilding Chelmsford jail. By one part of the law the new jail was to be built from the material of the old one; by another part of the law, the prisoners were to be kept in the old jail until the new jail was finished.

2563—John Bunyan, while in Bedford jail, was called upon by a Quaker desirous of making a convert of him.
"Friend John," said he, "I come to thee with a message from the Lord; and after having searched for thee in all the prisons in England, I am glad I have found thee at last."
"If the Lord has sent you," answered Bunyan, "you need not have had so much pains to find me out, for the Lord knows I have been here for twelve years."

SEE ALSO   RELATED SUBJECTS
Drinking 53   Courts 2471–2473
Honesty 293   Law Enforcement 2546–2548
Speeches 771   Police 2551–2552
Authors 1215   Criminals 2571
Woman's Suffrage 2051 Stealing 2581–2590
Insurance 2138
Criminals 2571
Stealing 2590

HANGING

2566—"It is very hard, my lord," said a convicted felon at the bar to Judge Barnet, "to hang a poor man for stealing a horse."

"You are not to be hanged, sir," answered the judge, "for stealing a horse; but you are to be hanged that horses may not be stolen."

2567—Allen, the Quaker, waited upon the Duke of Sussex to remind him of his promise to present a petition to abolish capital punishment. The Duke did not seem to like the job, and observed that Scripture has declared,

"Whoso sheddeth man's blood, by man shall his blood be shed."

"But please note," replied the Quaker, "that when Cain killed Abel he was not hung for it."

"That's true," rejoined the Duke, "but remember, Allen, there were not twelve men in the world then to make a jury."

2568—When Lord Bacon was Chancellor of England, a witty criminal was brought before him. "Your Honor should let me go," he observed. "We're kin. My name is Hogg, and Hogg is kin to bacon."

"Not until it's hung," said Bacon.

SEE ALSO	RELATED SUBJECTS
Lateness 324	Death 1746–1749
Courtship 855	Courts 2471–2473
Family 950	Law Enforcement 2546–2548
Bishops 1492	Criminals 2571
Trials 2484	Murder 2576
	Justice 2601

CRIMINALS

2571—A young criminal in Samuel Leibowitz's charge entered a plea of guilty. When the judge, on the set day, some days later, pronounced sentence dispatching the prisoner to Elmira, the latter spoke up unexpectedly, saying, "I don't see why I should go to jail, I am innocent."

"How about it?" demanded the judge.

Leibowitz replied, "He's guilty all right, your Honor, but since he entered his plea of guilty, he has been in the Raymond Street jail and the boys there have given him a post-graduate course in law. They tell him it is lovely at Sing Sing and terrible at Elmira. And now that you've sentenced him to Elmira, he wants to get out of it."

SEE ALSO
Conscience 146
Ingratitude 268
Honesty 293
Rough and Ready 721
Lawyers 2535
Hanging 2568

RELATED SUBJECTS
Courts 2471–2473
Trials 2476–2485
Lawyers 2526–2537
Law Enforcement 2546–2548
Police 2551–2552
Jail 2561–2563
Hanging 2566–2568
Murder 2576
Stealing 2581–2590
Stool Pigeons 2591–2592

MURDER

2576—In France the Comte de Charolais shot a tiler on the roof of a house for the pleasure of seeing him fall off. Louis XV pardoned him, saying, "Understand me well. I will likewise pardon any one who shoots you."

SEE ALSO
Kings 1981
Loans 2161
Juries 2517

RELATED SUBJECTS
Death 1746–1749
Trials 2476–2485
Hanging 2566–2568
Criminals 2571

STEALING

2581—Lord Chatham rebuked a dishonest Chancellor of the Exchequer by finishing a quotation the latter had commenced. The debate turned upon some grant of money for the encouragement of art, which was opposed by the Chancellor who finished his speech against Lord Chatham's motion by saying, "Why was not this ointment sold, and the money given to the poor?"
Chatham rose and said "Why did not the noble lord complete the quotation, the application being so striking? As he has shrunk from it, I will finish the verse for him:
"'This Judas said, not because he cared for the poor, but because he was a thief and carried the bag!'"

2582—Dr. Whipple, long Bishop of Minnesota, was about to hold religious services at an Indian village in one of the Western states, and before going to the place of meeting asked the chief, who was his host, whether it was safe for him to leave his effects in the lodge.

"There is no white man within a hundred miles of here," answered the chief.

2583—A man was once attending a formal dinner party. Finding himself next to a banker with whom he had very little acquaintanceship, he attempted to establish a friendly footing by remarking:

"I used to know Mr. Jones, who was with your firm. I understand he is a tried and trusted employee—"

The banker immediately assumed an air of cold unfriendliness.

"He was trusted, yes; and he will be tried, if we're fortunate enough to catch him."

2584—A certain celebrated New York night club proprietor is known for his laxness in the disciplining of his waiters on the point of honesty. It is in effect an extension of the tipping principle. Said he, on one occasion, "Most of the stealing they do is from the customers, so what do I care?"

2585—Balzac was once lying awake in bed when he saw a man enter his room cautiously and attempt to pick the lock of his writing desk. The rogue was not a little disconcerted at hearing a loud laugh from the occupant of the apartment whom he supposed asleep.

"Why do you laugh?" asked the thief.

"I am laughing, my good fellow," said Balzac, "to think what pains and risks you are taking in the hope of finding money by night in a desk where the lawful owner can never find any by day."

2586—President Lincoln had not forgotten some of the gossip once heard from Thad Stevens. Stevens and Simon Cameron had come into the Republican party from opposite sides. In conversation the Representative (Stevens) had relieved himself of some unkind expressions.

"You don't mean he'd (Cameron) steal!" exclaimed Lincoln, who had formed an accurate estimate of his aide's probity and knew that common theft was not one of his failings.

"He wouldn't steal a red-hot stove," retorted old Thad bitterly.

It was the sort of joke that helped make Lincoln's task bearable. He thought the Secretary of War should have a little fun, too, but the gentle Simon was not amused.

He raged, and in his rage sent off an impulsive demand
for a retraction. Unfortunately he found Stevens only
too ready to oblige.

"I said you would not steal a red-hot stove," the apology
ran. "I now take that back."

2587—The motto which was inserted under the arms of William,
Prince of Orange, on his accession to the English crown,
was, Non rapui sed recepi, ("I did not steal but I
received").

This being shown to Dean Swift, he said with a sarcastic
smile, "The receiver's as bad as the thief."

2588—Brahms' gold watch was stolen one day from his rooms
which he never locked. When the police came and urged
him to take the matter up officially, he simply said:
"Leave me in peace! The watch was probably carried
away by some poor devil who needs it more than I do."

2589—One of the most celebrated courts-martial during the Civil
War was that of Franklin W. Smith and his brother,
charged with defrauding the government. These men
bore a high character for integrity. At this time, however, courts-martial were seldom invoked for any other
purpose than to convict the accused, and the Smiths
shared the usual fate of persons whose cases were submitted to such arbitrament. They were kept in prison,
their papers seized, their business destroyed, and their
reputations ruined, all of which was followed by a
conviction.

The finding of the court was submitted to President
Lincoln who, after a careful investigation, disapproved
the judgment and wrote the following endorsement upon
the papers:

"Whereas, Franklin W. Smith had transactions with the
Navy Department to the amount of a million and quarter
of dollars; and

"Whereas, he had a chance to steal at least a quarter of a
million and was only charged with stealing twenty-two
hundred dollars and the question now is about his stealing one hundred, I don't believe he stole anything at
all.

"Therefore, the record and findings are disapproved, declared null and void and the defendants are fully discharged."

2590—Floyd Odlum, prominent authority on securities and exchange, once had a couple of Gainsboroughs and Watteaus stolen from him by a butler. The culprit ultimately landed in Sing Sing, and was there occupied in writing a novel. His former employer sent him pocket money and he, in turn, would forward to Odlum portions of his manuscript for his opinion.

"You write very well," Odlum once wrote to him, "but your style is a trifle stilted."

SEE ALSO	RELATED SUBJECTS
Long-Windedness 344	Honesty 286–294
Quick Thinking 487	Police 2551–2552
Clothing 716	Jail 2561–2563
Authors 1188, 1190, 1205	Criminals 2571
Buying and Selling 2066	
Chiseling 2128	
Debt 2172	
Wealth 2182	
Witnesses 2503	
Hanging 2566	

STOOL PIGEONS

2591—A disciple came to Mohammed and said:

"Master, my six brethren are all asleep, and I alone have remained awake to worship Allah."

Mohammed replied:

"And you too had better been asleep, if your worship of Allah consists of accusations against your brethren."

2592—One day M. Villemain, the Secretary of the French Academy, was declaiming in the library in a vigorous manner against Napoleon III. Leverrier, who was an ardent imperialist, chanced to overhear some of his remarks, and demanded:

"How dare you speak in this manner of the emperor in a public building?"

Villemain looked up carefully and replied:

"And who are you?"

"You know me, sir," said the astronomer.

"Your face may be familiar to me, but I don't exactly recall your name."

"Leverrier is my name."

"Oh, yes, Leverrier. Astronomer, I think. In his day I was intimately acquainted with Laplace; he was an astronomer too, and a gentleman."

"Sir," said Leverrier, "I despise wit, but if you continue speaking thus I warn you that I shall report your words to the proper authorities."

"Well," said Villemain, shrugging his shoulders, "every one has his way of making a living."

SEE ALSO   RELATED SUBJECTS
Honor 298   Cowardice 156–160
                      Honor 296–298
                      Witnesses 2501–2506
                      Evidence 2521–2523
                      Police 2551–2552
                      Criminals 2571

LAWS

2596—Lord John Russell said to David Hume, the philosopher: "What do you consider the object of legislation?"

"The greatest good to the greatest number."

"What do you consider the greatest number?"

"Number one," replied Hume.

2597—Mayor Frank Hague of Jersey City has been one of America's more notorious characters for many years. He is noted for his peculiar interpretations of the law, beginning with his insistent, "I am the law" policy. He pursues his legal interpretations into more specialized channels however. He has cut down Jersey City's murder statistics at the expense of manslaughter by rigidly classifying all inter-marital killings as manslaughter, "When a man kills his wife that's not murder, that's manslaughter," says Hague.

2598—Lincoln was once arguing a case against an opponent who tried to convince the jury that precedent is superior to law, and that custom makes things legal in all cases. Lincoln's reply was one of his many effective analogies in the form of a story. He told the jury that he would argue the case in the same way as his opponent, and began: "Old Squire Bagley came into my office one day and said: 'Lincoln, I want your advice as a lawyer. Has a man what's been elected justice of the peace a right to issue a marriage license?'

"I told him no. Whereupon the old squire threw himself back in his chair very indignantly and said, 'Lincoln, I thought you was a lawyer. Now Bob Thomas and me had a bet on this thing, and we agreed to let you decide, but if this is your opinion I don't want it, for I know a thunderin' sight better. I've been a squire eight years, and I've issued marriage licenses all that time.'

2599—A rather celebrated case tried by the Supreme Court involved a decision upholding the Virginia statute providing for the sterilization of imbeciles. The majority opinion was written by Justice Oliver Wendell Holmes and O.K.'d by all except Justice Pierce Butler, who was a Roman Catholic.

Speculating about this, Holmes is said to have remarked to a colleague, "He knows the law is the way I have written it. But he is afraid of the Church. I'll lay you a bet the Church beats the law."

Professor Powell of Harvard was in the habit of reading Holmes' opinions to his Law classes, " 'Three generations of imbeciles are enough,' " he would read, adding, "Mr. Justice Butler dissenting."

SEE ALSO	RELATED SUBJECTS
Behavior 1	Congress 1941–1948
Drinking 42	Courts 2471–2473
Endurance 216	Judges 2486–2497
Honesty 289	Lawyers 2526–2537
Vanity 625	Law Enforcement 2546–2548
Gossip 823	Justice 2601
United States 2031	Wills and Testaments 2606–2607
Chiseling 2132	
Courts 2471	
Trials 2482	
Judges 2492	
Jail 2562	

JUSTICE

2601—A French nobleman had been satirized by Voltaire and meeting the author soon after gave him a severe caning. Voltaire immediately complained to the Duke of Orleans and begged him to do him justice. "Sir," replied the duke, "you have had it done you already."

SEE ALSO	RELATED SUBJECTS
Murder 2576	Freedom 2036–2042
	Equality 2046
	Courts 2471–2473
	Laws 2596–2599

WILLS AND TESTAMENTS

2606—The merchant Guyot lived and died in the town of
Marseilles in France. He amassed a large fortune by the
most laborious industry and by habits of the severest
abstinence and privation. His neighbors considered him
a miser and thought he was hoarding up money from
mean and avaricious motives. The populace, whenever
he appeared, pursued him with hootings and execrations,
and the boys sometimes threw stones at him. At length
he died and in his will were found the following words:
"Having observed from my infancy that the poor of
Marseilles are badly supplied with water which they can
only purchase at a high price, I have cheerfully labored
the whole of my life to procure for them this great blessing, and I direct that the whole of my property be laid
out in building an aqueduct for their use."

2607—The will of Stephen Girard, endowing Girard College in
Philadelphia, prohibits clergymen from coming onto the
premises. Horace Greeley one day approached the
campus in his customary, somewhat clerical-looking
garb. The gatekeeper challenged him, calling out, "You
can't enter here."
"The hell I can't!" retorted Greeley.
"I beg your pardon, sir," replied the guard. "Pass right in."

SEE ALSO	RELATED SUBJECTS
Extravagance 232	Death 1746–1749
Playwrights 1380	Wealth 2181–2187
Bankruptcy 2196	Taxes 2191–2194
	Lawyers 2526–2537
	Laws 2596–2599

INDEX OF NAMES

Abernethy, Dr. John 362, 366, 1718, 1719, 1728
Adams, John Quincy 677, 1711
Adams, Maude 872
Adams, Walter 262
Addison, Joseph 124, 195
Ade, George 882, 1473, 2204
Adler, Jacob 1424
A. E. (George Russell) 38, 1189
Aeschylus 1388
Agassiz, Louis 1106
Ahasueros 406
Ahlwardt, Rector 447
Aldington, Richard 1096, 1099
Aldrich, Gene 2430
D'Alembert, Jean le Rond 1657
Alexander III 1977
Alexander the Great 1088
Alfred, King 1061
Alighieri, Dante 1090
Allen, Ethan 1609
Alvanley, Lord 801
Anacharis 866
Andersen, Hans Christian 882
Andrews, Roy Chapman 1661
Anglesea, Henry William 917
D'Annunzio, Gabriele 197, 626, 627
Antheil, George 1348
Antoinette, Marie 726, 737, 892
Apelles 1296
Archelaus 808, 809
Argyle, Duke of 721
Aristides 2491
Aristippus 236
Aristotle 191, 241
Armour, P. D. 276
Arne, Thomas Augustine 1766
Arnold, Benedict 2433, 2437
Ashburton, Lord 2482
Asquith, Margot 743
Astor, John Jacob 556
d'Auteroches, Comte de 2372

Bacon, Francis 1188
Bacon, Leonard 1454
Bacon, Lord 2568
Baillie, Matthew 1212
Baker, Judge Giles 2152

Balcarass, Lord 2433
Baldwin, Lady 2023
Baldwin, Stanley 763, 2007, 2023
Balfour, Lord Arthur J. 766, 797
Balzac, Honoré de 1265, 1301, 2585
Bamberger, Leon J. 341
Bannerman, Campbell 39, 766
Bannister, John 1410
Barnet, Judge 2566
Barnum, P. T. 539, 614, 2407
Barrie, James M. 18, 758, 1378, 1413, 1979
Barrymore, John 519, 831, 1401, 1414, 1425, 1431, 1436
Bates, Edward 1951
Beals, Carleton 2067
Beard, Charles A. 1670
Beatty, Admiral David 2389
Beaverbrook, Lord 836
Bede, The Venerable 1616
Beecher, Henry Ward 759, 1461, 1474, 1576, 1651, 2287
Beerbohm, Max 373, 669
Beethoven, Ludwig von 115, 389
Bell, Clive 684
Benchley, Robert 507, 884, 1217
Benjamin, Park 1461
Bennett, James Gordon 2232
Benton, Senator Thomas Hart 143, 497, 673
Berlioz, Hector 1323, 1775
Bernhardt, Sarah 207, 702
Beveridge, Senator 1668
Bible, Dana X. 1856
Bion 1608
Birkenhead, Earl of 2481
Bismarck, Prince Otto von 170, 404, 802
Blake, William 1207, 1765
Boileau (-Despreaux), Nicholas 1210
Bok, Edward W. 842
Bonaparte, Napoleon—See Napoleon
Bonaparte, Pauline 446, 607, 901, 916
Bonner, Edmund 2024
Booth, Edwin 843, 1647
Booth, Junius Brutus 704
Booth, William 572
Boothe, Clare 1379

Boswell, James 1191, 1222, 2218
Boufflers, Mme. de 111
Bourget, Paul 986
Bourrienne, Louis de 461
Boxall, William 551
Boyle, Robert 1119
Brahms, Johannes 247, 248, 316, 426,
    437, 857, 1306, 1313, 1314, 1318, 1319,
    1322, 1347, 2588
Brandeis, Justice Louis D. 672
Brasidas 152
Brevoort, James 1975
Brewster, Bishop 2307
Bridges, Robert 1244, 1384
Briggs, Dean 757
Bright, John 609
Brisbane, Arthur 1247
Brooks, Noah, 336
Brooks, Phillips 67, 1497, 1654
Broun, Heywood 136, 966, 1240
Broun, Heywood Hale 966
Brown, John 1652
Browne, Lewis 908
Browning, Elizabeth Barrett 359
Browning, Robert 372, 591
Bryan, William Jennings 786, 2022
Buckingham, Duke of 931, 1991
Buckland, Francis Trevelyan 306
Bull, Ole 1363
Bunyan, John 2563
Burke, Edmund 345, 489, 1996
Burne-Jones, Edward, Sir 2107
Burns, Bob 134
Burns, George 832
Burns, Robert 372, 2547
Burnside, Gen. Ambrose E. 2383
Burr, Aaron 854, 862, 988
Burton, Richard 1216
Busby, Richard 693, 1056
Bushman, Francis X. 529
Butler, Benjamin Franklin 2441
Butler, Nicholas Murray 790, 1168
Butler, Pierce 2599
Butler, Smedley D. 2426, 2466
Byrnes, Inspector 2130
Byron, Lord (George Noel Gordon)
    564, 606, 687, 703, 969, 1190, 1756,
    1892

Cadman, S. Parkes 1464
Caedmon 1616
Caesar, Julius 157, 2003
Cairns, John 377
Calamy, Edmund 2006

Calhern, Louis 909
Calhoun, John C. 497, 732
Caligula 1986
Cambon, Jules Martin 106
Cameron, Basil 1334
Cameron, Simon 2586
Campbell, Mrs. Patrick 1429
Cannon, "Uncle Joe" 1846
Cano, Alonzo 1773
Cantor, Eddie 1396
Caraway, Hattie 789
Cardozo, Benjamin 2537
Carey, Gen. Sam 761
Carleton, Henry Guy 711
Carlyle, Thomas 1098
Carnegie, Andrew 1561, 2057, 2269
Caroline, Princess 856
Carter, Mrs. Leslie 1429
Caruso, Enrico 21, 77, 1423
Casanova, Jacques 1170
Catherine the Great 818, 1366, 2042
Cato, Marcus Porcius 382, 928, 2161
Cavour, di Camillo Benso, Count 248
Cervantes, Miguel de 2354
Cézanne, Paul 1269
Chalmers, Thomas 999
Chamberlain, Joseph 334, 770, 1782
Chamberlain, Neville 334, 2002
Chapin, E. H. 1248
Chaplin, Charlie 1423
Chapman, Dr. 1729
Charles I 694, 948, 1935
Charles II 1056, 1550, 1981
Charles V 1989
Charolais, Comte de 2576
Chase, Ilka 909
Chase, Salmon P. 384, 636
Chatelet, Mme. du 1013
Chatham, Lord William Pitt 331, 2581
Chatterton, Thomas 2211
Chaucer, Geoffrey 1970
Chesterfield, Lord 663, 666, 1496, 1547,
    1778
Chesterton, G. K. 1898
Cheyne, George 1
Choate, Joseph 333, 423, 1343, 2533,
    2545
Choate, Rufus 2529
Christina, Queen 1095
Churchill, Lady Randolph 667
Churchill, Winston S. 211, 334, 503,
    767, 807, 1801, 2375, 2481
Cibber, Colley 796
Cicero, Marcus Tullius 671, 2161

Cimabue 436
Clark, Champ 471
Clay, Henry 71, 351, 420, 590, 2162
Clay, Mrs. Henry 71
Clemenceau, Georges 2076, 2320
Clement, Pope 1501
Clive, Robert 2041
Cnidus 1302
Cobden, Richard 2032
Cockburn, Lord 352
Cocteau, Jean 2340
Cody, William (Buffalo Bill) 223
Coffey, Titian G. 1951
Coghlan, Charles 902
Cohalan, Daniel F. 1897
Colbert, Jean Baptiste 2236
Coleridge, Samuel Taylor 712, 1093, 1223, 1555, 1631
Collard, Royer 424
Comfort, William Wistar 1041
Compton, Karl 1157
Comstock, Anthony 2355
Condorcet, Marie Jean de 1657
Conneau 1984
Conrad, Joseph 2193
Constant, Benjamin 1987
Cook, Captain James 1141
Coolidge, Calvin 132, 133, 212, 484, 589, 617, 765, 813, 816, 1167, 1936, 1938, 1939
Coolidge, Mrs. Calvin 1939
Cooper, Thomas 391
Cooper, Gary 1391
Cooper, Grey 349
Copeland, Charles Townsend 1031
Corneille, Pierre 1388
Cornwall, Barry 1203
Correggio 1261, 1282
Cornell, Katherine 1429
Corwin, Thomas 421
Cotlow, Lewis 879
Coutades, Mme. de 607
Coward, Noel 146
Cowl, Jane 1414
Craven, Lord 1173
Creighton, Bishop 65
Cremony, John 226
Cromwell, Oliver 1611, 1900, 2006
Cronzas, Mme. de 682
Cruikshank, George 1622
Cumberland. Duke of 490, 712
Cumberland, Richard 1383
Curran, John Philpot 664, 1482, 1767
Cuvier, Georges 1089

Darrow, Clarence 177, 2541
Darwin, Charles 1121
Davidson, Bishop 7
Davies, Scrope 606, 1756, 1771
da Vinci, Leonardo 390
Davis, Cushman K. 780
Davis, Jefferson 314, 1935
Davis, Judge 327, 2473, 2483, 2495
Davis, Richard Harding 196, 552, 669
Davy, Humphrey 1278
Dawes, Charles 474
Defoe, Daniel 1172
Degas, Hilaire 972, 1256, 1263, 1286, 1293
della Scala, Prince 1090
Demetrius 1705
Demosthenes 776
Depew, Chauncey 777, 1156, 1846, 2267, 2379
de Valera, Eamon 771
Dewey, Parson 1609
Dibdin, Tom 123
Dickens, Charles 1162, 1166
Dickey, T. Lyle 2031
Dickinson, Emily 1167
Diderot, Denis 358, 818
Diller, Roland 272
Dillingham, Charles 1776
Ding (J. J. Darling) 237
Diogenes 236, 456, 1001, 1085, 1088, 2531
Disraeli, Benjamin 485, 609, 622, 767, 1717, 1920, 1988, 1990, 1998, 2300
Dixon, Harold F. 2430
Doane, Bishop 1542
Dolby, George 1166
Dolgorouki, Vassili 1976
Dollabella, Fabia 671
Donatello 1271, 1276
Donne, John 1770
Dorrance, Ward 1218
Douglas, Stephen 441, 492, 695, 1712
Douglass, Frederick 452
Doyle, Alexander 1481
Doyle, Arthur Conan 2556
Dressler, Marie 685
Drew, John 373
Dreyfus, Max 1311
Drummond, Henry 878
Dryden, John 1183, 1206
Duchâtel, Comte 271
Duke, James 566
Dumas, Alexandre (père) 505, 947, 1677

Dumas, Alexandre (fils) 273
Duncan, Isadora 197, 951, 1371
Dunne, Finley Peter 1371
Du Pont, Pierre S. 132
Durocher, Leo 643
Duse, Eleanora 958
Dvorak, Anton 316

Eddy, Mary Baker 1538, 1617
Edison, Thomas A. 62, 706, 744, 1127, 1128, 1129, 1130, 1131, 1136, 1138, 1149, 1527, 1601, 2079, 2183, 2261
Edward VII 506
Einstein, Albert 1148, 1150, 1151, 1152, 1153
Eldon, John Scott 769, 2515
Eliot, Charles W. 1017
Eliot, T. S. 1099
Elizabeth, Queen 288, 676, 1188, 2000
Ellenborough, Lord 2493
Elman, Mischa 1359, 1360, 1361
Emerson, Edward 1081
Emerson, Ralph Waldo 1081, 1094
Engel, Jerome D. 1470, 1472, 1535, 1537, 1577
Epstein, Jacob 1148
Erskine, John 1029, 1196
Erskine, Lord 2484
Escoffier, A. 23
Esther 406
Eugénie, Empress 1984
Euripides 1209, 1388
Evarts, William Maxwell 37, 768
Eyre, Edward John 1896

Fabry, Colonel 2417
Faraday, Michael 1127
Farinelli, Carlo 368
Faxe, Simon 1770
Fellows, Dexter 2104
Fellows, Col. John R. 2299
Fénelon, François 557
Field, Eugene 11, 17, 1104, 1245, 2302
Field, Marshall 540
Fields, James T. 8
Fields, W. C. 43, 1446
Fischer, Louis 2331
Fish, Mrs. Stuyvesant 1239
Fitch, Clyde 506
Foch, Ferdinand 156, 416, 937, 2317, 2396
Foote, Samuel 490, 850, 927, 1367, 1430
Fontanne, Lynn 1408, 1420

Fontenelle, Bernard 662, 1781
Ford, Henry 2266
Fosdick, Harry Emerson 1477
Fouché, Joseph 168
Fournier, Pierre 2372
Fox, Charles 501, 753, 1072, 2173
France, Anatole 1185, 1297
Francis I 534, 2024
Franck, César 1326, 1339
Franklin, Benjamin 111, 231, 1610, 2163, 2179
Franklin, Sidney 1831
Frederick the Great 244, 1013, 1486
Frederick William I 293
Frederick William IV 348
Freedman, David 529
Fréron, Louis Marie 901
Fry, General 324
Fuchs, Robert 316, 1318
Fuller, Margaret 444
Fuller, Justice Melville 1455, 2471
Fulton, Robert 411, 1126

Gabin, Jean 2316
Gable, Clark 1409
Gabrielli, Caterina 1366
Galilei, Galileo 1628
Gann, Dollie 376
Gannett, Frank 2007
Garfield, James A. 1020
Garland, Hamlin 20
Garrick, David 1549, 1999
Garrison, William Lloyd 764, 781
Garth, Samuel 1666, 1757
Gay, John 200
Gehrig, Lou 1821
Genlis, Mme. de 380, 863
George III 769, 1837
George IV 856
George V 498, 1971, 1973, 1985, 2408
George, Lloyd 788, 1142, 2052
Gershwin, George 206, 616, 619, 1154, 1311, 1312, 1321, 1325
Gibbon, Edward 357, 682
Gibbons, Cardinal 114
Gigli, Beniamino 1346
Gilbert, W. S. 1204
Giles, William 502
Gilmore, Patrick 114
Girard, Stephen 2607
Gladstone, William E. 402, 485, 1584, 1990
Gladstone, Mrs. William E. 1584
Glass, Carter 496

Gluck, Willibald 1313
Godwin, Mary 904
Godwin, William 564
Goering, Hermann 520
Goethe, Johann W. 1504
Goldsmith, Oliver 1171, 1199, 1200
Goldwyn, Samuel 665, 1177, 1376, 1391, 1393, 1395, 1396
Goodwin, Nat 199, 711
Goosens, Eugene 1337
Gorky, Maxim 1786, 2298
Gosse, Edmund 538, 591
Gounod, Charles 1323
Grammont, Comte de 1305
Grant, Cary 896
Grant, Ulysses S. 314, 571, 1304, 1583, 2386, 2397, 2406, 2416
Gray, Thomas 208
Grenfell, Robert 2375
Greeley, Horace 427, 731, 2607
Greeley, Mrs. Horace 444
Grimaldi, Joseph 366
Guest, Edgar A. 1211
Gunther, John 2351
Gustavus III 1116
Guyot 2606

Hacker, Maria 852
Haggard, Rider 996
Hague, Frank 2597
Hale, Edward Everett 1941
Hall, Radcliffe 1393
Hall, Robert 516
Halleck, Gen. Henry 2387
Haller, Albrecht von 1170
Hallstead, William F. 2078
Hambourg, Mark 1345
Hancock, John 399
Handel, Georg Friedrich 1336
Hanna, Mark 472
Harcourt, William Vernon 807
Hardrada, Harold 2390
Hardy, Thomas 1219
Harlan, Justice John M. 1762, 2521
Harmodius 546
Harriman, E. H. 232, 2235, 2543
Harris, Frank 1185, 1205, 1215
Hart, Moss 1386
Harte, Bret 117
Hartley, David 345
Harvey, Peter 1934
Hastings, Warren 1072, 1222, 2041
Hatch, O. M. 2404
Hawthorne, Nathaniel 1180

Hay, Lord 2372
Hayes, Helen 1407
Hazlitt, William 126
Healey, Father 628
Hearn, Lafcadio 242
Hearst, William Randolph 1428
Heifetz, Jascha 1359, 1360, 1362
Heine, Heinrich 1775
Heine, Peter 2421
Heinze, Fritz Augustus 2081
Helvetius 2353
Henderson, John 598
Henderson, Leon 2356
Hendrick, King 2082
Henri III 2380
Henry IV 625
Henry VIII 910, 2024
Henry, Patrick 502
Hepburn, Katherine 1431
Hereford, Bishop of 301
Herford, Oliver 97, 187, 524, 847
Herndon, William H. 2536
Herodotus 1748
Heyward, Du Bose 1211
Hill, Edwin C. 851
Hill, Rowland 1548
Hirschmann, Ira 2231
Hitchcock, Alfred 14
Hitchcock, Tommy 1841
Hitler, Adolf 520, 2001, 2002, 2337, 2344
Hobhouse, L. T. 703
Hobson, Richard Pearson 2420
Hofmann, Josef 1360
Hogarth, William 435, 1283, 2207
Hogg, Governor 243
Holland, Lord 1768
Holmes, Dr. Oliver Wendell 745, 1672
Holmes, Justice Oliver Wendell 672, 2526, 2599
Homer 110
Hood, Thomas 12
Hook, Theodore 2194
Hooker, Gen. Joseph 2387, 2391
Hopper, De Wolf 480, 1385
Horton, Edward Everett 312
Houdini, Harry 1776
House, Col. Edward 1943
Houston, Sam 1912
Howe, Julia Ward 112
Howells, William Dean 477, 1190, 2279
Howells, Mrs. William Dean 2279
Hoyt, Julia 909
Huddleston, Sisley 684

Hughes, Charles Evans 376, 2496
Hugo, Victor 424, 1297, 2336
Hull, Cordell 91
Hume, David 203, 1652, 2596
Hutton, Barbara 896
Huxley, Aldous 1099
Huxley, Julian 1452
Huxley, Thomas Henry 90

Ibn Ezra, Abraham 2198
Ibsen, Hendrik 1103
Ingersoll, Robert 1226, 1651, 1654
Iphicrates 546
Irving, Henry 419, 791
Iscariot, Judas 2581

Jackson, Andrew 774, 2326
Jackson, Gen. "Stonewall" 2409, 2422
Jacob, Max 2206
Jacoby, Oswald 1838
Jaffe, Sam 1403
James I 1983
James, Henry 611, 1169
James, William 1006
James,Mrs. William 1006
Janin, Jules 782, 1418
Jay, John 1592
Jebb, Richard 22
Jeffers, William 2270
Jefferson, Thomas 1942
Jeffries, Judge 2489, 2490
Jerrold, Douglas 123, 189, 190, 266,
   405, 653, 752, 1098, 1176, 1202, 1387,
   1622, 2086
Jessel, George 832
Joachim, Joseph 247, 1347
Joffre, Marshal 2376
John the Baptist 2526
Johnson, Congressman 471
Johnson, Hiram 346
Johnson, General Hugh 2111
Johnson, Jack 448, 1886
Johnson, John G. 2543
Johnson, Samuel 36, 141, 166, 188, 194,
   379, 386, 489, 523, 811, 855, 881, 921,
   1105, 1171, 1182, 1191, 1199, 1200,
   1222, 1224, 1303, 1353, 1430, 2046,
   2129, 2186, 2218
Johnson, Sir William 2082
Jones, Edgar De Witt 1469
Jonson, Ben 1173, 1184, 1203
Jowett, Benjamin 1021, 1656
Joyce, James 1099

Jumel, Mme. 854, 862
Junot, Marshal 901

Kahn, Otto 528
Kalbeck, Max 437
Kaufman, George S. 1386
Keats, John 466
Keller, Frances 610
Kelvin, William T. 1120
Kemble, John 1412, 1415
Kemble, Roger 1427
Kendrick, Archbishop 1494
Kennedy, Joseph 2023
Kent, Rockwell 1292
Khayyam, Omar 110
Killigrew, (Jester) 483
Kingsley, Charles 1268
Kipling, Rudyard 434, 842
Klein, S. 2105
Klemmer, Harvey 2337, 2338, 2342
Klopstock, Friedrich 1195
Knox, Frank 182
Knudsen, William S. 2268
Koo, Wellington 756
Kreisler, Fritz 1341, 1358

Laboulaye, Edouard 1942
Lackaye, Wilton 360
Lafayette, Marquis de 255, 1975
Lamb, Lady Caroline 597
Lamb, Charles 12, 122, 253, 321, 564,
   712, 956, 1111, 1186, 1203, 1555
Lamon, Ward 1948
Landis, Frederick 762
Landor, Walter Savage 202
Lang, Andrew 1008
Lansdowne, Lord 880
Laplace, Pierre de 2592
La Rochefoucauld-Liancourt, Duc de
   2061
Laski, Harold 2041
Latimer, Hugh 153
Laud, Archbishop 694
Lauder, Harry 565
Lauderdale, Lord 1550
Lawrence, D. H. 1099
Lawson, Sir Wilfred 42
Leacock, Stephen 26, 1671
Lebreton, Mme. 1984
Leclerc, General 916
Lee, Robert E. 2373, 2387, 2397
Liebowitz, Samuel 268, 2502, 2503,
   2506, 2522, 2523, 2534, 2571
Leotychidas 1635

Leslie, Constance 1277
Lessing, Gotthold Ephraim 82
Levant, Oscar 616, 619, 624, 1325
Leverrier, Urbain 2592
Lewis, Sinclair 836
Levi, Hermann 1313
Lillie, Beatrice 73, 513, 515
Lincoln, Abraham 96, 160, 161, 176,
    186, 245, 272, 274, 294, 314, 315, 322,
    324, 326, 327, 336, 356, 381, 383, 384,
    452, 491, 492, 535, 541, 571, 596, 601,
    623, 636, 647, 651, 652, 654, 695, 696,
    723, 762, 779, 867, 923, 946, 1010,
    1156, 1284, 1511, 1596, 1606, 1627,
    1633, 1707, 1901, 1931, 1933, 1934,
    1935, 1937, 1939, 1948, 1951, 1952,
    1966, 1967, 1968, 1969, 2031, 2037,
    2151, 2187, 2201, 2208, 2286, 2327,
    2332, 2333, 2383, 2386, 2387, 2388,
    2391, 2392, 2393, 2403, 2404, 2407,
    2411, 2414, 2415, 2416, 2418, 2419,
    2441, 2442, 2461, 2473, 2483, 2495,
    2536, 2542, 2544, 2586, 2589, 2598
Lincoln, Thomas 176
Lindsey, Ben 40
Liszt, Franz 1342
Livingston, Edward 1919
Lodge, Henry Cabot 1944
London, Jack, 612, 1251
Long, Huey 346, 1899
Longfellow, Henry Wadsworth 837
Longworth, Alice Roosevelt 376, 816
Lorimer, George Horace 1252
Louis XI 482
Louis XIV 483, 1305, 1769, 2027
Louis XV 2576
Louis XVI 726, 737, 2374
Louis, Joe 775
Louis Napoleon, Prince 968, 1076,
    1659, 1978, 1984
Louis Philippe 1975
Lucas, Lord 1416
Lully, Jean-Baptiste 1305
Lunt, Alfred 1408, 1420
Luther, Martin 1466
Lyndhurst, Lord John 1896

MacArthur, Judge 2471
Macaulay, Catherine 2046
Macaulay, Thomas Babington 1918
MacDonald, Bill 2546
Macgregor, Rob Roy 1774
Machiavelli, Nicolo 2003
Mackenzie, Morell 1669

Maclaurin, Prof. Colin 1028
Macready, William 733
Malcolm, John 1222
Malinowski, Bronislaw 2319
Mankiewicz, Herman 1386
Mann, Thomas 388, 583
Manning, William T. 1498
Mansfield, Lord 2482, 2492
Marks, Laurie 2130
Marlborough, Duke of 2381
Marmontel, Jean 2377
Marquis, Don 1861
Marsh, Sir Edward 1801
Marshalov, Boris 1946
Marshall, John 502
Marston, Gilman 353
Martinelli, Giovanni 2102
Marx, Groucho 517, 686, 742, 2141
Marx, Harpo 1528
Mary, Queen 1971
Mascagni, Pietro 1315
Matisse, Henri 2205
Matthews, Brander 1102, 1168
Matthews, Montague 835
May, Samuel J. 764
Maynard, John 1074
McCarthy, Lillah 1189, 1416, 2323
McClellan, George B. 696, 2391, 2392,
    2393, 2404
McCulloch, Hugh 2151
McKenna, Justice Joseph 1864
McMaster, John Bach 1933
McReynolds, Justice James C. 2526
Meighan, Tom 853
Melba, Nellie 23
Melchior, Lauritz 852
Mendelssohn, Felix 1316
Menjou, Adolph 1406
Metaxas, Georges 88
Meyers, Daniel 676
Michelangelo 1101, 1501
Milan, Duchess of 910
Millais, John Everett 1277
Miller, Clyde 432
Millikan, Robert A. 1122
Millikan, Mrs. Robert A. 1122
Milton, John 705, 931
Mirabeau, Honoré de 287, 803
Mirabeau, Count de 2283
Mohammed 2591
Moiseivitch, Benno 1345
Mola, Emilio 1636
Moncey, Marshal 691
Montague, Matthew 835

Montefiore, Moses 450
Moody, Dwight L. 1515
Moore, George 1189
Moore, Thomas 597
Morgan, J. P. 84, 213, 475, 560
Morold, Abbé 973
Morris, Clara 1411
Morris, Lewis 1193
Morris, William 1301
Morrow, Anne 84
Morrow, Dwight 81, 87
Morrow, Mrs. Dwight 84
Morse, Samuel F. B. 1272
Moseley, Oswald 2004
Mozart, Wolfgang Amadeus 114, 1317, 1320
Mueller, Max 63
Munsey, Frank 1239, 2091
Munthe, Axel 1356
Mussolini, Benito 2003, 2005, 2008, 2010

Napier, Charles 2401
Napoleon 406, 461, 691, 916, 959, 1076, 1388, 1601, 1932, 1980, 1993, 2003, 2237, 2413
Napoleon III 968, 1978, 1984, 2592
Nasby, Petroleum V. 623
Nelson, Horatio 722
Nevinson, C. R. W. 684, 1345, 1701, 2205
Newcastle, Duchess of 256
Newcastle, Duke of 1084
Newton, Sir Isaac 15
Nicholas II 1977, 1982
Nietzsche, Friedrich 1320
Norris, George W. 291, 1907
North, Lord Frederick 331, 349
Nottebohm, Gustav 437
Nye, Bill 54, 224

O'Connell, Morgan 801
Odlum, Floyd 724, 2590
O'Keefe, Georgia 205, 1273, 1280
O'Leary, Father 1482
Omar, Caliph 1629
Onslow, George 1996
Orlando, Vittorio 2016
Orleans, Duke of 2601
Orozco, Clemente 1270
Orpen, Sir William 1266
Otway, Thomas 1183

Pace (Jester) 288
Paderewski, Ignace Jan 115, 389, 478, 1344, 1351, 1354, 1357

Paganini, Nicolò 1352
Palmer, Robert 1410
Park, Mungo 169
Parker, Dorothy 514, 741, 746, 806, 1217, 1421
Parker, Francis Wayland 1046
Parker, Quanah 943
Parson, Professor 1030
Pascal, Blaise 1147
Pascal, Gabriel 1392
Pastula, Anthony 2430
Paten, Parson 1593
Paul, Maury H. B. 822, 824, 825, 826, 1239
Peck, E. S. 716
Peech, Dr. 2166
Penn, William 51
Pershing, Gen. John J. 136, 407, 1696
Peter the Great 1976
Phelps, William Lyon 772, 1026
Philip I 368
Phillips, Wendell 449, 1242
Picasso, Pablo 1264, 1274, 2206, 2340
Pinchot, Mrs. Amos 941
Pinkham, Lydia E. 1538
Piron 1100, 1175
Pitt, William 181, 675, 2318
Plato 387, 456, 1094
Poe, Edgar Allan 2202
Pope, Alexander 200, 246, 488
Porter, Mrs. Elizabeth 855
Potter, Henry C. 886
Powell, Professor 2599
Proust, Marcel 1099, 1764
Putnam, Israel 2121

Rabelais, François 531
Rachel, Elizabeth 271, 273, 275, 1418, 1439
Raleigh, Sir Walter 251
Rand, James H. 2091
Randolph, John 13, 420, 1919
Randolph, Lady 31
Raphael 1261, 1451
Récamier, Mme. 586
Reed, Thomas B. 333, 1945
Reichenbach, Harry 2355
Reicher, Frank 1291
Rembrandt 1705, 2344
Reynolds, Frederick 1212
Reynolds, James B. 2026
Reynolds, Joshua 668
Reynolds, Quentin 211
Rhodes, Cecil 10

Richardson, Samuel 1187
Richardson, Seth 2537
Richelieu, Cardinal Armand 298, 557
Richmond, Leigh 2219
Ridley, Nicholas 153
Ritz, César 23
Robertson, William 489
Robespierre, Maximilian 287
Rockefeller, John D. 992, 1526
Rodin, Auguste 1297
Rogers, Samuel 518, 751, 814, 880
Rogers, Will 16, 498, 949, 1428
Roosevelt, Eleanor 1237, 1940
Roosevelt, Franklin D. 109, 211, 355, 1531, 2021, 2191
Roosevelt, Theodore 107, 252, 447, 615, 620, 621, 943, 1065, 1911
Roosevelt, Col. Theodore 1802
Root, Elihu 2026
Rose, Billy 1394
Rosenwald, Julius 2184
Rossetti, Dante Gabriel 1288
Rossetti, W. M. 538
Rothenstein, William 1152
Rothschild, Baron 2182
Rouen, Countess de 1763
Rousseau, Jean Baptiste 1179
Rousseau, Jean Jacques 203, 1224
Rubinoff, David 1362
Rubinstein, Anton 1355
Russell, Dora 1036
Russell, Lord John 936, 2596
Rutledge, Archibald 313
Ryan, Patrick J. 374, 877, 1494
Ryan, John D. 2081

Sage, Russell 558, 2176
St. John, Lord 2276
Sales, St. Francis de 602
Salisbury, Bishop of 1493
Salisbury, Lord 1492
Sarasate, y Nevascues 1356
Sargent, Malcolm 1333
Savage, Minot J. 871
Saxe, John Godfrey 1795
Saxe, Marshal 2377
Scheele, Karl Wilhelm 1116
Schenck, Nicholas 853
Schildkraut, Mrs. Joseph 588
Schleiermacher, Friedrich 1108
Schoenberg, Arnold 1324
Schumann-Heink, Ernestine 21, 689
Schwab, Charles M. 499, 2269
Scott, Robert Falcon 1142

Scott, Walter 193, 564, 603, 1174
Scott, Winfield 2372
Secker, Archbishop 1593
Selden, John 1453
Selwyn, George 1768
Sévigné, Mme. de 361
Seward, William H. 441, 1935, 2037
Seymour, Jane 910
Shakespeare, William 582, 1184, 1186, 1204, 1416
Shaw, George Bernard 18, 31, 433, 674, 736, 951, 1103, 1178, 1189, 1198, 1376, 1384, 1392, 1441, 1891
Shay, Luke 2040
Shelley, Harriet 15, 989
Shelley, Mary Wollstonecraft 15
Shelley, Percy Bysshe 903, 904, 989, 1137, 1194, 1892, 1893, 2086
Shelley, Timothy 989
Sheridan, Richard Brinsley 357, 363, 481, 718, 1380, 1383, 1997, 2063, 2171, 2174
Sheridan, Thomas 1380, 1917
Sherman, William T. 2411
Shuter, Ned 457
Siddons, Sarah 668, 1422, 1427
Siebold, Agathe von 857
Sieyes, Abbé 1086
Simmons, J. Edward 2176
Sixtus V, Pope 1503
Skinner, Cornelia Otis 527
Skinner, Otis 527
Smith, Albert 1176
Smith, Alfred E. 2561
Smith, Franklin W. 2589
Smith, Logan Pearsall 1099
Smith, Robert 1676
Smith, Sydney 751, 778, 1468, 1565, 1676
Smithson, James 1721
Smollett, Tobias 286
Smoot, Reed 1240
Smyth, Alexander 351
Socrates 876, 887
Solon 866
Sophocles 1201, 1388
Southampton, Earl of 1181
Spenser, Edmund 1181
Spooner, John C. 787
Spurgeon, Charles 1541
Squire, Jack 1099
Staël, Mme. de 586, 664, 823, 841, 848, 959
Stamp, Sir Josiah 342, 970

Stangan, Temple 124
Stanislawski, Constantin 1401
Stanley, Henry M. 1601
Stanton, Edwin 596, 1952, 2415
Steel, John 2378
Steiglitz, Alfred 205, 1273
Stein, Gertrude 1274, 2340
Steinmetz, Charles 61
Stern, J. David 83
Sterne, Lawrence 1084
Sterne, Simon 2222
Steuer, Max 2487
Stevens, Alexander H. 692
Stevens, Thaddeus 347, 348, 1761, 1906, 2476
Stevenson, Robert Louis 171, 1208, 2306
Stokowski, Leopold 908, 1335
Strangford, Lord 597
Strauss, Isadore 173
Strauss, Mrs. Isadore 173
Streicher, Julius 303
Stromberg, Hunt 1391
Stuart, Gilbert 861
Suetonius 1986
Sullivan, Arthur 41
Sullivan, John L. 1887
Sumner, Charles 1583
Sunday, Billy 1516
Sussex, Duke of 2567
Sutton, Rev. Dr. 2166
Swift, Jonathan 9, 200, 246, 1456, 1551, 2587
Swinnerton, Frank 1099

Tacitus 1188
Taft, William Howard 681, 688, 690
Talleyrand, Périgord de 147, 158, 168, 192, 521, 586, 823, 841, 863, 922, 1086
Tamagno, Francesco 1368
Tarkington, Booth 1236
Tasso, Bernardo 1075
Tasso, Torquato 1075
Tate, Alfred O. 2261
Taylor, Deems 1348
Tennyson, Lord Alfred 63
Terborch, Gerard 551
Tessan, Lieut. de 2417
Thackeray, William Makepeace 8, 2216
Thalberg, Irving 1324
Themistocles 967
Thomason, F. L. 487
Thompson, Francis 204
Thoreau, Henry David 1595

Thurber, James 1447
Thurlow, Lord 1072, 1222
Tintoretto 1267
Titian 1267
Togo, Admiral Heihachiro 2022
Toiras, Marshal 159
Toler, Sydney 2528
Tolstoy, Count Leo 1262
Took, Horne 1837
Toscanini, Arturo 1331, 1338, 1339
Tree, Sir Herbert Beerbohm 532, 1377, 1402, 1417
Trelawney, Edward 687, 1194, 1893
Triboulet, (Jester) 534
Tumulty, Joseph P. 1897
Turenne, Marshal 2278
Turner, Joseph M. 436, 1268, 1290
Twain, Mark 19, 54, 66, 101, 121, 125, 221, 344, 419, 431, 477, 646, 725, 777, 807, 815, 942, 948, 950, 977, 986, 1011, 1073, 1109, 1110, 1213, 1221, 1279, 1542, 1585, 1747, 1848, 2101, 2203, 2249
Tyndall, John 1130

Ulysses 1146

Vanderbilt, Cornelius 2132, 2267
Vanderbilt, Mrs. Cornelius 824
Vanderbilt, Mrs. Graham Fair 822
Vanderbilt, W. K. 2267, 2277
Van Loon, Hendrik Willem 1022
Vasari, Giorgio 390
Vespasian 400
Victor Emanuel, King 1972, 2008
Victoria, Princess 1973
Victoria, Queen 536, 1351, 1988, 1990
Villars, Marshal 2027
Virchano, Rudolf 802
Vollard, Ambroise 1293
Voltaire (François Marie Arouet) 358, 476, 663, 666, 1013, 1170, 1179, 1657, 2164, 2353, 2601
von Sternberg, Joseph 1403
Vossius 1095
Vyazemsky 2042

Wade, Senator 1948
Wagner, Richard 1313, 1320
Walewska, Marie 406
Wallace, Edgar 1449
Wallace, Henry A. 2430
Wallace, William 551
Wallenstein, Alfred 1332
Waller, Edmund 256

Walpole, Horace 675
Walpole, Hugh 1099
Walpole, Robert 675
Walter, Bruno 1332
Warbeck, Peter 1985
Ward, Artemus 1107
Ward, Samuel 1352, 1418
Warrender, George 2389
Washington, Booker T. 252, 445
Washington, George 401, 522, 549, 1932, 2346, 2371, 2402
Watterson, Henry 113
Watts, Richard 1379
Wayne, Arthur 313
Webb, Sidney 2056
Webster, Daniel 6, 108, 479, 1007, 1711, 1847, 1934, 2162, 2542
Webster, Noah 108, 1082, 1091
Welles, Orson 1438
Wellington, Duke of 2378
Wells, H. G. 716, 1192, 2323
Wesley, John 1462, 1557, 1619
Westcott, Senator 333
Westley, Helen 1291, 1419
Whalen, Grover 2234
Whatley, Archbishop 778
Whipple, Bishop 2582
Whistler, James McNeill 198, 506, 547, 618, 717, 1205, 1279, 1281, 1285, 1287, 1288, 1290, 1669
White, Col. John R. 937
Whitefield, George 701, 1496, 1547, 1549, 1556

Whitman, Walt 957
Widmann, Josef 248, 426
Wiggam, Albert Edward 142
Wilde, Oscar 198, 425, 522, 618, 1185, 1193, 1198, 1205, 1382
Wile, F. W. 376, 2016, 2496
Wilhelm, Kaiser 1979
Wilks, Matthew 2504
Wilkes, John 1466
William of Orange 2587
Williams, Jane 903
Williams, Valentine 532
Williams, Walter 773
Wilson, Edith Bolling 2557
Wilson, Woodrow 292, 790, 1016, 1071, 1822, 1897, 1943, 2016, 2557
Winchell, Walter 833
Windsor, Edward 167, 2425
Winkelried, Arnold von 2382
Winthrop, Robert 1304
Woollcott, Alexander 512
Wordsworth, William 359, 564, 1093, 1186
Wright, Wallace 1617
Wu Ting Fang 587
Wynn, Ed 578

Xerxes 1748, 2036
Yeats, William Butler 1189
York, Duke of 1981
Young, Roland 1448
Zanuck, Darryl 1396
Ziegfeld, Florenz 1776

INDEX OF SUBJECTS

INDEX OF SUBJECTS

A

Ability 501, 1919
Abolitionists 1242
Absent-Mindedness 81-90
Accidents 1736
Accuracy 91, 92
Actors 1406-1431
Adoption 981
Advertising 2101-2108
Age 671-678
Agnostics 1651-1659
Airplanes 88
Alligators 306
Ambassadors 106, 474, 587, 756
Ambition 96, 97
America ..396, 550, 780, 2031, 2032
American Revolution, The
                       2346, 2371
Amsterdam 2344
Anarchists 538
Ancestors (see Family)
Anecdotes ...1156, 1168, 1185, 1243
Angel 1292, 1676
Anti-Trust Act, The 2543
Apoplexy 1861
Appendicitis 1673, 1691
Applause 1422
Appomatox Court House. 2397
"Arabian Nights, The" ... 1216
Architecture 1301, 1302
Armistice 2396, 2397
"Arms and the Man" 1441
Army, The 2401-2404
Art 1256
Aspirin 1947
Astrologers 482, 2001
Atheists 1651-1659
Athletics (see Recreation
    & Sports)
Auctions 55
Audiences 1436-1441
Authority 2246
Authors 1166-1219
Autographs 527, 536

Automobiles 251, 1811
Autopsy 1706, 1721

B

Babies 956
Baggage 221
Bakeries 201
Balloons 1633, 2343
Bananas 132
Bands 114
Bankruptcy 2196-2198
Banks 2151-2158
Banquets and Dinners ... 751-753
Baptism 1571, 2386
Baptists, 1472, 1578, 1594, 1624, 2386
Barbers 336, 808, 809, 1110
Bargaining 2076-2082
Barrel-Organ 1315
Baseball 1821-1824
Bataan Peninsula, The ... 2431
Bathrooms 579, 898
Battles 2371-2385
Bears 225, 1585, 1876, 1877
Beauty 661-669
Bedbugs 2111, 2298
Beer 42, 560
Begging 2216-2219
Behavior 1
Behemoth 2306
Belgium 2345
Believers 1591-1596
Better Business Bureau,
    The 2125
Bible 1581-1586
Bigamy 936
Bigotry 1626-1629
Billiards 1826, 1827
Birthdays 1011-1015
Births 1011-1015
Bishops 1491-1498
Black Hawk War, The ..2442, 2461
Blacksmiths 530, 737, 2529
Blindness 533, 705, 931
Boarding-Houses 11, 17

Boastfulness 101–103
Boats 92, 1816
Bohemians 741
Boners 106–119
Books 1221–1224
Boots 213, 718
Bores (see Dullness)
Borrowing 121–126
Bosses 2231–2235
Boston 425, 548, 613
Brains 1266, 2184
Brass 516
Bread 15
Brevity 131–134
Bricklayers 1491
Bridge 1838, 1840
Bromo-Seltzer 43
Bull Fighting 1831
Bunker Hill 577
Businessmen 2236, 2237
Butchers 1993
Butterflies 1687
Buying ....2066, et seq.

C

Cab Drivers, 90, 254, 683, 684, 685,
       812, 2026, 2339, 2556
Cabinet Members 1951–1953
Cabs 90, 254, 684
Caddies 1863, 1867
Caesar's Commentaries .. 1076
Cafeteria 2297
Cakes 201
Calamity Howlers 411
Calendar 2063
California 403
Cambridge 1022
Camel 1792
Camouflage 2340
Camp 2451
Campaigning 1911–1920
Canada 1794
Candy 972
Cannibal 2319
Capitalists 1898
Card Playing 1836
Carelessness 136
Caricature 1283
Catholics, 1483, 1486, 1538, 1594,
        1858, 2599
Cats 589, 2123
Cemeteries 1239, 1677, 1998
Censors 2351–2355

Champagne 2022
Chandelier 1567
Checks 2152, 2154, 2155, 2156
Cheerfulness 141–143
Cheese 437
Chicago 613
Children 951, 952, 966–977
Chinese 587, 756, 773
Chiseling 2121–2132
Choirs 620
Christianity 2009, 2545
Christian Science 1538, 1617
Churches 1526–1528
Churchmen 1451–1456
Church Services 1531–1538
Cigar-Box 2203
Cigars 61, 62, 212, 1782
Circus 262, 1050, 2104
Civilians in War 2331–2346
Civilization 167, 169
Civil War 2326–2329
Classrooms 1051–1053
Clermont, The 411, 1126
Clocks 1989
Clothing 716–726
Clubs 170, 342, 360
Cobbler 1296
Coffee 13, 19, 40, 589, 1781
Coffins 207
Coins 1900
Collection 2176–2179
Collections 1561–1569
College Life 1041
Colleges 1016–1022
Comedians 366, 457
Common Sense 1156, 1157
Competition 2116
Compliments 661, 662, 667, 668
Composers 1311–1326
Concerts 1341–1348
Coney Island 1786
Conductors 1331–1339
"Confessions" (Rousseau) 1224
Congress 1941–1948
Conscience 146, 147
Constitution, The 2031
Contempt of Court 2476, 2485
Contests, Miscellaneous ..1881–1883
Conundrums 1772
Conventions 322, 341, 654
Conversions 1621–1625
Cook 1191
Coroner 2512
Corporation Law 289

Corruption 1919
Cough 1767
Courage 151–153
Courts 2471–2473
Courtship 851–855
Courts-Martial 2589
Cow 1048, 1081, 2392
Cowardice 156–160
Crab 1089
Credit 2166, 2167
Criminals 2571
Critics 1096–1105
Crucifix 1773
Crying 957, 960, 973, 1412
Curiosity 161
Customers 201
Cynicism 166–170

D

Dada 1096
Dancers 1371
Dancing 1841
Dandelions 2313
Deafness 706, 1536, 1554, 2480
Death 1746–1749
Death, Accidental 1751
Death, Natural 1756, 1757
Deathbed Scenes 1761–1775
Debt 2171–2174
Declaration of Independ-
  ence 399
Dedications 1202
Degrees 1016, 1671
Delirium Tremens 1446
Dentists 1456, 1696, 1697
Department of Agriculture 2313
Desertion 2478
Detectives 2556, 2557
Devil, The, 1137, 1548, 1634, 1646,
  1920
Devotion 171–173
Devout Persons 1601, 1602
Dictators 2001–2011
Dictionary, 108, 386, 391, 1071, 1089,
  1232, 1542
Dieting 687
Diligence 176, 177
Diplomats 2021–2027
Directors 1401–1403
Discipline 2441, 2442
Discretion 181, 182
Diseases 1721
Divorce 906–911

Doctors 1666–1679
Doctor's Fees 1681
Dogs, 281, 486, 744, 1236, 1669, 2072,
  2479, 2547
"Don Quixote" 2354
Doubles 646
Draft, The 1406
Drawing 1261–1293
Dreams, 647, 941, 975, 1208, 1992,
  2082
Drill 2461, 2462
Drinking 36–55
Druggists 733, 1679
Dueling 801–803
Dullness 186–195

E

Eagles 1879
Earache 1703
Ears 607
Earthquakes 242, 371, 1926
East India House, The .. 321
Eating 6–23
Eccentricity 196–209
Economy 211–213
Editors, 117, 1241, 1247, 1248, 1251,
  1252
Education 1046
Efficiency 2266–2270
Eggs 97, 2308
Egress 539
Egyptians 435, 1792, 1793
Eiffel Tower, The 1301
Elections 1921
Electricity 1120
"Elegy In a Country
  Churchyard" 2201
Elephants 262
Emancipation Proclama-
  tion, The 2037
Emperors 1971–1993
Employment 2226–2228
Encyclopedia Britannica,
  The 1092, 2446
Endurance 216
Enemies 1198, 2027
Engagement 856, 857
England, 405, 476, 549, 550, 663, 666,
  2032, 2337, 2342, 2343
Episcopalians 1471
Epitaph 884, 886
Equality 2046
Erudition 1071–1076

Eskimo Pies   2522
Eternity   352
Ethics   290
Evangelists 1511–1516
Evidence 2521–2523
Exaggeration   221
Examination Papers   1026
Executives 2231–2235
Experience 881, 1073
Experimenters 1136–1138
Explorers 1141, 1142
Explosion   1736
Extravagance 231, 232

F

"Faerie Queen, The"   1181
Fairy Tale   2321
Family 946–950
Farmers and Farming ...2311–2313
Fascism 2004, 2009, 2011
Father 986–990
Fatness 681–690
Fever 1672, 1705, 2147
Fighting 152, 466
Film ....1376, et seq.
Fire Department   541
Fires, 101, 143, 204, 208, 372, 376,
    1238, 1557, 2138, 2139, 2140, 2301
Firing 2246–2249
First Aid 1741, 2341
Fishing, 49, 1453, 1467, 1846–1854,
                              2038
Fish-Market   2523
Fiume 1943, 2016
Flattery 236, 237
Flea   1397
Flirtation 861–863
Flute   904
Fools 514, 578, 786, 1474, 1999
Football 1856–1858
Foot Racing 1881, 1882
France, 405, 476, 663, 666, 2026, 2316,
                              2335
Franco-Prussian War ...2336, 2339
Freedom 2036–2042
Friendship 866, 867
Frogs   2122
Fuchsias   1546
Fundamentalism   1477
Funerals 1776–1778
Furs   222

G

Gambling   71–74
Garbage   2282
Garters 722, 826
Generosity 241–248
Genius 1351, 1356
Gentlemanliness 251–256
Georgia   2126
Germans   2345
Gettysburg   324
Ghosts   1631
Ghost Writers   1177
Gibbet   169
Gin   40
Girard College   2607
Gloves   444
Gold   563
Gold-Fish   197
Golf 1861–1869
"Good Earth, The"   1324
Gossip 821–826
Gout   1728
Government ....1896, et seq.
Governors   1956
Grand Canyon, The   937
Grant's Tomb   1371
Gratitude 261–268
Gravedigger   929
Greece   967
Greed 271–276
Guides 1792, 1793
Guitar   275

H

Habeas Corpus   823
Habits   31
Hair 507, 606, 916
Handicaps and Afflictions. 701–707
Handkerchief 2008, 2182
Hands   665
Handwriting 731–733
Hanging 2566–2568
Hangovers   43
Harper's Ferry   2387
Harvard 1017, 1031, 1793
Hat 532, 716, 717, 2064
Hate   253
Haverford College   1041
Headaches   1947
Headlines   1246

Heaven 1511, 1541, 2003, 2010
Hell, 68, 374, 484, 496, 1346, 1501,
    1511, 1513, 1541, 1557, 1948
Helpfulness 281
Hippopotamus 209
Hiram College 1020
Hiring 2246–2249
Hissing 1111
"Hobson's Kisses" 2420
Hollywood 1446–1449
Holy Ghost, The 1514
Home Life 996–1001
Homeliness 651–656
Homeopath 1668
Homestead Law 216
Honesty 286–294
Honor 296–298
Hope 881
Horse Racing 1871, 1872
Horses, 601, 643, 683, 1093, 2128,
    2286–2288, 2415, 2456, 2566
Hospitality 1006–1008
Hospitals 1674, 1691
Hotels 1899, 2296–2302
"Huckleberry Finn" 1221
Human Nature 1, 168
Humility 1277
Hunchback 701
Hunting 1876–1879
Husband 916–918
Hypochondriacs 1716–1720
Hypocrisy 301–303

I

Ice-Wagon 2288
Idaho 548
Ideas 194
Ignorance 1454
Imagination 306
Inauguration 1936
India 2041
Indians 226, 617, 943, 2582
Infidelity 901–904
Ingratitude 261–268
Injury 1741
Inquisition, The 1628, 2354
Insomnia 26
Instincts 759
Instrumentalists 1351–1363
Insurance 2136–2140
International Relations .. 2016
Introductions 786–791
Inventors 1126–1131

Irishmen 442, 707, 1189, 2276
Israelites 435
Italy 2321, 2322

J

Jail 2561–2563
Japanese, The, 332, 2296, 2351, 2430
Jersey City 2597
Jesters 288, 483, 534, 694
Jews, 303, 442, 443, 447, 450, 981,
    1486, 1487, 2001, 2366, 2545
Jockey 1476
Judges 2486–2497
Juries 2511–2517
Justice 2601

K

Kaiser, The 1979
Kangaroo 1141
Kentucky 504
Kidnapping 925
Kindness 311
Kings 1971–1993
Kiss 843, 847, 861, 2417, 2420
Koran 1629, 1634
K. P. 2466
Kreplach 1686
Kuhn, Loeb & Company.. 475

L

Laissez Faire 2236
Land 274
Language 1231–1233
Laryngitis 2412
Lawyers 2526–2537
Lateness 321–324
Latin 774
Law Enforcement 2546–2548
Laws 2596–2599
Lawyers' Fees 2541–2545
Laziness 326, 327
Learned Men 1081–1095
Lectures 1106–1111
Legs 695, 1534, 1720
Lesbians 1393
Letters 596, 636, 731, 1091
Liars 49, 224, 331–336
Liberty 152, 313, 2040
Libraries 1226
"Life of Johnson, The" .. 1222
Lighthouse 27, 1302, 1675

Lightning Rods 1527
Listening 810, 814
Literature 1161, 1162
Living Buddha, The 1661
Loans 2161–2164
Lobsters 264
London 2334, 2338, 2342
Longevity 1781, 1872
Long-Windedness 341–363
Love 846–850

M

Machinery 2271
Magazines 1251, 1252
Magician 2293
Manners 31, 501, 589
Manufacturing 2261
Marches 2456
Marines, The 2434, 2436
Marriage 876–888
Marseilles 2606
Martyrs 153
Mathematicians 1146–1154
Mayflower, The 949
Mayors 1961
Medicines 1726–1731
Melancholy 366–368
Memory 371–375
"Messiah, The" 1333
Metaphor 780
Methodists 1594
Metropolitan Opera House 1239
Mexicans 267, 879, 981, 2067
Milk 1150, 1770
Ministers 1461–1477
Miracles 1616–1619
Mirrors 580, 2181
Missionaries 1521
Mocking-Birds 313
Modernism 1477
Modesty 376–390
Money, 296, 367, 1106, 1127, 1376,
     2176, 2187, 2423, 2541, 2544, 2545
Morals ....1451, et seq.
Morgan & Company 475
Mormons 942
Mother 991–993
Mother-in-Law 936, 937
Mount Vernon 522, 549
Mouth 587
Mules 572, 2406, 2419
Munich Conference, The. 2002
Murder 2576

Museum 1050
Mushrooms 20
Music 1303–1306
Mustaches 373, 503, 587
Mutton 10

N

Nail-Biting 690
Names 831–838
Nature 686, 1285, 1287
Navy, The 182, 2401–2404
Nazis 1148, 2038, 2344, 2366
Negroes, 252, 417, 441, 442, 445, 446,
     448, 451, 452, 475
Neighbors 601
Netherlands, The 378, 2344
New Orleans 255
Newspapers 1236–1248
New Year's Eve 1231
Niagara Falls 161
Nose 84, 653, 704, 1670
Nourmahal, The 2191
Nudists 720
Nullification 2326
Nuts 243, 272, 540

O

Obituaries 117, 614
Officers 2406–2427
Office Seekers 1966–1970
"Old Curiosity Shop, The" 1162
Old Maids 871–873
Operas 1341–1348
Operations 1674
Oranges 2067, 2302
"Otello" 1368
Oxford 1021, 1656
Oysters 8

P

Painting 1261–1293
Pagan Gods 1661
Pall-Bearers 2196
Panama 2226
Pancakes 1036
Pants 2209
Parables 1852
Paralysis 1720
Paris 2335, 2336
Parliament 1996–2000
Parrots 2291–2293

Parties 741–746
Partnerships 290, 2241, 2242
Patience 391
Patriotism 396–407
Patrons 1210
Pawnbrokers 2204
Pearls 513, 1032
Peddlers 422
Pennies 529
Perfume 2072
Pessimism 411
Philosophers, 141, 191, 1083, 1088,
1452, 1749
Phonograph, The 1131
Photographs 646, 2003
Physical Characteristics.. 646–648
Pianists (see Instrumentalists)
Piano 389
Pickpockets 2502, 2503
Pigeons 641
Pigtails 587
Pin 1401, 2249
Plagiarism ..1168, 1185, 1188, 2340
Plays 1386–1388
Playwrights 1376–1385
Poker 74, 1836
Police 2551, 2552
Politeness 416–420
Political Parties 1906, 1907
Politics 1896–1901
Polo 1841
Polygamy 941–943
Pompousness 421–427
Poor Health 1711, 1712
Poor-House 472
Popes 1501–1504
Pornography 1216
Porters 1806
Posterity 1179
Potatoes 786
Poverty 2201–2211
Practical Joking 431–437
Prayer 1606–1612
Precedent 2598
Prejudice 441–452
Preparedness 2402
Presbyterians 1594
Presidents 1931–1940
Press-Agents 2355
Price 2086
Pride 456, 457
Priests 1481–1483
Principle 501
Prisoners 2366

Prize Fighting 1886, 1887
Procrastination 461
Producers 1391–1397
Profanity 66–68
Professors 1026–1032
Prohibition 2548
Prohibitions and Restric-
tions 1641, 1642
Proof-Reading 1218, 1245
Protestants 1483, 1486, 1858
Providence ...265, 1527, 1795, 1816
Prunes 11, 2210
Psalms 1053
Psychiatrists 1036, 1686, 1687
Publicity 378, 614
Public Offices 1926
Public Relations 2111, 2112
Pupils 1061
Purgatory 877, 1501
Pyramids 1793

Q

Quakers 562, 878
Quarrelsomeness 466
Questions 987, 1036
Quick Thinking 471–492

R

Rabbis 1486–1488
Rabbits 281
Raffle 2251
Ranches 2312
Rationing 2356–2358
Real Estate 2141, 2142
Recantation 402
Recreation ....1786, et seq.
Red Sea 435
Refugees 2361, 2478
Regulations 2446
Reindeer 2281
Relativity 1150
Religion ....1451, et seq.
Reporters 119, 133
Reputation 76
Restaurants 2296–2302
Revivals 1576–1578
Revolutions 2061–2064
"Rhapsody in Blue" 1312, 1321
Rheumatism 1703
Richmond 2327
Rome 2066
"Romeo et Juliette" 1323

Rooster 759
Rouge 602
Rough and Ready 496–507
Rudeness 511–524
Rum 2121
Russo-Japanese War 1982, 2022

S

Sailors 116, 2430–2437
St. Louis 581
St. Vitus' Dance 1703
Salaries 2251–2254
Salesmen 2091–2097
Sandwiches 2299
Sausages 436, 802
"Scarlet Letter, The" 1180
Scenery 2141, 2142
Schools 1046–1050
Scientists 1116–1122
Scotchmen 559, 561, 1536, 2218
Sculpture 1296, 1297
Sears, Roebuck 2226
Seasickness 1702
Secret Service 2557
Selling ....2066, et seq.
Sentry 2451, 2479
"September Morn" 2355
Sermons 1541–1559
Servants 2276–2283
Shay's Rebellion 2040
Sheriffs 78
Shoes 724, 1296, 1636, 2103
Shortness 691–695
Shrewdness 526–541
Shrimps 422
Shushima 1982
Sickness 1701–1707
Sidewalk-Pitch Men 526
Silence 778, 808, 809, 811
Silver 2181
Sin and Sinners 1646, 1647
Sincerity 287, 1652
Singers 1366–1368
Sing Sing 2561, 2571, 2590
Slang 1495
Slavery, 334, 371, 417, 781, 2031,
                              2037, 2039
Sled 1052
Sleeping 26, 27
Sleeping Cars 2111
Small Children 966–977
Smoke 581
Smoking 61–65

Snake-Charmer 897
Snakes 45, 47, 263, 1635
Snobbishness 546–551
Snoring 261, 958, 1550
Social Activities 736, 737
Socialism 2056, 2057
Society 796, 797
Socks 723
Soldiers 2430–2437
Specialists 1670, 2272
Spectacles 375
Speeches 756–782
Spelling 972
Spirits 387
Sports ....1821, et seq.
Statistics 2221, 2222
Statues 382
Stealing 2581–2590
Steam 766, 2401
Sterilization 2599
Stinginess 556, 566
Stocks and Bonds 2146, 2147
Stool Pigeons 2591, 2592
Stores 2071, 2072
Storm Trooper 2335
Storytellers 419
Strategy 2386–2393
Stratford-on-Avon 582
Strawberries 11, 2210
Stubbornness 571, 572
Students 1036
Stupidity 576–583
Stuttering 711–713
Suburbs 1008
Subways 641
Success 782, 1153
Sugar 2358
Suicide 1394
Sunday School 1571
Superstition 1631–1636
Supreme Court, The 2496, 2526,
                                    2599
Surrealism 1096
Swimming 1891–1893
Swindling 2121–2132
Switzerland 2353, 2382
Symptoms 1716
Synonyms 1169

T

Tact 586–591
Talent 1097, 1551
Talking 806–818

Tallness 696
Taxes 2191–2194
Taxicab Drivers (see Cab Drivers)
Taxicabs (see Cabs)
Tea 13, 84, 745
Teachers 1056, 1057
Teeth 612, 1512, 1696
Telephones 211
Temper 596–598
Temperance 52
Texas 44, 243, 1796
Texas Rangers, The 2546
Theatre ....1376, et seg.
Theologians 1452
Thinness 189
Ticonderoga 1609
Time 352
Tips 1806
Tires 416, 2356, 2357
Titanic, The 173
Titles 622, 797
Tobacco 1018
Tolerance 601–603
Tombstone 886
Tongue-Twistedness 1533
Toothache 1703
Trafalgar 2423
Traffic Tickets 537, 2488, 2494
Trains 1801, 1802
Traitor 2433, 2437
Travel 1791–1796
Trees 312
Trials 2476–2485
Triplets 970
Trolley Cars 251
Trousers 491
Truth 2505
Turkey 768
Twins 970, 977
Typists 2248
Typographical Errors, 107, 109, 113, 117
Tyrants 236

U

Umbrella 2002
Underground Railway, The 1794
Understudy 1413
Union Pacific Railway ... 2270
United States, The 2031, 2032
Universities 1016–1022

V

Vanity 606–628
Vegetarians 15, 18
"Vicar of Wakefield, The" 1171
Violinists (see Instrumentalists)
Vitamins 2108
Vulgarity 603

W

Waiters 2306–2308
Wall Street 76, 2146
War and the Military, 2316, et seq.
War of 1812 2372
Washing 478, 479
Washington Monument .. 576
Watch 2204, 2588
Water 1622, 2022, 2606
Wealth 2181–2187
Weather 477, 760, 815, 1052
Wedding 891, 892
"Well of Loneliness, The" 1393
Whiskey, 39, 44, 55, 263, 492, 561, 565, 2416, 2548
Whisper 996
Wife 921–933
William & Mary College. 1018
Will Power 631
Wills and Testaments ... 2606
Wind 223, 416
Wine 37
Wishes 563
Witchcraft 2492
Witnesses 2501–2506
Woman's Suffrage 2051, 2052
Women 841–843
Work 326, 387, 2226–2228
Working Conditions 2256
World's Fair, The 2023
Worm 444, 765
Worrying 636

Y

Yachts 2191
Yale 1793
"Yankee Doodle" 1304
Yosemite Valley 1791
Youth 674, 675

Z

Zanies 641–643
Zoos 209